To Improve the Academy

To Improve the Academy

Resources for Faculty, Instructional, and Organizational Development

Volume 27

Linda B. Nilson, Editor

Judith E. Miller, Associate Editor

Professional and Organizational Development
Network in Higher Education

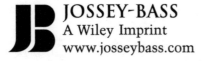

JOSSEY-BASS
A Wiley Imprint
www.josseybass.com

The Jossey-Bass
Higher and Adult Education Series

To Improve the Academy

To Improve the Academy is published annually by the Professional and Organizational Development Network in Higher Education (POD) through Jossey-Bass Publishers and is abstracted in ERIC documents and in Higher Education Abstracts.

Ordering Information

The annual volume of *To Improve the Academy* is distributed to members at the POD conference in the autumn of each year. To order or obtain ordering information, contact:

John Wiley & Sons, Inc.
One Wiley Drive
Somerset, NJ 08875-1272
Voice   877-762-2974
Fax   317-572-4002
E-mail   consumer@wiley.com
Web   www.josseybass.com

Permission to Copy

The contents of *To Improve the Academy* are copyrighted to protect the authors. Nevertheless, consistent with the networking and resource-sharing functions of POD, readers are encouraged to reproduce articles and cases from *To Improve the Academy* for educational use, as long as the source is identified.

Instructions to Contributors for the Next Volume

Anyone interested in the issues related to instructional, faculty, and organizational development in higher education may submit manuscripts. Manuscripts are submitted to the current editors in December of each year and sent through a blind peer-review process. Correspondence, including requests for information about guidelines and submission of manuscripts for Volume 28, should be directed to:

> Linda B. Nilson, Director
> Office of Teaching Effectiveness and Innovation
> Clemson University
> 445 Brackett Hall
> Clemson, SC 29634
> Voice   864-656-4542
> Fax   864-656-0750
> E-mail   nilson@clemson.edu

Mission Statement

As revised and accepted by the POD Core Committee on April 2, 2004.

Statement of Purpose

The Professional and Organizational Development Network in Higher Education is an association of higher education professionals dedicated to enhancing teaching and learning by supporting educational developers and leaders in higher education.

The Professional and Organizational Development Network in Higher Education encourages the advocacy of the ongoing enhancement of teaching and learning through faculty, TA, instructional, and organizational development. To this end, it supports the work of educational developers and champions their importance to the academic enterprise.

Vision Statement

During the twenty-first century, the Professional and Organizational Development Network in Higher Education will expand guidelines for educational development, build strong alliances with sister organizations, and encourage developer exchanges and research projects to improve teaching and learning.

Values

The Professional and Organizational Development Network in Higher Education is committed to:

- Personal, faculty, instructional, and organizational development
- Humane and collaborative organizations and administrations
- Diverse perspectives and a diverse membership
- Supportive educational development networks on the local, regional, national, and international levels
- Advocacy for improved teaching and learning in the academy through programs for faculty, administrators, and graduate students
- The identification and collection of a strong and accessible body of research on development theories and practices
- The establishment of guidelines for ethical practice
- The increasingly useful and thorough assessment and evaluation of practice and research

Programs, Publications, and Activities

The Professional and Organizational Development Network in Higher Education offers members and interested individuals the following benefits:

- An annual membership conference designed to promote professional and personal growth, nurture innovation and change, stimulate important research projects, and enable participants to exchange ideas and broaden professional networks
- An annual membership directory and networking guide
- Publications in print and in electronic form
- Access to the POD Web site and listserv

Membership, Conference, and Program Information

For information contact:

Hoag Holmgren, Executive Director
The POD Network
P.O. Box 3318
Nederland, CO 80566
Voice   303-258-9521
Fax   303-258-7377
E-mail   podnetwork@podweb.org

Contents

About the Authors

The Editors

Linda B. Nilson is founding director of the Office of Teaching Effectiveness and Innovation (OTEI) at Clemson University, where she also teaches a graduate course in college teaching. She authored *Teaching at Its Best: A Research-Based Resource for College Instructors,* now in its second edition (Anker, 2003; Jossey-Bass, 2007) and *The Graphic Syllabus and the Outcomes Map: Communicating Your Course* (Jossey-Bass, 2007). She also was coeditor of *Enhancing Learning with Laptops in the Classroom* (with Barbara E. Weaver, Jossey-Bass, 2005) and associate editor of Volumes 25 and 26 of *To Improve the Academy* (with Douglas R. Robertson, Anker, 2007, 2008). In addition, Nilson has published many articles and book chapters and has presented conference sessions and faculty workshops both nationally and internationally on dozens of topics related to teaching effectiveness, assessment, scholarly productivity, and academic career matters.

Before coming to Clemson, Nilson directed teaching centers at Vanderbilt University and the University of California, Riverside. Her chance to enter educational development came in the late 1970s, when her department (she was then a sociology professor at UCLA) selected her to establish and supervise its TA training program. Nilson has held leadership positions in the Society for the Study of Social Problems, Toastmasters International, Mensa, and the Southern Regional Faculty and Instructional Development Consortium. She earned her B.A. in sociology at the University of California, Berkeley, and her M.S. and Ph.D. in sociology at the University of Wisconsin, Madison. She can be reached at nilson@clemson.edu.

Judith E. Miller is associate dean for special academic initiatives at Clark University in Worcester, Massachusetts. She is a former biology faculty member; her current teaching includes courses in college teaching for graduate students. In 1998 she received the Outstanding Undergraduate Science Teacher award from the Society for College Science Teachers; in 2002 she was named the Massachusetts CASE Professor of the Year by the Carnegie Foundation for the Advancement of Teaching, and in 2004 she won Worcester Polytechnic Institute's Trustees' Award for Outstanding Teaching. Miller is the coeditor (with Jim Groccia and Marilyn Miller) of *Student-Assisted Teaching: A Guide to Faculty-Student Teamwork* (Anker, 2001) and (with Jim Groccia) of *On Becoming a Productive University: Strategies for Reducing Costs and Increasing Quality* (Anker, 2005). She has published and presented extensively on active and cooperative learning, learning outcomes assessment, team teaching, and educational productivity. She received her B.S. in biological sciences from Cornell University and her Ph.D. in microbiology from Case Western Reserve University. She can be reached at judmiller@clarku.edu.

The Contributors

Terre H. Allen is a professor of communication studies and director of the Faculty Center for Professional Development at California State University, Long Beach (CSULB). She has published numerous articles and book chapters on communication in the classroom, small-group communication, interpersonal, and organizational communication. Terre has worked as an instructional designer for several large organizations and is coauthor of USA Funds® Life Skills® curriculum for student success. Currently, she is serving as the faculty development coordinator for CSULB's Hispanic Serving Institution Title V development grant. She can be reached at tallen@csulb.edu.

Elizabeth Ambos is assistant vice chancellor for research initiatives and partnerships for the California State University (CSU) system office. In this capacity, she supports CSU research and sponsored programs efforts, focusing on multicampus collaborations. Prior administrative appointments included associate vice president for research and external support, graduate dean, and associate dean in the College of Natural Sciences and Mathematics—all at California State University, Long Beach (CSULB). She is also a professor in the Department of Geological Sciences at CSULB. She can be reached at eambos@calstate.edu.

Susan A. Ambrose is associate provost for education, director of the Eberly Center for Teaching Excellence, and a teaching professor in history at Carnegie Mellon University. She is responsible for advising the provost on educational issues; conducting institutional research that has an impact on policy and practice; identifying and responding to changing educational needs of the university; and maintaining the overall operation of the Eberly Center, the Intercultural Communication Center, and the Office of Academic Development. She can be reached at sa0n@andrew.cmu.edu.

Pamela E. Barnett is associate vice provost and director of the Teaching and Learning Center at Temple University. She was associate director of the McGraw Center for Teaching & Learning at Princeton University from 2004 to 2007, where she also taught courses in literary and cultural studies. Prior to her work in instructional development, she was associate professor of English and African American studies at the University of South Carolina. She can be reached at barnettp@temple.edu.

A. Jane Birch is assistant director for faculty development at the Brigham Young University Faculty Center. Among other programs and workshops, she directs the BYU Faculty Development Series—an intensive eighteen-month new-faculty program—and the Scholarship Workshop—a semester-long program on scholarly productivity. Birch helps faculty make connections between their religious faith and their work as teachers and scholars. She designed and developed a comprehensive faculty development database and continues to maintain it. She can be reached at jane_birch@byu.edu.

Phyllis Blumberg is director of the Teaching and Learning Center at the University of the Sciences in Philadelphia and a professor of social sciences. Her work focuses on learner-centered teaching and problem-based learning. She is a frequent presenter at POD and other conferences and has authored over fifty articles; she also published *Developing Learner-Centered Teaching: A Practical Guide for Faculty* (Jossey-Bass, 2008). She received her Ph.D. in educational and developmental psychology from the University of Pittsburgh. She can be reached at p.blumbe@usip.edu.

Michael Bridges is associate director for educational support in the Eberly Center for Teaching Excellence at Carnegie Mellon University. He is also an adjunct professor in the Department of Psychology, where he teaches courses in personality and stress and coping. He currently consults with faculty on course design and assessment, with a focus on issues related to learning and motivation. His research interests include survey design and methodology, scale development, personality, and happiness. He can be reached at mb4h@andrew.cmu.edu.

Bryan R. Cole is professor of educational administration in the Department of Educational Administration and Human Resource Development at Texas A&M University. He served as department head from 1996 to 2003 and has served in a number of other senior administrative capacities. His professional interests include continuous improvement in educational systems, educational law, and educational administration. He received his B.S. from the U.S. Military Academy at West Point and his M.Ed. and Ph.D. in educational administration (higher education) from Texas A&M. He can be reached at b-cole@tamu.edu.

Andrei Cerqueira Davis is a recent graduate of Western Washington University, with a master's degree in continuing and college education. He also holds a certificate in community and technical college teaching. His interest in faculty development has led him to research faculty learning communities and the scholarship of teaching and learning. He has also studied informal learning in formal learning settings. He can be reached at andrei_c_davis@hotmail.com.

Cynthia Desrochers is director of the Institute for Teaching and Learning of the California State University system. She taught at

UCLA's lab school (1975–1983) and was professor of education (1983–2007) and founding director of the Teaching and Learning Center (1996–2005) at California State University, Northridge. Desrochers' work focuses on translating research on learning into practice and on organizational understanding. She served on the POD Network Core committee (2004–2007) and chaired the Innovation Award subcommittee (2001–2005). She can be reached at cdesrochers@calstate.edu.

Michele DiPietro is associate director for graduate student support in the Eberly Center for Teaching Excellence and an instructor in the Statistics Department at Carnegie Mellon University. His work has focused on diversity in the classroom, faculty responses to tragic events, statistics education, student ratings of instruction, and the teaching consultation process. He was conference chair of the 2006 POD conference, "Theory and Research for a Scholarship of Practice." He can be reached at dipietro@andrew.cmu.edu.

Beverly Dolinsky has worked at Endicott College as the former dean of arts and sciences and as a professor of psychology for eighteen years. Her scholarship focuses on higher education curriculum, policy, and pedagogy. Dolinsky was appointed a visiting scholar to the New England Resource Center for Higher Education, where she studied innovative general education models. She currently serves as a task force adviser for the Policy Center on the First Year of College. She can be reached at bdolinsk@endicott.edu.

Phillip M. Edwards is a doctoral candidate at the Information School of the University of Washington. He received an M.S. in information (2003) from the University of Michigan, School of Information, and a B.S. in chemistry with a minor in mathematics (2001) from the University at Buffalo-SUNY. He is also an instructional consultant at the University of Washington's Center for Instructional Development and Research (CIDR); he consults with graduate TAs from the sciences, mathematics, and engineering. He can be reached at edwards@cidr.washington.edu.

Anne Fay is the director of assessment for the Eberly Center for Teaching Excellence and the Office of Technology for Education and an adjunct professor in the Psychology Department at Carnegie Mellon University. She received her Ph.D. in cognitive psychology from the University of California, Santa Barbara, and was a postdoctoral fellow for the James A. McDonnell Foundation in cognitive studies in educational practice. Her current focus is developing formative and summative assessments for programs and courses. She can be reached at af25@andrew.cmu.edu.

Karen Freisem is a senior consultant at the Center for Instructional Development and Research (CIDR) and coordinator of the center's work with math, science, and engineering departments. In addition to consulting with individual instructors, Freisem has helped conduct ongoing program assessment in many departments and develop teaching and learning materials in quantitative disciplines and in large class settings. She also works with TAs in CIDR's International TA Program. She can be reached at kfriesem@u.washington.edu.

Stanford T. Goto is an assistant professor in the Department of Educational Leadership at Western Washington University, where he coordinates a certificate program in community and technical college teaching. His professional interests include faculty development and professional identify formation among new college instructors. Currently, he is working with a local community college to cofacilitate a faculty learning community. He can be reached at stan.goto@wwu.edu.

Tara Gray serves as associate professor of criminal justice and as the first director of the Teaching Academy at New Mexico State University (NMSU). She has published three books, including her most recent, *Publish and Flourish: Become a Prolific Scholar* (New Mexico State University, 2005). She has been honored at NMSU and, at the national level, with eight awards for teaching or service. Gray has presented faculty development workshops to three thousand participants in more than twenty-five U.S. states and in Mexico, Guatemala, and Thailand. She can be reached at tgray@nmsu.edu.

Stacy Grooters is founding director of the Center for Teaching and Learning and holds faculty rank as an assistant professor in the Department of English at Stonehill College. She received her Ph.D. in English from the University of Washington, where she worked as an instructional consultant for the Center for Instructional Development and Research. Her scholarly interests include the role of instructor and student identity in the classroom, as well as the representation of education in literature and film. She can be reached at sgrooters@stonehill.edu.

Linda C. Hodges is director of the Harold W. McGraw Jr. Center for Teaching and Learning at Princeton University. A biochemist by training, she spent over twenty years as a professor in undergraduate education before transitioning into faculty development work in 2001. Hodges writes scholarly pieces on her pedagogical research, as well as reflective articles on teaching and faculty development. She can be reached at lhodges@princeton.edu.

Richard A. Holmgren is associate dean of the college and executive director of learning, information, and technology services at Allegheny College in Meadville, Pennsylvania. As associate dean, he has been involved in faculty development, programs for first-year students, academic support for students, and institutional assessment. As executive director, he oversees the library, computing services, and student support services. His primary professional interest is fostering the development of a campus culture and structures that support the work of students and faculty. He can be reached at richard.holmgren@allegheny.edu.

Wayne Jacobson is associate director of the Center for Instructional Development and Research at the University of Washington. He consults with departments, faculty, and TAs in math, sciences, and engineering, and teaches the graduate school's interdisciplinary courses on teaching and learning in higher education. He also works closely with the UW SoTL Forum and has recent publications on assessment of teaching, preparation and support for international TAs, and inclusive teaching in STEM disciplines. He can be reached at wjacobs@u.washington.edu.

Trav D. Johnson is a consultant in the Center for Teaching and Learning at Brigham Young University. He works with faculty, departments, and colleges to improve teaching and helps direct the BYU online student rating system. Before coming to BYU, Johnson worked at the University of Illinois in faculty and course evaluation. His research focuses on the use of evaluation in instructional improvement, including approaches that promote understanding, collegiality, and accountability. He can be reached at trav_johnson@byu.edu.

Steven K. Jones is the director of academic assessment in the Center for Educational Excellence (CEE), as well as an associate professor at the United States Air Force Academy. He is dedicated to creating and implementing assessment tools to improve the learning of undergraduate students. He has a Ph.D. in cognitive psychology from the University of Oregon. He can be reached at steven.jones@usafa.edu.

Audrey M. Kleinsasser directs the Wyoming School–University Partnership—a statewide consortium of seventeen school districts, the University of Wyoming, the Wyoming Community College Commission, the Wyoming Department of Education, and the Wyoming Education Association. She is also a professor of educational studies at the university. She preceded Jane V. Nelson as director of the Ellbogen Center. She can be reached at dakota@uwyo.edu.

Paul J. Kuerbis became the second director of the Crown Faculty Center at Colorado College in 1999. The center is located within the Learning Commons at Tutt Library, which also houses the Colket Student Learning Center. A professor in the Education Department, he is well known for his work in K–20 STEM (science, technology, engineering, and mathematics) reform. He has served on several committees with the National Academies and the National Research Council in Washington, D.C. He can be reached at pkuerbis@coloradocollege.edu.

Gail F. Latta is professor and former associate vice chancellor for academic affairs at the University of Nebraska-Lincoln. She teaches graduate courses on leadership development, organizational development and change, foundations of human resources, and research methods in leadership studies. Latta's research and consulting focus on organizational culture, leadership, and change, emphasizing the role of leader identity, adult development, and self-theories in emerging leadership theories and models of leadership development. She can be reached at glatta@unl.edu.

Marsha C. Lovett is associate director for faculty support in the Eberly Center for Teaching Excellence and associate research professor in the Psychology Department at Carnegie Mellon University. Her main activities at the Eberly Center include consulting with faculty on teaching and learning issues and applying research on student learning to improve instruction. She also teaches courses in cognitive psychology and mentors graduate students in the Program in Interdisciplinary Educational Research. She can be reached at lovett@cmu.edu.

Deborah S. Meizlish is the coordinator of social science initiatives at the Center for Research on Learning and Teaching at the University of Michigan. Meizlish consults with administrators, faculty, and GSIs (graduate student instructors) on course and curricular issues, plans university-wide programs on issues of teaching and learning, and conducts seminars on topics ranging from effective student presentations to peer review of teaching. Her research and writing focus on academic hiring, academic integrity, and political science pedagogy. She can be reached at debmeiz@umich.edu.

Kim M. Mooney is founding director of the Center for Teaching and Learning at St. Lawrence University, as well as special assistant to the president for assessment and associate professor of psychology. The center was established in 2001 during her five-year term as associate dean for faculty affairs. Mooney is also a founding member of the POD Small College Committee and, with her coauthors, designs and runs workshops on faculty development programs and centers at liberal arts and other small colleges. She can be reached at kmooney@stlawu.edu.

D. Brent Morris is the director of faculty development in the Center for Educational Excellence (CEE) at the United States Air Force Academy. He is a lieutenant colonel in the United States Air Force and holds a doctorate in nuclear engineering. His research interests are in physics education and student learning. He can be reached at douglas.morris@usafa.edu.

Ed Neal is director of Faculty Development in the Center for Teaching and Learning at the University of North Carolina at Chapel Hill. He leads faculty development workshops and seminars, writes articles and monographs on pedagogical issues, develops teaching assessment systems, designs program evaluations, and serves on university committees that deal with teaching, assessment, and the curriculum. He is also the editor of *The Journal of Faculty Development* and a member of the editorial boards of *The National Teaching and Learning Forum* and *Innovative Higher Education*. He can be reached at ed_neal@unc.edu.

Jane V. Nelson directs the Ellbogen Center for Teaching and Learning at the University of Wyoming. Prior to assuming this position, she directed the university's writing center, coordinated writing-across-the-curriculum courses, and taught literature and writing courses. She and Audrey M. Kleinsasser were codirectors of a FIPSE project that used a faculty development model to help instructors identify and understand the literacies that students need to succeed in their courses. She can be reached at jnelson@uwyo.edu.

Marie Kamala Norman is a teaching consultant and research associate at the Eberly Center for Teaching Excellence at Carnegie Mellon University. She is also an adjunct professor of anthropology in the Department of History, where she teaches courses in cultural anthropology, medical anthropology, theory, and methodology. She is particularly interested in teaching issues involving international students, international faculty, and adjunct faculty, as well as the use of qualitative methods in educational research. She can be reached at mnorman@andrew.cmu.edu.

Evelyn T. Patterson is assistant dean for curriculum planning and professor of physics at the United States Air Force Academy. She received her B.S. degree from Bucknell University, where she majored in physics and minored in music, and her Ph.D. in experimental cosmic ray physics from the University of Delaware. She joined the faculty of the Academy in 1993. Her research interests include improving the effectiveness of teaching and learning, particularly through the use of technology. She can be reached at evelyn.patterson@usafa.edu.

Larissa Pchenitchnaia is a curriculum renewal specialist in the Artie McFerrin Department of Chemical Engineering at Texas A&M University. She has a Ph.D. in educational administration (higher education). Her professional interests include faculty professional development, curriculum development, and assessment of teaching practices and learning outcomes. She can be reached at larissap@tamu.edu.

Iola Peed-Neal is associate director of the Center for Teaching and Learning at the University of North Carolina-Chapel Hill. Her responsibilities include managing center operations and developing university-wide organizational, faculty, and instructional development programs. She also conducts research, directs the Future Faculty Fellows Program, and consults with faculty and administrators on teaching and curricular issues. She is the editor of all center publications, including *Teaching for Inclusion*—a diversity handbook used in dozens of colleges and universities nationwide. She can be reached at iola@email.unc.edu.

Donna M. Qualters is director of the Center for Teaching Excellence and associate professor of education studies at Suffolk University. She is also senior editor of *Chalk Talk* and a board member of the New England Faculty Development Consortium. Qualters' research involves all areas of faculty life, including spirituality and ethical inquiry, as well as traditional areas of assessment, technology, and learning. She is currently co-principal investigator on a National Science Foundation grant to assess learning through computer-facilitated networked play among engineering students. She can be reached at dqualters@suffolk.edu.

Michael Reder is director of Connecticut College's Faculty Center for Teaching & Learning. He publishes and consults regularly on teaching and learning at small colleges, including starting successful centers and creating programs that address the needs of untenured faculty. He served as the inaugural chair of the POD Small College Committee and as faculty in the National Institute for New Faculty Developers and the Harvard Graduate School of Education's Management Development Program. He can be reached at reder@conncoll.edu.

Ann Riley is a Ph.D. candidate in adult and higher education in Educational Leadership & Policy Studies at the University of Oklahoma. Her interests lie in faculty development, including programs for TAs, international students, and new faculty. Her current research focuses on the holistic adult development and the place of spirituality among third-year faculty. She earned a special education degree and an M.S.W. from OU and practiced family psychotherapy for twenty years. She can be reached at annriley@ou.edu.

Erik Rosegard is an associate professor in the Department of Recreation and Leisure Studies at San Francisco State University. He has presented numerous papers in the areas of teaching, instructional methods, and community service learning and was recognized with the Faculty Award for Outstanding Community Service Learning. Rosegard was recently appointed a faculty associate with the Center for Teaching and Faculty Development. He is now focused on transferring his scholarly teaching to the scholarship of teaching and learning. He can be reached at rosegard@sfsu.edu.

Kenneth S. Sagendorf is the deputy director of faculty development in the Center for Educational Excellence (CEE) and an assistant professor at the United States Air Force Academy. His research interests include faculty development, strategies to facilitate student learning, and the scholarship of teaching and learning through focused reflection. He can be reached at kenneth.sagendorf@usafa.edu.

Mary Deane Sorcinelli is associate provost for faculty development and an associate professor in the Department of Educational Policy, Research, and Administration at the University of Massachusetts

Amherst. She is also founding director of UMass Amherst's award-winning Center for Teaching and author of several resources on teaching and learning, faculty development, and early career faculty. Sorcinelli, Jung Yun, and their provost, Charlena Seymour, are co-principal investigators of an Andrew W. Mellon Foundation grant to support mentoring for new and underrepresented faculty on their campus. She can be reached at msorcinelli@acad.umass.edu.

Cheryl A. Stevens has been a faculty member at East Carolina University for ten years. She is concerned with scholarly teaching and engagement, evidenced in part by her leadership role in park and recreation education toward establishing a pilot program for the blind peer review of scholarly teaching. Stevens has received five teaching awards and is the author of *Service Learning for Health, Physical Education and Recreation: A Step-by-Step Guide* (Human Kinetics Publishing, 2008). She can be reached at stevensc@ecu.edu.

David W. Stockburger is the deputy director of academic assessment at the United States Air Force Academy in the Center for Educational Excellence (CEE). An emeritus professor of psychology at Missouri State University, he continues to teach an online statistics course for that institution. His current interests include assessment of online statistics courses, item response theory, GIS, and student feedback to instructors. He has a Ph.D. from Ohio State University in mathematical psychology and statistics. He can be reached at steven.jones@usafa.edu.

Mark Wiley is a professor of English and is currently the associate dean of curriculum and personnel in the College of Liberal Arts at California State University, Long Beach (CSULB). A former director of CSULB's Faculty Center for Professional Development, he has coordinated CSULB's English composition program and assumed leadership roles in K–16 partnerships and general education reform. His research in rhetoric and composition has been published in journals such as the *Journal of Advanced Composition* and *Rhetoric Review*. He can be reached at mwiley@csulb.edu.

Michael Woodnick is associate professor of communication studies at Northeastern University and a founding member of the Communication Studies Department. He has developed and taught courses in communication and authenticity, spirituality, and communication and the quality of life. From 2000 to 2003, Woodnick served as the first university-appointed director of spiritual life. He can be reached at m.woodnick@neu.edu.

Mary C. Wright is an assistant research scientist and coordinator of GSI initiatives at the Center for Research on Learning and Teaching, University of Michigan. In addition to her work with graduate students, Wright consults with faculty and departments and directs a SoTL grants program. Her research interests include faculty-institutional alignment of values, retention in the sciences, and qualitative research. She is author of *Always at Odds? Creating Alignment Between Faculty and Administrative Values* (SUNY, 2008). She can be reached at mcwright@umich.edu.

Donald H. Wulff began his career in instructional development in 1980 as a graduate research assistant at the University of Washington. He joined the staff of the UW Center for Instructional Development and Research (CIDR) in 1984, and at the time of his death in February 2008, he was director of CIDR, associate dean of the graduate school, and affiliate faculty in the UW Department of Communication. He was past president of POD (1993–1994), 2002 recipient of the Bob Pierleoni Spirit of POD Award, and 2007 recipient of the University of Washington David B. Thorud Leadership Award.

Jung H. Yun is director of new-faculty initiatives in the Office of Faculty Development and a lecturer at the University of Massachusetts Amherst. Previously, she was an administrator at several not-for-profit organizations in New York City, including the New York Public Library, Lincoln Center for the Performing Arts, and the New York City Economic Development Corporation. Yun, Sorcinelli, and their provost, Charlena Seymour, are co-principal investigators of an Andrew W. Mellon Foundation grant to support mentoring for new and underrepresented faculty on their campus. She can be reached at jungy@english.umass.edu.

Preface

All the chapters in this volume fit under one of six themes: 1) our work and careers as educational or faculty developers, 2) new programs that enhance faculty work and careers, 3) improved tools we can use in our individual consultations with faculty, 4) variations in our work by institutional type, 5) innovative approaches to evaluating faculty on both teaching and the scholarship of teaching and learning, and 6) initiatives that nurture new and future faculty, as well as prospective educational developers.

Section I: For and About Educational Developers

Chapter One: This is my own research-grounded analysis of the cumulative impact of several current trends in higher education. The individual trends are familiar, but viewing them all together generates a much more challenging picture of the demands and expectations that both the faculty and educational developers are facing today. In fact, they are so challenging that it will take magic, I contend, to meet them.

Chapter Two: Ed Neal and Iola Peed-Neal bring a total of sixty-four years of experience to their summary of lessons learned *experientially* in the day-to-day practice of faculty development. Their advice is valuable, not only for the new director of a faculty development center but also for anyone who aspires to such a directorship. Even seasoned directors who move to a new institution will appreciate being reminded of the many things one must learn as part of the settling-in process.

Chapter Three: Gail F. Latta gives educational developers a crash course in organizational development (OD), particularly the theories of organizational change and cultural analysis that underpin the practice of OD. She forecasts that administrators will call on us, if they haven't already, to broaden our roles to encompass managing institution-wide change. This responsibility will require identifying and articulating the cultural norms of faculty and staff and developing strategies to use these norms to facilitate change.

Chapter Four: A. Jane Birch and Tara Gray detail the many ways—ten to be exact—that we can use a well-designed relational database to enhance our effectiveness and efficiency in managing and assessing center activities and programs. The new, inexpensive system tools that are available today can raise the quality and professionalism of the services we offer, streamline administrative tasks, and leave us more time and energy to work directly with faculty.

Chapter Five: Cynthia Desrochers picks up on the "magic" theme in analyzing why so many directors of teaching and learning centers in the twenty-three-campus California State University (CSU) system perform a disappearing act after just a few years. Drawing on historical CSU system reports and surveys of center directors, she examines how directors view their position, where they go when they leave it, and how organizational factors contribute to their leaving. She then proposes forty-seven factors in six categories that should help retain directors by preventing the burnout so prevalent among them.

Section II: Helping Faculty Thrive

Chapter Six: Phyllis Blumberg describes a successful, comprehensive system for helping faculty shift their teaching from instructor-centered to learner-centered. It is designed to prevent and even overcome resistance by providing faculty with concrete, learner-centered classroom practices, reflection questions, and self-assessment rubrics to help them determine how learner-centered their courses are at different times. The system includes a plan for making the changes of their choosing incrementally.

Chapter Seven: Elizabeth Ambos, Mark Wiley, and Terre H. Allen share their experience designing and directing the Scholarly Writing Institute—a three- to four-day, retreat-like program held during semester breaks to develop and support faculty writing. The Institute furnishes not only quiet writing time but also one-on-one editing and statistical help, relevant panel discussions, and self-assessment of one's writing progress. Aside from praising the Institute experience, many faculty renew their interest in scholarship and join writers' support groups.

Chapter Eight: Jane V. Nelson and Audrey M. Kleinsasser present an effective leadership development program designed just for faculty. Diverging from the business and industry approach, this model grooms those who excel intellectually, fostering their personal growth, confidence, and sense of competence, which then transfers into their committees and administrative roles. It draws on the transformative effects of the scholarship of teaching and learning, the educational renewal model, soft projects and social capital, and horizontal structures.

Chapter Nine: Donna M. Qualters, Beverly Dolinsky, and Michael Woodnick recount their year-long efforts to develop a web of inter-related activities around spirituality and meaning on a secular campus. They started by surveying faculty, administrators, and staff to assess the interest in exploring spirituality, then designed programs in response to the wide variety of needs expressed. Among the lessons they learned was how to create a climate that accepts and values spiritually oriented initiatives in a nonsectarian institution.

Section III: One-on-One with Faculty

Chapter Ten: Michele DiPietro, Susan A. Ambrose, Michael Bridges, Anne Fay, Marsha C. Lovett, and Marie Kamala Norman introduce an online consultation tool that may complement face-to-face consultations or more efficiently serve adjunct and off-site faculty. Once the teaching problem and its causes (selected from a list of possibilities) are identified, the tool links each cause to appropriate contextualized solutions, along with the learning principles behind each solution. The instructor not only acquires concrete strategies to solve the problem but also learns the peda-gogical theory and research that make them effective.

Chapter Eleven: Steven K. Jones, Kenneth S. Sagendorf, D. Brent Morris, David W. Stockburger, and Evelyn T. Patterson describe their role in promoting their institution's cultural trans-formation to an outcomes-driven, learning-focused paradigm. They developed a learning-focused classroom observation form, which differs considerably from traditional observation forms, over a lengthy process of testing, collecting feedback, and revis-ing the document again and again. They explain the many les-sons they learned in the process about classroom observation, effective teaching, and faculty development.

Chapter Twelve: Wayne Jacobson, the late Donald H. Wulff, Stacy Grooters, Phillip M. Edwards, and Karen Freisem answer the question we all ask ourselves sooner or later: Do we really make any long-term difference in the way our clients teach? Their survey of faculty and teaching assistants who consulted with their center one to five years ago revealed the answer is yes, but many former clients reported important benefits of their consultations beyond improving their teaching, such as the access to new information and resources, a sense of connection to like-minded colleagues, a renewed joy in teaching, and much more.

Section IV: Educational Development by Institutional Type

Chapter Thirteen: Stanford T. Goto and Andrei Cerqueira Davis look at two distinct programs that have fostered faculty engagement in the scholarship of teaching and learning at two community colleges. One approach employs a faculty learning community; the other encourages course-based research collaboration between faculty and students. Both have proven effective in generating research, as well as sustained discussions on teaching, despite the faculty's heavy course loads, limited institutional supports and rewards for research, and weak ties to collegial research communities.

Chapter Fourteen: Michael Reder, Kim M. Mooney, Richard A. Holmgren, and Paul J. Kuerbis extend Mooney and Reder's chapter in last year's edition of *To Improve the Academy* on the challenges and features of faculty development at small and liberal arts colleges. Here they propose thirteen practical strategies for starting and sustaining faculty development programming at small institutions, distilled from their own experiences and those of many of their colleagues, compiled over the past seven years. Their advice is particularly valuable for relatively new faculty developers.

Chapter Fifteen: Larissa Pchenitchnaia and Bryan R. Cole present the results of their nationwide survey of faculty development center directors at research-extensive universities. Their goal was to identify, using the Delphi method to maximize consensus, what these directors saw as "essential" programs, both currently and for the future, at their type of institution. The directors anticipated many more programming needs for the future than for now. This study's findings can help inform current and future faculty development planning at research-extensive universities.

Section V: Faculty Evaluation

Chapter Sixteen: Cheryl A. Stevens and Erik Rosegard propose a model integrating the course portfolio and the peer review of scholarly teaching for documenting and evaluating the scholarship of teaching and learning using a discipline-based, blind peer-review process. They argue convincingly that until SoTL becomes a public, cumulative endeavor that is peer reviewed and critiqued against agreed-upon scholarly standards, many faculty will continue to view it as evidence of teaching excellence and to eschew it for the greater rewards and recognition of disciplinary research.

Chapter Seventeen: Trav D. Johnson complements the learning-centered teaching paradigm with a learning-centered approach to evaluating teaching—one that replaces the traditional focus on instructor performance and course characteristics with an emphasis on student learning. Borrowing principles from program evaluation, it assesses teaching in terms of the alignment among learning goals, activities, assessments, and outcomes, integrating information from whatever sources are best suited to provide it, whether students, peers, administrators, or the teacher-under-review.

Section VI: For the Next Generation

Chapter Eighteen: Ann Riley hopes to help new faculty and increase their retention with her findings on changes in their support needs over their first year. She examines three types of needs: 1) *professional* (teaching, research, service), 2) *personal* (local community, personal or family adjustment, religious or spiritual issues), and 3) *relational* (social fit with colleagues, staff, and students). As these shift in priority during the year, she recommends that new-faculty development programs shift accordingly in their focus.

Chapter Nineteen: Jung H. Yun and Mary Deane Sorcinelli introduce a network-based mentoring model—"Mutual Mentoring"—that is designed to integrate new and underrepresented faculty in nonhierarchical, collaborative, and cross-cultural relationships with colleagues. Faculty of all ages and ranks participate and learn from each other. The program has proven very popular on their campus, involving about 20 percent of all pre-tenure and tenured faculty.

Chapter Twenty: Deborah S. Meizlish and Mary C. Wright present the results of their survey of former graduate teaching consultants who previously worked in the teaching center. Do such graduate employment opportunities foster future allies and leaders of faculty development? This study chronicles how these former consultants carried their teaching-center involvement into their first faculty jobs and emerged as leaders of departmental and institutional faculty development and pedagogical initiatives.

Chapter Twenty-One: Pamela E. Barnett and Linda C. Hodges document the transformation of the graduate student facilitators they trained to lead problem-solving-skills workshops for undergraduates. Like most faculty, these facilitators started out believing that their job was to promote students' mastery of the content and that the problem-solving process was obvious. Leading the workshops makes them realize the cognitive difficulties that novice learners face and the need for explicit instruction in disciplinary thinking processes.

Conclusion

We have some ingenious colleagues. After perceiving a human need, they work individually and often in teams to meet that need. It should be inspiring to us all to read about this varied assortment of innovative models, programs, research findings, and principles of practice. They are each easily transferable and applicable to at least a large subset of colleges and universities, and we may find among them solutions to problems we are facing now or will face soon.

Within *To Improve the Academy*, we can find opportunities to add to the joy of our jobs as educational developers. When we read this volume and mine its gemlike ideas for our own institution, we're not just keeping up with the literature; we're making the world of higher education a better place.

LINDA B. NILSON
Clemson University
Clemson, South Carolina
April 2008

Acknowledgments

An editor stands on the shoulders of her reviewers, and I was fortunate to have had many strong shoulders to stand on—45 sets of shoulders, to be exact. As a team, they provided over 130 reviews, most of which offered thoughtful, constructive, in-depth comments on each of their assigned manuscripts. Those who wrote two- to-three single-spaced pages of feedback and evaluation on each manuscript they reviewed certainly deserve some kind of award. The reviewers didn't always agree about a given manuscript, but they explained the values and standards they used to arrive at their recommendations. Here is the list of those unsung, behind-the-scenes heroes: Danilo Baylen, Laurie Bellows, Donna Bird, Phyllis Blumberg, Jeanette Clausen, Jodi Cressman, Bonnie Daniel, Cynthia Desrochers, Michele DiPietro, Sally Barr Ebest, Bonnie Farley-Lucas, Judy Grace, Elizabeth Yost Hammer, Jace Hargis, Eric Hobson, Wayne Jacobson, Frances Johnson, Kathleen Kane, Mick LaLopa, Marion Larson, Jean Layne, Virginia S. Lee, P. Rachel Levin, Deandra Little, Alice Macpherson, Vilma Mesa, Daniel Mercier, Bonnie Mullinix, Ed Neal, Ed Nuhfer, Leslie Ortquist-Arhens, Patrick O'Sullivan, Donna Petherbridge, Susan Polich, Nancy Polk, Edwin Ralph, Gerald Ratliff, Jen Schoepke, Ike Shibley, Jennifer Shinaberger, Judy Silvestrone, Karen St. Clair, Suzanne Tapp, Karen Ward, and Mary Wright.

Hoag Holmgren, executive director of the POD Network, furnished information, updates, and files I desperately needed. More than that, he was joy to work with and always a bright spot in my day.

On the publisher's side, David Brightman served as my editor at Jossey-Bass, patiently answering my many questions and keeping me on track. It was also a pleasure to work again with Carolyn Dumore, formerly of Anker Publishing, who guided the production process.

Douglas Reimondo Robertson, editor of the last two volumes of *To Improve the Academy*, was sitting just behind me, even though he didn't know it and most of the time was physically over four hundred miles away. In my communications with contributors, reviewers, and authors, I often recalled his experiences as editor and little pieces of advice he shared with me along the way. Before I acted, responded, or made a decision, I reflected on Doug's words and asked myself, "What would Doug do?" Then the best course of action became pretty clear.

Associate editor Judith E. Miller proved to me that I had selected a superb successor. Always prompt to respond and respectful of deadlines, she did an amazing amount of careful, close editing of just over half the manuscripts accepted. She also functioned as an additional reviewer, with her wise comments and suggestions for revisions. Just as valuable were her ideas about improving aspects of the *TIA* "operation." Judy brings a highly effective combination of practical and scholarly intelligence to all she does, so I didn't worry about a thing.

I wish I had staff members to thank for their assistance in preparing this volume, but Clemson's Office of Teaching Effectiveness and Innovation is pretty much a one-person unit. (I deeply appreciate the help and social interaction that William Weathers and Geraldine Hunter provided, even though they belonged to the instructional technology unit.) Therefore, my shifting from a paper-based to a wholly electronic operation was essential, and it worked out very well. All of those involved in producing this volume had a little more time to complete their tasks, whether writing, reviewing, or editing. In addition, I was able to provide the actual reviews (edited to preserve anonymity) to all the manuscript authors using copy-and-paste functions. Many thanks to the dozens of reviewers and authors for effortlessly making the change to an electronic production process.

Ethical Guidelines for Educational Developers

Preamble

Educational developers, as professionals, have a unique opportunity and a special responsibility to contribute to improving the quality of teaching and learning in higher education. As members of the academic community, we are subject to all the codes of conduct and ethical guidelines that already exist for those who work or study on our campuses and in our respective disciplinary associations. In addition, we have special ethical responsibilities because of the unique and privileged access we have to people and information—often sensitive information. This document provides general guidelines that can and should inform the practice of everyone working in educational development roles in higher education.

Individuals who work as educational developers come from different disciplinary areas. Some of us work in this field on a part-time basis or for a short time; for others, this is our full-time career. The nature of our responsibilities and prerogatives as developers varies with our position in the organization, our experience, interests, and talents, as well as with the special characteristics of our institutions. This document attempts to provide general ethical guidelines that should apply to most developers across a variety of settings.

Ethical guidelines indicate a consensus among practitioners about the ideals that should inform our practice as professionals, as well as those behaviors that we would identify as misconduct. Between ideals and misconduct is the area of dilemmas, where each of our choices seems equally right or wrong, or where our different roles and responsibilities place competing—if not incompatible—demands on us, or where certain behaviors may seem questionable but there is no consensus that those behaviors constitute misconduct.

It is our hope that these guidelines will complement individual statements of philosophy and mission and that they will be useful to educational developers in the following ways:

- In promoting ethical practice by describing the ideals of our practice
- In providing a model for thinking through situations that contain conflicting choices or questionable behavior
- In identifying those specific behaviors that we agree represent professional misconduct

Responsibilities to Clients

- Provide services to everyone within our mandate, provided that we are able to serve them responsibly
- Treat clients fairly, respecting their uniqueness, their fundamental rights, dignity, and worth, and their right to set objectives and make decisions
- Continue services only as long as the client is benefiting, discontinuing service by mutual consent; suggest other resources to meet needs we cannot or should not address
- Maintain appropriate boundaries in the relationship; avoid exploiting the relationship in any way; be clear with ourselves and our clients about our role
- Protect all privileged information and get informed consent from our client before using or referring publicly to his or her case in such a way that the person could possibly be identified

Competence and Integrity

Behavior

- Clarify professional roles and obligations
- Accept appropriate responsibility for our behavior
- Don't make false or intentionally misleading statements
- Avoid the distortion and misuse of our work
- When providing services at the behest of a third party, clarify our roles and responsibilities with each party from the outset

- Model ethical behavior with coworkers and supervisees and in the larger community
- Maintain appropriate responsibility for the behavior of those we supervise

Skills and Boundaries

- Be reflective and self-critical in our practice; strive to be aware of our own belief system, values, biases, needs, and the effect of these on our work
- Incorporate diverse points of view
- Know and act in consonance with our purpose, mandate, and philosophy, integrating them insofar as possible
- Ensure that we have the institutional freedom to do our job ethically
- Don't allow personal or private interests to conflict or appear to conflict with professional duties or the client's needs
- Continually seek out knowledge, skills, and resources to undergird and expand our practice
- Consult with other professionals when they lack the experience or training for a particular case or endeavor and in order to prevent and avoid unethical conduct
- Know and work within the boundaries of our competence and time limitations
- Take care of our personal welfare so we can take care of others

Others' Rights

- Be receptive to different styles and approaches to teaching and learning and to others' professional roles and functions
- Respect the rights of others to hold values, attitudes, and opinions different from our own
- Respect the right of the client to refuse our services or to ask for the services of another
- Work against harassment and discrimination of any kind, including race, ethnicity, gender, class, religion, sexual orientation, age, and nationality
- Be aware of and don't abuse the various power relationships with clients (for example, power based on position or on information)

Confidentiality

- Keep confidential the identity of our clients, as well as our observations, interactions, or conclusions related to specific individuals or cases
- Know the legal requirements regarding appropriate and inappropriate professional confidentiality (for example, for cases of murder, suicide, or gross misconduct)
- Store and dispose of records in a safe way, and comply with institutional, state, and federal regulations about storage and ownership of records
- Conduct discreet conversations among professional colleagues; don't discuss clients in public places

Responsibilities to the Profession

- Attribute materials and ideas to their authors or creators
- Contribute ideas, experience, and knowledge to colleagues
- Respond promptly to requests from colleagues
- Respect your colleagues and acknowledge their differences
- Work positively for the development of individuals and the profession
- Cooperate with other units and professionals involved in development efforts
- Be an advocate for institutional and professional missions
- Take responsibility when you become aware of gross unethical conduct in the profession

Conflicts Arising from Multiple Responsibilities, Constituents, Relationships, Loyalties

We are responsible to the institution, faculty, graduate students, undergraduate students, and our own ethical values. These multiple responsibilities and relationships to various constituencies, together with competing loyalties, can lead to conflicting ethical responsibilities. Here are some examples:

- An instructor is teaching extremely poorly, and the students are suffering seriously as a result.
  - *Conflict:* responsibility of confidentiality to client teacher versus responsibility to students and institution to take some immediate action

- A faculty member wants to know how a TA, with whom we are working, is doing in his or her work or in the classroom.
  - *Conflict:* responding to faculty's legitimate concern versus confidentiality with TA
- We know firsthand that a professor is making racist, sexist remarks or is sexually harassing a student.
  - *Conflict:* confidentiality with professor versus institutional and personal ethical responsibilities, along with responsibility to students
- A fine teacher is coming up for tenure, has worked with our center or program for two years, and asks for a letter to the tenure committee.
  - *Conflict:* confidentiality rules versus our commitment to advocate for good teaching on campus and in tenure decisions

In such instances, we need to practice sensitive and sensible confidentiality and do the following:

- Consult in confidence with other professionals when we have conflicting or confusing ethical choices.
- Break confidentiality in cases of potential suicide, murder, or gross misconduct (in such cases, to do nothing is to do something).
- Inform the other person or persons when we have to break confidentiality, unless to do so would be to jeopardize our safety or the safety of someone else.
- Decide cases of questionable practice individually, after first informing ourselves, to the best of our ability, of all the ramifications of our actions; work to determine when we will act or not act, while being mindful of the rules and regulations of the institution and the relevant legal requirements.

Conflicts Arising from Multiple Roles

As educational developers, we often assume or are assigned roles that might be characterized as, for example, teaching police, doctor, coach, teacher, or advocate, among others. We endeavor to provide a "safe place" for our clients; we are at the same time an institutional model and a guardian for a conscience for good teaching. These multiple roles can also lead to ethical conflicts.

Some educational developers, for example, serve both as faculty developers and as faculty members. As faculty we are on review committees but through our faculty development work have access to information that probably is not public but is important to the cases involved. Given these multiple roles, it is important always to clarify our role for ourselves and for those with whom we are working. When necessary, we must rescue ourselves.

A particular case of multiple roles needing guidelines is the summative evaluation of teaching. Faculty and administrators (chairs, deans, and so on) have the responsibility for the assessment of teaching for personnel decisions.

In general, educational developers do not make summative judgments about an individual's teaching. In particular, we should never perform the role of developer and summative evaluator concurrently for the same individual, other than with that person's explicit consent and with proper declaration to any panel or committee. However, we may provide assessment tools, collect student evaluations, help individuals prepare dossiers, educate those who make summative decisions, and critique evaluation systems.

Conclusion

These guidelines are an attempt to define ethical behaviors for the current practice of our profession. The core committee welcomes comments and suggestions, as we continue to refine this document in light of the changes and issues confronting us as educational developers in higher education. The guidelines will be updated on a periodic basis.

We would like to thank our many colleagues who offered their thoughtful comments on earlier drafts.

In creating this document, we have referred to and borrowed from the ethical guidelines of the following organizations: American Psychological Association, American Association for Marriage and Family Therapy, Guidance Counselors, Society for Teaching and Learning in Higher Education, Staff and Educational Development Association.

Note: Prepared by Mintz, Smith, & Warren, January 1999. Revised March 1999, September 1999, and March 2000.

To Improve the Academy

For and About Educational Developers

Chapter 1

Editor's Introduction
The Educational Developer as Magician

Linda B. Nilson
Clemson University

After so many changes in the academy, faculty and educational developers face chal-
lenges that require magic to meet. Faculty members are supposed to perform the magic,
and we educational developers are expected to teach them how. The trick is to teach more
in the same amount of time to disinterested and unprepared students, under the condi-
tions of larger classes, less authority, and lower rewards. College and university faculty are
under attack for falling short, and educational developers are next in line to feel the heat.
Perhaps we should start defending our faculties, explaining our challenges, and publiciz-
ing our efforts and inroads.

Ever think of yourself as a magician? Even if *you* don't, other people apparently do because they are entrusting us faculty and
instructional developers with such challenging tasks that it would
take a lot of magic to achieve what they want. In fact, they expect
us to be master magicians and to transform the faculty into at
least journeyman magicians themselves.

What's the trick? To teach, within the same four-year block as
years ago, more knowledge and skills than ever before to students who are unprepared to learn them, as well as disinterested
in learning them, under the conditions of larger classes, less
authority, and lower rewards than ever before.

Let's break that trick down.

No one would argue that the knowledge required to succeed in
professional, semiprofessional, technical, and managerial positions
has grown astronomically over the past fifty to seventy-five years.

And we in higher education are well aware that the public and our own accrediting agencies demand that we develop in students a host of skills—critical thinking, quantitative reasoning, ethical judgment, cultural sensitivity, written and oral communication, information literacy, and scientific literacy, for example—that we never had to address explicitly before. In fact, we didn't even talk about "skills" thirty years ago. Should this broader and more challenging learning process take the same four years that it used to? The government and the public seem to think that it should.

Now let's examine our students.

Students Today

A considerably higher proportion of high school graduates than ever before in the United States enter either two-year or four-year institutions of higher learning. In 1919, the figure was 32.8 percent, in 1927 32.0 percent, in 1939 20.1 percent, and in 1947 33.2 percent, then between 1951 and 1964, the percentage rose from 30.0 percent to 39.5 percent (Campbell & Seigel, 1967). Today, about 75 percent of high school graduates take some kind of postsecondary schooling within two years of graduation (Association of American Colleges and Universities, 2002)—an amazing increase of about 90 percent in four decades.

However, a much smaller percentage of high school graduates—32 percent—is actually college-ready by the most minimal yardstick, which means having completed the basic college-required courses and having acquired *basic* literacy skills (Greene & Forster, 2003)—obviously an inadequate definition of *college-ready*. Of those actually entering our colleges and universities, only 47 percent are ready in the sense that they have at least basic reading, writing, and math skills (Miller & Murray, 2005).

Many of us can recall when, for better or for ill, universities screened applicants for proficiency in academic skills. But probably none of us can recall when an eighth-grade education, let alone a high-school diploma, provided solid proficiency in English and math. In fact, with her American third-grade education and absolutely no intellectual bent, my grandmother (born in 1888) exceeded "functionally literate." What happened in the last hundred years? Even in 1995, only 29 percent of entering freshmen took at least one remedial reading, writing, or math course (National Center for Educational Statistics, 1996). But in 2005, 53 percent needed one or more remedial courses (Miller & Murray, 2005), which represents an 83 percent increase. What happened in those ten years?

Students come to us culturally unprepared as well, and they have been since the early 1990s, when the term *classroom incivilities* was coined. Like the generations before them, they behave in their college classrooms much the way they did in high school. But today's students have learned standards of behavior that show little respect for instructors or for fellow students who want to learn. High schools tolerate such conduct, perhaps because they no longer have the legal right to enforce behavioral rules in meaningful ways. In addition, students can't be expected to behave as politely in a setting in which they feel "forced" to be, and now that college feels almost as required as high school for many students, they attend for reasons other than genuine desire.

Not only are students less prepared for college-level work and behavioral expectations; they don't particularly value the knowledge and skills we have to offer. As we well know, the vast majority of them attend college for strictly instrumental reasons—to get a better-paying job than they could otherwise or to please their parents—and they aim for obtaining the diploma, not learning. They view that diploma as a necessary, though not sufficient, condition for living as well as or better than their parents do. Deluged for years with subtly high-pressure advertising, they value material success dearly. But few see serious learning as the means to achieve it. Because many of them skated through high school doing very little work for their good grades, they are not about to knock themselves out now. They eschew rigor, reading, and writing and feel entitled to the decent grades they believe they (or their parents) paid for. (Among the younger, middle-class students, many parents will aggressively back them up on their claim.) Not that students won't work. Most put long hours into their gainful employment and either family duties or Greek activities, electronic entertainment, and "beer and circus." But they certainly do not regard a full college course load as a full-time, life-engrossing pursuit, and they may even resent those who challenge their perception.

According to Biggs (2003), the current student profile is much the same in the British Commonwealth. He puts faces on the situation, as he describes two archetypical college students. Susan is every professor's dream—bright, curious, academically motivated, well-prepared, goal-oriented, reflective about her course material, and interested in deep learning. In 1980, 75 percent of the students in college classrooms were like Susan (Brabrand & Andersen, 2006). In contrast, Robert is pursuing a degree to get a decent job and is probably less academically talented than Susan. In any case, he comes to his classes with little (or at least much less) preparation, motivation, and interest in the subject matter. Rather than reflecting on and constructing the knowledge he receives, he prefers to surface-learn and memorize whatever material is necessary to get by. Robert's type made up only one-quarter of the student body in 1980—relatively few made it through or even attended college—but today it represents almost 60 percent, no doubt more in many colleges and universities (Brabrand & Andersen, 2006). Meanwhile, the Susans of the world make up less than 42 percent overall. For this day and age, Biggs defines *good teaching* as "getting most students to use the higher cognitive level processes that the more academic students use spontaneously" (2003, p. 5)—in other words, turning a lot of Roberts into Susans.

This is a noble goal, but how realistic is it? Robert doesn't want to change. He has different values and is probably busy with other pursuits of higher priority than his course work. Even if he did want to change, he might not be capable of thinking as deeply as Susan routinely does.

In recent years, we have studiously avoided acknowledging differences in students' raw ability to learn, and we believe that anyone can learn anything in the right learning environment. This may be true, but consider the time factor. Some students grasp complex concepts and relationships in their first exposure and can explain them to their slower peers in group work, while others *in the same learning environment* (same class, same instructor) never really "get it." We all have known students who have repeated a course, put genuine effort into it, and never "got it." How long can a person stay in school? The students who learn *immediately* and with little help from anyone, like Susan, may simply be more able than others.

Enter the Magician

Changing Roberts into Susans is where the magic comes in. And we faculty developers are supposed to teach faculty how to perform this magic act—one student at a time, again and again and again.

But perhaps nothing is impossible for our faculty with the proper institutional support and enough time with each student. So let's look at how our colleges and universities are trying to help their students get motivated and succeed. On the one hand, they have instituted more lenient policies on course withdrawals and repeat-course grade replacement, as well as student-support services and even personal coaches. But on the other, they are accepting greater numbers of students, thus creating a more anomic social environment. They are also accepting more heterogeneous student populations and crowding them into larger classes, especially in the freshman year, when students are most likely to fail or leave. Although large classes enhance the bottom line, the research consistently shows that they work against every positive student dimension you can think of: motivation, class attendance, attention in class, classroom civility, academic integrity, learning, academic performance, development of higher-order cognitive skills, long-term retention, teaching evaluations, college persistence, and satisfaction with the course, the discipline, and the institution—not to mention instructor morale (Cuseo, 2004). The faculty just cannot provide enough individual help and attention to so many students, nor can they pitch so much material to so many different levels of background and ability at once. So colleges and universities may giveth to students in some ways, but they taketh away in others.

Given the preparation and attitudes that students bring to college, plus their need to work a job or two, along with the double-edged support institutions provide, it is little wonder that today's students commonly take five or six years to graduate from college, if they graduate at all. According to a 2007 report by the

National Center for Higher Education Management, only 47 percent of those who enter four-year institutions right after high school graduate within six years (calculated from Figure 8 in the NCHEM report). Nor is it any wonder that most graduates are entering the labor market lacking basic skills. According to a 2006 study by the American Institutes for Research, fewer than 50 percent of students graduating from four-year colleges and fewer than 75 percent of those graduating from two-year colleges have attained literacy proficiency.

Many of today's students would never have completed, if they even had attended, college under the old system in operation over thirty years ago. Higher education was considered a privilege for the brightest and most diligent. It was also a screening device. Students who couldn't cut it, no matter how poor the instruction they received, simply flunked out or dropped out. This was expected, even *desirable,* as unofficial certification of an institution's selectivity and high standards. Back then, the students were solely responsible for their own learning. Colleges and universities were not held accountable for much of anything, least of all the effectiveness of instruction. Lecturing was *de rigueur* for the faculty. Yet, although we have no national literacy assessment data from "back then," employers and the public were not complaining about their graduates' poor literacy skills, sloppy reasoning, and shallow knowledge bases. These college survivors must have had well-honed learning skills, solid cognitive abilities, and plenty of self-motivation.

How times have changed. Despite what our students and institutions bring to the table today, faculty members are under fire, apparently, for failing to achieve the same results with their students that they used to. Neither the public nor the government seems to notice the drastic increases in ill-prepared and differently motivated students, class sizes, and heterogeneity, and the breadth of knowledge and skills needed to succeed in the educated labor force. Two recent reports—one issued by Jobs for the Future (Reindl, 2007) and the other by the National Center for Public Policy and Higher Education (2006)—sounded the alarm that the United States is falling behind other developed nations in college completion rates. Again, in view of the situation just described, it is little wonder. But what was the solution forwarded?

Get the federal government to fund more higher education costs, as is true in all of the seven nations with higher college completion rates? Beef up the K–12 system so more students leave high school truly college-ready? Institute some cultural change to exalt learning, knowledge, and excellence in school? Reduce class sizes and heterogeneity? No, the solution given was simply to increase its degree production by 37 percent (Reindl, 2007)—a measure guaranteed to worsen the situation that students, institutions, and faculty already face. Reindl did not propose any means or sources of support for so radically raising degree production without lowering standards. Rather, he blasted higher education for increasing spending and tuition, turning out poorly skilled graduates, and not providing sufficient access. In other words, American higher education is solely responsible for the problems in higher education, as well as for solving them. Expect no help.

The Faculty's Dilemma

This brings us to the faculty's loss of authority and rewards. It is within many of our living memories that students and the public at large held all levels of teachers—professors most of all—in the highest esteem. Although only modestly paid, K–12 teachers commanded respect for their above-average intelligence and their contribution to the greater social good. Professors, almost all of them tenured or tenure-track, enjoyed good or very good salaries, enviable job security, abundant free time, and the respect that was then widely accorded to highly intelligent individuals. Those who taught were role models who drew their motivation from a "higher source" than sheer materialism.

Fade to today. In many, perhaps most, high school settings, demonstrating intelligence and interest in learning is almost taboo. The most highly rewarded heroes in and out of school are athletes, rock musicians, and Paris Hilton or Brittany Spears look-alikes. Having certain things that money can buy, from tennis shoes to electronics, cements one's social status. Given this personal history, many of today's college students must look askance at us for investing so many years in our education in return for relatively low-paying jobs. The fact that we are seen as "service workers" expected to satisfy a rather demanding and stressed-out set of customers—one that our institutions competed for and desperately want to retain—does not enhance our prestige. Our administration wants us to please our students, even though many of them don't like taking the most effective medicine we can prescribe: active learning (Michael, 2007; Rhem, 2006; Thorn, 2003). If they do poorly, it's *our* problem because we are supposed to retain them. More accurately, we are supposed to make them retainable, despite our large, heterogeneous classes.

Along with suffering a loss of authority, faculty are being worked to death with sixty- to eighty-hour weeks. Except in community colleges, they are expected to publish and present more than ever before, despite the dearth of grant support and travel funds. At the same time, they are teaching heavier course loads and larger classes and are supposed keep abreast of and publish in not only their discipline but also the scholarship of teaching (Sorcinelli & Austin, 2006). In addition, they are less free than in the past to teach and assess as they see fit (Wilson, 2007). After all, their raises and promotions depend, at least to some extent, on their student ratings, and a number of students (it only takes a few) penalize their instructors for active learning strategies and "strict" grading methods (Johnson, 2003; Rhem, 2006; Thorn, 2003). Meanwhile, faculty salaries have been slipping for many years. Of course, the untenured experience these trends most sharply—in particular, the 46 percent of faculty (as of 2003) who work part-time for pitiful pay and no benefits (American Association of University Professors, 2005–06). Many of these are road warriors piggybacking multiple jobs.

As higher education faculty become an economically weaker, more politically frail, and less respected force in American society, they are an easy target for blame. Employers, the federal and state governments, report-generating centers, and the general public collectively point the finger at the quality of instruction for the poor overall quality and insufficient numbers of college graduates (Carey, 2007; Eaton, 2007). Faculty receive little recognition—none at all from outside academe—for student-centering their teaching, and they are faulted for pursuing research, even though their professional survival depends on it.

Blaming the faculty means blaming us. We have dodged the bullets thus far only because we have not been particularly visible to academe's critics. But our obscurity cannot last for long. Will we be the next scapegoats? Will we be held responsible for the lengthening time-to-degree, students' unsatisfactory persistence rates, the stagnant numbers and percentages of college graduates, and the downward spiral in their literacy levels? After all, aren't we the ones who are supposed to train and "fix" the faculty to train and "fix" the students? Didn't we get to our positions because *we* worked magic with students? Where's our magic now? If we were performing our tricks right, our society wouldn't be in the educational pickle it's in today, right?

Conclusion

Perhaps we should think about defending our faculties, about informing our nonacademic constituencies about the challenges instructors—and we—face from our ill-prepared students, the knowledge economy's burgeoning expectations of them, our money-driven institutions, and our own industry's broken labor market. All these conditions preclude the magical results everybody wants. Even if we educational developers ran the universities, it is unclear what we could accomplish with our current students and resources.

To Improve the Academy showcases our best efforts to achieve magical results. As the evaluation results show, these efforts do make headway. Those who discount the fruits of academe's labor as puny need to know about these innovative programs. They need to know about the array of successful, ongoing programs that have attracted faculty year after year. And they need to know how dedicated today's faculty are to making whatever magic they can with their Roberts.

References

American Association of University Professors. (2005–06). *Annual report of the economic status of the profession.* Washington, DC: Author.

American Institutes for Research. (2006). *The literacy of America's college students.* Washington, DC: Author.

Association of American Colleges and Universities. (2002). *Greater expectations: A new vision for learning as a nation goes to college.* Washington, DC: Author.

Biggs, J. B. (2003). *Teaching for quality learning at university* (2nd ed.). Berkshire, UK: Society for Research into Higher Education and Open University Press.

Brabrand, C. (Co-Producer/Writer/Director), & Andersen, J. (Co-Producer). (2006). *Teaching teaching and understanding understanding* [DVD]. Denmark: University of Aarhus and Daimi Edutainment.

Campbell, R., & Seigel, B. N. (1967). The demand for higher education in the United States, 1919–1964. *American Economic Review, 57*(3), 482–494.

Carey, K. (2007, September/October). Truth without action: The myth of higher-education accountability. *Change, 39*(5), 24–29.

Cuseo, J. (2004). *The empirical case against large class size: Adverse effects on teaching, learning, and retention of first-year students.* Retrieved August 6, 2007, from www.ulster.ac.uk/star/curriculum_development/cuseo_class_size.pdf

Eaton, J. (2007, September/October). Institutions, accreditors, and the federal government: Redefining their "appropriate relationship." *Change, 39*(5), 16–23.

Greene, J. P., & Forster, G. (2003, September). *Public high school graduation and college readiness rates in the United States* (Education working paper No. 3). Retrieved August 6, 2007, from Manhattan Institute for Policy Research Web site: www.manhattan-institute.org/html/ewp_03.htm

Johnson, V. E. (2003). *Grade inflation: A crisis in college education.* New York: Springer-Verlag.

Michael, J. (2007). Faculty perceptions about barriers to active learning. *College Teaching, 55*(2), 42–47.

Miller, M. A., & Murray, C. (2005). *Advising academically underprepared students.* Retrieved November 12, 2007, from NACADA Clearinghouse of Academic Advising Resources Web site: www.nacada.ksu.edu/Clearinghouse/AdvisingIssues/Academically-Underprepared.htm

National Center for Educational Statistics. (1996). *Remedial education at higher education institutions in fall 1995* (Report No. NCES 97–584). Washington, DC. Summary retrieved November 12, 2007, from www.ecs.org/clearinghouse/25/33/2533.htm

National Center for Higher Education Management. (2007). *The emerging policy triangle: Economic development, workforce development, and education.* Boulder, CO: Western Interstate Commission for Higher Education.

National Center for Public Policy and Higher Education. (2006). *Measuring up: The national report card on higher education.* San Jose, CA: Author.

Reindl, T. (2007). *Hitting home: Quality, cost, and access challenges confronting higher education today*. Washington, DC: Jobs for the Future, Knowledge Center/Publications.

Rhem, J. (2006). The high risks of improving teaching. *National Teaching and Learning Forum, 15*(6), 1–4.

Sorcinelli, M. D., & Austin, A. E. (2006, November). Developing faculty for new roles and changing expectations. *Effective Practices for Academic Leaders, 1*(11), 1–6.

Thorn, P. M. (2003). *Bridging the gap between what is praised and what is practiced: Supporting the work of change as anatomy and physiology instructors introduce active learning into their undergraduate classroom*. Unpublished doctoral dissertation, University of Texas, Austin.

Wilson, R. C. (2007, September 12). AAUP goes to bat for "freedom in the classroom." *Chronicle of Higher Education*. Retrieved November 12, 2007, from http://chronicle.com/daily/2007/09/2007091202n.htm

Chapter 2

Experiential Lessons in the Practice of Faculty Development

Ed Neal, Iola Peed-Neal
University of North Carolina at Chapel Hill

The practice of faculty development, as distinct from its theoretical and empirical principles, must largely be learned experientially, through an often painful process of trial and error. In this chapter, we offer some of the lessons we have learned in our combined total of sixty-four years as faculty developers, in hopes that others might benefit from our experience.

In spite of a history that reaches back almost fifty years, faculty development as a profession is still poorly defined. Perhaps it would be more accurate to say that it is *variously* defined. The Web site of the Professional and Organizational Development (POD) Network requires over 3,600 words to provide definitions of *faculty development,* describe types of development programs, and posit ethical guidelines for the profession.

Of course, there are some excellent books on the practice of faculty development, most notably *A Guide to Faculty Development: Practical Advice, Examples, and Resources* (Gillespie, Hilsen, & Wadsworth, 1997), *Face to Face: A Sourcebook of Individual Consultation Techniques for Faculty/Instructional Developers* (Lewis & Povlacs Lunde, 2001), and *Practically Speaking: A Sourcebook for Instructional Consultants in Higher Education* (Brinko & Menges, 1997). The POD annual, *To Improve the Academy,* also provides invaluable advice and guidance about the practice of the profession. However, organizational history, culture, and politics create unique environmental conditions at each institution, and a given program may have little in common with programs at other schools, even those of the same size and type. As a result, even experienced developers may find themselves at a loss when confronting new situations in their work—a state of affairs reflected in the frequent requests for help and guidance posted on the POD listserv.

Faculty development is a craft that must be mastered largely experientially, through imitation, observation, and trial and error, like bartending or dog walking. However, as an old saying goes, the problem with learning from experience is that you get the test first and the lesson afterward. As a way to help other developers avoid some of the more painful lessons, we would like to share a few insights about the practice of our peculiar profession. The information we present next is based primarily on our experience and that of our colleagues in our own teaching center— the Center for Teaching and Learning at UNC Chapel Hill—but many of these ideas are shared by our colleagues in POD. We caution the reader that this is by no means an exhaustive treatment of the subject and that, owing to space limitations, we have had to omit many details.

What Our Teaching Center Does

We have worked for a combined total of sixty-four years at a large public research university in a teaching center that serves 3,000 faculty members and 1,500 teaching assistants (TAs) across dozens of schools and departments. The center provides a full range of faculty development programs, including professional development consultations for all instructors, new-faculty orientations, TA orientations, a Future Faculty Fellowship program, an Explorations in Teaching workshop series, support for departmental TA development programs, a videotaping program for assessing classroom teaching, formative and summative evaluation of teaching, mentoring for career development, and support for department- and school-based faculty development initiatives.

The Faculty Development Program also assists faculty members who are preparing dossiers for promotion and tenure, writing research grant proposals, and assuming formal and informal leadership roles. It also offers a comprehensive "boot camp" for new administrators. Each of these areas is supported by a peer-to-peer mentoring program. The center's Curriculum Development Program supports an array of initiatives that focus on curricular change and revision, from graduate and undergraduate program reviews to the creation and revisions of interdisciplinary curricula or issue-based curriculum projects. These initiatives also actively support the inclusion of student perspectives in the review, revision, and development of curricula and related courses.

The Instructional Development Program serves the planning needs of instructors and teaching teams by providing substantial consultation and support for the development and implementation of particular courses or course sequences. It addresses instructor and student expectations, course organization and syllabus design, the implementation of specific teaching and learning strategies and student experiences, and the development of instructional materials and technologies, course Web sites, and evaluation measures. Instructors may create teaching resources and technologies with the expert help of instructional designers and instructional technology professionals, or they may work independently in the Teaching Resource Lab—a staffed, up-to-date instructional technology facility. Instructional development serves instruction that occurs in the traditional classroom settings, online or through distance education programs, and in the community, laboratory, clinic, or field-research setting.

These programs grew gradually over three decades in line with the principles outlined next. The existence of our center has been seriously threatened several times in its history, and we believe its survival is evidence that these principles work.

Principles That Work

As difficult as it might be, you should conduct an honest self-assessment to inventory your capabilities and shortcomings as a professional developer, and the earlier, the better. Consider the questions in the next section as a starting point.

Develop Your Competence

How thoroughly have you studied the literature on teaching improvement and faculty development? For example, how extensive is your knowledge of subjects such as testing theory, student evaluation of teaching, the scholarship of teaching and learning, teaching portfolios, process consulting, organizational change, leadership, communities of practice, and accreditation?

How thoroughly have you studied the literature on student learning? For example, how much do you know about the principles of cooperative learning, collaborative learning, inquiry-based learning, and problem-based learning, including their similarities, distinctions, and differences?

How much do you know about teaching in disciplines other than your own, including the kinds of challenges that instructors face in these disciplines? For example, if you have a degree in the social sciences or humanities, you need to learn about teaching in the science, technical, engineering, and mathematical (STEM) disciplines and the health sciences, and vice versa. Even within the STEM disciplines, you will find substantial differences between teaching in an engineering school and teaching in a mathematics department. Similarly, within the health sciences, teaching in medicine differs in many ways from teaching in dentistry and nursing.

Ultimately, the process of mastering these areas is a career-long process, because practices change and new theories constantly come to light. Every time you embark on a project in an area in which you have little or no experience, you will have an opportunity to add to your competencies and your professional repertoire. Don't be afraid to stretch your abilities.

However, knowledge of the field must be accompanied by appropriate personal traits and interpersonal skills. Effective developers must be tenacious, resilient, flexible, trustworthy, and completely committed to their work. Good listening skills, the ability to suspend judgment, frame problems, work collaboratively, and manage your time efficiently are also essential to success.

Once your skills inventory is complete, the next step is to create a plan that will enable you to increase your competencies over time. The Internet can help fill many gaps in your knowledge very quickly, but it cannot replace a systematic study of the published literature; having a structured reading plan is essential. POD members are an excellent source of help and expertise, and they can suggest key books and articles for your reading program. If you feel that you need to work on certain personal traits and interpersonal skills, you can develop these through conscious practice, especially if you have a colleague willing to help you— or a good therapist.

Know Your Environment

You should be familiar with the policies and rules that govern your institution.

Know the Institutional Rules and Regulations. In addition to its instructional policies, you need to learn the regulations that govern fiscal processes, employment practices for faculty and staff (especially tenure and promotion rules), methods of institutional assessment and accountability, the applicability of public records laws, applicable federal laws (for example, the Family Educational Rights and Privacy Act, or FERPA), the regulation of grants and contracts, policies regarding conflicts of interest, and so on. These policies, rules, and regulations affect the lives of the people with whom you work, even though many faculty members may not be very knowledgeable about them. Your ability to help your clients is compromised if you do not know the policies that govern the institution. Moreover, your knowledge of the rules may allow you to exploit opportunities that will benefit your program and avoid threats to its health.

Know the Structure. You should learn the organizational structure of your institution and keep abreast of changes in that structure. Who reports to whom can change quickly, and you need to know the potential consequences for your program and for your clients and their departments.

If your institution has a faculty council or senate, learn its role in campus governance. Find out what functions the undergraduate and graduate student governments serve and how alumni are substantively involved in campus affairs. Learn as much as you can about the role of the chancellor or president and any bodies that oversee that office. Remember, too, that the governance of public institutions is quite different from that of private and church-affiliated schools. If you have experience working in one type of institution and have changed to a different type, don't assume that it operates in the same way.

Know Your Administrator. Obviously, the first rule of success in any job is to pay close attention to the administrator to whom you report and look to that person for the clarification and elaboration of your duties. Find out his or her expectations and strive to meet—and exceed—them. As many administrators are unfamiliar with our discipline and our capabilities—or worse, have bizarre notions about them—try to educate your supervisor about faculty development and how it is practiced (for example, our confidentiality ethics). Assess your degree of programmatic autonomy as early as possible; exercise autonomy to the extent that you are comfortable with it. If your administrator wants to rethink every program idea you have, start planning your move to another job unless you're happy being continually micromanaged and second-guessed.

Never surprise your boss. Alert your administrator to any problems that you encounter as soon as they arise. Never surprise powerful deans or department chairs either; they can make your life very difficult, even if you don't report to them directly.

Make your supervisor look good, and help him or her look good to higher-ups. Give away a good idea that could be used to better advantage by your boss than it could by you. In addition to the idea itself, provide the background for presenting the idea to others, the rationale for implementation, findings from peer institutions, a cost-benefit analysis, and so forth.

Some administrators are very hands-on, but more often they have responsibilities at many different levels and cannot devote too much time to one area. It's best to assess which kind of administrator you report to as quickly as possible, but if you can't do that, you should assume that this is a busy person. Don't make an appointment to "run an idea" past your boss before thoroughly researching it, connecting it to a perceived local need, and having at least some supporting documentation at hand.

In the last analysis, however, remember that *faculty* are the people you need to serve. Administrators come and go, but faculty members persist, often into advanced age, and if you serve them well, they will support you in time of need. The tension between what faculty members want and what administrators desire is inherent in every institution of higher education, and your survival will depend on how well you negotiate between the needs of the two groups.

Know Your Faculty. We don't intend to stir up controversy, but most faculty development "needs assessments" are a waste of time, especially if the institution is large and diverse. Needs assessments can be valuable tools for decision making in areas such as resource support, the suitability of classroom equipment, and instructional technology assistance. But faculty members rarely understand the kinds of programs and services we might provide if they haven't seen them before, and their responses on survey instruments may only reflect their ignorance of the possibilities rather than rational choices among programs.

Instead, you should talk to faculty members—as many as you can, as often as you can, individually and in groups. Find out what's on their minds, their hopes, their fears, their challenges, then ask what you can do for them. If they are unresponsive, be prepared to offer ideas for programs and services and draw them into a conversation about the potential benefits. This strategy takes longer than a quick, online survey, but it yields far richer, more meaningful results.

Know Your Students. If you teach courses (and you should), you will inevitably learn something about the students at your institution. However, if your school is large and diverse, you will encounter only a small portion of the student body. Talking to faculty members in various departments will yield valuable information about more students, but your school's institutional research office can often provide helpful statistical profiles of various subsets of the student body and data from institutional and national surveys, such as the National Survey of Student Engagement (NSSE). Reading the student newspaper and serving as the faculty adviser to student groups can also better acquaint you with the students. The more you know about them, the more effective you will be with your clients.

Know Your Role. Job descriptions in faculty development are often vaguely worded or maddeningly unspecific about what the institution wants you to do. Read your contract carefully, because it is likely to differ from the description used for recruitment. Ask how your performance will be assessed, and request clarification of any points you don't understand. Find out where your program fits in the organizational structure and where your boundaries are drawn.

Find out the extent to which you own the copyright of materials that you develop. If you plan to do any consulting for other institutions, you also need to know the regulations governing external activities for pay. Employment policies are rarely consistent across institutions (and are rarely available from a single source), but investigating the policies that govern the specific type of position you hold is a good way to ascertain your basic rights and responsibilities.

Although you should always be open to collaboration (see the Advocate and Collaborate section), you should also avoid getting involved with projects and initiatives that don't have measurable outcomes or that are not aligned with institutional goals. These projects will sap your energy and may actually create ill will. Their work usually vanishes from institutional memory without a trace, and your contributions will disappear with them.

Be an effective steward of resources under your control. Be prepared to justify any expenditure that you make by tying it to how your work or programs support institutional goals. And never, ever engage in what might be deemed extravagance.

Rules of Consulting

Consulting is three parts mentoring and one part psychotherapy, consequently the rules of consulting are somewhat fluid. However, as a starting point, the consultant and the client must share a clear picture of the purpose and the dimensions of the relationship. The purpose should be negotiated and mutually agreed on, either formally or informally. Establish what you are going to call success and how you will measure it.

Establish the Relationship

The relationship with a client may, and perhaps *should,* have social aspects that go beyond its professional dimensions. Meeting over coffee or lunch, talking about other aspects of personal life, and even sharing hobbies can add important elements to the association. Unlike psychotherapists, developers should not avoid social interactions with clients, as this aspect of the relationship is beneficial and reflects the broader collegiality of the academy.

Often scheduling and agenda setting are very informal ("Let's meet in two weeks, and you can tell me how your students are responding to your new discussion technique"). Whether you prefer formal or informal methods, it is important to schedule meetings and agree on their purpose to ensure that progress will be made in a timely fashion.

Empower Your Clients

In consulting work, you must be explicit about your availability, the extent to which you can be a resource for your client, and the kinds of resources that you can provide. Keep in mind the limitations on your time and energy; you have many obligations and responsibilities and often less free time than the average faculty member. The easiest (and often most personally rewarding) response to client needs is to provide all the strategies, tools, and information resources yourself, but you should avoid the temptation to do so. Although you may expect that the duration of a consulting relationship will be fairly short or limited in scope, if you don't train your clients to be self-reliant, they may call on you to solve routine problems long after the initial relationship is over.

Employ collaborative problem-solving techniques to enable clients to take ownership of tasks and projects and to identify other campus resources that your client can use (for example, the writing center, the learning center, or the counseling center). It can be useful to have clients categorize the kinds of help that they think they will need and "fill in" support resources under each category. The categories may be as broad as course planning, assessment, or classroom presentations or as specific as how to use classroom equipment or how to evaluate online writing assignments.

This strategy creates a useful resource for clients and gives the developer a picture of how faculty members conceptualize their needs. The technique also gives the consultant an opportunity to discuss omissions, correct misconceptions, and frame issues from the client's perspective.

Teach your clients the pedagogical concepts that underlie the solution to a given instructional problem. If they understand that some principles apply to many different situations, they can solve future problems by themselves.

Commit to Confidentiality

Confidentiality is absolutely essential in the consulting relationship, and clients need to be assured that nothing shared in consultations will become public. Violations of this rule can ruin faculty members' careers and destroy a faculty development program. Most faculty development programs publish formal statements of their confidentiality policies, and if your program lacks such a statement, you should construct one immediately. The POD Web site and listserv archives are good sources of information to help you develop a statement, but remember that it must conform to the conditions that pertain to your own institution. Engage other personnel in your office in creating the policy, because it will have little meaning unless everyone agrees and strictly adheres to it. Finally, make sure that you clear the policy with the campus legal counsel to ensure that it conforms to institutional policies and applicable state laws.

Ask for permission to use the products of your work with clients (for example, syllabi, rubrics, instructions for assignments) to use as exemplars with other clients. This practice affirms your commitment to the confidentiality of your relationship, shows your clients that you place a high value on the outcome of your work together, and will also make them very, very happy.

When a department chair refers a junior faculty member to you for help, issues of trust and confidentiality immediately arise. At minimum, you should be prepared for your client to approach the relationship with reluctance, and you need to think of ways to reassure him or her that the relationship is both private and collegial in nature. Let the faculty member know that he or she is your client, not the department chair or anyone else, and that you will not divulge anything about your exchanges unless the client wants you to share it with someone else.

Occasionally, a department chair will refer a faculty member to you to avert a disciplinary action, and the chair will need documentation to fulfill legal requirements. In such cases, the best course of action is to negotiate a letter of agreement among the parties that reflects what you can offer the faculty member and provide the necessary documentation in strict accordance with the agreement. Resist the temptation to overstate the outcomes of your work together. Simply submit—or have the faculty member submit—evidence that supports change or improved outcomes, and allow the evidence to speak for itself.

Suspend Judgment

Your perspectives, knowledge, capabilities, and limitations shape how you frame issues and solve problems, but as a consultant, you should try to ensure that your own experiences and preferences do not create a barrier to exploring the alternatives that your clients wish to explore or blur the domains into which issues fall.

You should seek to meet your clients' needs at the level that they define them in order to 1) resolve their immediate concerns, 2) increase the probability that they'll come back with higher-level needs or with ideas they wish to explore, and 3) help establish an ongoing development relationship with each client. For example, you may feel strongly that your clients should learn to use interactive or group-based strategies instead of lectures, but you are likely to be more effective in the long run if you help them improve their lecture techniques and course materials, if that's what they really prefer at this stage in their development. Like a good mentor, you can help clients benefit from your knowledge and experience, taking things that resonate with their teaching philosophies and postponing things that they are not ready to explore. This approach also helps you reinforce the message that they can continue development efforts on their own at their own pace.

Share Your Own Goals

Consulting, like mentoring, should be a two-way street. Tell your clients what you personally hope to gain from the relationship; share your own experiences in teaching and encourage your clients to share what they have learned. This kind of dialogue helps establish a common bond as teachers and promotes the idea that your relationship is collegial rather than therapeutic. This approach also shows that you respect your clients and value the things they can teach you.

Practice Active Listening and Directive Engagement

Obviously, faculty developers need to listen carefully and genuinely hear what their clients are saying, as well as summarize their clients' communication periodically to validate that they have heard them correctly. However, successful consulting also requires *directive engagement* with clients, which means drawing them into purposeful discussions of the issues so as to lead them to solutions that you consider the most appropriate for the individual. Directive engagement implies equal participation of both parties, reducing the possibility that either you or your client will dominate the conversation and focus on only one aspect of the issue at hand.

Actively promote dialogue by asking open-ended questions and directive questions such as these:

- What do you think is the main concern here?
- What evidence led you to that conclusion?
- Could you give me an example?
- How do you think your students feel about this situation (issue, problem)?
- Have you tried this? or How did that work for you?
- How did you feel about that outcome (result)?
- What problems did you encounter, and how did you handle them?
- What kinds of assessment could (did) you use in your class to monitor this situation?
- What do you think needs to be done to resolve this issue?
- Can you think of any alternative solutions?

Accentuate the Positive

Be positive, be encouraging, and be believable. Many clients have struggled with their teaching alone, with limited success, and often feel that there is no hope for progress. Junior faculty members are frequently so overwhelmed by everything they must do to gain tenure that they don't see how they can possibly find the time or the energy to work on their teaching. Instructors who are required by their departments to teach in new, unfamiliar ways, such as problem-based learning in the health sciences, are often bewildered and frightened by the prospect of change. In short, many of the instructors who seek our help are, to a greater or lesser extent, discouraged and frightened, and developers need to provide positive, encouraging messages to their clients.

To be effective, a positive outlook should not be forced, nor should you raise false hopes for impossible gains. However, you can point out improvement when you see it (even if the gains are small) and, metaphorically or literally, give clients pats on the back for their achievements. If their progress is slow and bumpy, it is especially important to let them know that your faith in their abilities is still strong. If your clients think that you believe in them, they will work harder and *will succeed,* just as students do when they think their teachers believe in them. They are also more likely to experiment with new techniques and methods if they know you believe they can handle them successfully.

Program Goals

You can establish your credibility and reputation in an institution relatively quickly by providing programs and services that target your constituents' expressed needs, as long as they are within the scope of your charge. However, as a professional developer, you should also try to ascertain needs that are *not expressed* and create programs that address these as well. Remember that your program goals should be closely aligned with institutional goals. Explore the Web sites of teaching centers in your institution's peer aspiration group for program ideas and services you can offer.

Discover Wants and Needs

Initiating conversations with deans, chairs, faculty members, and TAs is the best way to discover what they want. On the basis of these interviews, you can prioritize their ideas and plan the programs to implement immediately or in the future. From here you can put together a five-year plan.

However, you should also perform an "environmental scan" of your institution to determine hidden needs. If your institution has published the names of schools in its peer aspiration group, conduct a comparative study of your institution and those in this aspiration group to help you see the big picture of your institution's goals. Then set targets for how you might help your school achieve those goals. Read the back issues of the student newspaper and, if one exists, the official institutional paper for the faculty; delve into the faculty senate archives and administrative memos to the faculty; interview students and retired faculty; read local and area newspapers as well. This kind of research can reveal structural and organizational problems of which most faculty are only dimly aware. You may also uncover issues that have been buried long ago but nonetheless continue to have an impact on the institution and can affect the success of your programs.

Advocate and Collaborate

Become an advocate for special constituencies and institutional initiatives that seek to enhance the academic climate. For example, if students have organized a service-learning program, you may be able to help them grow the program and institutionalize it, bringing in faculty support. Try to visualize teaching issues and instructional needs from a pan-institutional perspective. Faculty developers are uniquely placed to support multidisciplinary, inter-institutional dialogues, projects, courses, and programs for faculty and students. From this base you can accomplish institutional change on a large scale by exercising leadership and by collaborating with other centers within the institution. Moreover, such collaboration helps establish a network of supporters for your own program.

Evaluate Your Work

To judge by conversations with many faculty developers in POD, we are, as a group, terrible at evaluating our work and worse at keeping detailed records that document it. Although evaluation and documentation will not prevent a determined president or provost from abolishing your program, the lack of data like these places it at considerable risk, even in the best of times.

It is safe to say that all faculty development programs evaluate their workshops, seminars, and group events, and some also evaluate other services such as consultations and publications. However, in most cases the evaluations are limited to questionnaires that survey satisfaction with the event or the experience. This kind of information can be dismissed by critics as "smile data" that reflect the faculty's positive feelings about workshops or services rather than what they learned. These data do provide important feedback on the quality of the workshop and a rough measure of faculty interest in a particular subject. However, faculty development programs also need to evaluate and document their impact in terms of expanding pedagogical knowledge, altering teaching practice, and improving the teaching and learning environment.

Faculty should gain knowledge about pedagogy from workshops and consultations, and this kind of learning can be assessed with well-designed surveys. Follow-up assessments, including student ratings, classroom observations, and student performance data, can document positive changes in teaching behavior. Keeping track of the number of faculty development clients who go on to win teaching awards is another measure of the program's impact on teaching behavior. Institutional impact is more difficult, but not impossible, to assess. For example, if you help a department revise its curriculum and the result receives positive feedback from teachers and students, those data can be presented as evidence of institutional change. Campuswide student surveys, such as the NSSE, mentioned earlier, and the Faculty Survey of Student Engagement, can show trends in key indicators of teaching practice such as active learning and critical thinking.

Keep Good Records

Keeping track of the clients you work with each year is helpful in many ways: the record can provide the documentation that you need to request a funding increase; it can show the extent and depth to which you are reaching (or failing to reach) your constituencies, and it can help improve the overall performance of your office. Using a spreadsheet or similar software that allows you and your colleagues to sort data in a number of ways, you can track your work by entering each occurrence of engagement with your clients; at a minimum you can enter the client's name, department, rank, and the category of service that he or she received. You can also track participation in workshops or other group events by entering data from a sign-in sheet or registration record.

Assessing the records in your client roster will enable you to gauge where your ever-disappearing time is going, how much time you are giving to one or two clients or departments, and how much time you are spending on different categories of service or strategies that reach different constituencies or produce different results. This assessment will help you set next year's performance goals to remediate any problems you've discovered.

By compiling records of all consultants in an office (after deleting any confidential information) and sharing them internally, your office can improve its practice by enabling you to identify important trends. For example, learning that two consultants in your office are meeting with clients on the same issue, from the same department, provides an opportunity to initiate a more programmatic or collaborative approach to the issue (rather than individual consultations). Sharing records internally can also help you avoid embarrassment if your advice differs substantially from that provided by another consultant in your office, or if clients extol the virtues of another consultant and you are uninformed about the relationship. Examining these records can reveal an overall picture of the balance of services, the extent to which your office has "penetrated the market" (served the disciplines and types of instructors represented), and how it has done so. Assessment of documentation can also drive program development, help set the direction your office will take in the coming year, promote a shared vision, and support the creation of measurable long-term plans.

Make Friends

Build a base of support among the faculty; after all, the junior faculty you help today will be the deans and department chairs of tomorrow. Working one-on-one with faculty, trying not to say no (at least not too often), and being as accessible as possible are critical to winning their support. Although workshops and other kinds of group programs are more visible than one-on-one consultations, individual work with teachers is the most effective way to improve teaching, and it also inspires intense loyalty from those you help. Fifty percent of your time is not an unreasonable amount to spend on individual consultations.

Constantly sell your program to those in the highest level of the administration. If your work is not well known and well respected at this level, your program, budget, and position could all disappear in times of fiscal exigency.

Give others credit. When you collaborate with faculty groups or other centers, make sure you give them an appropriate share of the limelight. They will do the same for you if you have done it for them.

Conclusion

The principles described here are based on lessons we learned from real events and occurrences, pleasant and unpleasant, during our faculty development careers. One final principle, which is also derived from long experience, is that you try not to be discouraged if things don't go as well as you planned. Being in the people business, we deal with the most variable entity on earth. Each faculty member and administrator is a unique individual, and, as in health professions, one person's medicine may be another one's poison. We can't always know in advance how a client will respond to our best-intended advice. So when a given day falls short of our hopes, always keep in mind Winston Churchill's definition of success: "Success is going from failure to failure without a loss of enthusiasm."

References

Gillespie, K., Hilsen, L., & Wadsworth, E. (Eds.). (1997). *A guide to faculty development: Practical advice, examples, and resources.* Bolton, MA: Anker.

Lewis, K., & Povlacs Lunde, J. (Eds.). (2001). *Face to face: A sourcebook of individual consultation techniques for faculty/instructional developers.* Stillwater, OK: New Forums Press.

Brinko, K. T., & Menges, R. J. (Eds.). (1997). *Practically speaking: A sourcebook for instructional consultants in higher education.* Stillwater, OK: New Forums Press.

Chapter 3

Maturation of Organizational Development in Higher Education
Using Cultural Analysis to Facilitate Change

Gail F. Latta
University of Nebraska-Lincoln

Organizational development (OD) is fundamentally about increasing institutional capacity for change. Organizational culture is a pivotal variable mediating the success of institutional change initiatives. Faculty and OD professionals are poised to address the need for increased understanding of organizational culture and change in higher education institutions. This chapter presents a conceptual guide to theories of change and cultural analysis that inform OD practice. Distinctions between content and process theories of change, as well as normative and idiomatic approaches to cultural analysis, are reviewed with respect to their utility for facilitating change in the academy. Implications for the maturation of OD in higher education are discussed.

Organizational development (OD) is fundamentally about increasing institutional capacity for effecting change—change in individuals, in organizational units, and in institutional strategic direction (Bennis, 1969; Warzynski, 2005). The need for effective leadership of organizational change has become a preoccupation of academic administrators throughout the higher education community (Astin & Astin, 2000; Gayle, Tewarie, & White, 2003; Kellogg Commission,

2006). Increasingly, academic support units working to promote faculty development within the academy are being called on to respond to the need for internal facilitators of organizational change (Blackwell & Blackmore, 2003; Chism, 1998; Diamond, 2005; Ruben, 2005). Understanding and managing organizational culture has emerged as a pivotal issue in ensuring the success of these organizational change efforts (Eckel & Kezar, 2003; Kezar & Eckel, 2002; Latta, 2006). Mastering the skills and techniques of assessing organizational culture and managing change have become essential components of the knowledge base for individuals responding to the demand for assistance planning and facilitating OD in academic institutions.

New Roles for Faculty Developers

The need to increase institutional capacity for effecting successful organizational change is helping define new roles for individuals working in academic support units to foster faculty development in the academy (Blackwell & Blackmore, 2003; Chism, 1998; Diamond, 2005; Frantz et al., 2005; Patrick & Fletcher, 1998; Warzynki, 2005). Traditionally focused on enhancing individual skills for teaching and learning, these units are being called on to expand the scope of their services to encompass all areas of institutional mission in support of broader strategic goals (Chism, 1998; Ruben, 2005). Individual faculty development efforts are giving way to opportunities for working with intact academic units (Dwyer, 2005; Latta & Myers, 2005), targeted administrative groups such as department chairs (Austin, 1994; Yen, Lang, Denton, & Riskin, 2004), leadership development initiatives (Turnbull & Edwards, 2005), and senior planning teams (McLean, 2005; Warzynski, 2005). The intent of these efforts extends beyond attention to immediate results, to address the strategic goals of developing future leadership capacity and supporting long-term institutional objectives (Chesler, 1998; Gardiner, 2005; Patrick & Fletcher, 1998).

The expansion of traditional roles for academic support units and faculty developers in the academy requires a new orientation toward developing human resources and enhancing organizational capacity for change (Chism, 1998; Gilley, Eggland, & Gilley, 2002). Faculty developers are being challenged to extend their knowledge base beyond training and development efforts to incorporate other areas of practice in human resource development. This shift toward a focus on planned, organization-wide development within the academy represents a trend toward maturation of OD practice in higher education (Baron, 2006; Diamond, 2005; Torraco & Hoover, 2005).

Facilitating organizational change is a core component of OD and human resource practice in all types of organizations (Gilley, Eggland, & Gilley, 2002; Swanson & Holton, 2001). Increasingly, individuals responsible for supporting the development of faculty and academic units in the academy are being called on to enhance organizational capacity for effecting positive institutional change (Diamond, 2005; Ruben, 2005; Turnbull & Edwards, 2005). Understanding organizational culture has emerged as an essential component of managing planned change (Bate, 1990; Eckel & Kezar, 2003; Pondy, 1983; Schein, 1996; Tierney, 1990; Trice & Beyer, 1991). Demand for internal consultants with the insight and technical expertise to apprehend and interpret elements of organizational culture will increase in academic institutions, as the internal and external demands on these communities continue to mount (Chesler, 1998). Faculty developers who invest in mastering the cognitive tasks of cultural analysis will be poised to respond to this demand (Diamond, 2005). As Patrick and Fletcher (1998) observe, "since faculty developers come from the ranks of the faculty, they are well positioned to serve a mediating role between the faculty and administration" (p. 164).

Organizational development requires the presence of human resource facilitators at every stage of diagnosis, planning, and implementation (Gardiner, 2005; Rothwell, Sullivan, & McLean, 1995; Smith, 1998). Academic professionals working in OD, including faculty developers, have not always had the opportunity to contribute throughout the full range of the planning cycle (Baron, 2006; Middendorf, 1998). Responding to these shifting institutional demands requires that individuals acquire new skills in organizational assessment, intervention, and change management (Diamond, 2005). Two essential components of this expanded knowledge base for academic professionals working in OD include being familiar with change management and understanding organizational culture.

Change Management

Two types of knowledge inform OD with respect to orchestrating change: 1) content knowledge and 2) process knowledge. *Content knowledge of change* refers to the substance of a change initiative; it defines what and who is expected to change and to what degree. Process knowledge of change outlines the procedural stages involved in implementing specific change initiatives. Process models describe the steps in planning and implementing change and identify the factors that must be managed throughout implementation (Burke, 2002).

Content Theories of Organizational Change

Content theories of change concern two dimensions of human performance affected by organizational change: behavior and cognition. Behavioral change addresses specific human resource outcomes targeted by an OD intervention. Cognitive change involves the thought processes, attitudes, beliefs, and tacit unconscious mechanisms that mediate behavioral change.

Behavioral Change. Behavioral change is implicit in any change initiative. However, the challenges of specifying and measuring the behavioral outcomes of organizational change have plagued OD researchers and practitioners alike. Determining exactly who, what, and how much change will occur is complicated by the recognition that organizations function as loosely coupled systems, making it difficult to specify the impact of change in one part of the organization on other dimensions (Birnbaum, 1988). The consequences of loose coupling are manifest at both the individual and organizational levels (Weick, 1969). At the individual level, the consequences of loose coupling are evident in the lack of correspondence between learning and performance outcomes (Fenwick, 2006), as well as in the disconnect between attitudes and behavioral change (Gladwell, 2005). At the organizational level, the challenges of identifying and overcoming barriers to transfer of training in organizations is continuing evidence of the difficulty of linking planned change interventions to behavioral change (Bunch, 2007; Hatala & Fleming, 2007).

In an attempt to develop more precise methods of assessing the behavioral impact of organizational change, Golembiewski, Billingsley, and Yeager (1976) conceptualized three types of change, termed *alpha, beta,* and *gamma* change. Although Golembiewski's theory is generally understood as a designation of the degree of behavioral change resulting from a change intervention, it is more accurately described as a theory of measurement respecting the behavioral outcomes of OD. This perspective reflects the fact that change interventions not only modify behavior but simultaneously alter the ways in which behavior is perceived.

Alpha change represents incremental change that can be measured using existing tools of subjective assessment. Beta change is accompanied by the extension of the subjective instruments of assessment that members of an organization use to monitor and evaluate their own and others' behavior. Gamma change occurs when the behavioral change effected is so great that it requires the adoption of new outcome measures of accomplishment. The subjective changes associated with alpha, beta, and gamma change are not required to produce the behavioral change itself but rather occur as a *collateral* result. Thus, although not technically a measure of the magnitude of behavioral change, Golembiewski's theory serves as a conceptual framework for specifying the impact of change on how organizational behavior and outcomes are subjectively assessed.

Cognitive Change. In addition to behavioral change, OD interventions are concerned with effecting cognitive change. Cognitive theories of change invoke the notion of "schemata" (Bartunek & Moch, 1987) or "theories-in-use" (Argyris, 1976) as *mediating* the impact of change. These mental constructs serve to focus attention, interpret experience, and assign meaning to events. In the context of organizational change, schemata "affect how change agents understand and engage in planned change" (Bartunek & Moch, 1987).

Argyris (1976, 1982) conceptualized cognitive change in organizations as occurring within a system of single- or double-loop learning (Argyris, 1982). Single-loop learning occurs whenever individuals adapt to change without altering their cognitive frameworks. Double-loop learning occurs when organizational problems are approached in a way that allows decision makers to achieve new levels of insight to inform thinking, reasoning, and decision making (Argyris, 1976, 1982). Double-loop learning requires suspending familiar theories-in-use that tacitly govern behavior, in favor of a conscious exploration of the typically unexamined assumptions underlying one's own and others' actions (Argyris, 1976). Because double-loop learning requires relinquishing existing cognitive frames that "represent a source of confidence that one has in functioning effectively in one's world" (Argyris, 1976, p. 370), it involves increased risk and requires leaders who exhibit reduced defensiveness and greater willingness to share power. In this regard, effecting double-loop learning in organizations depends on individuals who have themselves achieved higher levels of cognitive development (Kegan, 1982, 1994).

Bartunek and Moch's (1987) orders-of-change theory adds another dimension to the cognitive model of change. The degree of cognitive change required by an organizational intervention is conceptualized in this model as first-order, second-order, and third-order change. These orders capture both the magnitude and character of the cognitive modifications required of individuals affected by a change initiative. First- and second-order changes are roughly similar to Argyris's single- and double-loop learning but described from the perspective of the OD practitioner. Thus, first-order change involves "tacit reinforcement of present understandings," whereas second-order change effects "the conscious modification of present schemata in a particular direction" (Bartunek & Moch, 1987, p. 486). Third-order change requires "the training of organizational members to be aware of their present schemata and thereby more able to change those schemata as they see fit" (Bartunek & Moch, 1987, p. 486). In each case, the order of magnitude is determined by the nature of the change initiative.

Integration of Behavioral and Cognitive Change. Behavioral and cognitive aspects of human experience underlying the implementation of change have heretofore been conceptualized as independent dimensions of organizational change. Figure 3.1 offers a theoretical framework for illustrating the combined impact of change

Figure 3.1. Integration of Behavioral and Cognitive Theories of Change Illustrating the Impact of Organizational Culture

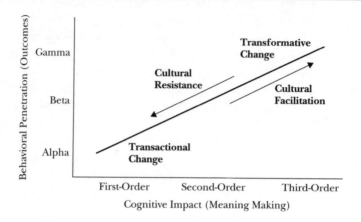

initiatives on behavioral and cognitive aspects of organizational life. The degree of transformative change is determined by plotting behavioral change (alpha, beta, and gamma change) against cognitive change (first-, second-, and third-order change) on a two-dimensional graph. The former represents the extent of behavioral penetration affected by the change initiative, whereas the latter characterizes the magnitude of cognitive impact required to effect the change. The slope of the line connecting the degree of change on each of these dimensions represents the magnitude of change involved. Every change initiative can be characterized by its placement along this penetration-impact gradient.

Some OD initiatives require limited cognitive change but significant behavioral change, while others require little change of behavior but dramatically new ways of thinking. Initiatives that require minimal modification of behavior and cognitive schemata are characterized as continuous or transactional. The greater the behavioral and cognitive change required, the more transformative (discontinuous) the change initiative (cf. Burke, 2002; Eckel & Kezar, 2003). Understanding the interplay of the behavioral and cognitive demands required to implement a change initiative affords leaders a means of assessing the magnitude of change required to implement strategic objectives. OD practitioners can use these theoretical frameworks to help members of an organization anticipate the impact of strategic organizational objectives and plan effective intervention strategies.

Impact of Organizational Culture on Change. The integrated theoretical content model of change proposed here provides a means of conceptualizing the impact of organizational culture on efforts to implement specific change initiatives. Cultural elements in organizations mediate the implementation of change in a way that either facilitates or inhibits the institutionalization of change, altering the slope and magnitude of the change trajectory (see Figure 3.1). The influence of organizational culture on the content of change can thus be conceptualized as either facilitating or creating resistance to change along the penetration-impact gradient. Understanding the tacit processes of sense making that underlie organizational culture can afford change agents insight into the factors influencing the successful behavioral and cognitive modifications necessary to implement strategic initiatives.

To illustrate the orders-of-change magnitude and the impact of organizational culture, consider the behavioral and cognitive implications of two initiatives currently being implemented at many institutions of higher education: 1) integrating instructional technologies and 2) introducing interdisciplinary curricular reform. The former certainly requires the acquisition of new technical skill, as well as adoption of alternative conceptual approaches to curricular design, requiring both behavioral and cognitive change. But although mastery of these techniques may lead to the adoption of new instructional strategies, it does not necessarily require a redefinition of disciplinary content or instructional goals, or the adoption of new outcome measures of success. In terms of change magnitude, these reforms occur closer to the transactional end of the penetration-impact gradient. Integrating interdisciplinary perspectives into the curriculum, on the other hand, requires a far more penetrating level of change, both in terms of redefining behavioral outcomes of learning (penetration) and with respect to the nature of the cognitive frames required to embrace new interdisciplinary perspectives (impact). This represents a far more transformative change that is therefore more vulnerable to the facilitative or resistant dimensions of organizational culture.

Process Models of Organizational Change

Process models of organizational change designate the sequence of events required to effect organizational change. These models reflect differing levels of granularity with respect to the process of effecting organizational change, but each recognizes distinctive stages of change implementation (Burke, 2002; Hurley, 1990; Lueddeke, 1999; Neumann, 1995). A generic process model of organizational change delineates a sequential progression through six stages: 1) assessing readiness for change, 2) creating a vision for change, 3) specifying intervention initiatives, 4) developing implementation strategies, 5) institutionalizing the effect of change, and 6) assessing the impact of change.

Process models of organizational change increasingly incorporate elements of organizational culture and the inherent processes of meaning making that it embodies as one of many component factors affecting change implementation. Some of these models acknowledge the influence of tacit dimensions of organizational life at one or more stages of the change process, without explicitly identifying organizational culture. The influence of these forces is implicit in Lewin's (1947) classic "unfreeze-change-refreeze" theory of change, as well as in subsequently popularized "vision" models, such as Kotter's (1996) eight-step strategy for leading change, Senge's "fifth discipline" (1990), and Kouzes and Posner's (2002) "leadership challenge."

Integrated process models of organizational change (Burke & Litwin, 1992; Kanter, Stein, & Jick, 1992; Tichy, 1983), including some specific to institutions of higher education (Baker, 1998; Eckel & Kezar, 2003; Hurley, 1990; Latta, 2006; Lueddeke, 1999; Shults, 2006), have been developed to inform OD practitioners' understanding of the impact of cultural dimensions on processes of implementing organizational change. These models vary with respect to whether behavior or cognitive change is expected to occur first (Burke, 2002). Other theorists have developed "culturally sensitive" process models that locate organizational culture as the target of change initiatives (Bate, 1990; Bate, Kahn, & Pye, 2000; Wilkins & Dyer, 1988). Still others suggest that cultural considerations may be more important in effecting some types of change than others (Beer & Nohria, 2000; Kezar, 2001).

Organizational culture has consistently emerged as a crucial ingredient in the success of efforts to implement institutional change (Curry, 1992; Fullan & Miles, 1992; Heracleous, 2001; Johnson, 1987; Pascale, Milleman, & Gioja, 1997). Latta (2006) has recently developed a process model of organizational change in cultural context (OC^3 Model) that takes into consideration the mediating influence of organizational culture at every stage of change implementation (see Figure 3.2). This model applies whether culture is the target of change or not. A central assumption of this model is that cultural knowledge is a prerequisite for leading effective change. Although space does not permit full elaboration of the OC^3 Model (see Latta, 2006), it is reproduced here to illustrate visually the integral link between organizational culture and change.

Figure 3.2. OC^3 Model of Organizational Change in Cultural Context: The Critical Role of Understanding Organizational Culture

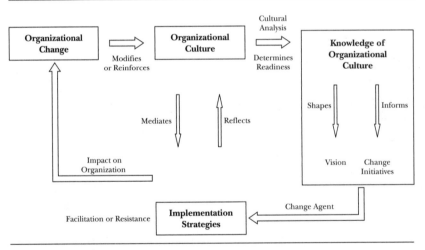

Source: Adapted from Latta (2006).

Understanding organizational culture emerges as a crucial component of effecting organizational change from the perspective of both content and process models of change. These models predict that creating profiles of organizational culture and documenting variations among subcultures within the academy constitute critical contributions to the success of efforts to effect lasting institutional change. Because cultural knowledge is largely tacit, it often requires the mediation of an outside facilitator to elicit

(Heracleous, 2001; Schein, 1999, 2004). Internal facilitators, familiar with the techniques of cultural analysis, can also be effective in conducting a cultural self-assessment or audit (Austin, 1990; Fetterman, 1990; Kuh & Whitt, 1988).

Faculty working in academic support units are well poised to respond to the need for internal facilitators to help academic units understand the cultural norms that mediate the implementation of change (Diamond, 2005). Creating integrated cultural profiles can also provide academic administrators insight into the meaning-making norms embedded in the culture of the institutions they lead (Birnbaum, 1989; Neumann & Bensimon, 1990). By revealing the underlying thought processes, decision making, and behavioral norms of an institution, cultural analysis can provide academic leaders the knowledge they need to serve as effective agents of change (Baird, 1990; Bensimon, 1990; Neumann, 1995).

The Nature and Functions of Organizational Culture

Culture is fundamentally about meaning making. Common to all definitions of *culture* in organizations is the assertion that culture is a socially constructed reality rooted in cognitive processes of meaning making (Alvesson, 2002; Heracleous, 2001; Martin, 2002; Neumann, 1995; Schultz, 1995). Scholars in many disciplines operate from the epistemological position that human beings are innately disposed to impose meaning on their experiences (Schultz, 1995). Bolman and Deal (1991) assert that the human need for meaning is more basic than any others identified in Maslow's (1943) hierarchy of needs. Culture embodies the systems of shared meaning embedded in organizations (Peterson & Smith, 2000). These systems of meaning are jointly created and collectively preserved by individuals working together toward common goals (Schulz, 1995).

The processes of meaning making that culture sustains afford regularity and familiarity to everyday life. However, cultural knowledge differs from many other subjective realities that define human experience in being largely tacit (Trice & Beyer, 1991). Thus, unlike emotion, attitudes, and reason, which constitute the primary substance of conscious awareness, cultural knowledge operates primarily at a subconscious level (Rousseau, 1990). Although it informs decision making and actions, cultural knowledge does not routinely constitute the focus of introspective rumination. Consequently, most people find it difficult to articulate the cultural norms, values, and basic beliefs that inform their own actions, beyond those embodied in institutional mission statements or declarations of organizational values.

Challenges of Studying Organizational Culture

The challenges of studying organizational culture derive largely from its tacit character. Because of its implicit nature, organizational culture is transmitted indirectly through inductive means (Schein, 2004). The behavior of new members of any culture-sharing group is shaped through successive approximations of assimilation—a process made easier when existing norms are consistent with prior experience. This inductive method of transmission renders cultural knowledge difficult to articulate, requiring elaborate techniques to elicit. As Schein (1999) notes,

> What really drives the culture—its essence—is the learned, shared, tacit assumptions on which people base their daily behavior. It results in what is popularly thought of as "the way we do things around here," but even the employees in the organization cannot without help reconstruct the assumptions on which daily behavior rests. (p. 24)

This latter assumption that most individuals require assistance articulating cultural knowledge has given rise to a host of techniques for eliciting the cultural tenets that govern meaning making and behavior in organizations.

Two intellectual skills are required for conducting cultural analysis in organizations: 1) the ability to discern and document elements of culture extant within the academic community and 2) familiarity with the conceptual frameworks for deciphering the cultural forms that emerge from such an analysis and interpreting the meaning systems embedded in these cultural forms. The remainder of this chapter provides a conceptual guide for mastering these skills and representing the results of cultural analysis in a usable format.

Approaches to Cultural Analysis in the Academy

Cultural analysis is not a uniform set of procedures, perspectives, and practices but a diverse assortment of epistemological strategies or "ways of knowing" that can be employed by OD practitioners for understanding patterns of sense making in organizations. Understanding the conceptual variations and distinctions inherent in these different approaches to deciphering organizational culture will enable organization developers to select and use appropriate strategies that align with particular institutional purposes and settings. Many of the interrelationships among the various perspectives on organizational culture discussed in this chapter are portrayed graphically in Figure 3.3.

Figure 3.3.   Interrelations Among Conceptual Frameworks: Elements of Organizational Culture

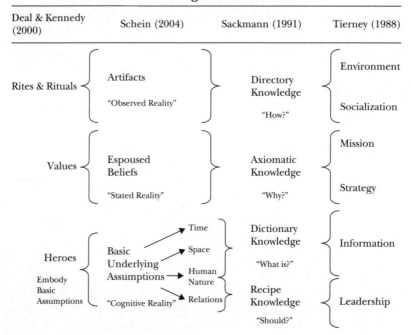

Deal & Kennedy (2000)	Schein (2004)	Sackmann (1991)	Tierney (1988)

Elements of Organizational Culture

The study of organizational culture focuses on "the beliefs, values and meanings used by members of an organization to grasp how the organization's uniqueness originates, evolves, and operates" (Schultz, 1995, p. 5). Driskell and Brenton (2005) catalog many elements of culture that constitute the object of cultural analysis in organizations. Trice and Beyer (1993) make a distinction between *ideological* and *concrete* elements of culture. The former refers to beliefs and values, whereas the latter encompasses an extensive array of artifacts, which they call cultural forms. Deal and Kennedy (2000) incorporate this dichotomy into their taxonomy of cultural elements, focusing on rites and rituals (concrete elements) and values (ideological elements), while adding an emphasis on the role of heroes in manifesting concrete human embodiments of ideological dimensions of organizational culture.

Schein (2004) consolidated the basic elements of organizational culture identified by others, classifying them into three broad categories and arranging them into a hierarchical model. The three broad categories of cultural elements in Schein's hierarchy are 1) artifacts, 2) espoused belief and values, and 3) basic underlying assumptions. These categories correspond to manifestations of observed reality (artifacts), stated reality (espoused beliefs), and cognitive reality (basic assumptions), organized according to increasing levels of conceptual abstraction (see Figure 3.3).

Schein (2004) asserts that organizational culture emerges from the institutional struggle to survive against internal and external threats. He maintains that the core of culture reveals itself through these struggles, in the form of basic assumptions relating to five ontological dimensions of human existence: 1) truth, 2) time, 3) space, 4) human nature, and 5) relationships. All other cultural aspects of organization life are postulated to devolve from shared beliefs concerning these elemental dimensions. Other theorists echo this view that underlying the primary functions of problem solving and sense making in organizations is the fundamental role of culture in defining the nature of reality (Alvesson, 2002; Sackmann, 1991).

Cultural Elements in Higher Education Institutions

Tierney (1988) developed a taxonomy of cultural elements specific to the context of higher education. This framework, "delineating and describing key dimensions of culture," sought to outline "essential concepts to be studied at a college or university" in conducting ethnographic research (Tierney, 1988, p. 8). Six dimensions of organizational culture emerged as essential to such an analysis: 1) environment, 2) mission, 3) socialization, 4) information,

5) strategy, and 6) leadership. The elements of this framework serve equally well as a guide for OD professionals creating profiles of organizational culture in institutions of higher education.

The six dimensions in Tierney's (1988) taxonomy can be mapped onto Schein's (2004) hierarchical model of organizational culture (see Figure 3.3). Institutional norms relating to environment and socialization represent specific types of artifacts. Institutional mission and strategy embody the espoused values and beliefs of an organization. Questions relating to "what constitutes information, who has it, and how [it is] disseminated" (Tierney, 1988, p. 8) correspond to basic assumptions about the nature of reality in Schein's hierarchy. Finally, Tierney's attention to institutional leadership, particularly the use of symbolic communication to garner support for aspirational goals, suggests a link to Schein's basic assumptions about truth.

Cultural Typologies in Higher Education Institutions

Cultural analysis involves more than merely enumerating the cultural elements that characterize a particular organization. Rather, it is the interrelationships among these elements and how they function as an integrative whole that determines the specific cultural forms exhibited (Alvesson, 2002). Cultural forms emerge when elements of culture are interpreted in light of the rules of sense making employed by members of a culture-sharing group (Geertz, 1973; Lévi-Strauss, 1969). Interpreting cultural elements requires an understanding of these rules and how they are used by members of an organization to create meaning from experience in the context of organizational life (Neumann, 1995; Peterson & Spencer, 1990).

Two approaches characterize the application of cultural analysis in organizations: 1) normative and 2) idiomatic. The normative approach seeks to identify cultural forms that span multiple organizations, providing a basis for comparative analysis. Idiomatic cultural forms result in distinct cultural profiles and reflect emergent constructs that operate uniquely in the context of a single institution. The application of cultural analysis techniques to academic organizations has fostered the derivation of a number of useful typologies of normative cultural forms, called archetypes. Distinctions among these normative typologies are detailed in Table 3.1 and will be reviewed before turning to a discussion of the processes involved in deriving idiomatic cultural profiles.

Table 3.1. Typologies of Normative Cultural Forms in the Academy

Kuh & Whitt, 1988 "Cultural Tapestry"	Birnbaum, 1988 "Cognitive Frames"	Bergquist, 1992 "Six Cultures"
Faculty	Collegial	Collegiate
Basic assumption: rational	Basic assumption: egalitarianism	Basic assumption: rationality
Values: academic freedom, truth seeking, autonomy	Values: consensus, shared power, common aspirations, consultation	Values: autonomy, shared governance, collaboration
Characteristics: intellectual scrutiny, collegiality, shared governance	Metaphor: "community of scholars"	Purpose: conduct research and scholarship, encourage student learning and development
Purpose: disseminate knowledge, criticize society, foster life of the mind	Characteristics: self-governance, collegiality, institutional loyalty, reciprocity, loose coupling	Artifacts/ceremonials: grants, publication, commencement
Subcultures: disciplinary affiliations	Administrative presence: minimal hierarchy, informality, deliberation	
	Leadership: leader is "first among equals"; expert and referent power	
Administration	Bureaucratic	Managerial
Basic assumption: separatism	Basic assumption: efficiency	Basic assumption: efficiency
Values: leadership, balance priorities	Values: certainty, predictability, compliance	Values: fiscal responsibility, effective supervision, planning, competence

(*Continued*)

**Table 3.1. Typologies of Normative Cultural
Forms in the Academy (*Continued*)**

Kuh & Whitt, 1988 *"Cultural Tapestry"*	*Birnbaum, 1988* *"Cognitive Frames"*	*Bergquist, 1992* *"Six Cultures"*
Administration	*Bureaucratic*	*Managerial*
Characteristics: multiple constituencies, stewardship	*Metaphor:* "rational organization"	*Purpose:* inculcate in undergraduates the knowledge and skills for vocational success
Purpose: manage resources and personnel	*Characteristics:* division of labor, codification of rules, vertical administrative loops, tight coupling	*Artifacts/ceremonials:* enrollments, revenue generation, bureaucracy
Subcultures: task-related academic, student affairs, fiscal, campus facilities	*Administrative presence:* hierarchy determines information access, objectives, rewards merit	
	Leadership: based on rationality, competence, expertise; legitimate power, delegation of authority	
		Developmental
		Basic assumptions: growth/maturation
		Values: student-centered learning, demographic systems of planning
		Purpose: maximize cognitive, behavioral, and affective potential
		Artifacts/ceremonials: institutional research, faculty/program development

Table 3.1. Typologies of Normative Cultural Forms in the Academy (*Continued*)

Kuh & Whitt, 1988 "Cultural Tapestry"	Birnbaum, 1988 "Cognitive Frames"	Bergquist, 1992 "Six Cultures"
Students	Political	Advocacy
Basic assumption: peer influence	*Basic assumption:* negotiation	*Basic assumption:* egalitarianism
Values: hedonism, informality, flexibility, autonomy, support	*Values:* social exchange, mutual dependence, decentralized power	*Values:* confrontation, fair bargaining, mediation, academic capital
Characteristics: informal, fluid, social experimentation	*Metaphor:* "shifting kaleidoscope"	*Purpose:* to progressively substitute liberating social attitudes and structures for repressive ones, service learning
Purpose: promote social networking, affiliation, coping, information sharing, personal validation	*Characteristics:* interest groups and coalitions; emerging issues	*Artifacts/ceremonials:* policies, benefits, collective bargaining agreements, community involvement
Subcultures: affiliations influenced by personal interests, ideology, living arrangements, recreation	*Administrative presence:* loosely coupled coalitions and negotiation	
	Leadership: informal, intuitive	
	Anarchical	Virtual
	Basic assumption: irrationality	*Basic assumption:* open systems
	Values: fluidity, self-interested participation, persistence	*Values:* responsiveness in the face of fragmentation and ambiguity
	Metaphor: "organized anarchy"	*Purpose:* foster global education, online learning, knowledge dissemination

(*Continued*)

**Table 3.1. Typologies of Normative Cultural
Forms in the Academy (*Continued*)**

Kuh & Whitt, 1988 *"Cultural Tapestry"*	*Birnbaum, 1988* *"Cognitive Frames"*	*Bergquist, 1992* *"Six Cultures"*
	Anarchical	*Virtual*
	Characteristics: lack of control or coordination; vague goals, unclear technology, fluid participation	*Artifacts/ceremonials:* networks, technological resources, partnerships
	Administrative presence: individual autonomy, minimal oversight; open participation; loose coupling	
	Leadership: bounded rationality; decision making in uncertainty; symbolic over instrumental action	
		Tangible
		Basic assumption: parochialism
		Values: tradition, standards, ancestry, reputation, identity, work itself
		Purpose: institutional growth, resident education, preservation of roots
		Artifacts/ceremonials: physical campus attributes, historical memorabilia, commencement exercises

Normative Cultural Forms in Institutions of Higher Education

Kuh and Whitt (1988) focused on the distinct cultural forms represented by three subpopulations within the academy: 1) faculty, 2) students, and 3) administrators. The faculty culture "provides a general identity for all faculty" (p. 76) but is characterized by fragmentation among disciplinary subcultures. The student culture is a heterogeneous cultural form that affords students a "means to cope with the difficulties of college life by providing students with social support and guidelines to live by" (p. 89). It can serve as either a conservative influence or force for change within the institution. Administrative subculture is characterized by a separatism from both faculty and student cultures in the academy, which tends to foster cultural norms not reflective of the values held by the majority of those affected by leadership decisions.

Birnbaum (1988) conceptualized four cultural forms he considered exemplary of the range of institutional types extant within the higher education community: the 1) collegiate, 2) bureaucratic, 3) political, and 4) anarchical cultures. He then proposed a fifth, emerging culture—the cybernetic culture—which he portrayed as an "ideal" type (see Table 3.1). Birnbaum asserted that these cultural archetypes rarely exist in pure form in the academy but that this "purposeful simplification" affords clarity to the salient aspects of each, while highlighting "the essential limitation faced by any administrator or researcher who takes a single frame approach to understanding higher education" (Birnbaum, 1988, p. 84).

Bergquist's (1992) analysis, which initially yielded four cultures of the academy, has recently been revised to account for the emergence of two additional cultural archetypes (Bergquist, 2006). The six currently extant cultural forms identified by Bergquist (1992, 2006) are the 1) collegiate, 2) managerial, 3) developmental, 4) advocacy (formerly negotiating), 5) virtual, and 6) tangible forms (see Table 3.1). Each of these cultural forms is held to exist to some degree within every academic institution, functioning to sustain a particular set of institutional assumptions relating to identity and mission. Bergquist (2006) has recently developed a diagnostic instrument for detecting the presence of the six cultural forms identified in his research, thus providing a new tool for analysts wishing to use a normative, descriptive approach to cultural analysis.

Considerable overlap exists among all three of these typologies of academic culture, affording convergent validity to these normative cultural forms. Both Birnbaum (1988) and Bergquist (1992) produced extensive narrative descriptions of the cultural forms identified through their research and explored the implications of each for organizational development, change, and leadership in institutions of higher education. Kuh and Whitt (1988) conclude that organizational culture is integral to institutional history, integrity, decision making, and leadership. Although space limitations preclude a comprehensive treatment of these separate cultural forms, the essence of each is summarized in Table 3.1.

Based on their findings, these normative cultural theorists all challenged the assumption of cultural uniformity, asserting that separate cultural forms coexist interdependently and vie for dominance within the academy. Their work is significant in that it draws attention to the existence of distinct subcultures within the academy. Organizational subcultures emerge in relation to structural boundaries (departmental, college affiliations), role identification (administrators, faculty, students), and disciplinary perspectives (humanities, sciences, social sciences, technology), as well as intangible dimensions (philosophical, ideological, political). Describing the interactions and power relations among subcultures in organizations is an essential component of conducting a cultural analysis (Howard-Grenville, 2006; Kuh & Whitt, 1988; Sackmann, 1997; Trice & Beyer, 1993).

The frameworks that have emerged from normative studies of organizational culture have been employed by researchers in higher education (Kezar & Eckel, 2002; Smart & St. John, 1996). Most recently, Kezar and Eckel (2002) used Bergquist's (1992) cultural archetypes, in conjunction with Tierney's (1988) elemental framework, to differentiate the cultural profiles derived from their ethnographic study of institutional change strategies at six higher education institutions. They discussed the advantages and disadvantages of these two approaches as tools for organizational development:

> When using both frameworks together, they provide a more powerful lens than when using only one in helping to interpret and understand culture. The archetypes provide a ready framework for institutions unfamiliar with cultural analysis; the framework establishes patterns for them to identify. The Tierney lens provides a sophisticated tool for understanding the complexities of unique institutions. Although Tierney's framework is an important framework, it may be more difficult for practitioners to use readily. (Kezar & Eckel, 2002, p. 440)

This work draws attention to the utility of employing normative cultural frameworks as a means of understanding and interpreting the attitudes, behavior, and assumptions that characterize many academic communities without requiring extensive cultural analysis.

In the context of facilitating OD, awareness of pervasive cultural norms within the academy yields insight into the complexities of implementing organizational change. Normative approaches to cultural analysis provide an effective means of understanding the competing values and underlying assumptions that create sources of facilitation or resistance to change initiatives. Normative approaches to cultural analysis enable facilitators of OD to describe and test certain assumptions about values and expectations as a means of helping faculty and administrators understand differences of perspective and negotiate toward common ground.

Idiomatic Approaches to Cultural Analysis

The normative approach to cultural analysis has yielded many insights and provided a useful platform for understanding the commonalities of organizational culture that characterize institutions of higher education. Despite these common elements, culture in organizations is ultimately unique. Normative approaches to cultural analysis often obscure the idiosyncrasies that give institutions their distinctive character. Researchers adopting an idiomatic approach to cultural analysis strive to overcome this limitation by constructing cultural profiles that uniquely describe particular academic communities.

In Schein's (2004) view, culture can best be *apprehended* by starting with the most visible and least abstract elements (artifacts) and progressing to successively more conceptual and abstract dimensions (basic assumptions). He stressed, however, that the *interpretation* of cultural elements must progress in an inverse manner, from the most abstract underlying assumptions to the behavioral norms and visible artifacts: "In other words, if I understand the pattern of shared basic assumptions of a group, I can decipher its espoused values and its behavioral rituals. But the reverse does not work. One cannot infer the assumptions unless one has done extensive ethnographic research" (Schein, 1991, p. 252).

The power of ethnographic analysis lies in its potential to yield a unique cultural profile of an organization, reflecting the self-understanding and implicit rules governing behavior, decision making, and meaning making in organizations (Heracleous, 2001; Howard-Grenville, 2006; Neumann, 1995; Neumann & Bensimon, 1990). Such analysis can result in the construction of a cultural profile that more directly mirrors the language and everyday behavior of organization members (Alvesson, 2002; Schultz, 1995).

Ethnographic Analysis. Conducting an ethnographic analysis of organizational culture requires documenting and interpreting organizational behavior from both an emic (insider) and etic (outsider) perspective (Fetterman, 1990, 1998). Documenting these elements requires conducting unobtrusive observation and systematic interviews with key informants (Latta, 2006). These ethnographic interviews involve more than reflective listening; they are actively investigative. Informants must be willing to engage in penetrating dialogue intended to surface the cognitive, motivational, and affective tenets that constitute the bases for individuals' behavior, attitudes, and decisions, as well as the interpretations and meaning they attribute to organizational experiences and events.

The ethnographic approach to apprehending the tenets of organizational culture is distinguished by three characteristics: 1) researcher reflexivity, 2) reactions of principle members, and 3) iterative hypothesis testing (Heracleous, 2001). The researcher records observations but also keeps track of his or her own reactions. The interviewer continuously formulates and tests hypotheses about the nature of cultural tenets at work in the community by asking questions informed by observations, experiences, and interactions with others. Methodological guides are available to assist in mastering the techniques of conducting ethnographic investigations using observations and interviews with key informants (Alasuutari, 1995; Creswell, 2008; Fetterman, 1990, 1998; Rhoads & Tierney, 1990; Wolcott, 1999).

Constructing Idiomatic Cultural Profiles. Transforming ethnographic observations into idiomatic cultural profiles is an interpretive process (Alasuutari, 1995). Three analytical perspectives inform this approach to cultural analysis: Sackmann's (1991) cultural knowledge taxonomy, Martin's (1992, 2002) three-perspective analysis, and Latta's (2006) cultural profile-matrix approach. These approaches share a dependence on ethnographic analysis but offer alternative means of integrating and rendering cultural insights visible. The conceptual distinctions among these approaches are outlined in Table 3.2.

Sackmann's (1991) cultural knowledge taxonomy was derived using a "quasi-ethnographic" approach to cultural analysis. The taxonomy consists of a four-dimensional matrix for representing the results of ethnographic analysis in organizations, focusing on four types of information transmitted by culture: 1) dictionary, 2) directory, 3) axiomatic, and 4) recipe knowledge. Dictionary knowledge concerns the nature of reality and answers the question, What is? It relates to organizational purpose, membership, strategy, and design. Directory knowledge relates to cultural norms governing interpersonal relations, learning, adaptation, and change. Axiomatic knowledge reveals insights about underlying organizational purpose and encompasses aspects of culture that correspond to the question, Why? The fourth type of cultural knowledge—recipe knowledge—represents the presence or absence of aspirational or subversive elements in organizational culture, existing in the form of expectations concerning how things "should" be (see Table 3.2). Sackmann (1991) asserts that high-performing organizations with internally consistent cultures will be characterized by smaller

Table 3.2. Idiomatic Approaches to Cultural Analysis: Conceptual Dimensions

Sackmann, 1991 "Knowledge Taxonomy"	Martin, 2002 "Multiple Perspectives"	Latta, 2006 "Cultural Profile-Matrix"
Dictionary Knowledge	Integration Perspective	Dominant Cultural Profile
What is?		
Purpose	Shared aspects of culture	Unique idiomatic cultural profile
Members	Organization-wide consensus	Emergent tenets of organizational culture
Design	Internal consistency	Pervasive elements of culture that sustain basic cultural tenets
Directory Knowledge	Differentiation Perspective	Matrix of Subcultural Variations
How to?		
Accomplish tasks	Subcultural consensus	Variations from dominant cultural profile
Manage relations	Organization-wide variations ·	Divergence and convergence among subcultures
Learn		
Recipe Knowledge	Fragmentation Perspective	
What should be?		
	No clear consensus	
	Irresolvable inconsistencies	
Axiomatic Knowledge		
Why?		

amounts of recipe knowledge than those experiencing cultural discord.

Sackmann's (1991) taxonomy provides a bridge between normative and idiomatic methods of cultural analysis. The types of knowledge delineated by Sackmann's taxonomy can be mapped onto the elements of Schien's (2004) basic hierarchical model of cultural forms in organizations (see Figure 3.3): directory knowledge is revealed through cultural artifacts; axiomatic knowledge embodies espoused beliefs and values; dictionary knowledge concerns basic assumptions relating to the nature of time, space, relationships, and human nature. The identification of recipe knowledge separates basic assumptions about truth from other fundamental beliefs, adding a dimension of vision regarding what should be and thus also aligns with the role of leaders and heroes in the taxonomies of Tierney (1988) and Deal and Kennedy (2000). Yet the four categories in Sackmann's (1991) cultural knowledge taxonomy differ from the categories defined in normative approaches to cultural analysis by focusing on the dimensions of meaning embodied in organizational culture, rather than the cultural forms themselves.

Sackmann's (1991) work further departs from normative approaches to analyzing culture in organizations by drawing attention to the fact that cultural knowledge encompasses dimensions pertaining to both the current and future desired states of an organization. Although Sackmann's cultural knowledge taxonomy has not been widely used by researchers or practitioners, it holds promise as a tool for facilitating organizational development in the context of change management. The inclusion of aspirational norms (recipe knowledge) affords added utility to employing this model of organizational culture as a means of identifying performance gaps in the context of planned change (Bate, Kahn, & Pye, 2000; Gilley & Maycunich, 1998; Rothwell, 1996).

Martin's (2002) three-perspective conceptual model of organizational culture represents a more dramatic departure from normative approaches than Sackmann's. Martin advanced her multidimensional model of cultural analysis as an alternative to the analytical, descriptive approach to isolating separate cultural forms. Martin (1992) championed the notion that culture does not manifest as separate, objective, reified forms in organizations but instead constitutes a multidimensional, subjective reality that should be analyzed simultaneously from three different perspectives. These perspectives reflect the degree of integration, differentiation, and fragmentation that exists within the fabric of the organization's culture. The analysis resulting from this multiple-perspectives approach emphasizes the notion that elements of uniformity, diversity, and discontinuity coexist within the culture of an organization, which obviates the need to develop cultural typologies to account for differences within the organization's meaning-making systems.

The three dimensions of meaning emphasized by Martin's approach highlight different aspects of organizational culture (see Table 3.2). The integration perspective highlights those aspects of culture that pervade the organization, cutting across hierarchy, roles, and organizational units. The differentiation perspective, on the other hand, acknowledges the existence of subcultural variations along certain salient dimensions where integration exists only within formally or informally defined groups within the organization. Finally, the fragmentation perspective focuses on "ambiguity as the essence of organizational culture" (Martin, 1992, p. 12), explicitly acknowledging dimensions of the organizational life where no clear consensus exists.

Using Martin's approach to cultural analysis, it is possible to document that an academic community may share a pervasive cultural commitment to maintaining a prestigious level of research achievement (integration perspective), yet harbor considerable subcultural variation among academic units with respect to the value placed on teaching excellence (differentiation). At the same time, there may be a complete lack of consensus about the role and value of outreach (fragmentation). Martin's three-perspective approach to cultural analysis is designed to reveal these qualitatively different dimensions of cultural manifestation. Although Martin's three-perspective approach has been largely ignored by researchers studying culture in the academy, the cultural perspectives defined by Martin's work have broad applicability in large, complex organizations such as institutions of higher education.

One limitation of Martin's approach that may account for its underuse is its failure to yield an integrative cultural profile that represents both cultural integration (uniformity) and differentiation (subcultures) along comparable cultural dimensions. The problem of how to treat subcultures in organizations pervades the literature of cultural analysis (Hatch, 1997; Howard-Grenville, 2006; Kuh & Whitt, 1988; Sackmann, 1997) and deserves special attention by those facilitating cultural analysis in the context of organizational change (Bergquist, 1992; Latta, 2006; Sackmann, 1997). Some have explored the presence of subcultures as a potential source of institutional weakness (Deal & Kennedy, 2000; Tierney, 1988; Toma, Dubrow, & Hartley, 2005). Others, however, "caution against building a unified institution that is dominated by one culture . . . and fails to honor the legitimate claims and considerable benefits provided by" other cultural forms (Bergquist, 2006, p. 7).

The typical approach to addressing internal cultural variations results in the creation of separate subcultural profiles for each extant group within the organization (Bergquist, 1992, 2006; Birnbaum, 1988; Kuh & Whitt, 1988; Martin, 1992; Neumann & Bensimon, 1990; Smart & St. John, 1996). Yet this approach makes it difficult for researchers and institutional leaders to understand subtle variations in sense making that occur between seemingly comparable groups across the institution (that is, departments and colleges or faculty with different disciplinary affiliations). Thus, two academic departments, each exemplars of the collegiate cultural form, may differ significantly in the particulars of how that culture manifests. Employing normative analysis in this instance has the drawback of obscuring the distinctive aspects of institutional culture necessary for understanding nuances that exist within the organization as a whole. Martin's (2002) three-perspective approach, on the other hand, treats cultural integration as separate from subcultural variations. Latta (2006) developed an integrated approach to idiomatic cultural analysis that overcomes both these limitations.

Latta's (2006) cultural profile-matrix approach involves first documenting the hierarchical relations among elements of organizational culture as a whole, then delineating variations in the

degree to which each dimension of the overall culture is manifest within organizational subcultures (see Table 3.2). The first
step results in a profile of the dominant organizational culture,
detailing the relationship among basic beliefs (assumptions) and
the underlying cultural elements (artifacts, values, behavior norms,
and so on) that sustain these beliefs (see Table 3.3). The second
step involves creating a matrix detailing the degree to which each
subcultural group within the institution conforms or diverges from
the tenets of this dominant cultural profile (see Table 3.4).

**Table 3.3. Example of an Idiomatic Cultural Profile:
Dominant Tenets of Organizational Culture
and Elements That Sustain Each Tenet**

Dominant Cultural Tenets	*Cultural Elements That Sustain Each Tenet*
Pervasive paternalism	Dominance of business officers
	Respect for administrative hierarchy
	Advisory role of faculty senate
Culture of prestige	Aversion to pubic debate of issues
	Sense of industry and competition
	Reciprocal institutional loyalty
	Intolerance for nonconformity
Land-grant identity	Balance of teaching and research
	Dominance of applied disciplines
Decentralization of power	Unit level self-determinism
	College subcultures
	Differential power among colleges

Source: Latta (2006).

The utility of Latta's (2006) approach is that it permits both
the emergence of a unique cultural profile (the goal of idiomatic
analysis), while at the same time providing a means of describing
subcultures along comparable cultural dimensions (the strength
of normative approaches). If the example were extended, the
dominant cultural profile would include elements of culture
relating to the nature of the organization's overall commitment
to research, teaching, and outreach. Deviation from, or consistency

Table 3.4. Example of an Idiomatic Matrix of Cultural Variations Among Institutional Subcultures

Cultural Elements	Engineering	Science	Technology	Business	Liberal Arts	Agriculture
Prestige	very strong	strong	weak	very strong	moderate	moderate
Paternalism	strong	strong	strong	strong	strong	strong
Aversion to debate	strong	moderate	strong	strong	weak	strong
Industriousness	very strong	strong	weak	very strong	moderate	moderate
Teaching/Research	moderate	strong	very strong	moderate	very strong	very strong
Land grant	strong	weak	strong	moderate	weak	strong
Self-determinism	very strong	strong	strong	very strong	strong	strong
Loyalty	strong	strong	strong	strong	strong	strong

Source: Latta (2006).

with, these overall cultural commitments would then be documented in a matrix of organizational subcultures. Tables 3.3 and 3.4
provide examples of the types of cultural representations resulting
from Latta's cultural profile-matrix approach to cultural analysis.

Together, the dominant cultural profile and the matrix of subcultural variations provide a visual representation of the organization's unique cultural makeup, capturing both the substance
and internal dynamics moderating the processes of institutional
sense making. These tools of cultural analysis supplement the
traditional "thick description" narratives characteristic of ethnographic research (Fetterman, 1998; Geertz, 1973). Although illustrating the application of the cultural profile-matrix approach to
cultural analysis is beyond the scope of this chapter, Latta's
(2006) research on institutional change at land grant universities
provides numerous examples that demonstrate the utility of this
form of cultural analysis for identifying the mediating influence of
culture at every stage of a planned change process. The approach
has particular value as a tool for identifying the sources of cultural
facilitation and resistance to change implementation. Although
the utility of this approach to cultural analysis has not yet been
demonstrated beyond the academic environment, it is expected
to have broad applicability in organizations characterized by distinct subcultural factions.

Conclusion

Change management and cultural analysis have become main-
stream practices in organizational development outside the academy (Cummings & Worley, 2000; French & Bell, 1999). Both are
essential tools for effective leadership in academic institutions as
well (Astin & Astin, 2000; Eckel, Hill, Green, & Mallon, 1999).
Understanding content and process models of change affords
increased awareness of the importance of considering the impact
of organizational culture on the success of change initiatives.
Emerging models of organizational change in cultural context
draw increased attention to the importance of integrating cultural analysis into the practice of facilitating OD in institutions of
higher education (Bate, Kahn, & Pye, 2000; Latta, 2006; Wilkins &
Dyer, 1988).

Mastering the craft of interpreting elements of organizational culture has thus become an essential tool for leaders of organizational change, enabling them to maximize their potential to effect positive change that will have lasting results (Curry, 1992). Two alternative approaches to cultural analysis—normative and idiomatic—provide options for individuals called upon to support the implementation of change initiatives. Normative approaches provide the advantage of using preexisting cultural typologies, common to many academic institutions, for anticipating and interpreting reactions to institutional change. Normative cultural typologies benefit from a high degree of face validity, without requiring investment in extensive assessment and analysis.

However, normative cultural analysis lacks specificity and fails to capture unique aspects of institutional culture that may be essential for understanding and implementing change. Idiomatic approaches to cultural analysis require a greater investment in assessment but offer the advantage of capturing unique nuances of organizational culture that may be essential to the success of OD initiatives. Idiomatic cultural analysis provides greater insight into differences among institutional subcultures. Understanding unique aspects of organizational culture can help OD professionals interpret the behavior of individuals and organizational units, permitting them to understand motivations and pinpoint the underlying causes of dysfunction or discontent, while anticipating sources of facilitation or resistance that may arise in advancing strategic initiatives (Latta, 2006).

Using cultural analysis techniques to support institutional change initiatives in the academy represents an effective strategy for furthering the maturation of organizational development in institutions of higher education. Faculty developers and other members of the academy working to facilitate organizational development can capitalize on their roles as internal facilitators to help academic leaders understand the implicit rules that govern behavior and meaning attribution within the larger organizational context (Baron, 2006; Chism, 1998; Hurley, 1990). This review of change theories and recent advances in cultural analysis provides a conceptual overview of the variety of theoretical perspectives and methodological approaches available for discerning and representing the essence of culture and change in the academy. Further research on the use of these various techniques will further inform the selection of effective tools for particular situations. Mastering the techniques of cultural analysis and applying them within the context of organizational change will spur the maturation of OD in institutions of higher education (Rousseau, 1990).

References

Alasuutari, P. (1995). *Researching culture: Qualitative method and cultural studies.* Thousand Oaks, CA: Sage.

Alvesson, M. (2002). *Understanding organizational culture.* Thousand Oaks, CA: Sage.

Argyris, C. (1976). Single-loop and double-loop models in research on decision making. *Administrative Science Quarterly, 21,* 363–375.

Argyris, C. (1982). *Reasoning, learning, and action.* San Francisco: Jossey-Bass.

Astin, A. W., & Astin, H. S. (2000). *Leadership reconsidered: Engaging higher education in social change.* Washington, DC: Kellogg Foundation.

Austin, A. E. (1990). Faculty cultures, faculty values. In W. G. Tierney (Ed.), *New directions for institutional research: No. 68. Assessing academic climates and cultures* (pp. 61–73). San Francisco: Jossey-Bass.

Austin, A. E. (1994). Understanding and assessing faculty cultures and climates. In M. K. Kinnick (Ed.), *New directions for institutional research: No. 84. Providing useful information for deans and department chairs* (pp. 47–63). San Francisco: Jossey-Bass.

Baird, L. L. (1990). Campus climate: Using surveys for policy-making and understanding. In W. G. Tierney (Ed.), *New directions for institutional research: No. 68. Assessing academic climates and cultures* (pp. 35–45). San Francisco: Jossey-Bass.

Baker, G. A. (1998). *Managing change: A model for community college leaders.* Washington, DC: Community College Press.

Baron, L. (2006). The advantages of a reciprocal relationship between faculty development and organizational development in higher education. In S. Chadwick-Blossey & D. R. Robertson (Eds.), *To improve the academy: Vol. 24. Resources for faculty, instructional, and organizational development* (pp. 29–43). Bolton, MA: Anker.

Bartunek, J. M., & Moch, M. K. (1987). First-order, second-order, and third-order change and organization development interventions: A cognitive approach. *Journal of Applied Behavioral Science, 23*(4), 483–500.

Bate, P. (1990). Using the culture concept in an organization development setting. *Journal of Applied Behavioral Science, 26*(1), 83–106.

Bate, P., Khan, R., & Pye, A. (2000). Towards a culturally sensitive approach to organization structuring: Where organization design meets organization development. *Organization Science, 11*(2), 197–211.

Beer, M., & Nohria, N. (2002). *Breaking the code of change.* Boston: Harvard Business School Press.

Bennis, W. G. (1969). *Organization development: Its nature, origins, and prospects.* Reading, MA: Addison-Wesley.

Bensimon, E. M. (1990). The new president and understanding the campus as a culture. In W. G. Tierney (Ed.), *New directions for institutional research: No. 68. Assessing academic climates and cultures* (pp. 75–86). San Francisco: Jossey-Bass.

Bergquist, W. (1992). *The four cultures of the academy.* San Francisco: Jossey-Bass.

Bergquist, W. (2006). *The six cultures of the academy.* San Francisco: Jossey-Bass.

Birnbaum, R. (1988). *How colleges work: The cybernetics of academic organization and leadership.* San Francisco: Jossey-Bass.

Birnbaum, R. (1989). The implicit leadership theories of college and university presidents. *Review of Higher Education, 12*(2), 125–136.

Blackwell, R., & Blackmore, P. (2003). *Towards strategic staff development in higher education.* London: Society for Research into Higher Education and Open University Press.

Bolman, L. G., & Deal, T. E. (1991). *Reframing organizations: Artistry, choice, and leadership.* San Francisco: Jossey-Bass.

Bunch, K. J. (2007). Training failure as a consequence of organizational culture. *Human Resource Development Review, 6,* 142–163.

Burke, W. W. (2002). *Organization change: Theory and practice.* Thousand Oaks, CA: Sage.

Burke, W. W., & Litwin, G. H. (1992). A causal model of organizational performance and change. *Journal of Management, 18*(3), 532–545.

Chesler, M. A. (1998). Planning multicultural audits in higher education. In M. Kaplan & D. Lieberman (Eds.), *To improve the academy: Vol. 17. Resources for faculty, instructional, and organizational development* (pp. 171–201). Stillwater, OK: New Forums Press.

Chism, N. V. N. (1998). The role of educational developers in institutional change: From the basement office to the front office. In M. Kaplan (Ed.), *To improve the academy: Vol. 17. Resources for faculty, instructional, and organization development* (pp. 141–154). Stillwater, OK: New Forums Press.

Creswell, J. W. (2008). *Educational research: Planning, conducting, and evaluating quantitative and qualitative research* (3rd ed.). Upper Saddle River, NJ: Prentice Hall.

Cummings, T. G., & Worley, C. G. (2000). *Organization development and change* (7th ed.). Mason, OH: South-Western College Publishing.

Curry, B. K. (1992). *Instituting enduring innovations: Achieving continuity of change in higher education.* (Report No. 7), ASHE-ERIC Higher Education. Washington, DC: George Washington University.

Deal, T. E., & Kennedy, A. A. (2000). *Corporate cultures.* New York: Perseus.

Diamond, R. M. (2002). Faculty, instructional, and organizational development: Options and choices. In K. H. Gillespie (Ed.), *A guide to faculty development: Practical advice, examples, and resources* (pp. 2–8). Bolton, MA: Anker.

Driskell, G. W., & Brenton, A. L. (2005). *Organizational culture in action: A cultural analysis workbook.* Thousand Oaks, CA: Sage.

Dwyer, P. M. (2005). Leading change: Creating a culture of assessment. In S. Chadwick-Blossey & D. R. Robertson (Eds.), *To improve the academy: Vol. 23. Resources for faculty, instructional, and organizational development* (pp. 38–46). Bolton, MA: Anker.

Eckel, P. D., & Kezar, A. (2003). *Taking the reins: Institutional transformation in higher education.* Westport, CT: Praeger.

Eckel, P. D., Hill, B., Green, M., & Mallon, B. (1999). Reports from the road: Insights on institutional change. *On Change,* No. 2. Washington, DC: American Council on Education.

Fetterman, D. M. (1990). Ethnographic auditing: A new approach to evaluating management. In W. G. Tierney (Ed.), *New directions for institutional research: No. 68. Assessing academic climates and cultures* (pp. 19–34). San Francisco: Jossey-Bass.

Fetterman, D. M. (1998). *Ethnography* (2nd ed.). Thousand Oaks, CA: Sage.

Frantz, A. C., Beebe, S. A., Horvath, V. S., Canales, J., & Swee, D. E. (2005). The roles of teaching and learning centers. In S. Chadwick-Blossey & D. R. Robertson (Eds.), *To improve the academy: Vol. 23. Resources for faculty, instructional, and organizational development* (pp. 72–90). Bolton, MA: Anker.

French, W. L., & Bell, C. H. (1999). *Organizational development* (6th ed.). Upper Saddle River, NJ: Prentice Hall.

Fullan, M., & Miles, M. (1992, June). Getting reforms first: What works and what doesn't. *Phi Delta Kappan,* 745–752.

Gardiner, L. F. (2005). Transforming the environment for learning: A crisis of quality. In S. Chadwick-Blossey & D. R. Robertson (Eds.),

To improve the academy: Vol. 23. Resources for faculty, instructional, and organizational development (pp. 3–23). Bolton, MA: Anker.

Gayle, D. J., Tewarie, B., & White, A. Q. (2003). *Governance in the twenty-first century university: Approaches to effective leadership and strategic management.* (ASHE-ERIC Higher Education Report, Vol. 30, No. 1). San Francisco: Jossey-Bass.

Geertz, C. (1973). *The interpretation of cultures.* New York: Basic Books.

Gilley, J. W., Eggland, S. A., & Gilley, A. M. (2002). *Principles of human resource development* (2nd ed.). New York: Basic Books.

Gilley, J. W., & Maycunich, A. (1998). *Strategically integrated HRD: Partnering to maximize organizational performance.* Reading, MA: Addison-Wesley.

Gladwell, M. (2005). *Blink: The power of thinking without thinking.* New York: Little, Brown.

Golembiewski, R. T., Billingsley, K. R., & Yeager, S. (1976). Measuring change and persistence in human affairs: Types of change generated by OD designs. *Journal of Applied Behavioral Science, 12,* 133–157.

Hatala, J., & Fleming, P. R. (2007). Making transfer climate visible: Utilizing social network analysis to facilitate the transfer of training. *Human Resource Development Review, 6*(1), 33–63.

Hatch, M. J. (1997). *Organization theory: Modern, symbolic, and postmodern perspectives.* New York: Oxford University Press.

Heracleous, L. (2001). An ethnographic study of culture in the context of organizational change. *Journal of Applied Behavioral Science, 37,* 426–446.

Howard-Grenville, J. A. (2006). Inside the "black box": How organizational culture and subculture inform interpretations and actions on environmental issues. *Organization Environment, 19,* 46–73.

Hurley, J. J. P. (1990). Organizational development in universities. *Journal of Managerial Psychology, 5*(1), 17–22.

Johnson, G. (1987). *Strategic change and the management process.* Oxford: Blackwell.

Kegan, R. (1982). *The evolving self.* Cambridge, MA: Harvard University Press.

Kegan, R. (1994). *In over our heads.* Cambridge, MA: Harvard University Press.

Kellogg Commission on the Future of State and Land-Grant Universities. (2006). *Public higher education reform five years after the Kellogg Commission on the Future of State and Land-Grant Universities.* Washington, DC: National Association of State Universities and Land-Grant Colleges.

Kezar, A. (2001). *Understanding and facilitating organizational change in the 21st century: Recent research and conceptualizations.* (ASHE-ERIC Higher Education Report, Vol. 28, No. 4.) San Francisco: Jossey-Bass.

Kezar, A., & Eckel, P. D. (2002). The effect of institutional culture on change strategies in higher education. *Journal of Higher Education, 73*(4), 435–459.

Kotter, J. P. (1996). *Leading change.* Boston: Harvard Business School Press.

Kouzes, J. M., & Posner, B. Z. (2002). *Leadership challenge.* San Francisco: Jossey-Bass.

Kuh, G. D., & Whitt, E. J. (1988). *The invisible tapestry: Culture in American colleges and universities.* (ASHE-ERIC Higher Education Report, Vol. 17, No. 1.) Washington, DC: The George Washington University, Graduate School of Education and Human Development.

Latta, G. F. (2006). *Understanding organizational change in cultural context: Chief academic officers' acquisition and utilization of cultural knowledge in implementing institutional change.* Unpublished doctoral dissertation, University of Nebraska–Lincoln.

Latta, G. F., & Myers, N. F. (2005). The impact of unexpected leadership changes and budget crisis on change initiatives at a land-grant university. *Advances in Developing Human Resources, 7*(3), 351–367.

Lévi-Strauss, C. (1969). *The elementary structures of kinship.* Boston: Beacon Press.

Lewin, K. (1947). *Field theory in social science.* New York: Harper & Brothers.

Lueddeke, G. R. (1999). Toward a constructivist framework for guiding change and innovation in higher education. *Journal of Higher Education, 70*(3), 235–260.

Martin, J. (1992). *Cultures in organizations: Three perspectives.* New York: Oxford University Press.

Martin, J. (2002). *Organizational culture: Mapping the terrain.* Thousand Oaks, CA: Sage.

Maslow, A. (1943). A theory of human motivation. In J. M. Shafritz, J. S. Ott, & Y. S. Jang (Eds.), *Classics of organization theory* (pp. 159–173). New York: Wadsworth Press.

McLean, G. N. (2005). Doing organization development in complex systems: The case at a large U.S. research, land-grant university. *Advances in Developing Human Resources, 7*(3), 311–323.

Middendorf, J. K. (1998). A case study in getting faculty to change. In M. Kaplan & D. Lieberman (Eds.), *To improve the academy: Vol. 17. Resources for faculty, instructional, and organizational development* (pp. 203–223). Stillwater, OK: New Forums Press.

Neumann, A. (1995). Context, cognition and culture: A case analysis of collegiate leadership and cultural change. *American Educational Research Journal, 32*(2), 251–279.

Neumann, A., & Bensimon, E. M. (1990). Constructing the presidency: College presidents' images of their leadership roles, a comparative study. *Journal of Higher Education, 61*(6), 678–701.

Pascale, R., Milleman, M., & Gioja, L. (1997, November/December). Changing the way we change. *Harvard Business Review, 75*(6), 127–138.

Patrick, S. K., & Fletcher, J. J. (1998). Faculty developers as change agents: Transforming colleges and universities into learning organizations. In M. Kaplan & D. Lieberman (Eds.), *To improve the academy: Vol. 17. Resources for faculty, instructional, and organizational development* (pp. 155–169). Stillwater, OK: New Forums Press.

Peterson, M. F., & Smith, P. B. (2000). Sources of meaning, organizations, and cultures. In N. M. Ashkanasy, C. P. M. Wilderon, & M. F. Peterson (Eds.), *Handbook of organizational culture and climate* (pp. 101–115). Thousand Oaks, CA: Sage.

Peterson, M. F., & Spencer, M. G. (1990). Understanding academic culture and climate. In W. G. Tierney (Ed.), *New directions for institutional research: No. 68. Assessing academic climates and cultures* (pp. 3–18). San Francisco: Jossey-Bass.

Pondy, L. (1983). The role of metaphors and myths in organizations and in the facilitation of change. In L. Pondy, P. Frost, G. Morgan, & T. Dandridge (Eds.), *Organizational symbolism* (pp. 157–166). Greenwich, London: JAI Press.

Rhoads, R. A., & Tierney, W. G. (1990). Exploring organizational climates and cultures. In W. G. Tierney (Ed.), *New directions for institutional research: No. 68. Assessing academic climates and cultures* (pp. 87–95). San Francisco: Jossey-Bass.

Rothwell, W. J. (1996). *Beyond training and development: State-of-the-art strategies for enhancing human performance.* New York: American Management Association.

Rothwell, W. J., Sullivan, R., & McLean, G. N. (1995). *Practicing organizational development: A guide for consultants.* San Francisco: Pfeiffer.

Rousseau, D. M. (1990). Assessing organizational culture: The case for multiple methods. In B. Schneider (Ed.), *Organizational climate and culture* (pp. 153–192). San Francisco: Jossey-Bass.

Ruben, B. D. (2004). *Pursuing excellence in higher education.* San Francisco: Jossey-Bass.

Sackmann, S. A. (1991). *Cultural knowledge in organizations: Exploring the collective mind.* Newbury Park, CA: Sage.

Sackmann, S. A. (Ed.). (1997). *Cultural complexity: Inherent contrasts and contradictions.* Thousand Oaks, CA: Sage.

Schein, E. H. (1991). What is culture? In P. J. Frost, L. F. Moore, M. R. Louis, C. C. Lundberg, & J. Martin (Eds.), *Reframing organizational culture* (pp. 243–253). Newbury Park, CA: Sage.

Schein, E. H. (1996). Culture: The missing concept in organizational studies. *Administrative Science Quarterly, 41,* 229–240.

Schein, E. H. (1999). *The corporate culture survival guide.* San Francisco: Jossey-Bass.

Schein, E. H. (2004). *Organizational culture and leadership* (3rd ed.). San Francisco: Jossey-Bass.

Schulz, M. (1995). *On studying organizational cultures: Diagnosis and understanding.* New York: Walter de Gruyter.

Senge, P. (1990). *The fifth discipline.* New York: Doubleday.

Shults, C. (2006, October). *Towards organizational culture change in higher education: Introduction of a model.* Paper presented at the meeting of the Association for the Study of Higher Education, Anaheim, CA.

Smart, J. C., & St. John, E. P. (1996). Organizational culture and effectiveness in higher education: A test of the "culture type" and "strong culture" hypothesis. *Educational Evaluation and Policy Analysis, 18*(3), 219–241.

Smith, B. L. (1998). Adopting a strategic approach to managing change in learning and teaching. In M. Kaplan & D. Lieberman (Eds.), *To improve the academy: Vol. 18. Resources for faculty, instructional, and organizational development* (pp. 225–242). Bolton, MA: Anker.

Swanson, R. A., & Holton, E. F., III. (2001). *Foundations of human resource development.* San Francisco: Barrett-Koehler.

Tichy, N. M. (1983). *Managing strategic change: Technical, political and cultural dynamics.* New York: Wiley.

Tierney, W. G. (1988). Organizational culture in higher education: Defining the essentials. *Journal of Higher Education, 59*(1), 2–21.

Tierney, W. G. (Ed.). (1990). *New directions for institutional research: No. 68. Assessing academic climates and cultures.* San Francisco: Jossey-Bass.

Toma, J. D., Dubrow, G., & Hartley, M. (2005). *The uses of institutional culture.* San Francisco: Jossey-Bass.

Torraco, R. J., & Hoover, R. E. (2005). Organizational development and change in universities: Implications for research and practice. *Advances in Developing Human Resources, 7*(3), 422–437.

Trice, H. M., & Beyer, J. M. (1991). Cultural leadership in organizations. *Organization Science, 2*(2), 149–169.

Trice, H. M., & Beyer, J. M. (1993). *The cultures of work organizations.* Upper Saddle River, NJ: Prentice Hall.

Turnbull, S., & Edwards, G. (2005). Leadership development for organizational change in a new U.K. university. *Advances in Developing Human Resources, 7*(3), 396–413.

Warzynski, C. C. (2005). The evolution of organizational development at Cornell University: Strategies for improving performance and building capacity. *Advances in Developing Human Resources, 7*(3), 338–350.

Weick, K. E. (1969). *The social psychology of organizing.* Reading, MA: Addison-Wesley.

Wilkins, A. L., & Dyer, W. G., Jr. (1988). Toward culturally sensitive theories of culture change. *Academy of Management Review, 13*(4), 522–533.

Wolcott, H. F. (1999). *Ethnography: A way of seeing.* Walnut Creek, CA: Alta Mira.

Yen, J. W., Lang, S. E., Denton, D. D., & Riskin, A. (2004, June). *Leadership development workshops for department chairs.* Paper presented at the meeting of Women in Engineering Programs and Advocates Network Conference, Albuquerque, NM.

Chapter 4

Ten Ways to Use a Relational Database at a Faculty Development Center

A. Jane Birch
Brigham Young University

Tara Gray
New Mexico State University

The authors thank Julene Bassett, Nancy Chism, Jean Conway, Jenith Larsen, Leslie Ortquist-Ahrens, Kathryn Plank, and Lynn Sorenson for their comments.

Providing quality support to faculty requires attention to administrative details and event logistics. As professionals, we must also assess the impact of our work and be prepared to report to those who will judge its worth and allocate resources. To do this we need current, accurate data that are easy to access and easy to use. We also need a simple way to manage faculty development activities and evaluate the outcomes. The best technology for achieving these goals is a relational database. This chapter describes ten ways a relational database can be used to support faculty developers in their various roles and activities.

As faculty developers, our priority is serving faculty. Though we'd like to keep administrative details to a minimum, we cannot escape them altogether. If we are to serve faculty well, we must be organized. Faculty developers need current, accurate data that are easy to access and easy to use (Chism & Szabó, 1996). This includes having a simple way to record our activities and assess the outcomes (Plank, Kalish, Rohdieck, & Harper, 2005). It also includes reporting what we are doing to those who will judge its worth and allocate resources (Frantz, Beebe, Horvath, Canales, & Swee, 2005). The best technology for achieving these goals is a relational database (a database that contains multiple tables of data that are related to each other). In this chapter we describe ten ways a relational database can be used to support the activities of a faculty development center.

Most faculty developers currently employ assorted low-tech tools to administer and assess faculty development programs (Chism, 2003). These tools may include file folders full of paper, text documents, spreadsheets, or even flat-file databases (simple databases in which all data are recorded in a single table). These tools are limited and inflexible and make generating reports very difficult. Their simplicity makes them suitable for small tasks, such as managing single events, but they are not sophisticated enough to efficiently manage a variety of events or services over a longer time span. Using these tools, one center reported that their program coordinator took eight weeks to complete their annual report (Plank et al., 2005).

Relational databases are substantially more powerful, flexible, and expandable than alternative methods of tracking data. For instance, relational databases virtually eliminate data replication because data (such as names, addresses, and dates) can be entered (or updated) once and become immediately accessible throughout the system. Without a relational database, the same data are inevitably entered multiple times, drastically increasing complexity, time needed for maintenance, and possibility for inconsistencies. In addition, because of the simple, efficient way in which data are organized in a relational database, the data can be used, reused, combined, searched, sorted, edited, displayed, and printed in a variety of ways that are difficult, if not impossible, to do with alternative methods of organization.

A well-designed database provides the power and flexibility to accomplish a wide variety of administrative tasks for any number of people and events over an unlimited time span. A good database can help faculty developers serve faculty better while significantly reducing the time needed to accomplish related administrative tasks (by our estimates, a 30 to 90 percent time saving, depending on the task). In this way, the database is a workhorse and is like having an extra staff member at the center (Eynon & Chism, 2007). Although setting up such a database system is not easy (it may take several months of concerted effort), it is well worth the investment.

Brigham Young University (BYU) and New Mexico State University (NMSU) have created relational databases to serve the ongoing administrative and assessment needs of their centers. Both databases were created using FileMaker Pro—a powerful and user-friendly relational database program. FileMaker Pro is flexible enough to handle almost any conceivable data need in a faculty development center and can be used with both Macintosh and Windows operating systems. However, other relational database programs, such as Microsoft Access or MySQL, can be used. The ideas in this chapter apply to most relational database software applications on the market today.

The purpose of this chapter is to assist faculty developers in establishing or improving faculty development databases. Next are ten important ways a database can assist a faculty development center. It is not necessary for a database to do *all* of the following, so consider each item in light of current needs. The items are divided into record keeping and managing events:

Record Keeping

1. Record all useful data.
2. Quickly locate needed data.
3. Organize data for assessment, strategic planning, and reporting.
4. Increase accuracy and eliminate redundant data entry.

Managing Events

1. Track details needed to administer events.
2. Manage correspondence.
3. Enable participants to register online.
4. Create name tags and other customized materials.
5. Learn names by using photos.
6. Create a membership system.

Record Keeping

Like a well-managed home, a well-managed office has a place for everything and everything in its place. A relational database provides a logical, efficient location to store all useful data; it also makes those data accessible to everyone at the center.

Record All Useful Data

Most centers record data about the clients whom they serve. A database can store information about the center's activities in order to better administer, report on, and archive events. At a minimum, the name of each program, an outline of the activities, the date, and the participants' names can be recorded. To track more data at BYU, we can include the learning objectives, a detailed description and evaluation of what happened, publicity used, media handouts, cost, innovations, and future plans. We can also track all the people involved in the activity, including participants, cosponsors, presenters, event administrators, student assistants, and people who were invited or who planned to attend but did not for one reason or another.

A relational database is an excellent system for recording data for activities with multiple concurrent participants (such as workshops), but most faculty development centers provide many other services and resources. A database can also assist with these. For example, a faculty development database can be used to do the following:

1. Record notes about each session with each client, along with follow-up notes on things to do and a method for tracking their completion.
2. Recall information about individual clients and their previous interactions with the center before they arrive at the office for a consultation.
3. Share resources used by staff members in working with clients.
4. Manage complex programs such as Students Consulting on Teaching (Sorenson, 2000), where student schedules must be matched with faculty schedules, equipment checked in and checked out, and reports managed.

5. Keep records of how staff members use their time to better "measure, track, and report the work that centers do" (Plank et al., 2005, p. 174).
6. Record costs associated with each activity, along with evaluation data gathered.
7. Manage a large library collection to more easily locate resources and to facilitate a convenient check-out process with automatic e-mail reminders about due dates.
8. Keep records of one-time or recurring projects that do not include either clients or participants (for example, creating a database for the center).

The amount of data stored in a database depends on the resources and objectives of the center. The accompanying Web site (fc.byu.edu/jpages/database) contains an extensive list of the types of data that might be included in a faculty development database.

Entering data into a database can be done in a variety of ways. NMSU has clients enter contact information about themselves using online registration. BYU imports (or manually enters) a great deal more information, not just about clients but also about each unit on campus and each activity of the center. With the right permission and technical assistance, you can link your database directly into the institutional database, thereby enabling dynamic access to data housed by the university without having to enter it at all. To obtain data from the university, be prepared to demonstrate genuine need and provide convincing evidence that the data will be carefully safeguarded. (This process may take many months, so start early.)

It may take time to get the needed data into a database but, depending on your needs, it can be very useful to have all data in one place. For example, including demographic information about clients is invaluable for determining which populations are being served (Chism, 2003) and for targeting specific audiences (Holton, 2002). As a rule of thumb, we recommend entering all the data that will be useful for your purposes, but no more. Including excess data that no one uses increases the work needed to maintain the database and decreases the motivation to use it (Chism, 2003).

Quickly Locate Needed Data

The central reason for storing data is to use them at a later date. Because a relational database can hold all of the data important to the center in one location, it eliminates most of the guesswork (not to mention frustration) of remembering where important data are stored. In addition, because of the highly efficient way a good relational database stores data, it is easy to access the data quickly through database searches or queries.

How much data are entered will determine the kind of searches that can be performed for data retrieval. For example, the BYU database can be used to locate "all professors promoted within the past 5 years." This search could not be done on the NMSU database because only current rank has been entered; the year that rank was obtained has not been entered. A Web site that supplements this chapter (fc.byu.edu/jpages/database) shows a representative listing of the kind of searches that can be done with a well-designed database. Consider carefully what questions you need answered before designing your database.

Organize Data for Assessment, Strategic Planning, and Reporting

A well-designed database system shines as a tool to document and analyze the work of a center and to assess and report on its impact (Plank et al., 2005). Data generated from the database create a useful portrait showing which faculty members are served, how they are served, and the cost of the service. The level of analysis can range from how the center serves the campus as a whole to any specific group of people or even to any individual. Data organized in a database can be used to evaluate which colleges or departments are underrepresented among participants, which services cost a lot in time or money but attract little use, and which services participants find most helpful. Having current, accurate data at your fingertips is invaluable for conducting internal reviews, cost-benefit analyses, budget requests, and strategic planning (Chism, 2003; Chism & Szabó, 1996, 1997; Frantz et al., 2005; Mullinix, 2006; Plank et al., 2005).

Administrators also need an accurate picture of what the center is doing and the impact of its work (Frantz et al., 2005). By using a database, needed data are likely to be more accurate and comprehensive and take far less time to compile (Plank et al., 2005). Data in a database can be used to respond to appropriate requests for information from any level of administration, as well as in annual reports, budget proposals, and other reports. Data generated by the database provide a body of evidence that can be used by the center to document careful use of resources or to justify requests for further budget increases (Frantz et al.). This information can assist a center in "tooting its own horn"—a role most centers shun but one that may become important to the survival of some centers (Bartlett, 2002; Plank et al., 2005).

At NMSU, the center uses its database to raise money from the deans by showing them a report that documents the percentage of participation that comes from each college. These percentage stats are used to determine "fair share pledging" for each college. For example, if a college were using 10 percent of the center's resources in year one but 12 percent of the resources in year two, the college would be asked to pay 12 percent (rather than 10 percent) of the total donated that year by deans. Over time, this allows the amount that deans appropriately pay to increase as the costs to the center increase. NMSU now raises about $100,000 from colleges and other units on campus (Gray & Conway, 2007).

Plank and colleagues (2005) note that just as we remind faculty that "we can no longer (if we ever could) be excellent simply by assertion" (p. 186), so must faculty development centers provide evidence of the impact of their work. Shortly before the thirty-year-old teaching and learning center at the University of Nebraska was discontinued, the director of the center was told that she had "a week to write a report—not to exceed two pages— explaining why [the center's] work was valuable to the university" (Bartlett, 2002, p. A10). Eventually, most centers may be held accountable for the resources that they use. If we postpone gathering concrete statistics until others demand them, it may be too late (or too difficult) to produce accurate data (Frantz et al., 2005). Data should be collected systematically as part of the natural workflow (Chism & Szabó, 1996, 1997; Plank et al., 2005). By incorporating the use of a database into the everyday work of the center, data are kept up to date and readily accessible.

Increase Accuracy and Eliminate Redundant Data Entry

As mentioned earlier, a relational database allows data to be entered just once to be instantly available to every authorized member of the center for any relevant project or activity. For example, once a client's name or department is entered, it is instantly available for an unlimited number of future uses: e-mails, letters, name tags, seating charts, gift certificates, reports, and so forth. Without a database, consider how many times the same information is typed (and proofread) over and over again.

Having accurate data is important, so it is critical to develop simple protocols for data entry and to train staff on the importance of accuracy (Chism, 2003). Modern database applications are designed to facilitate accuracy by providing users with simple data-entry methods, such as drop-down menus, rather than requiring them to type everything by hand. In addition, good database programs employ a variety of data-testing techniques that can be used to immediately identify and resolve common mistakes (for example, illogical dates, empty fields, and duplications).

Managing Events

There are a myriad of details involved in sponsoring successful faculty development events (Hilsen & Wadsworth, 2002). A database proves indispensable in helping to manage these details. In addition to helping track RSVPs and attendance, the database can be used to organize participant groups, handouts, seating, food requests, survey data, and any idiosyncratic information needed for the specific purposes of an activity.

Track Details Needed to Administer Events

The BYU database helps to manage presentations by tracking all information needed to coordinate with the presenters for each specific event, including requests and responses, travel arrangements, media, handouts, equipment, introductions, and thank-you letters. The database is also used to help select appropriate presenters for future events by storing information about possible presenters, such as areas of expertise, past evaluation data, demographics, and contact information.

Relational databases facilitate other logistical tasks, such as quickly gathering lists of people to contact; printing programs, agendas, seating charts, attendance rolls, and participant directories; exporting or merging data; and handling all follow-up tasks, including gathering and storing evaluation data, sending follow-up memos, recording ideas for making the event better next time, noting expenses, and updating the inventory of materials that can be used in the future. A database is also particularly suited to drastically simplifying management of all correspondence to participants, presenters, and others (this function is described in detail next).

Beyond supporting logistical tasks, a database can be used as a project management tool. At BYU, the database stores structured "to-do lists" for some of the more complicated programs that the center administers. Each such program has a set of tasks with detailed notes about what needs to be done, who is responsible for doing it, and when it should be completed. Each task includes multiple subtasks with further details, which helps users to complete each item quickly and effectively. Once they are completed, tasks are checked off. Because everyone accesses the same data through the database, all members of the team see exactly what has been done and what still needs doing.

Manage Correspondence

At many faculty development centers the amount of communication among staff, participants, and clients can be enormous. Correspondence for workshops may include invitations, reminders to RSVP, confirmations of registration, reminders to attend, and requests for feedback. This type of correspondence is significantly simplified by using a database system. In fact, when properly set up, the database does all of this via e-mail, with minimal effort from staff members. By using a database, each piece of correspondence can be effortlessly customized for individual recipients. Beyond e-mail, the database assists in quickly producing customized letters, memos, faxes, envelopes, and labels.

Any text used in correspondence at BYU can be saved in the database and reused in the future. The next time the same or similar event occurs, quick modifications to the stored text are made, and the database is ready to e-mail or print the new set of correspondence. The database can also keep a record of exactly what correspondence has been sent to each individual, as well as any responses from that person.

Enable Participants to Register Online

Developing a database-driven online registration system requires extensive technical expertise and development time, but the pay-off can be substantial. At NMSU, about 700 people register for an average of three or four workshops each, for a total of 2,672 unique registrations per year. In the past, participants registered by phone and e-mail. That's a lot of phone calls and e-mail messages! Now the database interfaces with a Web site, which allows participants to register online. Having participants register online is much easier and more accurate because participants input their own data. As an added benefit, participants can check their registration online or modify it, which saves additional phone calls and e-mail messages.

The database at the Office for Professional Development at Indiana University–Purdue University Indianapolis (IUPUI) allows for online registration and database-generated event confirmations. With their e-mail confirmation, participants receive an Outlook vCal file that they can use to automatically insert information about the upcoming event into their electronic calendars (N.V.N. Chism, personal communication, May 21, 2007). In addition to allowing participants to register online and be reminded of their registrations, Monmouth University takes online interface with a database a step further. They use online surveys to allow potential participants to indicate topics of workshops that they are interested in attending and to indicate when they are available to attend them. This allows the faculty developers to design workshops specifically targeted to the needs of participants, at times when the participants are available (Mullinix, 2006).

In addition to its uses for registration, a database can be used in conjunction with the Internet to provide other services. The IUPUI database allows faculty to apply online for grant proposals and awards, thus drastically reducing paperwork (J. S. Eynon, personal communication, May 23, 2007). There are also many elements of the extensive IUPUI Web site that are driven by their database, making the site easily changeable, dynamic, and tailored to individual user needs (Eynon & Chism, 2007).

Create Name Tags and Other Customized Materials

Once participants are registered, it is easy to create database-generated participant name tags—a few mouse clicks will send them directly to the printer. Creating name tags (or name plates, if preferred) through a database is also more professional. Our name tags have the person's name and department, as well as the center logo, and can be printed in color. Databases also allow us to customize other materials for participants, including certificates, gift cards, thank-you notes, and binder labels.

Learn Names by Using Photos

Faculty developers know and appreciate the importance of teachers learning the names of their students (Auster & MacRone, 1994). By adding photos to the database, faculty developers can easily memorize names, faces, and any needed information about the individuals served through their centers. At BYU, photos are displayed throughout the database, so users can easily associate names with faces whenever the database is accessed. Before each event, we can use the database to quickly generate electronic "flash cards," which help us to refresh our memories. In just a few minutes, we are prepared to greet most participants by name. The database is also used to print photo directories of any group of people for use away from the computer.

Getting photos for a database may or may not be easy. Most institutions take digital photos of all employees for I.D. or directory purposes. Using these photos may result in the best collection, but getting permission to use them can be difficult. One alternative is to download digital photos that appear on departmental Web sites. If nondigital photos are available, they may be scanned into the computer, or centers may purchase a digital camera and take the photos themselves (perhaps starting with the new faculty). Once you have the photos, importing them into the database is a relatively simple procedure.

Create a Membership System

At NMSU, the task force that created the faculty development center indicated that they didn't mind participating in professional development but they wanted credit for it. The center responded by creating a membership system. Memberships are earned by participation in the center activities and awarded on a yearly basis. The database is used to track which participants have earned membership in the center: a basic membership (ten hours or more of participation), a sustaining membership (twenty hours or more of participation), or a distinguished membership (forty hours or more of participation).

The membership system allows the center to offer various kinds of recognition and awards for various levels of membership. The system has created quite a bit of interest. At the end of each year, over two hundred members are honored. The database enables each member to receive a report documenting his or her participation at all center events, along with encouragement to use the information to strengthen vitae and annual reports. Similar reports are sent to each department head and dean (Gray & Conway, 2007). Individual faculty members often request a printed list of all activities in which they have participated during the current year (which is available to them online) and past years (which must be printed for them).

Overcome Challenges

The design, development, and maintenance of a relational database of the scope described here is not a small project. We estimate that the time to develop a comprehensive system (especially one linked to a dynamic Web site) requires approximately two to six months of full-time work if starting from scratch (depending on the skill level of the developer). Not every faculty development center has the resources or desire to create such a comprehensive system, but developing a system narrower in scope can drastically cut the development time. In fact, a simple database with just client contact information could be designed and up and running within a few hours! If time and resources are tight, consider designing a simple database that focuses on just a few of the functions that are highest priority; later, the database can be expanded to include additional functionality.

When it becomes possible to create a more comprehensive, robust database system, consider working with a professional database designer. Unless a center is lucky enough to employ someone with excellent technical skills, most faculty developers probably will not want to build a database totally in-house (note that this is not an acceptable project to assign to a temporary student worker). Fortunately, it is not difficult to find competent professionals with the necessary technical expertise, and joining forces with a similar center is a good way to get the job done. The California State University system developed a faculty development center management tool (named Depot) to be used systemwide on twenty-three campuses (C. Desrochers, personal communication, July 25, 2007).

There are several other ways to reduce database development time. One option is to build on the success of teaching centers that have successfully implemented comprehensive database systems. Such centers may be willing to share design elements, including screen shots of their databases and Web interfaces. The Ohio State University faculty development center generously provides a CD with information about their database and others modeled on it. BYU has developed a Web site with detailed information about the design of their database system (fc.byu.edu/jpages/database). Using such detailed information as a blueprint could cut development time by as much as 25 to 50 percent.

Still another route is to adopt a database developed at another center. The databases at NMSU and BYU are available (with restrictions) for other centers to use. Remember, however, that a database should be customized to a particular center's needs, so another center's database must be modified to fit a new center. When adopting a database, adequate time and money must be budgeted for learning how to use it and tailoring it to particular needs. Keep in mind that this additional investment is not insignificant.

In whatever way a database system is designed and developed, actively involve everyone who will ultimately use it (Plank et al., 2005). This includes discussing the purpose of the database and how it will support the mission of the center, needed functions and reports, and the design of the user interface. None of these important elements should be left to the discretion of the database developer! Involving the entire staff will result in a much more functional, user-friendly database that better meets their needs. It will also build support and excitement for making the transition to new ways of doing things.

A necessary precaution when using databases is to back up data regularly. This is true of all data stored on hard drives, but it is particularly true of data that are accessed and changed frequently and on which the entire staff depends for daily operations. At BYU, the database is backed up automatically every hour. Once a week, the entire database is burned to a CD and stored off campus.

Finally, in designing the database, carefully consider the need to respect the confidentiality of the data collected (Chism, 2003). Strict policies and protocols should be planned in advance to make sure that staff is well trained and that the data are secure. Good relational database software will include multiple ways to protect data and provide multiple layers of access so that sensitive data are available only to those who need it.

Conclusion

The primary job of a faculty developer is not administering and assessing programs; the primary job is supporting faculty. Nevertheless, the effective faculty developer must do all three. Because a well-designed database system helps a faculty developer be far more effective and efficient in administering and assessing programs, more time and energy can be devoted to helping faculty. The service provided can also be at a higher level of quality and professionalism. Affordable tools needed to develop a comprehensive, user-friendly database system were not readily available even ten years ago. Now, relatively powerful, inexpensive relational databases can enable every faculty developer to handle administrative tasks with the minimum of time and effort—and possibly even to enjoy these aspects of the job!

References

Auster, C. J., & MacRone, M. (1994). The classroom as a negotiated social setting: An empirical study of the effects of faculty members' behavior on students' participation. *Teaching Sociology, 22,* 289–300.

Bartlett, T. (2002, March 22). The unkindest cut. *The Chronicle of Higher Education,* p. A10.

Chism, N. V. N. (2003). *How professional development units keep track of their services (based on responses to an e-mail inquiry on the POD listserv, December 30, 2002).* Unpublished manuscript, Indiana University–Purdue University Indianapolis.

Chism, N. V. N., & Szabó, B. (1996). Who uses faculty development services? In L. Richlin (Ed.), *To improve the academy: Vol. 15. Resources for student, faculty, and institutional development* (pp. 115–128). Stillwater, OK: New Forums Press.

Chism, N. V. N., & Szabó, B. (1997–98). How faculty development programs evaluate their services. *Journal of Staff, Program, and Organization Development, 15*(2), 55–62.

Eynon, J., & Chism, N. V. N. (2007, October). *Tracking purpose and priorities: Database systems for monitoring our work.* Paper presented at the 32nd annual meeting of the Professional and Organizational Development Network in Higher Education, Pittsburgh, PA.

Frantz, A. C., Beebe, S. A., Horvath, V. S., Canales, J., & Swee, D. E. (2005). The roles of teaching and learning centers. In S. Chadwick-Blossey & D. R. Robertson (Eds.), *To improve the academy: Vol. 23. Resources for faculty, instructional, and organizational development* (pp. 72–90). Bolton, MA: Anker.

Gray, T., & Conway, E. (2007). Build it [right] and they will come: Boosting attendance at your teaching center by building community. *Journal of Faculty Development, 12*(3), 179–184.

Hilsen, L. R., & Wadsworth, E. C. (2002). Staging successful workshops. In K. H. Gillespie (Ed.), *A guide to faculty development: Practical advice, examples, and resources* (pp. 108–122). Bolton, MA: Anker.

Holton, S. A. (2002). Promoting your professional development program. In K. H. Gillespie (Ed.), *A guide to faculty development: Practical advice, examples, and resources* (pp. 100–107). Bolton, MA: Anker.

Mullinix, B. B. (2006). Building it for them: Faculty-centered program development and eManagement. In S. Chadwick-Blossey & D. R. Robertson (Eds.), *To improve the academy: Vol. 24. Resources for faculty, instructional, and organizational development* (pp. 183–200). Bolton, MA: Anker.

Plank, K., Kalish, A., Rohdieck, S., & Harper, K. (2005). A vision beyond measurement: Creating an integrated data system for teaching centers. In S. Chadwick-Blossey & D. R. Robertson (Eds.), *To improve the academy: Vol. 23. Resources for faculty, instructional, and organizational development* (pp. 173–190). Bolton, MA: Anker.

Sorenson, D. L. (2000). Student collaboration in faculty development: Connecting directly to the learning revolution. In E. C. Wadsworth (Ed.), *To improve the academy: Vol. 8. Resources for student, faculty, and institutional development* (pp. 97–121). Stillwater, OK: New Forums Press.

Chapter 5

Magicians of the Golden State

The CSU Center Director Disappearing Acts

Cynthia Desrochers
The California State University

The California State University (CSU) Teaching and Learning Center directors perform daily feats of magic, often culminating in one particularly dramatic trick at the end of the academic year—their own disappearing acts. This chapter traces the history of the center director position in the CSU system, reports where directors go when they leave the position after only a few years, and proposes how frequent turnover might be reversed through organizational factors aimed at promoting retention of these Magicians of the Golden State.

The date is January 2000, and seventeen California State University (CSU) Teaching and Learning Center directors (henceforth called center directors) are gathered for their semi-annual meeting of the Faculty Development Council (FDC), this one being held at CSU Sacramento. The FDC is an unofficial affinity group composed of all twenty-three center directors in the CSU system. The day's topic is "A Discussion of Center Director Burnout." Forty-seven ideas for avoiding burnout are generated and subsequently organized into six major themes. The follow-up report on this session reads, "The discussion was far-ranging, positive in focus, and energizing to participants" (Faculty Development Council Report, 2000).

Fast-forward the calendar to fall 2007, and we find that only one of the original seventeen center directors remains on the roster; this represents a 94 percent turnover in seven years. In addition, two new center directors have just been appointed, and four additional center directors have resigned over the summer, leaving their posts vacant as the academic year begins.

Although there are many benefits to being a center director in the CSU system—the twenty-three center directors communicate often, meet semi-annually, and receive support at the CSU system level—the CSU center director position is a challenging one. Centers have typically two employees: the center director, who may be part-time (.2 to .8) and an administrative support assistant, who may also be part-time (.5 to 1.0). Consequently, the demand for center services is often greater than a center is able to provide. Moreover, because historically our directors come from the ranks of CSU tenured faculty, they perform daily feats of magic, not only for their centers but also for their academic departments and colleges, as they fulfill teaching, scholarship, and service responsibilities.

The "magic" and their "bag of tricks" might look like this on any given Monday. Begin the day with an 8:00 A.M. college personnel meeting; scurry off to Costco to buy inexpensive snacks for a workshop; run to class to teach thirty students in a freshman seminar, meeting Mondays and Wednesday, 10:00 to 11:30; be back at the center by noon to lead a session on classroom civility; meet at 2:00 P.M. with three faculty who are writing an NSF grant and need to include a faculty development component; arrive late to the faculty senate meeting but just in time to deliver the commercial for the center-sponsored mini-grants; feel a bit under the weather by day's end but can't call in sick tomorrow because there are no "substitutes" to facilitate tomorrow's workshop session on course redesign, and now it's off to the car and home, grateful not to be teaching that 4:00 to 7:00 P.M. class, like last semester. Then, after a few comparable semesters, like many magic acts, these center directors stage their most dramatic finale—their own disappearing acts.

This chapter is guided by the assumption that frequent and often unanticipated turnover of center directors both impedes the overall functioning of teaching and learning centers and prevents smooth transitions between center directors. What follows is a systemwide study that relies on CSU reports, surveys, and personal interviews to investigate and provide partial answers to the following questions: 1) What, exactly, is the CSU center director turnover rate? 2) Where do CSU center directors go when they leave the position? 3) What role do workload, resources, and stress play in the high turnover rate? 4) What changes in organizational conditions might result in higher retention of CSU center directors?

The CSU Teaching and Learning Center

The twenty-three-campus CSU is the nation's largest and most diverse university system, with approximately 40,000 faculty and 450,000 students. Student enrollments at individual campuses range from approximately 800 students to 36,000 students. Our first Teaching and Learning Center was established at California State University, Long Beach (CSULB) in the late 1970s. By 2000, all twenty-two campuses in the system at that time (the twenty-third campus opened in 2002) had either a coordinator or director of teaching and learning, with differentiated amounts of released-time provided them to promote campuswide instructional enhancement endeavors. The rapid development of campus centers was the result of a few highly motivated leaders in the CSU who spread the word regarding the importance of establishing a Teaching and Learning Center. In the mid-1980s, the CSU chancellor created the Institute for Teaching and Learning (ITL). Under the leadership of the ITL faculty director, with an advisory board of academic senators, campus administrators, and system administrators, ITL's mission was to support systemwide, discipline-specific research on teaching and learning. In the early to mid-1990s, as new centers sprang up throughout the CSU system, the ITL directors informally mentored the new center directors. In 1994, the ITL held a meeting and discussed impressive goals for their future direction, including becoming the "preeminent system faculty development operation in the country through

- Research
- Exchange/Dissemination of ideas and information

- Renewal
- Mentoring
- Focus on learning
- Promoting reflection about the nature and process of teaching and learning" (Institute for Teaching and learning, 1994, p. 1)

By all accounts, the CSU was trailblazing in its goals. Eight years later, Cook and Sorcinelli (2002) would highlight many of the same benefits derived from establishing an effective Teaching and Learning Center, as synthesized here:

- Plays a key role in creating a campus culture that values and rewards teaching and learning
- Provides an overview of campus best practices in order to highlight and disseminate them campuswide
- Fosters faculty conversations across disciplines
- Addresses unique campus interests and needs in support of educating students
- Takes responsibility for staying abreast of and communicating the literature on student learning
- Assists faculty on a confidential basis
- Offers a comprehensive program to support faculty professional development, including workshops and seminars, new-faculty orientation programs, grant competitions to stimulate teaching improvements, and publications to share basics and innovations
- Provides the institutional memory that allows for continuity in teaching support services as department chairs, deans, and provosts come and go

Throughout my twelve years of involvement with CSU faculty development, first as the founding director of a campus center (1995 to 2005) and currently as the director of the Institute for Teaching and Learning, I have witnessed many of these same benefits provided by our established centers, except for one— institutional memory. Unfortunately, many of our centers suffer from amnesia due to frequent turnover of center directors. Acknowledging that two campuses have three-year-rotating director positions that permit term renewal, the other campuses have no such policies to prevent center directors from remaining in

**Figure 5.1. Number of Directors at CSU Campus
Centers, 1995–2007**

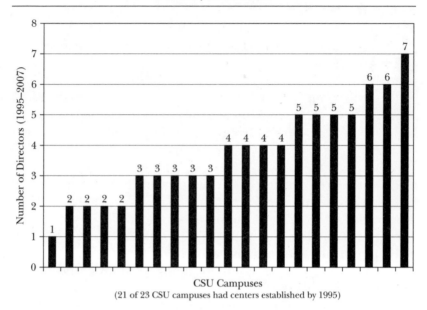

CSU Campuses
(21 of 23 CSU campuses had centers established by 1995)

the position indefinitely; however, few remain for long. In the 2006 survey of center directors, of the nineteen responding, 53 percent had been in the position two years or less, and 32 percent had been in the position three to four years (Faculty Development Council Survey, 2006). Figure 5.1 depicts the historical roster of the twenty-one established CSU campuses from 1995 to 2007.

The longevity of center directors varies considerably, ranging from no turnover during this time period to a campus that has had seven different directors over the same twelve-year period. (*Note:* This campus is currently experiencing stability, having had the same director for over three years.)

Director Disappearance Act

Where do CSU center directors go when they leave the position? A search of historical reports, coupled with interviews of past CSU leadership, resulted in information about forty former directors between 1995 and 2007.

Exit Goals

The major exit goal, representing 42 percent of those departing, as illustrated in Figure 5.2, was to assume a higher-level administration position within the CSU system. These data confirm that the CSU center directorship is a stepping-stone position to becoming an associate dean, dean, associate vice president, assistant provost, or system-level director in the CSU system. Although exact reasons for each exit may remain confidential for many, informal interviews reveal two publicly expressed reasons for their exits. First, the center director position is a positive administrative experience; hence, some directors are motivated to seek higher-level administrative positions because they find that they enjoy administrative work. Second, some center directors, working on partial released-time, seek a full-time administrative position in order to enjoy greater job focus, compensation, and status. Regardless of the underlying reasons that center directors exit the position in favor of administrative roles, however, this practice results in a high turnover rate for CSU center directors. Moreover, I would argue that as beneficial as it may be to have campus administrators who are knowledgeable about teaching

**Figure 5.2. Where CSU Center Directors Go
Directly After Leaving the Position, 1995–2007**

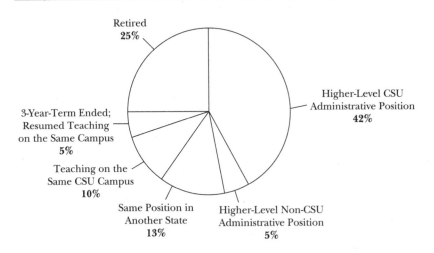

and learning, it severely retards the cumulative faculty development expertise in the CSU system.

The next greatest departure destination, at 25 percent, was to
retirement. This indicates that directors tend to take the center
directorship toward the end of their careers. Many report that
the directorship is a vehicle for giving back to the university by
sharing one's accumulated wisdom with newer faculty. Next, of
the 13 percent who left the center director position in order to
take a similar job in another state, their reasons included the
desire to move closer to family or to leave an unhealthy work
environment. And finally, the 10 percent who returned to teaching have tended to be midcareer faculty who reported that they
missed teaching and discipline-based research. There are no
doubt other reasons for leaving the center director position that
are personal and have gone unreported, such as being ineffective
or not enjoying the work.

Underdeveloped Expertise

How does a novice center director become an expert? Bransford,
Brown, and Cocking (2000), presenting research from the cognitive sciences, caution that expertise falls on a continuum, from
novice to expert, and is field-dependent; hence, it typically does
not transfer directly from one field to another. Moreover, the
nature of expertise is such that experts in a field have developed
a well-organized knowledge base that they thoroughly understand, can easily call on and use, and often adapt to fit different
conditions. Given the requirements needed for a center director
to develop expertise in this role, and given the long-running performance of the "Center Director Disappearing Acts," the CSU
system needs to address factors that may increase center director
retention in the position so that directors attain an operational
level of expertise, leading to that systemwide preeminence, as
envisioned by CSU visionaries in 1994.

Historically, our center directors have been recruited from the
ranks of campus tenured faculty with outstanding teaching records
and interest in faculty development; however, few have experience
in directing a center and even fewer a well-organized knowledge
base in designing curriculum, instruction, and assessments for a

variety of disciplines. In the 2006 survey of center directors, of the nineteen responding, one came from the field of education, three from educational technology, and one from educational administration. The other disciplines represented include computer science, communication studies, sociology, English, history, political science, plant science, nursing, and business law. Hence, with expertise in a wide range of disciplines not directly related to faculty professional development, new center directors get on-the-job training in order to develop expertise in learning theory, instructional strategies, course design, assessment, working with faculty and administrators, and managing a center. Nancy Chism (2006) made this comment in a POD session: "For the School of Medicine, we don't say, 'You're healthy; let's make you dean of the school.' However, in faculty development we often say, 'You teach well; let's make you head of our center.'" Perhaps the CSU is guilty of doing this, as currently only one campus out of twenty-three employs a director who was hired as an experienced faculty developer through a nationwide search. Might this practice of selecting inexperienced faculty developers contribute to our revolving door of center directors? Would director longevity improve if experienced faculty development professionals were hired to fill the CSU center director positions? Would these individuals need to hold tenured faculty positions to be perceived as credible by our disciplinary faculty?

Mullinix (2008) is exploring the perceived impact of center director faculty status on director credibility with discipline-based faculty, and she finds that a significant majority of experienced faculty development professionals "perceived faculty status to be an important contributor to their credibility, effectiveness, and interactions with faculty colleagues" (p. 190). This may lead us to conclude that if experienced faculty development professionals are hired by the CSU in the future, it is important that they be tenure-track in order to increase center director retention rates without compromising center director effectiveness with faculty.

Magicians on Overload

The responsibilities of our center directors are numerous and varied. Surveys conducted in 1996, 2002, and 2006 confirm a high level of center productivity. In the most recent 2006 survey, with nineteen center directors responding, the majority of center directors (50 to 100 percent) reported the following activities as "major responsibilities" of their centers:

- Providing pedagogical workshops
- Establishing faculty learning communities
- Conducting individual faculty consultations
- Providing academic technology workshops
- Organizing fall-term new-faculty orientations
- Providing new-faculty programs throughout the year
- Administering mini-grants and follow-up
- Supporting Retention, Tenure, and Promotion portfolio development
- Promoting scholarship of teaching and learning projects (Faculty Development Council Survey, 2006)

Moreover, 42 percent report major responsibility for providing service learning support and 32 percent for coordinating program assessment. In addition, 37 percent report having a peer-review or peer coaching program, and 32 percent run book groups. In order to provide these faculty development programs, 80 percent of our centers have at least one dedicated room; however, the other 20 percent have no room dedicated to their use.

Do our center directors feel overloaded? And if so, does this overload lead to stress, and ultimately, director burnout in early stages of careers, accounting for some of the CSU center director turnover? The systemwide study provides answers to these questions.

Job burnout starts with stress, which is often the result of being faced with too many demands, a lack of rewards, and a feeling of powerlessness (Potter, 1998). Eventually, an individual's coping skills are strained, and she may burn out and quit the job. *Merriam-Webster's Online Dictionary* defines *burnout* as "exhaustion of physical or emotional strength or motivation usually as a result of prolonged stress or frustration." Recalling the center directors' meeting where Center Director Burnout was the topic, key ideas from this discussion appear in Table 5.1 and suggest why sixteen of the seventeen center directors in attendance have since left the position.

Table 5.1. Themes and Suggestions for Avoiding Center Director Burnout

Theme I. Network with colleagues.

1. Attend dean and associate dean meetings with your provost.
2. Become a member of campus committees and the faculty senate.
3. Recruit good advisory board members and promise not to overload them with excessive demands.

Theme II. Just say no.

1. Have a clear view of your mission and only accept responsibilities and opportunities consistent with it.
2. Tie new initiatives to resources (only agree to support an effort with additional staff or budget).
3. Don't stretch so far that you undermine the quality of what you are already doing.
4. Negotiate your role with your supervisor. If you have multiple roles, negotiate less than full-time expectations with each supervisor. Invite your supervisors to meet with you all together, so they have a better understanding of their joint expectations of you.
5. Set deadlines and limits (for example, do not provide last-minute assistance to grant writers).

Theme III. Get the human resources you need to do your job well.

1. Know the tasks performed by other units on campus and refer appropriate inquiries to them.
2. Develop skills in others (for example, recruit faculty who will assume responsibility for some programs).
3. Recruit workshop leaders. Don't try to do everything yourself.
4. Delegate some responsibilities to student assistants.

Theme IV. Take care of yourself.

1. Make hard decisions about your continued role in your discipline. Don't try to be a full-time expert in your discipline and a full-time faculty developer.
2. Find an intersection between your discipline and faculty development (for example, become active in teaching-related aspects of your discipline).
3. Make hard decisions about your continued role as a teacher. Don't try to teach more than you can cope with in addition to your faculty development role.
4. Protect your health with appropriate exercise and diet.
5. Recognize that you can't do everything.

(Continued)

Table 5.1. Themes and Suggestions for Avoiding Center Director Burnout (*Continued*)

Theme V. Advocate for your center.

1. Advocate for yourself through periodic reports to the right people.
2. Advocate for yourself through a flashy brochure and a newsletter or Web site.
3. Get others to advocate on your behalf. When people express gratitude for your work, suggest that they let those above you know about it, too.
4. Schmooze your provost. What initiatives are important to him or her? What resources can he or she provide you to make them happen?
5. Walk about campus with an administrator; let him or her see your connections to the faculty.

Theme VI. Replace yourself.

1. Mentor your own replacement to ensure continuity when you take a sabbatical or leave the position.
2. Develop skills in other faculty so you can delegate responsibilities to them.
3. Get resources for an associate director, program coordinator, or graduate student intern.

These suggestions for combating burnout imply that these hard-working center directors created self-protective radar screens in order to identify and eliminate tasks that placed excessive demands on their time and well-being; moreover, they resorted to myriad informal social connections and marketing tactics in order to earn administrative approval and gain resources to run their centers. Where are the clear position descriptions and sufficient, predictable budgets that might alleviate some of the stress associated with directing these centers? Perhaps part of the reason they are lacking lies in our history, as many of the CSU Teaching and Learning Centers sprang up virtually overnight in the early to mid-1990s. At that time, many director position descriptions were merely one-paragraph blurbs defining general duties, such as "to support faculty in their multiple roles," with a modest budget allocation to match. These limitations aside, the development of Teaching and Learning Centers on each CSU campus signaled an interest in faculty professional development and student learning, and many of us were excited to be a part of this new teaching and learning focus in higher education.

Retention Motivators for Center Directors

Having just returned from a POD conference excursion to Fallingwater—Frank Lloyd Wright's acclaimed architectural masterpiece in Pennsylvania—I cannot help but reflect on the degree to which pre-planning resulted in a magnificent concrete home cantilevered above a roaring waterfall among huge rocks. Similarly, can our faculty development centers become attractive and stable units if we plan now by surveying the landscape, situating ourselves on a strong foundation, and avoiding large overhanging boulders? The current reality of having many novice center directors in the CSU presents not only a challenge to mentor them but also a critical point for change if we can identify and implement institutional conditions that might foster retention of directors.

To better understand what factors might motivate a center director to remain in this position for five more years, a short anonymous survey was conducted at a systemwide center directors' semi-annual meeting in late fall, 2007. Fifteen of the nineteen permanent center directors, representing 80 percent of the permanent-director group, responded to the following question:

> What would *motivate* you personally to stay in the Center director position for five more years versus moving to a new position? Think in terms of anything your university could realistically do for you/ your Center as being possible. List five *motivators*, if possible.

Most directors were able to list five motivators, resulting in a total of fifty-eight items. In analyzing these items, those listed by only one center director were removed from the sample. Subsequently, items were categorized, and percentages of the total remaining were calculated, yielding the following results, as shown in Table 5.2. Moreover, these responses were analyzed according to the years of experience as a center director. Of those responding, 30 percent were considered "experienced" faculty developers (five years or more experience), whereas the

**Table 5.2. Motivators for Center Directors to Stay
in This Position for Five More Years**

Motivator	Percentage	Examples
More resources	40% (half responded *increased budget*)	Increased budget, released-time, staff time, and faculty associate time
Enacted institutional mission that values faculty development (FD)	30%	Institutional actions that show support and commitment for FD (such as encouraging faculty participation), as well as growth of FD
Enhanced decision-making responsibility in the university	15%	Report to provost; value center director input and expertise, not just a midwife for campus initiatives
Center physical space	15%	Provide a permanent physical space; better location

other 70 percent were combined, representing either "novice" (up to two years experience) or "moderately experienced" (from two to five years experience).

Experienced faculty developers' motivators to remain in the position differed from those of the less experienced developers in that they had an *institutional focus*. For example, experienced faculty developers listed motivators such as the following: a stable administration, an institutional decision-making role, administrative support, and higher-level reporting lines. The novice and moderately experienced faculty developers' motivators were more *center-focused*. For example, these newer developers typically listed the following: staff support, released time, increased budget, more faculty associates, and dedicated center space. This indicates a developmental path toward the desire for greater institutional involvement and impact as individuals mature in the center director position. Also of interest was that none of our center directors listed what might be termed self-serving motivators, such as greater salary compensation, elevated rank, or high-status title.

Potential Solutions

How can the picture I have described here—The Case of the CSU Center Directors' Disappearing Acts—be interpreted and what possible solutions can be offered? General job satisfaction reports, organizational development literature, and experienced educational developers provide insights.

The Society of Human Resource Management (SHRM) annually interviews employees and human resource professionals in order to publish a Job Satisfaction Survey Report. Its purpose is to identify factors that contribute to job satisfaction so organizations can implement measures to retain skilled employees. The SHRM 2007 Report lists the top five "very important" job satisfaction aspects, in order of importance, as the following: compensation, benefits, job security, work-life balance, and communication between employees and senior management (Meisinger, 2007). This list demonstrates how unique higher education employment opportunities and faculties are, in that only the last one on the top-five list—"communication with senior management"—appears comparable to a motivational need cited by our center directors, identified as "institutional support." That our center directors do not mention the other top-three satisfaction aspects may indicate that either they are well compensated, with benefits and security, or that these are not their top-priority job-satisfaction needs. It is less clear that work-life balance goes unnoticed by center directors, as this area was not investigated directly; however, directors do report a need for more human resources in order to provide center services. Moreover, center directors typically come to campus five days per week, whereas their previous teaching schedules often permitted an on-campus schedule of three to four days per week. And recalling that all of our center directors are discipline-based faculty, directors with five-days-per-week center-director schedules must relegate disciplinary-scholarship projects to the weekends, which by most definitions constitutes a work-life imbalance.

Nelson (1988) states that the goal of organizational development is to improve the functioning of the entire organizational system. For colleges and universities, this means students, faculty, administrators, and staff. Moreover, organizational development is based on the assumption that an organization is most effective when both individual goals and organizational goals are integrated (Nelson, 1998). This suggests that if greater student learning and talent development are a high priority for the university, the Teaching and Learning Center director holds a pivotal role in this goal's attainment.

Chism (1998) addresses the role of center directors in promoting institutional change, noting the importance of achieving the following to be most effective in that role: alignment of center goals with institutional priorities, development of center director authority, as derived from credibility and respect, and development of enabling conditions, such as access, which she defines as "ready channels of communication with individual faculty, governance bodies, and curriculum/course design decisionmakers and participation on task forces and committees that deal with these issues" (p. 146) and resources.

Bolman and Deal (1992) cite many of the same factors as Chism, listing the following as necessary characteristics for effective teamwork: "clear goals, open communication, shared leadership, and a comfortable, informal atmosphere" (p. 35). Recalling the CSU center director reports of desiring a meaningful decision-making role within the university, it is critical that center directors become integral team members on the provost's cabinet if student-learning initiatives are a high priority of the university.

The Whole Picture

Table 5.3 provides a graphic to visually depict, organize, and suggest outcomes for factors contributing to center director satisfaction and retention. Nilson (2007) argues persuasively that a well-crafted graphic enhances our ability to both comprehend and draw inferences about information. Those are the goals of this matrix. In developing the Center Director Retention Matrix, I have borrowed from the business world by adapting Ambrose's (1987) change matrix format. Moreover, this matrix draws substantively from organizational development and change principles (Bolman & Deal, 1992; Nelson, 1988), the work of Chism, CSU Reports, and CSU center director surveys and personal interviews,

Table 5.3.   Center Director Retention Matrix: Institutional Factors to Consider to Retain Center Directors

1 Center Director is Credible, **Skilled**, and Respected	2 Center has Sufficient and Stable **Budget**	3 Center has Sufficient **Human Resources**	4 Center has **Space** and Good Location	5 Center Programs are **Aligned** with Campus Goals	6 Campus Actions Show that the Center is **Valued**	7 Center Director is a Member of the Campus **Decision-Making Team**	Center Director is Likely to Feel:
							Satisfied w/Position
Limited or Missing	Sufficient Budget	Human Resources	Center Space	Programs Aligned	Center Valued	Team Member	**Anxious**
Skilled	**Limited or Missing**	Human Resources	Center Space	Programs Aligned	Center Valued	Team Member	**Frustrated**
Skilled	Sufficient Budget	**Limited or Missing**	Center Space	Programs Aligned	Center Valued	Team Member	**Stressed**
Skilled	Sufficient Budget	Human Resources	**Limited or Missing**	Programs Aligned	Center Valued	Team Member	**Frustrated**
Skilled	Sufficient Budget	Human Resources	Center Space	**Limited or Missing**	Center Valued	Team Member	**Peripheral**
Skilled	Sufficient Budget	Human Resources	Center Space	Programs Aligned	**Limited or Missing**	Team Member	**Angry**
Skilled	Sufficient Budget	Human Resources	Center Space	Programs Aligned	Center Valued	**Limited or Missing**	**Mistrusting**

as reviewed throughout this chapter. The resulting matrix identifies seven center director satisfaction factors to consider in order to retain center directors. Appearing horizontally across the top of the matrix, these seven factors include the following:

1. The center director is credible, skilled in the tasks required of the position, and respected by faculty and administrators.
2. The center director has a sufficient and stable budget in order to operate and provide the services necessary to run an effective faculty development center.
3. The center has sufficient personnel, both professional and administrative support, in order to provide high-quality services to the college or university.
4. The center has dedicated space, including offices, conference rooms, and computer labs as needed, and these workspaces are located where faculty can easily attend workshop sessions.
5. The center programs are aligned with campus goals, which assumes that 1) the campus has stated goals, 2) the campus enacts these stated goals, 3) the campus communicates to the center about furthering the campus goals that are related to faculty development, and 4) the center designs programs that are aligned with these campus goals.
6. The campus actions show that the center is valued, which may include allocation of resources, recognition and rewards, and policies and practices.
7. The center director is a member of the campus decision-making team that formulates important campuswide policies and procedures related to faculty development.

The Center Director Retention Matrix suggests center director feelings as outcomes that may result when each of the seven factors on the matrix is either limited or missing for the center director within the institution. Note that these are suggested outcomes, and others may be experienced. Moreover, serving as a heuristic to analyze problematic conditions existing for a center director within the university's organizational structure, this matrix has the potential to predict center director satisfaction or dissatisfaction in the position, the latter leading to center director resignation and, ultimately, increased center director turnover rates and compromised faculty development programs.

Conclusion

This discussion of center director disappearing acts must be placed in the context of our goals for higher education. How much do we value good faculty development that leads to good teaching and good learning? Bok (2006), former president of Harvard University, states that our colleges are underachieving and accomplishing far less for students than they should. Reflecting on the quality of undergraduate education, he asks, "Has the quality of teaching improved? More important, are students learning more than they did in 1950?" To these questions Bok responds, "The honest answer is that we do not know" (p. 30). Bok describes a tendency for faculties and academic leaders to focus on subject matter and neglect pedagogy with a "studied disregard of the research on student development in college" (p. 50). Noting that changing instructional methods requires a lot of effort, Bok determines that neither university faculties nor administrators are motivated to discover better ways of educating students, so business as usual continues.

Fink (2003) discusses barriers to change in teaching faced by faculties themselves, including overcoming habitual teaching patterns, receiving no encouragement to rethink their assumptions about teaching, finding the time to learn and prepare for alternative ways of teaching, and being confronted by uncooperative students who reject an innovative teaching strategy with which they are unfamiliar.

Holding firm the belief that all faculties can change instructional methods in favor of those designed to improve student learning and recognizing that there are many challenges to overcome, I conclude that the CSU must strengthen the connection between our CSU Teaching and Learning Centers and campuswide initiatives related to teaching and learning. Center directors are the principal campuswide teachers of and advocates for instructional innovations, encouraging others to keep a laser's focus on intentional teaching, curriculum and assignment design, and outcomes assessment. It is, therefore, critical that we provide our Teaching and Learning Center directors with the necessary resources—human and financial—to effectively operate the CSU centers and campuswide programs. In addition, we must allow directors a respite from non-center-related university-service tasks in order for them to become experts at center directing and pedagogy, leading to career-long center director roles on CSU campuses. In some instances, center director impact and longevity will increase through hiring experienced professional faculty developers and giving them a tenured faculty position. If we eagerly support these steps, the CSU system will edge closer to the lofty goal expressed in 1994—that of "becoming the preeminent system faculty development operation in the country."

References

Ambrose, D. (1987). *Managing complex change.* Pittsburgh, PA: The Enterprise Group, Ltd.

Bok, D. (2006). *Our underachieving colleges: A candid look at how much students learn and why they should be learning more.* Princeton, NJ: Princeton University Press.

Bolman, L. G., & Deal, T. E. (1992, Autumn). What makes a team work? *Organizational Dynamics, 34–44.* Retrieved October 18, 2006, from www.fromccl.org/leadership

Bransford, J. D., Brown, A. L., & Cocking, R. R. (Eds.). (2000). *How people learn: Brain, mind, experience, and school* (Expanded ed.). Washington, DC: National Academy Press.

Chism, N. V. N. (1998). The role of educational developers in institutional change: From the basement office to the front office. In M. Kaplan (Ed.), *To improve the academy: Vol 17. Resources for faculty, instructional, and organizational development* (pp. 141–154). Stillwater, OK: New Forums Press.

Chism, N. V. N. (2006, October). *If there's a scholarship of professional development, why don't we educate for it?* Concurrent session at the 31st annual meeting of the Professional and Organizational Development Network in Higher Education, Portland, OR.

Cook, C. E., & Sorcinelli, M. D. (2002). *The value of a teaching center.* Retrieved September 25, 2007, from www.podnetwork.org/faculty_development/values.htm

Faculty Development Council. (2007, February). *Defining the field: The CSU faculty development center survey 2006.* Summary report, p. 3.

Faculty Development Council (January 2000). Report on a discussion of center director burnout.

Fink, L. D. (2003). *Creating significant learning experiences: An integrated approach to designing college courses*. San Francisco: Jossey-Bass.

Institute for Teaching and Learning. (1994, October). Summary of the October 7, 1994, discussion on the future direction of the ITL.

Meisinger, S. (2007, October). Job satisfaction: A key to engagement and retention. *HR Magazine, 45*(10), 8.

Merriam-Webster's Online Dictionary. Definition of *burnout*. Retrieved October 16, 2007, from www.m-w.com/dictionary/burnout

Mullinix, B. B. (2008). Credibility and effectiveness in context: An exploration of the importance of faculty status for faculty developers. In D. R. Robertson & L. B. Nilson (Eds.), *To improve the academy: Vol. 26. Resources for faculty, instructional, and organizational development* (pp. 173–195). Bolton, MA: Anker.

Nelson, G. (1988). Organizational development: Working with change agents. In E. Wadsworth (Ed.), *A handbook for new practitioners* (pp. 175–180). Stillwater, OK: New Forums Press.

Nilson, L. B. (2007). *The graphic syllabus and the outcomes map. Communicating your course*. San Francisco: Jossey-Bass.

Potter, B. A. (1998). *Job burnout: What it is and what you can do about it? Summary*. From *Overcoming job burnout: How to renew enthusiasm for work* (pp. 1–2). Ronin Publishing. Retrieved August 28, 2007, from www.docpotter.com/art_bo-summary.html

Helping Faculty Thrive

Chapter 6

Practical Tools to Help Faculty Use Learner-Centered Approaches

Phyllis Blumberg
University of the Sciences in Philadelphia

Instructors often resist dramatic changes in their teaching, and learner-centered approaches are not intuitive for most instructors. They need tools to help them adopt these approaches. This chapter describes four tools—1) a list of components of Weimer's five practices of learner-centered teaching, 2) reflection questions to prepare instructors to determine the learner-centered status of their courses, 3) self-assessment rubrics, and 4) a Planning for Transformation form—to help instructors change their teaching. Taken together, these tools form a comprehensive system with which to plan for change. This system encourages and assists instructors to make incremental changes toward using learner-centered approaches in their teaching.

Although instructors complain that their students cannot apply what they have previously learned and are unable to learn on their own, they may not associate how they teach with these consequences. Traditionally, instructors have focused on what they do and not on what their students are learning. This emphasis on instructors often results in passive learning on the part of students. Educators call this traditional method instructor-centered teaching. In contrast, learner-centered teaching occurs when instructors focus on student learning. Learner-centered teaching, which is increasingly encouraged in higher education, emphasizes a variety of methods that shift the role of the instructor from giver of information to facilitator of student learning and creator of an environment in which learning can take place. When the focus is shifted to student learning, student retention improves and graduates are better prepared than those students who were more traditionally educated (Matlin, 2002; Sternberg & Grigorenko, 2002).

A survey of 494 North American faculty developers identified "promoting learner-centered teaching" as the most important issue they need to address in their work (Sorcinelli, Austin, Eddy, & Beach, 2006). Currently, most of these faculty developers offer assistance to their instructors in using learner-centered teaching (Sorcinelli et al., 2006). Faculty developers are changing the focus from how teachers instruct in the classroom to what the students are learning. Such a change in approach requires changes in how we help instructors teach and assess students (Fink, 2003; Gardiner, 1994). Given these issues, faculty developers are seeking guidance on how to help instructors transform their teaching to be more learner-centered.

The purpose of this chapter is to offer faculty developers some explicit tools for encouraging instructors to embrace more learner-centered approaches. First, I review the research supporting learner-centered teaching, discuss why faculty members resist its implementation, and show how such resistance can be overcome. Next, I offer four tools to help instructors implement learner-centered teaching. The chapter shows how to

1. Give instructors concrete components of learner-centered teaching to bring the abstract concepts into focus.
2. Organize these components into continua from instructor-centered to learner-centered, using self-assessment rubrics; this helps instructors identify the status of their courses.
3. Use questions comparing ideal situations with their realities to help instructors visualize alternatives to what they currently do.
4. Use additional questions that can help instructors plan the incremental changes they wish to make.

Finally, I describe a comprehensive system for change that faculty developers can use to help instructors transform courses, incorporating these four tools.

Why Should Instructors Use Learner-Centered Approaches?

Strong research evidence exists to support the implementation of learner-centered approaches instead of instructor-centered approaches. However, most instructors, especially those outside of psychology and education, do not know this literature. Informing faculty of this evidence helps them understand why they should incorporate more learner-centered approaches. This knowledge also helps them defend their teaching methods to their students and more traditional faculty peers.

A task force of the American Psychological Association integrated the research into fourteen Learner-Centered Psychological Principles, which can be summarized through the following five domains (Alexander & Murphy, 2000; Lambert & McCombs, 2000).

1. *The knowledge base.* The conclusive result of decades of research on building a knowledge base is that what a person already knows largely determines what new information he attends to, how he organizes and represents new information, how he filters new experiences, and even what he determines to be important or relevant (Alexander & Murphy, 2000). Therefore, learner-centered instructors will consider what their students already know and help their students assimilate new information in relation to what they have previously learned. In some cases, the learner-centered instructors have to explicitly show how the students' previous knowledge is incorrect or faulty.

2. *Strategic processing and executive control.* The ability to reflect on and regulate one's thoughts and behaviors is an essential aspect of learning. Successful students are actively involved in their own learning, monitor their thinking, think about their learning, and assume responsibility for their own learning (Lambert & McCombs, 2000). This domain has several important learner-centered implications. First, learner-centered instructors use activities that ask students to reflect on and monitor their learning. Second, although students prefer it when their instructors assume responsibility for their learning by providing lecture notes or detailed study guides, this practice does not benefit the students in the long run. Learner-centered instructors help students learn how to take responsibility for their own learning.

3. *Motivation and affect.* The benefits of learner-centered education include increased motivation for learning and greater satisfaction with school; both outcomes lead to greater achievement (Johnson, 1991; Maxwell, 1998; Slavin, 1990). Research shows that personal involvement, intrinsic motivation, personal commitment, confidence in one's abilities to succeed, and a perception of control over learning lead to more learning and higher achievement in school (Alexander & Murphy, 2000). Learner-centered approaches increase student engagement through active participation. Learner-centered instructors motivate their students to be intrinsically motivated to learn instead of being driven by grades; they help their students perceive that they have control over their own learning.

4. *Development and individual differences.* Individuals progress through various common stages of development, influenced by both inherited and environmental factors. Depending on the context or task, changes in how people think, believe, or behave are dependent on a combination of one's inherited abilities, stages of development, individual differences, capabilities, experiences, and environmental conditions (Alexander & Murphy, 2000). Learner-centered instructors use different teaching and learning activities and approaches to accommodate individual differences and capabilities.

5. *Situation or context.* Theories of learning that highlight the roles of active engagement and social interaction in the students' own construction of knowledge (Bruner, 1966; Kafai & Resnick, 1996; Piaget, 1963; Vygotsky, 1978) strongly support this learner-centered paradigm. Learning is a social process. Many environmental factors, including how the instructor teaches and how actively engaged the student is in the learning process, positively or negatively influence how much and what students learn (Lambert & McCombs, 2000). In comparison studies between students in lecture and active learning courses, there are significantly more learning gains in the active learning courses (Springer, Stanne, & Donovan, 1999). Active learning is a critical component of all learner-centered approaches. Learner-centered instructors routinely use activities where the students interact with each other, such as in small groups, while actively engaging with the content to be learned.

The swift growth in the number of institutions of higher learning using the National Survey of Student Engagement (NSSE) is evidence of the widespread acceptance of learner-centered teaching (Ewell, 2001). Results from 972 colleges and universities surveying more than 844,000 students led the NSSE researchers to develop five benchmarks of effective educational practices, including level of academic challenge, active and collaborative learning, meaningful student-faculty interactions, enriching educational experiences, and supportive campus environment (National Survey of Student Engagement, 2005). All these benchmarks are consistent with the fourteen learner-centered principles developed by the task force of the American Psychological Association (Alexander & Murphy, 2000; Lambert & McCombs, 2000) and the learner-centered practices I described earlier with each domain.

Learner-centered teaching is also consistent with the current accreditation process for institutions of higher education and for professional programs. The assessments of student learning outcomes are fundamental to this process, in that the regional and professional program accrediting bodies use learning outcomes to judge the quality of these programs. Accrediting agencies concentrate on student learning that transcends disciplines such as the development of problem solving and information literacy skills (Middle States Commission on Higher Education, 2003). Learner-centered approaches also focus on the students' developing these skills and learning how to learn for the present and the future. Learner-centered instructors explicitly help students develop these skills and assess students on their mastery of them.

Why Do Instructors Resist Changing to Learner-Centered Teaching?

Teaching that uses learner-centered practices requires the development of new skills and attitudes (Sorcinelli et al., 2006). My experience as a faculty developer shows that many instructors are confused about how to transform their instructor-centered teaching to be more learner-centered. For example, some faculty members believe that they only can implement such practices in small classes. Others feel that using learner-centered approaches would negatively influence the content and rigor of their courses because the students would spend time on active learning activities while reducing or dumbing down the content (Blumberg & Everett, 2005). For some instructors, their teaching is so unlike what we describe as learner-centered that they do not know how to make incremental steps.

When I first started to educate instructors about learner-centered teaching, I drew either-or comparisons between instructor-centered and learner-centered approaches. Instructors were unable to accept such a stark contrast between the learner-centered and instructor-centered approaches. Just listing learner-centered approaches may not suggest ways to change our teaching. For example, a key concept in learner-centered teaching is that students assume responsibility for their own learning (Weimer, 2002). Most instructors already believe that students should assume responsibility for their own learning but may not know how to help students do so. Instructors need concrete and incremental ways, not just theoretical constructs, to implement learner-centered approaches.

The choice of terminology can help or hinder instructor acceptance of learner-centered teaching. People choose different phrases for this approach. "Learner-centered teaching" places the emphasis on the person who is doing the learning (Weimer, 2002). "Learning-centered teaching" focuses on the process of learning. Both phrases appeal to faculty because they identify the critical role of teaching in the learning process. The phrase "student-centered learning" is also used in the literature, but some instructors do not like it because it suggests a consumer focus, seems to encourage students to be more empowered, and appears to remove the teacher from the critical role.

How Can Faculty Developers Help Instructors Implement Learner-Centered Teaching?

Educating instructors about what learner-centered teaching is can be helpful (Blumberg, 2004). Giving instructors the educational and psychological research foundation on which learner-centered approaches rest helps them understand why they should adopt it. Instructors also like teaching models and examples. Once instructors learn that courses can be learner-centered without sacrificing content and rigor, they are more likely to begin to accept these approaches. They also like hearing that there are many different ways to implement learner-centered teaching. Weimer's (2002) model of learner-centered teaching appeals to many instructors.

Weimer (2002) identifies five ways instructors need to change to achieve learner-centered teaching. These five areas are the 1) functions of content, 2) role of the instructor, 3) responsibility for learning, 4) processes and purposes of assessment, and 5) balance of power. This approach to learner-centered teaching focuses on how the students are learning and the conditions that facilitate or hinder learning.

Brief definitions such as the following overview of these learner-centered approaches in each of Weimer's five areas might motivate instructors to learn more about these practices.

1. *The functions of content* in learner-centered teaching include building a strong knowledge foundation and developing an understanding of why and how the content should be learned and used in the future.
2. *The role of the instructor* should focus on student learning and should be facilitative rather than didactic.
3. *The responsibility for learning* shifts from the instructor to the students. The instructor creates learning environments that motivate students to accept responsibility for learning.
4. *The processes and purposes of assessment* shift from only assigning grades to include constructive feedback and assistance with improvement. Learner-centered teaching uses assessment as a part of the learning process.
5. *The balance of power* shifts so that the instructor shares some decisions about the course with the students, such that the instructor and the students collaborate on course policies and procedures.

Are There Tools to Help Instructors Transition to Learner-Centered Teaching?

Four helpful tools are described next.

1. A List of Specific Instructor Behaviors

Although Weimer's (2002) model appeals to faculty, it does not provide concrete ways for instructors to implement the changes that they need to make (Wright, 2006). Because the practices are broad, abstract categories, they do not define specific learner-centered instructor behaviors at a sufficient level of detail for many instructors. Therefore, I decided to further define specific components of each practice.

Discussions with faculty developers, instructional designers, instructors, and administrators over four years led to the development of specific components of these practices. A total of over 250 faculty developers and instructors, who were in many different disciplines and who taught at all levels in higher education, offered feedback and validation. This cycle of seeking feedback and making corrections on the components validated the components and gave me confidence that the specific items transcend disciplines and different types of courses. Appendix A lists the components of each practice area.

2. Rubrics to Assess the Transition

Although Weimer's (2002) five components acquainted instructors with the specific aspects of each practice, they still did not give enough direction to help instructors transform their teaching. Therefore, I introduced these components, identifying incremental steps between instructor-centered and learner-centered teaching. Incremental steps allow instructors to make changes gradually over time, as they make a transition from instructor-centered to learner-centered teaching. The incremental approach I use describes two levels of transitioning between instructor-centered and learner-centered teaching for each component of each of the five practices. This approach makes the transformation process more manageable.

For example, here are the incremental steps between the learner-centered and instructor-centered approaches on a component in the Function of Content practice area, which describes the level to which students are engaged in the content. The instructor's expectations and student assessment strategies determine the level to which students engage in the content. In an instructor-centered approach, the instructor requires the students to memorize content, such as formulas or dates in history, without it necessarily having any meaning, and recall them on a test. In the lower level of transitioning, the instructor provides the content so that the students can actively learn it, perhaps by providing them with questions to which the answers come directly from the textbook or the lectures. In the higher level of transitioning, the instructor provides activities that help students transform some content to make their own meaning. For example, the instructor might ask the students to develop a chart or graph to summarize some material in the text. Finally, with a learner-centered approach, the instructor expects the students to develop associations between what they read or heard in class and their own lives or real-world phenomena, thus forming their own meaning of the content. When students engage in content at this level, they are more likely to remember it and be able to use it later.

Next, I organized the incremental steps into rubrics. Rubrics provide concrete, incremental steps between levels. I found using rubrics to be a very effective way for instructors to see how to make incremental changes. Instructors often are familiar with rubrics as an objective and effective way to grade student assignments. Therefore, I did not have to introduce a new concept to them. Instead of assessing student performance, rubrics can be used to evaluate the status of a course on the continuum from instructor-centered to learner-centered for the five learner-centered practices, and instructors can see incremental steps in the transformation process. Because each rubric lists several different components or methods, this tool shows various ways instructors can change their teaching. Among the components, different courses may be at varying points in their transition to learner-centered teaching. Moreover, I emphasize that instructors should not expect their courses ever to be at the highest standard in all categories with every component.

I constructed these rubrics based on Weimer's (2002) five practice areas, using the following rules:

1. Develop a separate rubric for each of her five practices. With separate rubrics for each practice, instructors can focus on one practice without having to consider changing their teaching in another practice area.
2. Each horizontal row of items is a separate or independent component of each practice area. The components of each

of the five practices help to identify specific examples of how teachers can transition to more learner-centered practices.

3. Each step of the rubrics explains what instructors can do to make their courses more learner-centered; the instructor's perspective should be the focus throughout.

Appendix A displays part of the rubric for one component from each of the five practice areas. The complete set of rubrics can be found at Blumberg (2008) or on the Web at www.usp.edu/learningmodules/lct.htm.

3. Reflection Questions to Answer Before Completing the Rubrics

As some instructors have trouble determining the learner-centered to instructor-centered status of their courses, I developed reflection questions to answer before using the rubrics. These questions ask instructors to think about ideal ways that each practice can be implemented, then to compare the ideal implementation with what they do now as a way to begin to think about the current status of their course and future changes to it.

4. A Planning for Transformation Form

This form helps instructors plan the components of all aspects of an anticipated change. Instructors record the current status of their course on the component they wish to transform; they plan what changes they want to make, as well as the projected learner-centered status once they make these changes. They address the tactical planning considerations given in Appendix B. Once instructors complete this Planning for Transformation form, they are ready to begin making changes to their courses.

Why Do These Tools Appeal to Instructors?

Gradual changes in teaching are more palatable to instructors than radical restructuring. By seeing their teaching along a continuum, instructors do not have to totally reject their current teaching methods. The levels of transitioning help them identify the status of a course and guide instructors to make the transition gradually. Incremental steps can be easy and practical to achieve, yet they can be transformative in their effect on a course.

Once instructors identify the current status of their courses, they may aim for the next level of transitioning within a specific component as a way to transform their teaching. Transforming one's total teaching may take several years, whereas moving from one level to the next on a specific component within a practice area in a single course may be a realistic short-term goal. Although each rubric describes four incremental levels from an instructor-centered to a learner-centered course, instructors do not need to make the transition using every level. They can skip one or more transitioning levels on a component and change the course to be learner-centered in one step.

How Can Faculty Developers Use These Tools?

These tools, taken together, form a comprehensive system for transforming courses. Faculty developers can use this system in ongoing interactions with faculty, such as in faculty learning communities, or they can begin the process in workshops and then give the instructors the rest of the tools to use on their own. I find that the following steps promote transformation to learner-centered teaching:

1. Educate instructors about learner-centered teaching. Help them understand why learner-centered teaching leads to superior student learning and retention, compared with approaches that are more traditional.
2. Help instructors decide that they want to make a change in their teaching approach by showcasing and discussing practical examples and supporting them to be courageous. This step can be emotionally difficult for instructors because it requires desire to change and trust that the changes will improve their teaching.
3. Educate instructors about the tools and how they can use them.

4. Ask instructors to choose a course they wish to modify. I recommend that instructors choose one that meets most of these criteria:

They have taught the course at least three times and expect to continue teaching it on a regular basis.

They are comfortable with the course content and enjoy teaching it.

The course is not in their own research area because they may be too close to the material to allow the course to become learner-centered.

They feel that they can improve the course so that students learn more or achieve better outcomes.

5. Ask instructors to complete the reflection questions comparing the ideal situation with their practices to prepare to assess the learner-centered status of their course.

6. Ask instructors to assess the learner-centered status of their course using the rubrics, reminding them that not all courses should be entirely learner-centered.

7. Ask instructors to select a few components they wish to transform. Instructors should choose components based on the type of course, the level of the students, personal insights, feedback from students, faculty peers, political considerations, or climate for change. The components can come from one practice area or from different practice areas.

8. Assist instructors to complete the Planning for Transformation (see Appendix B) form only for those components that they are considering changing. The instructors should complete a separate form for each component they might change. This form appears simple but actually requires much thought, and instructors might need to review it a few times.

9. Ask instructors to review their proposed changes to plan the next steps. Instructors might consider such questions as these: Can they be achieved together as a group? How practical are they to do at once? Should one be implemented before the others? Instructors might want to start with a few easy-to-implement changes as they plan for changes that are more comprehensive.

10. Assist instructors to secure the resources they will need. Ask them to begin planning how much time they need to make these changes.
11. Support instructors as they begin to make changes. This can be a scary process.
12. Encourage instructors to collect assessment data on their transformed courses.
13. Encourage instructors to conduct scholarship of teaching and learning on these courses. Encourage them to present their scholarship at relevant conferences, as well as in published form.

Conclusion

Weimer (2002) describes an approach to learner-centered teaching that includes five different practice areas. Although this model appeals to faculty, instructors may have difficulty knowing how to transform their own teaching to be more learner-centered because it does not offer pragmatic suggestions. If broad practice areas are divided into specific, concrete components, instructors can get an idea of different ways that such an approach can be implemented. An incremental approach, such as one given in rubrics, helps instructors begin to see where they can make changes. Faculty developers can use these components, rubrics, and associated tools to help instructors begin the transformation process. Using a comprehensive system for incremental change, instructors can transform their teaching to be more learner-centered.

Appendix A

The Components of Learner-Centered Teaching by Practice Area

Two tables are given for each of the five practice areas. The first table for each practice area lists the components and the learner-centered approach for each component. The second table for each practice area shows the rubric with two transitional levels between the learner-centered and the instructor-centered approaches for one component. The selected component is starred on the table listing the components.

Table A1. The Function of Content Practice Area

Specific components of this practice	Employs a learner-centered approach for this component
1. Varied uses of content In addition to building a knowledge base, instructor uses content to help students • Know why they need to learn content • Acquire discipline-specific learning methodologies, such as how to read primary source material • Practice using inquiry or ways of thinking in the discipline • Learn to solve real-world problems	In addition to building a knowledge base, instructor uses all four bulleted subcriteria of the varied uses of content listed in the left column.

Table A1. The Function of Content Practice Area (*Continued*)

Specific components of this practice	Employs a learner-centered approach for this component
2. Level to which students are engaged in content*	Instructor encourages students to transform and reflect on most of the content to make their own meaning out of it.
3. Use of organizing schemes	Instructor provides and uses organizing schemes to help students learn content.
4. Use of content to facilitate future learning	Instructor frames and organizes content so students can learn additional content that is not taught.

Table A2. A Sample Rubric for One Component of the Function of Content

Component 2. Level to which students are engaged in content			
Employs learner-centered approaches	Transitioning to learner-centered approaches		Employs instructor-centered approaches
	Higher level of transitioning	Lower level of transitioning	
Instructor encourages students to transform and reflect on most of the content to make their own meaning out of it.	Instructor assists students to transform and reflect on some of content to make their own meaning out of some of it.	Instructor provides content so students can actively learn material as it is given to them without transforming or reflecting on it.	Instructor allows students to memorize content.

Table A3. The Role of the Instructor Practice Area

Specific components of this practice	Employs a learner-centered approach for this component
1. Creation of an environment for learning • Through organization and use of material • By accommodating different learning styles	Instructor creates a learning environment by using both bulleted subcriteria listed in the left column.
2. Alignment of the course components: objectives, teaching/learning methods, and assessment methods for consistency	Instructor explicitly, coherently, and consistently aligns objectives, teaching/learning methods, and assessment.
3. Use of teaching/learning methods appropriate for student learning goals*	Instructor uses various teaching/learning methods that are appropriate for student learning goals.
4. Use of activities involving student, instructor, content interactions	Instructor routinely uses activities in which students actively interact with material, instructor, and each other.
5. Articulation of SMART objectives (**S**pecific, **M**easurable, **A**ttainable, **R**elevant, **T**ime-Oriented)	Instructor articulates SMART objectives in the course syllabus and refers regularly to them throughout the course.
6. Motivation of students to learn (intrinsic drive to learn versus extrinsic reasons to earn grades)	Instructor inspires and encourages students to become intrinsically motivated to learn.

Table A4. A Sample Rubric for One Component of the Role of the Instructor

Component 3. Use of teaching/learning methods appropriate for student learning goals

Employs learner-centered approaches	Transitioning to learner-centered approaches		*Employs instructor-centered approaches*
	Higher level of transitioning	*Lower level of transitioning*	
Instructor uses various teaching/ learning methods that are appropriate for student learning goals.	Instructor uses some teaching/ learning methods that are appropriate for student learning goals.	Instructor uses teaching/learning methods • Without regard for student learning goals • Without regard for conflict with the learning goals	Instructor • Does not have specified learning goals • Does not use active learning activities

Table A5. The Responsibility for Learning Practice Area

Component of this practice	Employs a learner-centered approach for this component
1. Responsibility for learning	Instructor provides increasing opportunities for students to assume responsibility for their own learning, leading to achievement of stated learning objectives.
2. Learning-to-learn skills or skills for future learning (including time management, self-monitoring, goal setting, doing independent reading and research, conducting original research)	Instructor facilitates students' development of various and appropriate skills for further learning.

(Continued)

Table A5. The Responsibility for Learning
Practice Area (*Continued*)

Component of this practice	Employs a learner-centered approach for this component
3. Self-directed, lifelong learning skills (including determining a personal need to know more, knowing who to ask or where to look for information, determining when need is met) and developing an awareness of students' learning abilities	Instructor helps students become • Self-directed, lifelong learners • Aware of their own learning and abilities to learn
4. Students' self-assessment of their learning*	Instructor motivates students to routinely and appropriately assess their own learning.
5. Students' self-assessment of their strengths and weaknesses	Instructor encourages students to become proficient at self-assessment.
6. Information literacy skills (framing questions, accessing and evaluating sources, evaluating content, using information legally) (Association of College and Research Libraries, 2004)	Instructor helps students become proficient in all five information literacy skills.

Table A6. A Sample Rubric for One Component
of the Responsibility for Learning

Component 4. Students' self-assessment of their learning			
Employs learner-centered approaches	Transitioning to learner-centered approaches		Employs instructor-centered approaches
	Higher level of transitioning	Lower level of transitioning	
Instructor motivates students to routinely and appropriately assess their own learning.	Instructor sometimes provides direction to help students assess their own learning.	Instructor does not direct students to assess their own learning.	Instructor • Believes that instructors alone assess student learning • Does not consider self-assessment of learning relevant

Table A7. The Processes and Purposes
of Assessment Practice Area

Component of this practice	Employs a learner-centered approach for this component
1. Assessment within the learning process	Instructor mostly integrates assessment within the learning process.
2. Formative assessment (giving feedback to foster improvement)*	Consistently throughout the learning process instructor integrates • Formative assessment • Constructive feedback
3. Peer and self-assessment	Instructor encourages students to use peer and self-assessments routinely.
4. Demonstration of mastery and ability to learn from mistakes	Instructor offers students many opportunities to learn from their mistakes and then demonstrate mastery.
5. Justification of the accuracy of answers	Instructor encourages students to justify their answers when they do not agree with those of instructor.
6. Time frame for feedback	Instructor and students • Mutually agree on time frame for feedback • Always follows time frame
7. Authentic assessment (what practitioners/ professionals do)	Instructor uses authentic assessment throughout the course.

Table A8. A Sample Rubric for One Component
of the Processes and Purposes of Assessment

Component 2. Formative assessment (giving feedback to foster improvement)

Employs learner-centered approaches	Transitioning to learner-centered approaches		*Employs instructor-centered approaches*
	Higher level of transitioning	*Lower level of transitioning*	
Consistently throughout the learning process instructor integrates • Formative assessment • Constructive feedback	Instructor gives students some constructive feedback following assessments.	Instructor • Uses a little formative assessment • Provides students with limited constructive feedback	Instructor • Uses only summative assessment (to make decisions to assign grades) • Provides students with no constructive feedback

Table A9. The Balance of Power (Control Issues)
Practice Area

Component of this practice	*Employs a learner-centered approach for this component*
1. Determination of course content	Instructor • Largely determines course content • Encourages students to explore additional content independently or through projects
2. Expression of alternative perspectives	Instructor encourages students to express alternative perspectives when appropriate.
3. Determination of how students earn grades*	Instructor uses mastery or contract grading to determine what grade students will earn.
4. Use of open-ended assignments	If appropriate, instructor routinely uses • Assignments that are open-ended or allow alternative paths • Test questions that allow for more than one right answer

Table A9. The Balance of Power (Control Issues)
Practice Area (*Continued*)

Component of this practice	Employs a learner-centered approach for this component
5. Flexibility of course policies, assessment methods, learning methods, and deadlines	Instructor is flexible on most course policies, assessment methods, learning methods, and deadlines. Instructor always adheres to what students agreed upon.
6. Opportunities to learn	Instructor helps students • Take advantage of opportunities to learn • Understand the consequences of not taking advantage of such learning opportunities (missing class)

Table A10. A Sample Rubric for One Component
of the Balance of Power

Component 3. Determination of how students earn grades

Employs learner-centered approaches	Transitioning to learner-centered approaches		Employs instructor-centered approaches
	Higher level of transitioning	*Lower level of transitioning*	
Instructor uses mastery or contract grading to determine what grade students will earn.	Instructor allows students to resubmit assignments for regrading.	Instructor allows students to drop one assessment but provides no alternative opportunities for them to demonstrate mastery.	All performance and assignments count toward students' grades.

Appendix B

The Planning for Transformation Form

1. What do you need to do or decide prior to making changes?

2. Identify obstacles or challenges that need to be overcome.

3. Identify strategies for overcoming obstacles.

4. Identify necessary resources.

5. How can you get students to accept this change?

6. Consider future outcomes of the change, such as its impact on other aspects of the course.

7. Consider possible future changes.

References

Alexander, P., & Murphy, P. (2000). The research base for APA's learner-centered psychological principles. In N. Lambert & B. McCombs (Eds.), *How students learn* (pp. 25–60). Washington, DC: American Psychological Association.

Association of College and Research Libraries. (2004). *Information literacy competency standards for higher education.* Retrieved October 5, 2004, from www.ala.org/ala/acrl/acrlstandards/informationliteracycompetency. htm

Blumberg, P. (2004). Beginning journey toward a culture of learning centered teaching. *Journal of Student Centered Learning, 2*(1), 68–80.

Blumberg, P. (2008). *Developing learner-centered teaching: A practical guide for faculty.* San Francisco: Jossey-Bass.

Blumberg, P., & Everett, J. (2005). Achieving a campus consensus on learning-centered teaching: Process and outcomes. In S. Chadwick-Blossey & D. R. Robertson (Eds.), *To improve the academy: Vol. 23. Resources for faculty, instructional, and organizational development* (pp. 191–210). Bolton, MA: Anker.

Bruner, J. (1966). *Toward a theory of instruction.* Cambridge, MA: Harvard University Press.

Ewell, P. (2001). Editorial: Listening up. *Change, 33*(3), 4.

Fink, L. D. (2003). *Creating significant learning experiences: An integrated approach to designing college courses.* San Francisco: Jossey-Bass.

Gardiner, L. F. (1994). *Redesigning higher education: Producing dramatic gains in student learning.* Washington, DC: The George Washington University, Graduate School of Education and Human Development.

Johnson, W. D. (1991). Student-student interaction: The neglected variable in education. *Educational Research, 10*(1), 5–10.

Kafai, Y., & Resnick, L. M. (1996). *Constructionism in practice.* Mahwah, NJ: Erlbaum.

Lambert, N., & McCombs, B. (2000). Introduction: Learner-centered schools and classrooms as a direction for school reform. In N. Lambert & B. McCombs (Eds.), *How students learn* (pp. 1–15). Washington, DC: American Psychological Association.

Matlin, M. W. (2002). Cognitive psychology and college-level pedagogy: Two siblings that rarely communicate. In D. F. Halpern & M. D. Hakel (Eds.), *Applying the science of learning to university teaching and beyond* (pp. 87–103). San Francisco: Jossey-Bass.

Maxwell, W. E. (1998, Fall). Supplemental instruction, learning communities and students studying together. *Community College Review.* Retrieved December 20, 2005, from www.findarticles.com

Middle States Commission on Higher Education. (2003). *Student learning assessment.* Retrieved July 18, 2008, from www.msche.org/publications/SLABook07070925104757.pdf

National Survey of Student Engagement. (2005). *Exploring different dimensions of student engagement.* Retrieved November 17, 2005, from http://nsse.iub.edu/pdf/NSSE2005_annual_ report.pdf

Piaget, J. (1963). *Origins of intelligence in children.* New York: Norton.

Slavin, R. E. (1990). *Cooperative learning theory, research and practice.* Needham Heights, MA: Allyn & Bacon.

Sorcinelli, M. D., Austin, A. E., Eddy, P. L., & Beach, A. L. (2006). *Creating the future of faculty development: Learning from the past, understanding the present.* Bolton, MA: Anker.

Springer, L., Stanne, M., & Donovan, S. (1999). Effects of small-group learning on undergraduates in science, mathematics, engineering, and technology (health sciences): A meta-analysis. *Review of Educational Research, 69*(1), 21–51.

Sternberg, R. J., & Grigorenko, E. L. (2002). The theory of successful intelligence as a basis for instruction and assessment in higher education. In D. F. Halpern & M. D. Hakel (Eds.), *Applying the science of learning to university teaching and beyond* (pp. 45–54). San Francisco: Jossey-Bass.

Vygotsky, L. S. (1978). *Mind in society: The development of higher psychological processes.* Cambridge, MA: Harvard University Press.

Weimer, M. (2002). *Learner-centered teaching.* San Francisco: Jossey-Bass.

Wright, R. (2006). Walking the walk: Review of learner-centered teaching, by Maryellen Weimer. *Life Sciences Education, 5*(311), 312.

Chapter 7

Romancing the Muse

Faculty Writing Institutes as Professional Development

Elizabeth Ambos, Mark Wiley, Terre H. Allen
California State University, Long Beach

We gratefully acknowledge the support of past and present colleagues at California State University, Long Beach, including Joy Phillips, James Till, and Kathy Smalley. The support and encouragement of Provosts Gary Reichard and Dorothy Abrahamse were essential to the success of the SWI.

A faculty professional writing program called the Scholarly Writing Institute (SWI) at California State University, Long Beach (CSULB) presents a replicable model to accelerate and support faculty writing. Based on Boice's (1990, 1994, 2000) work in faculty research productivity, the program combines individual writing time with editing and statistical consultation, panel discussions by prolific faculty, and reflective reporting of writing outcomes. Held over a three- to four-day period during semester breaks, the Institute is particularly accessible to faculty with family responsibilities. Evaluations indicate participant satisfaction with the experience and attitudinal change about successful writing strategies.

Higher education demands faculty accountability in both teaching and research (Kreber & Cranton, 2000), and faculty struggle with the degree to which these activities are complementary, as opposed to competitive (see Fox, 1992). The ideal outcome is the successful integration of teaching and research activities (Kreber & Cranton, 2000). So how can faculty development activities help faculty manage the balancing act that brings together teaching and research in mutual, rather than competitive, ways? Faculty development programs should address these primary aspects of faculty worklife, collaborating with other campus units to provide coordinated activities relating to teaching and research.

Why is the coordination of teaching and research activities of value to California State University, Long Beach (CSULB)? We are a large urban, comprehensive, master's-granting state university. We enroll approximately 37,000 students and employ 1,100 full-time and about 1,000 part-time faculty; the university has grown in stature and size during the last decade. CSULB ranks very favorably on a number of national and regional academic criteria, including for its combination of affordability and quality. Teaching is emphasized at the university, with routine teaching assignments of three to four courses per semester. Due to the increasing professional aspirations of recently hired tenure-track faculty and the competitiveness among applicants for coveted tenure-track positions, scholarship has gained more prominence and is a significant factor in tenure and promotion decisions.

The CSULB faculty development program partners with the Office of University Research to provide workshops and institutes on faculty research that complement the array of teaching workshops offered by faculty development. We believe that our united efforts communicate to faculty that teaching and research activities are mutual rather than competitive. We have codeveloped several programs that have been integrated into our faculty development menu and designed them to complement teaching-based programs. One of these programs—the Scholarly Writing Institute (SWI)—is the focus of this chapter. Other jointly sponsored programs include grant-writing and grant-management institutes.

After briefly reviewing the literature on writing productivity, with particular focus on Boice's (1990, 1994, 2000) work, we detail the activities of the SWI and faculty participants' evaluations of the Institute's effects and effectiveness. We conclude with a summary of lessons learned from offering SWIs and indicate future directions for our programs.

Anxiety About Writing

Writing is a necessary part of faculty life and, for many faculty, an important source of professional vitality and accomplishment. For others, it is more of a dreaded chore. The "publish or perish" maxim is a governing reality of faculty existence and a source of much anxiety. One must publish regularly and keep up with the competition or lose status and, possibly, employment. Although periodic anxiety may be a normal aspect of any career, high levels of it can paralyze faculty, particularly those engaged in professional writing post-Ph.D. and those navigating the perilous shoals of the tenure and promotion process. This anxiety is compounded when individual faculty members lack sufficient knowledge of publishing requirements and do not know how to deal with conflicting or negative reviews of their writing. In addition, many members of the professoriate need assistance in developing an efficient, structured, and time-effective writing process. For most new faculty members, few if any of these topics were covered in their doctoral programs—a critical deficiency, in our opinion (also see Bloom, 1985; Hjortshoj, 2001).

Boice's (1990) seminal work on professors as writers focuses on the premise that professors often approach writing as an overwhelming, singular, all-consuming experience. The reasons for this approach probably stem from writing a dissertation, which most Ph.D. candidates experience as a concentrated practice and foremost imperative in their lives for several years. Transitioning from Ph.D. candidate to the faculty ranks carries with it a shift to multiple roles and responsibilities and a change of focus from a single-minded pursuit of scholarship to obligations to teach and give service, in addition to conducting research. Moreover, as Hjortshoj (2001) points out, this transition is further complicated by faculty isolation: "[y]oung professors learn to write for publication much as they learn to teach: almost entirely through trial and error, with little direct guidance from colleagues" (p. 121).

Faculty may try to return to the single-minded focus but find that they cannot allocate writing time in the ways they formerly enjoyed. Thus, the "binge writer" is born—a faculty member who reserves a block of several days, usually at the end of a grueling semester, into which she pours her scholarly energy in exhausting, round-the-clock writing sessions, and from which she expects manuscripts ready for submission to foremost journals and publishing houses. Although binge writing is a successful strategy for some writers, it fails for most. Moreover, binge writers experience the "high" highs of the adrenaline rush of completing a difficult project and meeting a tight deadline, but after the latest challenge has been successfully surmounted, they sink into a "low" low, as they anticipate another writing project looming in the not-too-distant future—a future just far enough off to allow for substantial procrastination. Instead of being trapped in this emotional roller coaster, Boice (1990, 1994, 2000) persuasively advocates becoming a stable, consistent writer who practices "moderation"—that is, writing regularly for short periods of time.

Application of Boice's Research

We have adapted key features of Boice's (1990) model in the SWI by having participants practice focused writing for relatively brief periods over several days. The four key elements of Boice's extended, individualized program are infused into our concentrated writing institute. We focus on the first element of "automaticity"—the "getting writing going"—by sharing strategies for generating writing. We encourage participants to take on only small parts of larger projects during the Institute. This conscious division of large writing projects into smaller, more manageable tasks counters the tendency most faculty writers have to set unrealistic goals of writing quantity and perfection. The second element is "externality." During the Institute, the actual work of writing is given the highest priority, and participants are reminded continually about committing to that priority after the Institute. The third element, "self-control," and the fourth, "sociality," reinforce each other, as participants learn to monitor their own negative thoughts and substitute more positive thoughts about writing. This process occurs as participants get to know one another and begin sharing their own stories about writing habits, including all of their anxieties, self-doubts, and procrastinating behaviors. Through both informal shoptalk and formal panel discussions with faculty experts, participants learn more productive ways to think about themselves as writers and to deal with negative reviews. We also encourage them to read and respond to each other's work and to silence, as much as possible, that internal critic who, in the past, may have too easily derailed a writing project scarcely under way.

Based on SWI applications and on our discussions with faculty who have participated in these Institutes over the last five years, the single most frequently identified factor that affects an individual's writing productivity is the shortage of available time. When faculty members are on campus, they are in class or holding formal office hours, or they are in their offices with the door open. Students and faculty colleagues frequently take advantage of a faculty member's open-door practice. SWI participants cite other distractions at work, including telephone calls and the constant stream of e-mail. Many have repeatedly told us that they feel compelled to respond, whether to drop-in visitors, phone calls, or e-mail. This fragmentation of time leads to frustration when faculty face sustained writing projects, such as books and journal articles.

Through the Institutes, faculty begin to qualify and understand what they mean by "time to write" and to develop coping strategies to deal with the fragmentation of the writing process. Initially, they firmly attest that they require uninterrupted blocks of time to do their writing. Although we build in several two- to two-and-a-half-hour blocks for writing during the SWI, we also encourage participants to continue to devote smaller blocks of time to writing throughout the three- to four-day workshop. The productivity possible during relatively short writing time blocks is a revelation to most faculty. Prior to SWI, many assumed that six to eight hours of completely uninterrupted writing time are needed to make any progress in their writing. Discovery that as few as one or two solid hours can be as productive as six to eight fragmented hours leads SWI participants to "rewire" their writing process to use shorter time spans. Boice (1990) suggests that even thirty minutes of writing per day can be effective. However, most of our participants find this allotment of time insufficient and prefer at least one to two hours a day.

As a follow-up to the SWI, we also encourage participants to set aside small blocks of time for writing during each week, preferably each day, and to protect this time from all who might make demands on them, including colleagues, department chairs, and family. Certainly, it is easier for anyone to identify a one- to two-hour time block than a six- to eight-hour contiguous amount of time. We suggest that participants firmly communicate their writing intentions ahead of time to colleagues and family members.

Faculty participants have expressed gratitude to us for organizing these Institutes because they claim that *we* have given them "permission to write." The "we," by extension, includes the university administration. In addition, the clear message that resonates from the partnership of CSULB's Office of University Research and the Faculty Center for Professional Development is that teaching and research are both valued and supported by the administration.

The CSULB Scholarly Writing Institute

Boice's (1990) model for writing productivity provided the theoretical underpinnings for the development of the Institute. Our program mimics key elements of Boice's extended program (during which he might work with individuals for several weeks or months). However, ours takes a short-term approach intended to help faculty jump-start a stalled project or realize how they might alter their self-perceptions and behaviors as writers. Our Institute participants experience a mixture of group interaction, informal subgroup interactions, and substantial blocks of time set aside for individual writing.

Institute Design

We have offered the SWI ten times thus far on the CSULB campus. The first five Institutes were two and one-half days in length, although some faculty members stayed for a third day. However, in response to participants' evaluations, we added an extra full day to the most recent Institute. Although the design has varied from one Institute to another, depending on faculty needs, these elements have been maintained: sustained writing time, time for participants to talk with one another about the processes involved in producing scholarly writing, and resources for the participants such as assistance with editing, statistical analyses, and particular software programs. We also keep a ready supply of food and drink handy and try to minimize distractions. Funding for the Institute is provided by the Office of University Research from a special fund for research stimulation.

The application process occurs several months before the Institute. Applicants are asked to identify writing projects and to set realistic goals for the Institute. (See a typical application form at www.csulb.edu/divisions/aa/research/our/education/swi/.) What is a realistic goal? Of course, that depends on the nature of the writing project and the faculty member's degree of preparedness to write. Because faculty from across the university may participate, many from the natural and physical sciences have done all of their research in the laboratory and must now write up their findings. By contrast, humanities scholars may be composing long journal articles and regularly consulting text sources as they write, so their goals might be sections of a manuscript. Other participants intend to draft a grant proposal or a book prospectus to send out for review. We learned after the initial Institute to advise faculty that they should not expect to complete the final draft of that long-put-off journal article. We offer this caution because there are often psychological reasons that the writer has been putting the project off for months or years (see Boice, 1990)—reasons that may cause procrastination behavior during the Institute (for example, the temptation to take lots of breaks and spend more time talking to one of our editors than actually writing). We discuss the psychological barriers to writing during the Institute, bringing these nonproductive behaviors out in the open and thus beginning to change them.

Several SWIs have included a lunch meeting a few weeks before. The purpose of those meetings is to save a little of the precious Institute time in explaining to prospective participants the workshop format, what they can expect to happen during the Institute, and what we expect from them. We answer any questions and encourage faculty to talk about themselves and their interest in the Institute. This initial social bonding reduces individual anxiety and creates social networks to help faculty feel more comfortable talking about their writing and any attendant problems they might be having. Most important, we stress that the SWI is designed to help faculty accelerate their writing productivity or change their attitudes and behaviors toward writing; it is *not* a "remedial" activity for those who have failed at scholarship. No doubt, a few participants harbor these debilitating thoughts, so we consciously characterize the Institute as an opportunity to complete substantial work on a pressing project. Any perception of SWI as remedial has been dispelled by participation of a range of CSULB faculty, including practiced, productive writers.

Institute Activities

We accept most applicants—an average of thirty per Institute—as long as they present realistic writing goals on a significant project or two. Many participants repeat the experience. One Institute is offered in June near the beginning of the summer break and another in early January, just before the spring term—periods during which most faculty have the time to participate. Our June Institute is scheduled right after graduation ceremonies, before faculty are leaving for well-deserved vacations or summer research trips and well before summer break begins for children attending K–12. (Scheduling the SWI around K–12 school schedules is seen as an expression of the university administration's understanding of and commitment to the program.) We do insist that participants work in specific conference areas and not leave to return to their campus offices. The temptation to engage in other business in one's office is too great and allows for too many distractions.

During the opening session, participants introduce themselves and explain their personal goals for the Institute. The provost and vice presidents often make brief appearances to offer words of welcome, encouragement, and support, further enhancing the stature and prominence of this program. College deans may drop in to visit or to have lunch with participants.

Although we are still experimenting with the seating arrangement, we have previously seated participants side-by-side at small tables or kiosks. We encourage them to bring their laptops and research materials with them; we make a few laptops available for those who forgot to bring one or don't own one. Wireless Internet connectivity, printer capabilities (including color printers), and computing consultants are provided throughout the Institute.

We set aside at least two periods of two to two-and-a-half hours for individual writing per day, and participants are invited to stay after the final lunch on the third day to continue writing if they so choose, but without technical and editorial assistance. During the extended writing periods, participants are expected to work quietly on their own without disturbing others, but they are also free to meet for half-hour appointments with one of the writing editors or technical consultants. These consultants were selected, based either on recommendations from their department chairs, from their supervisors, or on our experiences collaborating with these experts on other projects. We also sought experts who we believed would work well with our participants and who expressed interest in and enthusiasm for these consultative activities. The consultation area is physically distinct from the main writing area so that conversations don't disturb active writers. These experts help participants with editing and proofreading, as well as statistical analyses, data presentation, and computer illustration and presentation software. Experienced faculty and administrators also offer consultations in human subject protocol and intellectual property, as well as researching journals for application formats and citation statistics, reference list software, information databases, and issues of retention, tenure, and promotion.

Finally, we offer an assortment of panel presentations on relevant topics such as overcoming writing barriers, responding to rejection comments by reviewers, managing time, and writing productively, featuring some of the university's most prolific faculty. We use participants' evaluations to modify our panel offerings and avoid repeating panels because some faculty attend more than one SWI. Table 7.1 presents a typical daily SWI schedule.

Table 7.1 Typical Daily Schedule for the Scholarly Writing Institute

Schedule	Activity	Description
8:30–9:00 A.M.	Breakfast, orientation, sign-in	Director, Office of University Research (OUR); Director, Faculty Center for Professional Development (FCPD)
9:00–9:30 A.M.	Introductions and expectations. What progress have you made in your writing? What work do you plan to do today? Do you have any special writing issues?	Directors joined by provost; each faculty attendee gives a one minute description of their writing project
9:45 –12:00 A.M.	Writing Session	Faculty experts available by appointment for editing and statistical consultation
12:00–1:00 P.M.	Lunch	Cohosted by OUR and FCPD
1:00–2:00 P.M.	Faculty panel discussion: "The Dark Side of Research and Writing"	Faculty panel moderated by FCPD Director talks about their experiences as writers, including dealing with adverse reviews and delays in journal publishing
2:00–4:15 P.M.	Writing Session	Faculty experts available by appointment
4:15–4:45 P.M.	Social Hour	Guest: Associate Vice President for Academic Personnel

Assessment of Institute Outcomes

We have conducted an assessment of outcomes from the first three years of our Institute (2004–2006), during which 163 faculty have participated one or more times. Twenty-six attended two or more Institutes, and one has participated in all six. About 13 percent of the participants are adjunct faculty, about 60 percent assistant professors, about 20 percent associate professors, and about 7 percent full professors. Females dominate attendance by about 4 to 1—a noteworthy statistic because only 48 percent of our faculty is female.

At lunch on the final day, we ask all participants to share their perceptions of the writing experience, reflect thoughtfully on their writing accomplishments, and complete a formal, written assessment survey of the Institute, containing both Likert-style and open-ended questions. Specifically, we ask how satisfied participants are overall with the experience, whether they accomplished their set goals, and what they liked most and least. There are also items about individual features of the Institute, such as the food, the venue, the editors, and specific sessions such as the panel discussion. Finally, we ask participants if they would attend another SWI and if they would recommend it to their colleagues.

The Institute assessment survey was distributed to 160 participants, 134 of whom returned completed forms, for a response rate of 83 percent. Ninety-seven percent of the respondents rated the Institute as highly valuable or valuable, and only one of these 134 indicated that it was not valuable. Literally 100 percent of the respondents said that they would recommend the Institute to colleagues, and 93 percent said they expected it to enhance their scholarly writing productivity. Participants were also asked to evaluate all the activities provided during the Institute, including panel presentations, small-group discussions, and editing and statistical consultations. Although small-group discussions received mixed ratings, 96 percent ranked the editing and statistical consultations as the most valuable Institute activity, beyond the time to write.

This precious writing time received the highest ratings. At first glance, this does not seem surprising or particularly interesting, but consider that we (those of us who sponsor and organize these Institutes) are not actually "creating" additional time for faculty writing. We simply invite participants to dedicate their time to write over three to five days. Are we, as Institute sponsors, being perceived as somehow giving these participants the permission to write? If this is the case, what does that say about the mind-set of our colleagues who cannot or will not allow themselves time to write if they perceive it as interfering with other duties, such as teaching, service, and family obligations?

In answering the open-ended questions, participants wrote that they appreciated the supportive environment, the consultant faculty, the general collegiality, and the constant supply of food. Following are two representative comments about what they found most valuable:

- A dedicated block of time, with comfortable work space, Internet hook-up, editors and statistics experts, food, good company, networking opportunity.
- Time to focus on research and be in an environment where others are challenging me to excel. The idea of common struggle is very helpful.

Although many faculty achieved their Institute goals, most qualified their accomplishments with the admission that their original goals were overly ambitious, perhaps a symptom of wishful thinking. Still, most participants made real progress on a paper or other product, as these comments suggest:

- Yes, I completed a first draft of a paper and got critical feedback so I can complete it with confidence.
- I think my goal was to finish a draft which was a bit lofty. I did, however, get about 1/2 to 2/3 of a draft done and more importantly feel I will hold myself accountable for getting it done.

The latter comment is evidence of an attitudinal change that can lead to a behavioral change in writing habits.

In fact, we asked participants to tell us about their changes in attitudes. These sample comments point to positive shifts:

- Try to set aside writing time. Try to do one project at a time with a clear goal.

- Work ethic. I am dedicated to scheduling frequent, manage-
  able writing blocks; less anxiety and a greater source of power
  in the review process.
- I can do it in small "chunks" of time; peer review is wonderful;
  I don't feel so alone—others have similar writing issues.
- I can do it; I can learn to break the binge writer habit.

Participants also described their barriers to writing and being
productive. Aside from the continual time demands of semesters,
they cited stress and the uncertainty of the tenure and promotion process. Some said that they could not say "no" to others'
requests for their time, or as a few expressed it, be "ruthless"
enough to write papers during the semester. A few others
expressed the lack of joy in writing and the relative unimpor-
tance of creating new knowledge, compared to meeting more
immediate professional obligations. Still, many faculty left the
Institute viewing these barriers as more self-imposed than externally imposed, and most intended to develop better writing habits, including writing more frequently. Typical is this comment:

- This is my third [SWI], and I have found that overall my writing is increasing gradually. Coming to these [Institutes] at
  least once a year tends to help maintain my momentum. I'm
  aiming to become more and more productive.

Conclusion

Given the tremendous success of the SWIs, we intend to continue
to offer them for the foreseeable future, maintaining the features
that faculty value most: space, sustenance, and editorial, statistical,
and coaching assistance. But we will also make changes based on
faculty feedback gathered during the final day's luncheon debrief-
ing and from the written evaluations. In addition, we intend to conduct formal research on the Institutes' long-term effects on faculty
productivity, satisfaction with scholarly work, and faculty retention.
Important questions remain. For example, what is the return on
investment in these Institutes, in terms of faculty productivity,
career advancement, and success in such professional milestones
as retention, tenure, and promotion? How does the productivity

of faculty scholars who participate in these Institutes compare with faculty who do not participate? Last, why do female faculty participate in such high numbers, in comparison to male faculty?

To help sustain the writing momentum, we sponsor monthly "Faculty Writing Fridays" at the faculty center and writers' circles that meet in small groups to read and discuss work-in-progress. These writers' groups are common faculty support mechanisms (see Gere, 1987, for a review and Eodice & Cramer, 2001, for an example of a writing support group). Our writers' circles spin off from the Institutes among faculty who have already established a good chemistry. Although some of these groups endure across departments and disciplines, the press of business during regular semesters sometimes intrudes on even the best of well-laid plans.

Perhaps the best reason to continue these SWIs is that our faculty get important work done in a short time and leave the experience with an authentic sense of accomplishment. They also leave believing they can be more productive scholars and more skilled time managers. Last, and just as important, they leave having met new colleagues with whom they have shared stories about disasters and triumphs in their scholarly work and built a community of writers. In short, our faculty complete the SWI well satisfied and with a substantially improved outlook for their professional scholarly success. We believe this outlook is key for the successful integration of teaching and research activities.

References

Bloom, L. (1985). Anxious writers in context: Graduate school and beyond. In M. Rose (Ed.), *When a writer can't write: Studies in writer's block and other composing-process problems* (pp. 119–133). New York: Guilford Press.

Boice, R. (1990). *Professors as writers: A self-help guide to productive writing.* Stillwater, OK: New Forums Press.

Boice, R. (1994). *How writers journey to comfort and fluency: A psychological adventure.* Westport, CT: Praeger.

Boice, R. (2000). *Advice for new faculty members: Nihil nimus.* Needham Heights, MA: Allyn & Bacon.

Eodice, M., & Cramer, S. (2001). Write on! A model for enhancing faculty publication. *Journal of Faculty Development, 18,* 113–120.

Fox, M. F. F. (1992). Research, teaching, and publication productivity: Mutuality versus competition in academia. *Sociology of Education, 65,* 293–305.

Gere, A. R. (1987). *Writing groups: History, theory, and implications.* Carbondale, IL: Southern Illinois University Press.

Hjortshoj, K. (2001). *Understanding writing blocks.* New York: Oxford University Press.

Kreber, C., & Cranton, P. (2000). Fragmentation versus integration of faculty work. In M. Kaplan & D. Lieberman (Eds.), *To improve the academy: Vol. 18. Resources for faculty, instructional, and organizational development* (pp. 217–230). Bolton, MA: Anker.

Chapter 8

Leadership for Learning
A New Faculty Development Model

Jane V. Nelson, Audrey M. Kleinsasser
University of Wyoming

The authors provide examples of a model that develops faculty leaders for learning in all institutions that prize research. The examples come from seven university-wide initiatives, which were sponsored by the institution's faculty development center. The initiatives spanned a nearly ten-year period. Based on four conceptual groundings—scholarship of teaching and learning principles, educational renewal, the production of social capital through soft projects, and horizontal structures—the model has the power to transform faculty into leaders. Elements of the model include a call to participate, a diverse cohort of participants, commitment to providing resources, conference center planners, and peer review and assessment. In contrast to leadership models borrowed from business and industry, the model prizes what the academy values most—collegiality, intellectual curiosity, and the generation of knowledge.

In the fall 2007 issue of *Liberal Education*, the authors of the article titled "Where Are the Faculty Leaders?" delineate a set of goals that most universities and colleges assuredly embrace: "high-quality teaching, innovative curriculum, cutting-edge research, intellectual enrichment, student engagement, improved student outcomes, greater faculty citizenship, a more democratic environment, a campus more responsive to community needs" (Kezar, Lester, Carducci, Gallant, & McGavin, p. 21). Just as assuredly, meeting these goals requires faculty leadership, but as the title of the article suggests, institutions often assume that faculty are natural-born leaders who will accept the call when it comes. In career paths already well defined by teaching, research, service, and extension responsibilities, how can faculty carve out time for leadership development? How can research institutions hope for anything more than the natural-born leaders stepping forward?

In this chapter, we describe a faculty development model that has shown potential for transforming faculty into leaders whose influence can be documented beyond their classrooms and their departments. In this model, faculty complete long-term inquiry projects that are intellectually rewarding and have transformative effects in their classrooms. Collaborating with colleagues outside their departments, they learn to value horizontal rather than hierarchical thinking. At the end of the projects, these individuals often exhibit the leadership characteristics identified by Tierney (1999): "good leaders are courageous, moral, willing to take risks, active listeners, excellent communicators, able to espouse a vision, and able to stimulate people" (p. 48). Enough of the participants in this model have created significant differences in university learning environments that we can propose an answer to the question, Where are the faculty leaders? Faculty will step into leadership roles when institutions invest in their leadership development.

Conceptual Groundings

Our faculty leadership model features four groundings: 1) the scholarship of teaching and learning, 2) educational renewal, 3) soft projects and social capital, and 4) horizontal structures. The groundings capture what is best about academic environments: intellectual curiosity, personal efficacy, and interest in community. The model helps to overcome the rigid vertical silos that often thwart change in higher education.

Scholarship of Teaching and Learning

Our leadership development model originates with international initiatives created by the American Association of Higher Education and the Carnegie Foundation for the Advancement of

Teaching, specifically the work of Pat Hutchings, Mary Huber, Barbara Cambridge, and Lee Shulman. In the mid-1990s, we had the great fortune of working closely with Hutchings when she was in residence at the University of Wyoming, working first for the American Association of Higher Education and then for the Carnegie Foundation. Her vision of scholarly teaching became embodied in the Carnegie Academy for the Scholarship of Teaching and Learning, known as the CASTL Program. Our model is patterned closely on a part of the CASTL initiative called the CASTL Scholars Program and the "teaching commons" described by Huber and Hutchings (2005) in *The Advancement of Learning: Building the Teaching Commons*. In this book, they document the ways in which faculty who are engaged in the scholarship of teaching and learning experience transformations as they move pedagogy to center stage. Assembling them into a teaching commons results in work that is "deeply intriguing, hope giving, and worthy of investment of faculty time and institutional resources" (p. 35). To this list of benefits we would add career enrichment that leads to leadership.

Educational Renewal

During the 1990s, John Goodlad and associates at the Seattle-based National Network of Educational Renewal, through its Institute for Educational Inquiry (IEI), developed a leadership program dedicated to preparing leaders who could advance educational renewal. Their work is described in *Leadership for Educational Renewal: Developing a Cadre of Leaders* (Smith & Fenstermacher, 1999). Goodlad uses the term *renewal* rather than *reform* because reform suggests a one-time event "with corruption at one end and completion at the other" (p. xiii). In contrast, renewal is ongoing and acknowledges the complex culture of schooling and its many components. Goodlad's model is distinguished by the goal of simultaneous renewal of P–12 schools, teacher education programs, and general education. Thus, a leadership cohort includes representatives of three groups who otherwise aren't asked to—and don't—talk with one another. The tripartite grouping, along with a set of readings new to all three groups, produces a leveling that, in turn, creates a different, more dynamic conversation. Like the Carnegie Foundation's CASTL Scholars Program of thirty-five to forty participants, IEI leadership programs were limited to twenty to twenty-five participants, meeting in multiple sessions over the course of a year. Participants made a commitment to read and discuss four or five books and articles for each session. They also conducted an inquiry project that they reported out during the final session.

In an analysis of the IEI leadership program, Smith and Fenstermacher (1999) report that participants developed a deeper understanding of teaching, appreciated collaboration across groups, and became agents of change in their institutions. Participants also developed ways to value their work, along with "capacities for collaboration" that included stewardship, nurturing, and access (p. 316). The national model developed by Goodlad and others was replicated by the Wyoming School–University Partnership—a founding member of the National Network for Educational Renewal.

Soft Projects and Social Capital

Our model is also founded on the work of educational policy theorist Bill Tierney, who has been examining university cultures and ways to produce change. In *Building the Responsive Campus: Creating High Performance Colleges and Universities,* Tierney (1999) advocates for the soft project as an "intense form of working relationships that can develop organizational excitement and camaraderie and ultimately produce demonstrable goals" (p. 73). Within the otherwise rigid structures of the institution, soft projects can be launched quickly by reassigning or supplementing the work that faculty already do. Throughout this book, Tierney frequently uses such terms as *radical* or *revolutionize* to indicate the need for a different kind of faculty structure to galvanize action. In his later work *Trust and the Public Good: Examining the Cultural Conditions of Academic Work,* Tierney (2006) argues that the work of both standing committees and soft projects should be designed to produce social capital in order to benefit both the individuals and the institution. "The challenge for those who work in academic organizations is to generate capital and overcome the concerns, fears, or objections of those who are reluctant to participate. . . . Low social capital suggests low levels of engagement, which in turn leads to disempowerment and low levels of trust" (p. 87). Both of Tierney's ideas—the soft project and the creation of social capital—help explain how a faculty member can be transformed from a dutiful, or perhaps even reluctant, committee member into a risk-taking leader with broad influence and a commitment to stewardship.

Horizontal Structures

The authors of the articles on faculty leadership published in the fall 2007 issue of *Liberal Education* explain a fourth concept that underlies our model: the importance of horizontal structures. Horizontal structures are those that exist across an organization to connect programs, departments, colleges, and institutional divisions. Examples include general education programs and committees, overall financial managements, tenure and promotion policies, and committees that oversee institutional accreditation.

Vertical structures run parallel to each other and might not connect. Almost always, universities are structured vertically, reflecting the administrative units of departments, colleges, and professional schools. The vertical nature of disciplinary structures has engendered the metaphor of *silo* to suggest how vertical structures can, unfortunately, create barriers of elitism, entrenchment, and intractability. Although disciplinary-based departments are powerful institutional structures, they are difficult to change. Moreover, the department committee work that makes up a large share of faculty service does not help faculty to "recognize opportunities to couple their specialized expertise to larger interests that can expand their own horizons, engage students, and advance their institutions" (Gaff, 2007, p. 9).

In contrast, horizontal structures that cut across disciplines, departments, and colleges develop "organizational citizens" with skills in "creating a vision, developing networks, and organizing multiple people" (Kezar et al., 2007, p. 16). Our faculty development model is intentionally designed to be horizontal for these more dynamic ends.

A Leadership Development Model for Faculty

The Ellbogen Center for Teaching and Learning—the University of Wyoming's faculty development center—has sponsored numerous soft projects to support both the scholarship of teaching and learning and the development of organizational leaders. The projects have been funded through a variety of sources. Internally, the Ellbogen Center has devoted a portion of its operating funds for these projects and has also received grants from other university organizations. External funding has resulted from successful grant proposals to regional and national private foundations and to the U.S. Department of Education's FIPSE (Fund for the Improvement of Postsecondary Education) program. Some of the projects have a specific curricular or pedagogical focus, while others are broadly conceived to allow for flexibility of interests among the participants. Although they vary slightly in length, purpose, and structure, they are all founded on the conceptual groundings described in the previous section. Table 8.1 lists some recent examples of these projects.

The faculty development model that we describe here departs significantly from the brown-bag or seminar structure that informs much of a typical teaching center's work. Brown-bag workshops or seminars help instructors to revise a course assignment, reframe a syllabus, and in general infuse energy into teaching, but they are not likely to develop scholarly leaders for teaching and learning. To achieve this more enduring goal, we have patterned a model on a grants process that requires mutual commitments of time, thought, and collegiality. This process consists of four features: 1) an invitation to participate, 2) a diverse cohort, 3) a commitment of resources, and 4) a dedication to peer review and assessment.

Invitation to Participate

We start a faculty development initiative by shaping a long-term, inquiry-based project around some broad themes. We then issue either a competitive call for written proposals or an invitation to participate, based on demonstrated previous work. Project participants understand that they are committing at least a

Table 8.1. Examples of Faculty Development
Projects in the Ellbogen Center

Project Name and Description	Funding	Cohort Length	Cohort Numbers and Dates	Number of Participants
inVisible College A year-long SoTL project with external consultants featuring stipends, readings, and a publicly presented project	Internal	1 year	3 cohorts: 2000–2003	8–23 for each cohort
e-Portfolios A year-long study, with external consultant and stipends to implement e-portfolios at the departments and program level	Internal	1 year	1 cohort: 2001–2002	6
Warming up the Chill A SoTL book project focused on diversity and the improvement of classroom learning environments	Internal and External (AAHE)	2 years	1 cohort: 2001–2003	6 plus 3 book editors
Senior Scholars A year-long SoTL project for senior faculty featuring stipends, readings, and a publicly presented project	External (private)	1.5 years	1 cohort: 2005–2006	7 plus collaborators
Connecting Learning Across Academic Settings (CLAAS) A three-year FIPSE project focused on general education resulting in numerous scholarly projects	External (FIPSE)	3.5 years	1 cohort: 2003–2007	6 plus collaborators
Kaiser Ethics Project A three-year project to embed ethics content into courses	External (private)	1 to 2 years	3 cohorts: 2006–2009	7 plus collaborators for each cohort

year's worth of work that will involve the scholarly tasks of reading, having discussions, engaging in research, and conducting assessment.

Diverse Cohort

The most successful calls or invitations encourage faculty to start with disciplinary problems in teaching and learning but also include the promise of cross-fertilization that might be multidisciplinary, intergenerational, cross-sector, and cross-institutional. Throughout its history, faculty have consistently thanked the Ellbogen Center for the opportunity to talk with other faculty from across campus or at other institutions, especially those in disciplines far removed from their own. What is true of single brown-bag discussions is tenfold more powerful for long-term development projects. In narrowly defined disciplinary groups, faculty leap too quickly to conclusions or outcomes, perhaps because they assume that everyone in the room shares values and knowledge. In more diverse groups that cross disciplines, faculty are willing to challenge each other, ask fundamental or beginning questions, seek clarification, and admit ignorance. In the ensuing discussions, faculty often start with puzzlement and then become risk takers as they sort through differences. Cross-fertilization helps faculty become innovators.

Resources

In return for the commitment of time, thought, and collegiality promised by faculty in their agreement to participate in a long-term project, the Ellbogen Center obligates resources to enable their achievement of project goals. In other words, the center must assume long-term investment risks to produce long-term results.

Acting as a Conference Center. To successfully sponsor significant faculty development projects, we understand what it means to be a convener of meetings. As chief worriers, we provide the scaffolding for a successful set of meetings, which includes creating the schedule, agenda, and structure for intellectual work. It also includes committing office staff to the dozens of tasks related to scaffolding: finding meeting rooms, providing catering, cleaning up, duplicating, working with university staff from multiple offices, creating Web sites, paying bills, managing spreadsheets, and communicating multiple times with participants by e-mail, phone, and snail mail. We cannot overstate the importance of this function. A high-quality leadership project requires considerable attention to detail.

Contracting Outside Expertise. Through our projects, we have confirmed the importance of anchoring faculty development in the intellectual work of others, especially those who have gained the respect of peers in published work. We are committed to finding powerful or provocative books published by leading scholars in teaching and learning, providing their books free to participants, and featuring book discussions as central parts of the project meetings. We also invite book authors and other experts to our meeting sites, where they not only give plenary talks to a community-wide audience but also meet in smaller sessions with project participants. We have invited such scholars as Mary Catherine Bateson, Larry Cuban, Bill Tierney, John Bean, Stephen Brookfield, Ken Bain, Pat Hutchings, Barbara Cambridge, and Lee Shulman. Among the wide-ranging benefits of this investment is the modeling of scholarly leadership that these invited experts provide.

Providing Stipends. The modest stipends we provide to faculty participants for many of our projects pay significant and ongoing dividends. For $1,000 to $3,000, faculty will commit to a project for fifteen and even twenty-four months. Only occasionally will a faculty member use the stipend for summer salary. A prized use of their stipends is travel, sometimes for disciplinary conferences, sometimes for specialized training. Frequently, faculty manage their stipends for more collaborative uses. They pull together their own working groups of peers, graduate students, and undergraduate students. They bring in outside experts to meet with these groups. As we analyze faculty use of stipends, we are often impressed by their ability to turn a quarter into a dollar and invest this earned interest in teaching and learning.

Peer Review and Assessment

The project structures described here, which involve mutual investments of time, thought, and resources, involve several forms of accountability. In project meetings over the course of one, two, or three years, faculty report to each other about the progress of their work. These reports often include early drafts for revised course materials, assessment instruments, conference papers, and articles for publication. The persuasive quality of these reports rises several degrees when we invite administrators to attend the meetings: deans and their associates, directors, vice presidents and their associates, even the university president and trustees. The quality escalates when we create public forums for their work in connection with on-campus visits of outside experts and when faculty use their stipends for presentations at conferences. Scholarly work is founded on peer review, and infusing peer review into teaching and learning projects guarantees an important measure of quality.

Most impressive to us has been a dedication to assessment that develops through the life of these projects. Starting in the early project meetings, assessment becomes the anchor for thinking about student learning. Faculty frequently develop major assessment projects. They use their stipends to hire a variety of collaborators that include undergraduate students, graduate students, and faculty peers. Some of these partners observe every class session of an instructor's course, providing a rich set of notes about student performance. Others help the instructors in data collection and analysis. Typically, by the end of a project, faculty participants are wholly committed to assessment as a central way of understanding teaching and learning. They also become spokespeople for assessment in their home departments and disciplines.

A Move into Leadership

One important effect of the leadership model is a change in identity. According to Gardner, Csikszentmihalyi, and Damon in *Good Work: When Excellence and Ethics Meet* (2001), a change in identity is really the development of competence and character in an individual: "The most developed individuals exhibit a sense of autonomy and maturity, while at the same time maintaining a connection to the wider community, to vital traditions of earlier times, and to people and institutions yet to come" (p. 243). At the start of an Ellbogen Center initiative, individuals sign on because they are curious, in need of help and nurturing, or simply looking for a way to fund an idea for a course they are teaching. At the end, these individuals often exhibit leadership characteristics that we cited in our introduction. They are "courageous, moral, willing to take risks, active listeners, excellent communicators, able to espouse a vision, and able to stimulate people" (Tierney, 1999, p. 48). They are able to persistently and effectively advocate for change in the teaching and learning culture.

Expanding Professional Roles and Identity: Two Profiles

In two noteworthy cases, faculty participants in our faculty development model are now directing innovative university-wide projects. Mark Lyford directs the Life Sciences program, and April Heaney directs the LeaRN program—an academic success center. These programs and their faculty leaders epitomize the possibilities for horizontal structures in the academy. They cut broadly and deeply across academic colleges and departments; they include statewide P–16 participants in their work and are carrying their local and regional success to national initiatives. These faculty leaders have communicated successfully with department and other university colleagues, persuading them to teach courses in substantively different ways. They cast their nets wide, establishing collaborations across several levels, and they create frequent, varied, and productive development opportunities for the faculty who teach in their programs. Both of these faculty have also created a comprehensive assessment culture in their programs as the bedrock for their decision making and for their faculty development projects.

Mark and April's identity transformations might be described as meteoric. Three to five years ago, they worked at the lowest faculty rank—temporary academic professionals. They now direct significant, complex university programs focused on student learning. In part, their transformation results from fortunate timing, which in the discipline of rhetoric studies is called *kairos*. Programs needed leaders at the same time Mark and April were demonstrating their interest, commitment, and leadership skills. Through the several years that we observed and reported on their work to the U.S. Department of Education FIPSE program, we also know that their participation in Ellbogen Center faculty development projects considerably shaped their leadership style. Both credit their participation in the three-year CLAAS (Connecting Learning for Academic Settings) faculty development project for teaching them how to plan for change in environments that include multiple disciplines and levels of expertise. They learned how to feature sustained faculty conversation as central to their work, how to develop a commitment to long-term collaborations and assessments, and how to create opportunities for others to be rewarded.

Examples abound of how they have adapted and transcended these lessons in their leadership. For the Life Sciences program, Mark has created a cross-department and cross-college executive committee and smaller stewardship committees that meet regularly to review teaching, learning, and assessment in the program's courses. Notable committee successes include the identification of common learning outcomes that cross course boundaries and the beginning of substantial conversation about assessment. For the Synergy program, which is a first-year learning community required of all conditionally admitted students, April runs a yearly summer faculty development institute to help the course instructors and peer mentors plan course connections. The success of Synergy has led top university administrators to envision an ambitious learning community concept for all first-year students—an initiative that April has been asked to lead.

At the regional level, Mark has collaborated with the Wyoming School–University Partnership to sponsor three years' worth of statewide science summits that include public school, community college, and university instructors. The focus of these meetings has been simple but powerful: at every meeting, the participants look at student work from all levels to locate the challenges of teaching life sciences. Among other values, participants have praised these summits for prizing the horizontal rather than top-down structure that results in a democratic discussion of ideas. With the same collaborative and horizontal model, April and the Partnership are now launching a series of statewide meetings called Teaching Writing in Wyoming.

At the national level, April assembled a winning nomination packet featuring the Synergy program for the TIAA-CREF's 2007

Theodore M. Hesburgh Award, which recognizes exceptional faculty development programs designed to enhance undergraduate teaching and learning. The award carries a $25,000 prize. Under Mark's leadership, he and two other biology faculty members were named as Education Fellows in the Life Sciences by the National Academies for completing a summer institute on innovative teaching. Mark has also assembled a group of colleagues from other major universities to form a national consortium of life sciences or biology program directors. Thus far, the directors represent eight large public universities, including the University of Wisconsin at Madison, the University of Illinois at Urbana-Champaign, Georgia State University, Michigan State University, the University of Massachusetts at Amherst, the University of Texas at Austin, the University of Michigan, and San Diego State University. The group plans to meet regularly, expand its membership, create materials for dissemination, collaborate on grant writing, and study such issues as the effectiveness of Advanced Placement biology courses and students' later success in college.

Leadership for Assessment

Thus far, we have demonstrated the transformations of individuals who move from faculty to leadership status in unique university programs. The profiles of April and Mark illustrate dramatic changes in leadership role and responsibility. Those changes directly result from their involvement in projects, based on our model's four groundings: the scholarship of teaching and learning, educational renewal, soft projects and social capital, and horizontal structures.

We can also document leadership transformations within the conventional university structure of departments and colleges. Of the fifty-four people who participated in at least one of the Ellbogen Center projects listed in Table 8.1, 22 percent, almost one-fourth, have become department heads, college deans and associates, program directors, and in one case an associate vice president. In most colleges and universities, of course, faculty routinely change or expand roles into leadership positions. Such changes depend on personal interest, timing, and institutional need. Faculty also take on leadership roles, based on peer pressure to "take their turn." Leaders transformed by the model we describe here go well beyond taking their turns at filling a position. Instead, these leaders play pivotal roles in leadership for learning.

One of the most significant features of their leadership for learning is the responsibility they take for assessment. Of the 22 percent we identify as institutional leaders, all but two are providing leadership for assessment work at the program, college, and university levels. As department heads and program directors, they have been the early adopters and advocates for completing a full cycle of assessment that includes identifying learning goals, collecting and analyzing data, and implementing change. Given the right circumstances and timing, they have sometimes been able to effect larger changes. For example, one of our faculty participants, now a department head and an associate dean, has led her college to complete assessment cycles and to prominently feature assessment of student learning at both the undergraduate and graduate levels on the college's Web site.

Of particular note is the role that the Ellbogen Center faculty participants have played in university-wide assessment efforts. The Office of Academic Affairs formed a university assessment coordinators committee more than ten years ago to help college and department leaders institutionalize ways to implement, document, and revise the assessment of student learning. In effect, the committee had the daunting challenge of selling the university community on the importance of student and program assessment and creating a university-wide presence that stewarded assessment conversations and action plans. Over the past eight years, faculty participants in Ellbogen Center programs have constituted 25 to 30 percent of this group, and they have helped to redefine the committee's role from vertical regulator or overseer to developer of an assessment culture. With their help, the assessment coordinators adopted the vision articulated in Peggy Maki's (2004) *Assessing for Learning: Building a Sustainable Commitment Across the Institution*. Maki argues that an institution will achieve an assessment culture by encouraging faculty to develop principles of commitment to student learning. Through a collaborative and iterative process, with "nested discussions, decisions, and actions" (p. 4), Maki envisions that an institution can adopt assessment as a central "way of knowing, learning, and evolving" (p. 8) as it pursues its primary mission of teaching and learning.

The assessment coordinators meet twice a month and engage in numerous activities. They attend national assessment conferences, sponsor university-wide assessments using national instruments, provide yearly reviews of every department's assessment efforts, develop workshops, and publish assessment news on a Web site and in a newsletter. They also sponsor major campuswide assessment forums and fund competitive grants to help departments achieve assessment outcomes. The forums have been successful events with broad attendance from all colleges and faculty levels. In the past few years, assessment experts for these forums have included Peggy Maki, Susan Hatfield, Linda Suskie, and Peter Ewell. In addition to working with these experts, participants in the forums learn from their campus colleagues who describe the results of local assessment projects, many of which were spawned through assessment assistance grants.

Although many departments and programs continue to struggle with assessment, several have profited from these efforts. They have adopted assessment as a way of developing their teaching to increase student learning and of determining curriculum revisions. In iterative and collaborative processes, they systematically commit to the collection and analysis of data about student learning, and they rapidly respond to the need for change. For these departments and programs, assessment has become a method for increasing their social capital. Significant leadership for this result has come from faculty members who learned about the power of assessment through the Ellbogen Center faculty development programs.

Conclusion

Models of leadership abound. In the current milieu, as colleges and universities come to be viewed as businesses, it is not surprising that they look to business and industry for ways to develop leaders. The faculty leadership model we describe here is distinguished by the principles that the academy values most: collegiality, intellectual curiosity, and the generation of knowledge. A structure that prizes intellectual work within a supportive, diverse cohort yields personal renewal and growth for individual faculty members. Faculty gain confidence and competence—qualities that transfer to other aspects of their work in and outside of the classroom.

Some might argue that convening small faculty cohorts into soft projects is a slow and costly way to grow leaders. We contrast the cohort model to typical leadership programs for which central administration selects a rising star to leave campus and participate in a one-time, intense summer program. Such programs enjoy considerable popularity and have good results. They are, however, genuinely expensive. They are not intended to create leaders for horizontal structures and fail to generate the kind of social capital our model creates. In fact, we assert that a university has an institutional obligation to invest in groups of faculty, working in cohorts around immediate instructional, curricular, and assessment issues. Who benefits? The institution, the faculty member, and, above all, students.

References

Gaff, J. G. (2007). What if the faculty really do assume responsibility for the educational program? *Liberal Education, 93*(4), 6–13.

Gardner, H., Csikszentmihalyi, M., & Damon, W. (2001). *Good work: When excellence and ethics meet.* New York: Basic Books.

Huber, M. T., & Hutchings, P. (2005). *The advancement of learning: Building the teaching commons.* San Francisco: Jossey-Bass.

Kezar, A., Lester, J., Carducci, R., Gallant, T. B., & McGavin, M. C. (2007). Where are the faculty leaders? *Liberal Education, 93*(4), 14–21.

Maki, P. L. (2004). *Assessing for learning: Building a sustainable commitment across the institution.* Sterling, VA: Stylus.

Smith, W. F., & Fenstermacher, G. D. (Eds.). (1999). *Leadership for educational renewal: Developing a cadre of leaders.* San Francisco: Jossey-Bass.

Tierney, W. G. (1999). *Building the responsive campus: Creating high performance colleges and universities.* Thousand Oaks, CA: Sage.

Tierney, W. G. (2006). *Trust and the public good: Examining the cultural conditions of academic work.* New York: Peter Lang.

Chapter 9

Searching for Meaning on College Campuses

Creating Programs to Nurture the Spirit

Donna M. Qualters
Suffolk University

Beverly Dolinsky
Endicott College

Michael Woodnick
Northeastern University

Discussing spirituality on a secular college campus can be risky. Yet faculty and students have expressed a need to explore meaning in their lives and work. This chapter describes one university's year-long efforts to develop a social web of activities around spirituality and meaning in community members' lives. We describe the process of determining needs and the resulting programs. But more important, we share lessons learned, including advice on creating the climate for spiritually oriented programming to gain acceptance and be viewed as an enhancement to campus life.

The late 1990s initiated a movement to "make spirituality public" and brought to light the need for faculty and staff to find meaning in their work and a deeper connection to the campus community. During this time, faculty questioned the traditional academic culture and felt burdened by unrealistic publication requirements and the simultaneous downgrading of the importance of teaching in the reward structure (Astin & Astin, 1999; Rice, Sorcinelli, & Austin, 2000). In spite of Parker Palmer's (1998) groundbreaking work exploring the inner landscape of authentic teaching, Astin and Astin (1999) found that faculty described spirituality more in terms of the outer world (social activism, good works, service learning) than the inner life of the individual.

Spirituality is not an easy topic to discuss on college campuses. Mentioning it, especially on secular campuses, raises the specter of violating the separation of church and state and can appear to cross boundaries, making some educators uncomfortable. Yet over the past decade, writers in higher education have identified the inextricable link between education and spirituality (Astin et al., 2002; Brown, 1999; Chavez, 2001; Lindholm & Astin, 2006). From these authors' viewpoint, spirituality is grounded in the human experience of living, suggesting that to be truly whole, faculty must find ways to connect with other like-minded individuals and identify ways to merge their academic work with their quest for meaning. To paraphrase Socrates, members of the academy are asking whether an unexamined academic life is worth living. They are seeking answers to questions that transcend how to teach well or achieve tenure. Of course, some believe that the life of the mind is the sole area of academic concern and the only content appropriate to education (Fish, 2003). But students and many colleagues are telling a different story. Students are asking faculty to help them explore the meaning of their life and work (Kuh & Umbrach, 2004; Parks, 2000), beyond learning the discipline. Faculty are seeking ways to find balance in personal and professional life and safe venues to discuss the meaning of their work in a larger context (Astin & Astin, 1999).

A recent study by Lindholm and Astin (2006) adds to the evidence of the faculty's interest in spiritual pursuits. Their survey of close to forty thousand faculty identified this interest and its prime obstacle: the faculty's lack of opportunity for such discussions and dialogues. In addition, they found that faculty who considered themselves spiritual regarded students' personal development as important as their intellectual and career development.

Although the primary mission of teaching centers is to promote excellence in teaching, many centers define a broader role and provide a more holistic approach to development through faculty life stages. A more recent conception of teaching centers as promoting learning communities (Cox, 2001), communities of practice (Wenger, 1998), and teaching commons (Hutchings & Huber, 2007) has at its core the need for faculty to have gathering places to learn and grow as teachers, researchers, professionals, and human beings. As part of this movement, some teaching centers have begun to explore spirituality in communal settings. Although programs such as book groups are welcome opportunities to explore this topic, they are often isolated activities. Creating a truly transformative experience requires the efforts of more than one entity (Miller, 2001). Teaching centers need to find ways to create what Stafford (2001) calls a "web of sociality." They have to intersect and interact with other university units to coordinate programming for multiple campus constituencies. Casting this broader net, these joint efforts can create campuswide interconnections that address the spiritual aspects of our work and lay the infrastructure to sustain the interest.

This chapter outlines Northeastern University's attempt to create this social web through collaboration. We describe the multiple activities that we developed to nurture the spirit on the campus and the important lessons we learned.

Addressing Spiritual Needs on Campus

The idea of creating forums for discussing the role of spirituality on the campus of Northeastern University was initially raised by the Spiritual Life Office (SLO)—part of the Student Affairs Division. The SLO wanted to deepen its mission to address the spiritual needs of faculty by creating a community that welcomed discussion about the need for human interaction and balance. To begin to change faculty perception of Spiritual Life as just a student organization, the SLO approached the Center for Effective University Teaching (CEUT) to discuss collaboration, first in an effort to raise campus awareness of the need to explore the search for meaning in work and life.

Our first challenge was finding ways to introduce the topic to faculty in a culturally acceptable way. Unless carefully conceived, this topic can become a flash point for many other agendas, unrelated to the initial intention of mutual exploration of meaning (Miller, 2001). Therefore, we decided to frame the project within the inquiry research model, which was familiar to our colleagues. We applied for a highly competitive internal grant from the president's office that funded projects promising to move the institution toward excellence. We argued that one way to achieve excellence was to help the community examine the meaning in their work and the connections between units and individuals. We proposed specific goals: 1) to gather baseline data on thoughts and feelings about the role of spirituality on the campus, 2) to begin to define spirituality in a welcoming and inviting environment on a nonsectarian campus, and 3) to initiate programming to promote community and connections among faculty, staff, and students. We also listed outcomes important to the mission of the institution: to develop a manuscript for a peer-reviewed journal to disseminate the work, to develop a model to inform and guide other campuses interested in developing spirituality on campus, and to provide venues to enhance the interaction between various community sectors, including staff, administrators, students, and faculty. To our delight, we received one of only five grants awarded that year. But even more important to our mission was the administration's recognition that the topic was important to the campus and could belong in a research institution.

Taking Steps to Make the Vision Real

To stay within the institution's research culture and the parameters of the grant, we first created a simple mail survey that asked participants (faculty, administrators, and staff) to reflect on the role of spirituality in their lives and areas on the campus where they felt it could be nurtured. We used the survey data to shape the programming for nurturing the spirit. At about the same time, Lindholm and Astin (2006) were asking similar questions in their 2004–2005 Triennial National Faculty Survey, conducted by UCLA's Higher Education Research Institute. The results of our single-institution study ($n = 285$, 19 percent return rate) were consistent with this larger survey of 37,827 full-time undergraduate faculty from 373 four-year colleges and universities. Participants strongly agreed that spirituality was synonymous with developing a meaningful philosophy of life and finding meaning. When asked if the university was a setting where spirituality should be nurtured, respondents split in their opinions. At our institution, community members tended to disagree with the proposition that administrative departments, research labs, research activities, academic departments, classrooms, and the health center were places where spirituality should be nurtured. Further analyses indicated that faculty disagreed significantly more than administrators or staff regarding the appropriate campus places for nurturing the spirit. Female community members were more receptive to different venues.

The survey data were eye opening for us. We realized that there were some very strong feelings about promoting a culture of spirituality. The process of surveying participants helped us understand some of these feelings, decide what to include in our programs, and understand our challenges. Clearly, the greatest challenge would be introducing the ideas in a context of teaching and academic departments. The mixed opinion led us to two operating principles. First, we needed to start slowly by introducing the idea into smaller venues and with self-selected individuals, and second, we had to conceptualize a variety of programming to appeal to the different needs. We began with a web matrix of interrelated activities to address the varied needs expressed in the survey (Figure 9.1). We wanted to design campuswide programming to build a social, interconnected web to help support and sustain the initiative (Stafford, 2001).

Our next challenge was naming the initiative. We wanted a title that would capture the need to come together in a community setting and at the same time convey that this was something beyond the "usual" community activities. We also knew from the survey that it was risky to use "spirit" in the title, but we took that risk. We finally settled on Nurturing the Spirit: Building Campus Community.

We then began to conceptualize a series of programs to provide different activities for the many constituents. Our goal was to break the isolation of our work and to bring people together to talk about

Figure 9.1. University Web of Sociality Spirituality Web

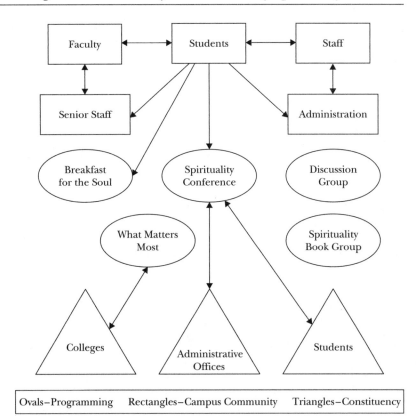

Ovals–Programming   Rectangles–Campus Community   Triangles–Constituency

life choices, community values, our students, and our own development and growth as a member of this campus community. Even though both individual and institutional change is hard, change theory provided some guidelines. If we were going to change the culture, we knew we had to create a variety of programming venues to engage individuals who are were in different stages of wanting to explore spirituality (Prochaska, DiClemente, & Norcross, 1992), including programming that allowed individuals to reflect on their assumptions and beliefs about the role of spirituality on a campus in a communal setting (Schein, 1995). Our slate of potential programming for the grant varied from small, intimate settings to a large campuswide conference. We planned short-term and long-term initiatives and one activity that brought faculty, staff, and students together. Our initial combination of activities encompassed different degrees of overt spiritualism in the hope that we would to find a successful mix. What follows is a brief description of the year-long programming.

Nurturing the Spirit Programming

We began slowly by bringing together those who were action-oriented or, in the words of Rogers (1995), early adopters of the idea that spirit can play a vital part in who we are and what we do in our academic life and work. Our first initiative was designed to test the results of the survey that the classroom was not an appropriate venue to explore spirituality. We solicited participants for a discussion group titled Nurturing the Mind and Spirit in the Classroom, to give us ideas to build on. To our amazement, forty classroom instructors and ten staff members attended. The lively exchange of ideas progressed to deeper levels, as participants shared their feelings of isolation and the need to connect with colleagues and students in more meaningful ways. With this event, we had our first group of supporters.

This initial success gave us the credibility and the support to move forward to another relatively low-cost program—the Spirituality Book Group—starting with the most famous book on authenticity and meaning, *The Courage to Teach* (Palmer, 1998). We sent out invitations to the community requesting those interested to commit to one semester, attend biweekly meetings, agree to be active participants, and share facilitation. Beginning with ten individuals, the Spirituality Book Group became one of the most enduring activities. It continued each semester for two years, with a core group of four or five returning participants, joined by two to three new members. Ranging across faculty rank and colleges, attendees included a number of respected senior professors and a former provost.

Concurrently, we developed a series of loosely structured, monthly gatherings for faculty and staff called Breakfast for the Soul. Participants came to explore, over a full breakfast, how to create deeper meaning in campus work and how to increase connections on the campus. The meeting was scheduled early so that staff members could participate. Because of the participants' varied needs to balance their work and life commitments, we structured the breakfast so that those who arrived late or left early would still feel that they had experienced community. Specifically, the beginning of each session was socializing and checking in, the middle portion was a focused activity (see Table 9.1) and group discussion, and the latter part was a summary of our ideas. We limited participation to twenty-five to allow everyone the opportunity to get to know each other. Our hope was to have at least enough people to begin a real dialogue, and the result was our most popular programs that year. Within twenty-four hours of e-mail notification of each breakfast, it had completely filled up. Again, a core group attended monthly, with others coming occasionally, as their schedules and hectic lives permitted.

When asked to evaluate this program, participants said it allowed them to pause during a very busy semester to reflect and to reach out to others around issues of meaning in our work. Staff particularly liked the idea of interacting with the faculty to talk about students and their common educational mission. Breakfast for the Soul was also identified as one of the few venues where faculty and staff could gather together on the campus as respected equals to discuss a shared agenda. Both faculty and staff felt that the breakfast provided them with balance, support, and professional nurturing.

Our third program—What Matters Most—brought students into the conversation. This initiative grew out of our concern that our students framed success in life as getting a good job and making money, and we wanted to offer an alternative perspective. Over pizza and soda, students heard invited faculty and staff explain what gave meaning to their lives and how they defined success. Our presenters included an academic dean, an athletic department member, and faculty members. Their stories were powerful and moving. One presenter was a senior staff member who had been a professional athlete and senior vice president in a large corporation before coming to the university. He opened his presentation by apologizing for having his cell phone on. He explained that, with his wife out of the country, he had to be available to his two young daughters in case of emergency. This personal sharing modeled the importance he placed on family and balance over prestige and salary.

Table 9.1. Breakfast for the Soul Activities

1. Focus Opening Activity

List the names of five people, living or dead, who have or had qualities/abilities that you admire and who are leading or led lives of meaning.

From the list, narrow to three.

For these people list the qualities/attributes/characteristics that made you identify them as special.

Elaborate on these qualities (e.g., if they are caring): how is this person caring in a way that another would not have been; what's special about this caring.

Look over what you've written in #4—are there similarities, common words, common themes?—list and then share together.

2. Token Sharing

Bring an item that has special meaning in your life; something that helps you connect to a deeper part of yourself—share with your group why the object is symbolic and why you brought it to share.

3. Heart Stones*

Take a heart stone from the pile—read the description in the book; share with a partner why you think you received this heart stone and how you can apply its message today in your work.

4. Parker Palmer views "education as spiritual formation—that the teacher is the living link between the knower and the known, the learner and the subject to be learned . . ."

Take a second to think about this statement; write your initial response(s), both positive and negative.

Now, write down ways you currently act as that link that allows students freedom to explore who they are.

Share in the group your ideas and actions as a teacher/mentor/guide that make education spiritual formation.

* Heart Stones – Sophia's Gift of the Spirit 1-877-440-990

The year-long series of activities culminated with our mini-conference (see the agenda in Table 9.2)—a day-long series of talks, interactive workshops, social events, and community-building activities to celebrate a year of exploring our communal quest for meaning. The call for proposals elicited a surprisingly wide variety of proposals from various constituents and departments, allowing us to choose presenters from each of the university colleges. With the strong support of both the president and provost, who welcomed and keynoted the conference, over one hundred faculty and staff attended during the final week of the semester. Our luncheon speaker had published a book on being passionate about teaching, and this topic attracted a large number of instructors to the luncheon. The final social event in the afternoon was a time to feed the body and to express the feelings of the soul. We posted a large piece of felt cloth with small, cut-out, felt gingerbread figures and asked people to write messages on the figures about meaning and spirit. This activity left us a beautiful visual reminder of the day that we could hang in various locations on campus.

On a 5-point scale, with 5 being "excellent," participants judged the value of the mini-conference sessions within the range of 2.8–5.0 and effectiveness of learning within the range of 3.0–5.0. As some of them wrote, "I was heartened to see that so many people are yearning for community and meaning in their lives" and "I think today has been a wonderful opportunity to come together and learn about community, I think all of us find it difficult to see, be part of, and establish community here." Another mentioned that "building community can happen in surprising and subtle ways."

Of course, these participant evaluations are strictly perceptual, and our lack of hard quantitative, longitudinal data is a limitation of this work. But we can say that the individuals who participated came from a wide variety of administrative offices, all six colleges in the university, and many individual disciplines. Our final numbers of attendees were the largest for any voluntary program that either the CEUT or the SLO had offered in recent memory. This added credence to our initial hypothesis that this kind of programming was needed and that combining our resources made sense. Based on the overwhelmingly positive

Table 9.2. Nurturing the Spirit: Building Campus Community Mini-Conference (President's Excellence Grant)

8:00 A.M.–8:30 A.M.	Registration
8:30 A.M.–9:00 A.M.	Welcome–President
9:00 A.M.–10:00 A.M.	Opening Plenary–Provost
10:00 A.M.–12:00 P.M.	Morning Breakout Sessions
	• Building People: Faculty and Students Engaging outside of the Classroom–College of Engineering
	• Listening and Telling Our Stories: Cultivating Community–College of Business Administration
	• The Role of the University in Creating Authentic Community–Spiritual Life Office and the Center for Effective University Teaching
12:00 P.M.–1:30 P.M.	Luncheon–Passionate Teaching
1:30 P.M.–3:30 P.M.	Afternoon Breakout Sessions
	• Spirituality and Community: Sources of Strength in Uncertain Times–College of Health Sciences
	• Cultivating Community Through Ethical Reflection–College of Arts and Science and Center for Experiential Education
	• Fostering Caring Connections on Campus–Center for Counseling and Student Development
3:30 P.M.–4:30 P.M.	Final Thoughts and Social Hour

feedback from participants, we believe that they felt the conference met a need to establish a sense of belonging and meaning on campus.

Learning from Mistakes

Through this initial programming, we learned a number of important lessons about bringing this vital topic of spirituality to a wide variety of constituents on a nonsectarian campus. As in most of life's lessons, there is much to be gained from our experiences, and we hope that by sharing we will help others who are contemplating advancing the concept of spirituality on their campus.

Early on, it became clear that gaining administrative support was of prime importance. Soliciting the support of the president and provost allowed us to get publicity that we might not have received. For example, both the university newspaper and the student newspaper wrote high-profile articles on the programs sharing the goals and reasoning behind this type of new programming on campus.

Although a campuswide survey was time-intensive, it was extremely valuable. The results gave us insight into the interested campus parties, the types of programming, and an idea of what would be accepted and what would be challenging. The survey also gave some academic legitimacy to the endeavor, because faculty saw our approach as rigorous, and the programming and the results were later accepted as a part of the university-wide research exposition. Though it was an unintended result, we received a number of comments attached to the survey, both positive and negative, that gave us additional insight into the process.

We discovered the importance of personally reaching out. We found that because of the potential misunderstanding of the topic, we needed to talk about it directly with people and explain our intentions so that it was not seen as a religious event. Every faculty or staff member whom we approached to offer a program, run a session, or facilitate a book group, accepted.

The need to spend more time on building an infrastructure became important. Keeping administrative support became all the more obvious when, during the next year, the provost stepped down, the director of the SLO returned to faculty, and the CEUT staff was diminished. As a result, and without longitudinal support, programming did not sustain itself outside the Spirituality Book Group, which continued mostly because of two instructors who were passionate about continuing.

In hindsight, we would have involved the advisory boards of both the CEUT and SLO more closely in the endeavor to create faculty champions to continue the work, regardless of administrative changes. We also would have requested more initial funding to institute more rigorous outcome assessment, even in the pilot stages, to give champions data to demonstrate the impact of this project.

Last, cost was not a significant factor in designing programs. Our most expensive projects were the survey construction and the mini-conference. The costs of running the Spirituality Book Group, the Teaching and Spirituality Workshop, Breakfast for the Soul, and What Matters Most were easily absorbed by our department budgets.

Conclusion

Engaging a campus in the quest for meaning and spirituality is not a project that lends itself to conclusions. Finding value and meaning in work is an ongoing human quest. The success of our year-long efforts highlighted the need of some faculty, staff, and students to explore the spiritual dimension. Despite sustainability issues, we were encouraged by the fact that about 150 individual faculty (20 percent) and 40 professional staff attended at least one event that grappled with the concept of meaning making. Adding student activities into the program provided venues for the entire campus community to come together around the common educational mission and to share their work struggles and quest for meaning.

Commitment and infrastructure were more important than money. No one requested course release or funding to participate or asked what they would gain from participation. The growth of the program rested on a few champions, a collaborative spirit in the programs, and a willingness to take risks. In other institutions, the viability of these programs will depend on the institution's commitment and its ability to overcome the usual inertia and unwillingness to change.

Could we have sustained Nurturing the Spirit? We continually ask ourselves that question. Multiple time demands, changing personnel, and uncertain life circumstances have made it difficult. But to relegate spirituality to the Student Affairs office or the Chaplaincy Office or a wellness committee is clearly *not* the way to meet an ever-growing need in an ever more hectic world. The literature suggests the need for this type of programming on the twenty-first-century campus, and we hope our project will smooth the way for others to create venues for spiritual dialogue and discussion.

References

Astin, A. W., & Astin, H. (1999). *Meaning and spirituality in the lives of college faculty: A study of values, authenticity, and stress.* Los Angeles: Higher Education Research Institute, University of California at Los Angeles.

Astin, A. W., Astin, H. S., Chambers, L., Chambers, T., Chickering, A., Elsner, P., et al. (2002, April). *A position statement from the initiative for authenticity and spirituality in higher education.* Retrieved August 15, 2007, from www.collegevalues.org/spirit.cfm?id=982&a=1

Brown, R. (1999, January). The teacher as contemplative observer. *Educational Leadership, 56*(4), 70–73.

Chavez, A. F. (2001). Spirit and nature in everyday life: Reflections of a mestiza in higher education. In M. A. Jablonski (Ed.), *New directions for student services: No. 95. The implications of student spirituality for student affairs practice* (pp. 69–80). San Francisco: Jossey-Bass.

Cox, M. D. (2001). Faculty learning communities: Change agents for transforming institutions into learning organizations. In D. Lieberman & C. Wehlburg (Eds.), *To improve the academy: Vol. 19. Resources for faculty, instructional, and organizational development* (pp. 69–93). Bolton, MA: Anker.

Fish, S. (2003, May 16). Aim low. *The Chronicle of Higher Education,* p. C5.

Hutchings, P., & Huber, M. (2007). *Building the teaching commons.* Retrieved August 15, 2007, from www.carnegiefoundation.org/perspectives/sub.asp?key=245&subkey=800

Kuh, G. D., & Umbach, P. (2004). College and character: Insight from the national survey of student engagement. In J. C. Dalton, T. R. Russell, & S. Kline (Eds.), *New directions for institutional research: No. 122. Assessing character outcomes in college* (pp. 37–53). San Francisco: Jossey-Bass.

Lindholm, J. A., & Astin, H. S. (2006). Understanding the "interior" life of faculty: How important is spirituality? *Religion and Education, 33*(2), 64–90.

Miller, V. (2001). Transforming campus life: Conclusions and other questions. In V. Miller & M. Ryan (Eds.), *Studies in education and spirituality* (pp. 299–312). New York: Peter Lang.

Palmer, P. (1998). *The courage to teach: Exploring the inner landscape of a teacher's life.* San Francisco: Jossey-Bass.

Prochaska, J. O., DiClemente, C. C., & Norcross, J. C. (1992). In search of how people change: Applications to addictive behavior. *American Psychologist, 47,* 1102–1114.

Rice, R. E., Sorcinelli, M. D., & Austin, A. E. (2000). *Heeding new voices: Academic careers for a new generation.* Washington, DC: American Association for Higher Education.

Rogers, E. (1995). *Diffusions of innovations* (4th ed.). New York: Free Press.

Schein, E. H. (1995). *Kurt Lewin's change theory in the field and in the classroom: Notes toward a model of managed learning.* Retrieved August 10, 2007, from www.solonline.org/res/wp/10006.html

Stafford, G. (2001). The college campus as a web of sociality. In V. Miller & M. Ryan (Eds.), *Studies in education and spirituality* (pp. 173–181). New York: Peter Lang.

Wenger, E. (1998). *Communities of practice: Learning, meaning, and identity.* Cambridge, England: Cambridge University Press.

One-on-One with Faculty

Chapter 10

Defeating the Developer's Dilemma

An Online Tool for Individual Consultations

Michele DiPietro, Susan A. Ambrose, Michael Bridges,
Anne Fay, Marsha C. Lovett, Marie Kamala Norman
Carnegie Mellon University

A very special thank-you to Judith Brooks, who masterfully designed the online tool.

This chapter introduces an online consultation tool that helps resolve the tension that developers often experience in consultations between offering quick fixes and providing in-depth but time-consuming conceptual understanding. The tool that the Eberly Center for Teaching Excellence has developed provides instructors with concrete teaching strategies to address common teaching problems, while also educating them about the pedagogical principles informing those strategies. The tool can be used to enhance traditional face-to-face consultations or, by itself, to reach a wider faculty audience, including adjunct and off-site faculty.

As faculty developers, we want to deliver concrete practical solutions to the teaching problems faculty experience, to use our time effectively, and to assist as many instructors as possible. Yet we also want to provide faculty with a deep understanding of the principles that underlie meaningful learning and guide effective teaching. These goals present developers with an apparent dilemma: Should we provide quick tips or seek to develop deep understanding of learning and pedagogy? The latter approach requires time and resources that many developers, not to mention instructors, simply do not have. Yet dispensing tips can backfire if instructors lack sufficient understanding of the problem and thus misapply techniques and strategies. How do we balance these two priorities when providing excellent teaching advice to reach the broadest possible audience?

Although this tension is not new to our profession (Cash & Minter, 1979), increased pressures on faculty time and limited financial resources have made it more acute. Sorcinelli, Austin, Eddy, and Beach (2006) address this issue when they point out that faculty developers will increasingly have to "connect, communicate, and collaborate to meet the challenge of how to do more with less while simultaneously maintaining excellence" (p. 158).

Our center has taken up this challenge. Capitalizing on the potential of the Internet to facilitate greater connection and communication, we have developed an online tool, based on the collaborative framework we employ in our face-to-face consultations with faculty. Our primary goal in developing this tool was to reach as many instructors as possible while preserving as much of the richness of the traditional consultation process as possible. Our secondary goal was to provide a useful resource for faculty developers. The tool combines 1) key elements of the collaborative consultation model, 2) a set of common teaching problems we frequently encounter in our consultations with faculty, 3) a three-step process for addressing these problems and identifying a range of appropriate, contextualized solutions, and 4) a set of learning and teaching principles, based on theory and research, that informs the solutions we suggest to instructors.

Our online tool allows users (whether instructors or faculty developers) to apply the three-step process to particular teaching problems, offering concrete and appropriate strategies, as well as their basic theoretical underpinnings. This chapter explains the online tool and offers it as a public resource for developers and instructors everywhere. The chapter is divided into four sections. The first section presents our consultation philosophy, situating it in relation to other consultation models. The second section illustrates our three-step consultation framework and applies it to one teaching problem commonly encountered by faculty with whom we consult. The third section introduces the online tool and its features. Finally, in the fourth section, we conclude with a discussion of the lessons learned from this process and their implications for faculty development.

Our Consultation Philosophy

Successful consultations demand a well-articulated and internally consistent consultation philosophy. Although we recognize that a number of different approaches can be effective, depending on the institutional context, we present ours because it forms the foundation for the online tool we developed. Our philosophy extends Brinko's (1991) work by characterizing one of her consultation models. Brinko identifies five models of consultation that pertain to faculty development:

1. *Provider of product.* This model views the faculty developer as the provider of a discrete product (for example, a checklist, template, or rubric) or a concrete tip that will solve problems in the classroom. Faculty developers who interact with instructors subscribing to this perspective are certainly familiar with these requests (for example, "Tell me the top three things I need to do to increase classroom participation").

2. *Prescriptive.* This model mimics the traditional medical model in which the doctor is seen as the all-knowing expert, capable of immediately and infallibly identifying the problem, diagnosing the underlying illness, and prescribing the appropriate remedies. Instructors with this outlook will often defer to the developer in all things pedagogical, waiting to be told what to do and how to do it.

3. *Collaborative.* In this model, both the instructor and the faculty developer are seen as experts—one in content and specific classroom context, the other in process and general pedagogy. The consultation is conceptualized as a genuinely joint effort, with the instructor having final authority on changes that affect her course.

4. *Affiliative.* This model originates from the psychotherapeutic literature and acknowledges that sometimes personal or professional issues affect an instructor's performance in the classroom. The faculty developer must therefore address those concerns with the pedagogical ones in a holistic vision of faculty development.

5. *Confrontational.* This model acknowledges that consultations sometimes become "stuck" because of faculty resistance or skepticism. The faculty developer's role in these cases is to openly challenge the instructor, by taking a devil's advocate position or by being blunt, in order to make progress.

Of these, we favor the collaborative model because it acknowledges the expertise and contribution of both the instructor and the faculty developer. Moreover, it often encompasses aspects of other models. In a bona fide collaborative effort, it is sometimes appropriate to offer products or, on occasion, be prescriptive. Certainly, some aspects of the affiliative and confrontational models belong in a true collaboration.

But if a collaborative consultation can, at times, resemble other kinds of consultations, what exactly characterizes this model at its core? We found this question worth exploring. The collaborative approach, as we employ it in our work, is as follows:

1. *Learner-centered.* We regard student learning as the center of the teaching process. Therefore, we aim to help instructors develop course objectives, assessments, and instructional activities that together support and promote student learning and performance.

2. *Educational.* We aim to help our colleagues gain a deeper understanding of the principles that underlie effective learning and teaching so they can make appropriate teaching decisions for their own courses (Knapper & Piccinin, 1999). We do not simply dispense teaching tips.

3. *Constructive.* We focus on providing constructive and practical feedback to help our colleagues succeed as educators. Our role is to support teaching, not to judge performance. We always highlight their strengths first and then identify areas for growth and concrete suggestions they can implement in the classroom.

4. *Data-driven.* We gather and analyze extensive data through classroom observations, student focus groups, and the examination of teaching materials. We then help instructors use these data to diagnose strengths and identify areas for improvement (Nyquist & Wulff, 2001).

5. *Research-based.* We apply state-of-the-art research from a range of disciplines (for example, cognitive psychology, organizational behavior, educational psychology, cross-cultural studies) to help instructors design and teach courses more effectively.

Our Three-Step Consultation Process

The features articulated earlier are at the center of our consultation process. We want to provide and share constructive and practical strategies, but we want those strategies to be informed by data, theory, and research, which we also want to share. The three basic steps we engage in when we employ this process are synthesized in Figure 10.1. The first step is to "Identify the Problem." Instructors sometimes come to the center with a vague sense that one of their courses is not working well or that students are unhappy, without being able to articulate the exact nature of the problem. Our twenty-seven years of experience at the center have illuminated a set of common, recurring problems that we refer to when helping faculty pinpoint the specific problem they are encountering. A sample of such problems includes the following (more problems are available at www.cmu.edu/teaching/solveproblem/index.html):

- Students don't participate in discussions.
- Students don't come to lecture.
- Students don't apply what they've learned.
- Students don't keep up with the readings.
- Students' background knowledge and skills vary widely.
- Students lack writing skills.
- Students may be cheating or plagiarizing.
- Students performed poorly on the first exam.
- Group projects aren't working.

In the second step, we employ a data-driven process to "Identify Possible Reasons" for the problem. This can involve collecting data to determine the cause or causes. In the third step, based on the identified reason and relevant data, the faculty developer and instructor work collaboratively to "Explore Strategies." The strategies we suggest are informed by principles of learning, as are the other steps.

Figure 10.1. Our Consultation Framework That Informed the Development of the Online Tool

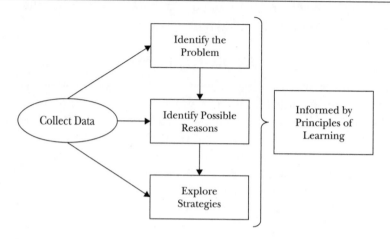

As an example, let's consider a common situation. A faculty colleague comes in with a vague sense of dissatisfaction about how his course is going. After some discussion, the instructor and faculty developer identify the key problem: students do not participate in discussions. To determine the cause of the problem, the developer collects data via classroom observations and focus groups with students. Some of the possible reasons might include the following:

1. Students did not complete the reading assignment.
2. Students did not focus on the relevant aspects of the reading assignment.
3. Students' individual styles or personalities may inhibit their participation.
4. Students' cultural values and norms may inhibit their participation.
5. Students may not have experience participating in discussions.
6. Students may not have the general background knowledge to participate.
7. Students come to class late and miss the framing of the discussion.
8. The instructor did not clearly articulate the goals of the discussion, define the structure, or effectively manage the process within the defined structure.

9. The intellectual environment is not conducive to participation.
10. The physical environment is not conducive to discussion.

Identifying possible reasons for the problem is a critical step in the consultation process. Because faculty members have rarely thought about all of the possible factors that could create or contribute to a problem, considering a broad range of possible explanations helps educate them about issues they may never have considered.

It is important to accurately identify the reason for the problem in order to choose appropriate interventions. If the reason students do not participate in discussions is that they do not keep up with the readings, the strategies might focus on integrating the readings more into the course and holding the students accountable for completing them. If the reason students do not participate is that they do not feel comfortable speaking up, volunteering unpopular opinions, or disagreeing with each other, the strategies must focus on creating a comfortable and productive classroom climate. If the reason students do not participate is because of a problem with the physical environment, the solution might be as simple as rearranging the chairs in the classroom. Sample reasons and strategies for this problem are listed in Table 10.1.

Table 10.1. Condensed List of Reasons and Strategies from the Sample Problem, "My students don't participate in discussions."

Sample strategies to address the problem "My students don't participate in discussions" based on possible reasons:

Students don't keep up with the reading.
"Scaffold" reading assignments.
Point out the relevance of the readings.
Hold students immediately responsible for readings.

Students did not focus on the relevant aspects of reading.
Provide strategies for reading.
Direct students' reading.
Model your reading strategy.

Students' individual styles or personalities may inhibit their participation.
Help students to prepare in advance.
Use groups.
Reward student participation.

(Continued)

Table 10.1. Condensed List of Reasons and Strategies from the Sample Problem, "My students don't participate in discussions." (*Continued*)

Students' cultural values and norms may inhibit their participation.
Define your expectations.
Articulate ground rules.

Students may not have experience participating in discussions.
Outline your goals.
Model appropriate behavior.
Allow students time to think.

Students may not have the general background knowledge to participate.
Assess prior knowledge.
Address lack of prior knowledge.

The instructor did not clearly articulate the goals of the discussion, define the structure, or effectively manage the process within the defined structure.
Prepare your questions in advance.
Identify why your questions are not effective.
Summarize the discussion.

The intellectual environment is not conducive to participation.
Tactfully correct inaccurate information.
Validate meaningful contributions.
Invite contradictory views.

Note. Descriptions for these and other reasons and strategies are available at www.cmu.edu/teaching/solveproblem/index.html.

Our Online Tool for Consultations

In their analysis of the history of faculty development, Sorcinelli and colleagues (2006) call the present period the Age of the Network, alluding to the ubiquitous presence of the Internet and its potential as a resource for faculty developers. We sought to exploit this potential by developing an online tool that walks users through the three-step consultation process described earlier.

We started brainstorming the list of common teaching problems our faculty has expressed to us over the years. We prioritized them according to frequency and developed the most commonly reported. In generating possible reasons and strategies, we drew on our collective expertise, both in faculty development and in our respective fields of specialization (the center staff includes cognitive, social, and developmental psychologists, a historian, a cultural anthropologist, and a statistician). After we developed the first version of the online tool, we conducted user tests to get feedback on it. We called on faculty members from various disciplines to go through the Web site with a specific teaching problem in mind and asked them to give us feedback on content, navigation, readability, and so on. The feedback was very positive, but it also highlighted some areas for improvement. We then revised the tool to incorporate the feedback and have since made it available to the campus community, presented it at conferences, and used it in our own consulting practice.

Our hope is that this tool can help to resolve the tension inherent in consultations by fostering a problem-solving process in which the teaching strategies offered are directly linked to the reasons underlying specific teaching problems and are firmly grounded in research and theory.

This tool is hosted by the Enhancing Education Web page—the joint Web site of our center and of the Office of Technology for Education—and is publicly available at www.cmu.edu/teaching/solveproblem/index.html.

As shown in Figure 10.2, the front page of the tool previews the three steps (problem, reason, strategies) and contains a link to the first step. Two sidebars on the right-hand side list the learning and teaching principles that underlie the inquiry process. This set of learning and teaching principles is included in Table 10.2.

Once the user clicks on the link, she is taken to a page asking her to choose from a menu of common classroom problems, grouped by categories, as shown in Figure 10.3. The principles are still presented in the sidebars. Once the user clicks on the relevant problem, she is taken to the next page, shown in Figure 10.4, which explores possible reasons the problem might be happening, still reinforcing the learning and teaching principles on the right. Once the user clicks on one of the possible reasons for the problem, she is then taken to the next page, shown in Figure 10.5. This page briefly elaborates on the reason, explaining in one paragraph the not-so-obvious reasons and providing some references when appropriate. Below this paragraph, one or more

Figure 10.2. The Front Page of Our Online Tool

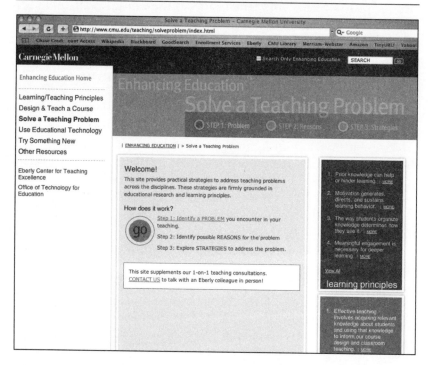

Table 10.2. Theory- and Research-Based Principles of Learning and Teaching

Theory- and Research-Based Principles of Learning
1. Prior knowledge can help or hinder learning.
2. Motivation generates, directs, and sustains learning behavior.
3. The way students organize knowledge determines how they use it.
4. Active engagement can promote deeper learning.
5. Mastery involves developing component skills and knowledge, synthesizing, and applying them appropriately.
6. Goal-directed practice and targeted feedback are critical to learning.
7. Learning requires that students monitor, evaluate, and adjust their learning strategies.
8. Students develop holistically.

Theory- and Research-Based Principles of Teaching
1. Effective teaching involves acquiring relevant knowledge about students and using that knowledge to inform our course design and classroom teaching.

Table 10.2. Theory- and Research-Based Principles of Learning and Teaching (*Continued*)

2. Effective teaching involves aligning the three major components of instruction: learning objectives, assessments, and instructional activities.
3. Effective teaching involves articulating explicit expectations regarding learning objectives and policies.
4. Effective teaching involves prioritizing the knowledge and skills we choose to focus on.
5. Effective teaching involves recognizing and overcoming our expert blind spots.
6. Effective teaching involves adopting appropriate teaching roles to support our learning goals.
7. Effective teaching involves progressively refining our courses, based on reflection and feedback.

Note. Explanations of the principles and the theory and research supporting them is available at www.cmu.edu/teaching/principles/learning.html and www.cmu.edu/teaching/principles/teaching.html.

Figure 10.3. Screenshot of Teaching Problems and Learning Principles (page scrolls down)

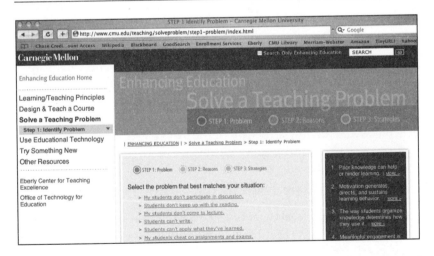

teaching strategies addressing that reason are offered. Some of the strategies link to relevant pages on the center's Web site (for example, designing and using rubrics, classroom assessment techniques). On this page's sidebars, the principles most pertinent to the reason are highlighted. The principles are also clickable,

Figure 10.4. Screenshot of One Problem and Possible Reasons (page scrolls down)

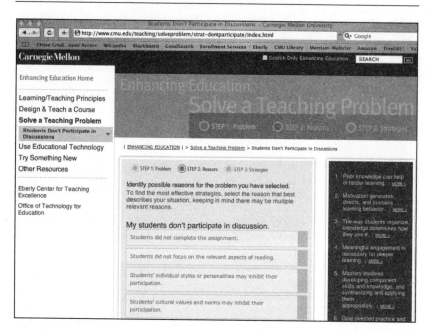

in case the user wants to learn more about learning theory in relation to her specific problem. Every subpage contains a text box at the bottom, inviting the user to contact the center if she wishes to know more or to tailor the consultation to her specific context. An important feature of the site is that the steps are sequential. Thanks to the link structure of the Web pages, one cannot jump to the strategy pages without exploring possible reasons first.

Discussion and Implications for Faculty Development

We have found the online tool to be useful and versatile, both for our faculty colleagues and for ourselves as faculty developers. In addition to providing contextualized solutions to common teaching problems, it has helped us bring the following points to the attention of instructors:

1. *A teaching problem can manifest itself for very different reasons.* As we mentioned before by way of example, students might not

Figure 10.5. Screenshot of Possible Strategies with Explanations and Relevant Learning Principles (page scrolls down)

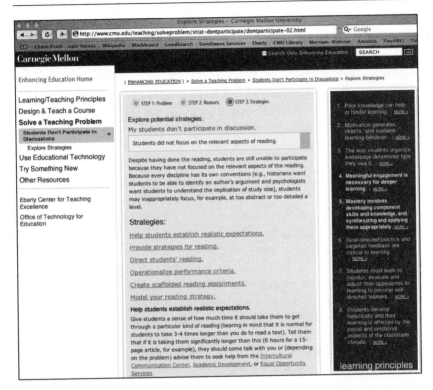

participate in a discussion because they have not done the relevant readings or because they find the classroom environment intimidating. Obviously, these are substantially different issues. Simply reading down the list of possible reasons for a problem alerts faculty to issues that might not have occurred to them.

2. *Effective strategies are intimately tied to the reasons that problems manifest themselves in the classroom.* For example, the strategies one would use to ensure that students do the assigned readings are not necessarily the same strategies one would use to create a more comfortable and inclusive classroom environment. If the reason for the problem is A and the instructor employs strategies meant to address B, it is likely that the original problem will not be resolved. This cautionary lesson is particularly important for those colleagues who are in search of quick fixes. We believe the

focus on *reasons* in our online tool engenders a more reflective approach to teaching problems.

3. *Reasons cluster into three general areas, all of which are critical for learning.* As faculty review lists of possible reasons for a problem, their attention is drawn to the cognitive-intellectual, social-emotional, and physical-environmental factors that impinge on learning. For example, students might not participate in discussions because of cognitive issues (for example, they lack critical background knowledge and skills, the questions are pitched at an overly abstract level), social-emotional issues (for example, students come from cultures in which classroom discussion is not employed or considered useful, students worry that their ideas will be dismissed), or physical-environmental issues (for example, students cannot hear or see one another). By highlighting all three dimensions of student learning, the online tool reinforces the point that effective teaching addresses the whole student.

4. *Some strategies can sometimes address several problems (or reasons) of a given type at once.* As faculty colleagues investigate specific teaching problems using the online tool, they find that some teaching strategies emerge in numerous contexts. For instance, a single strategy—aligning objectives, assessment, and instructional strategies—simultaneously increases learning, enhances student performance, increases student satisfaction, reduces cheating, and discourages grade grubbing. The simple fact that this strategy keeps reappearing reinforces its importance. At the same time, because the strategy's importance is contextualized within the discussion of a specific problem, rather than endorsed in the abstract (as, for example, in a list of best practices), we believe it is easier for faculty to understand, appreciate, and employ. Because the strategies originate from a small set of principles, instructors with a sufficiently large repertoire of strategies can solve many of their problems without having to always search for new strategies.

5. *The reasons and strategies are tied to learning and teaching principles.* Because the learning and teaching principles are always present in the sidebars to the right, highlighted selectively, depending on relevance to the specific situation, they convey the message that the process is not haphazard but systematic and grounded in theory and research on learning and teaching.

The tool itself can be used in the context of a consultation, but it is also publicly accessible online. Therefore, it is potentially useful in a variety of ways and to multiple audiences:

1. *It helps us reach underserved populations.* One such population is adjunct faculty, who may work in nonacademic jobs during the day and teach in the evening and thus are less able to avail themselves of on-site faculty development opportunities. Another underserved population includes professors teaching off-site in distance and satellite programs, which are proliferating across the globe. A third population includes those instructors on campus who are too embarrassed to ask for help but who could use the online tool safely and anonymously.

2. *It helps us use our time efficiently.* We often use the tool during our consultations because it puts a systematic analysis of a teaching problem, along with links to relevant materials (for example, sample rubrics and pretests, articles on pertinent issues) at our fingertips. We also sometimes use it before a consultation as a refresher on a particular subject. Consulting the online tool helps to ensure we consider all possible causes for a problem without jumping to conclusions, and it saves us from reinventing the wheel when we encounter different faculty experiencing the same problem. Finally, to make efficient use of face-to-face meeting time, it is sometimes helpful to direct a faculty colleague to a section of the online tool (for example, an explanation of clear, learner-centered objectives, advice on group work) in preparation for a consultation.

3. *It can be helpful to small teaching centers, where the staff experiences pressures on its own time and priorities.* At such centers, faculty developers are caught in a balancing act between programs that increase their visibility on campus and allow them to reach a broad audience (such as teaching workshops) and individual consultations that have a lasting and deep impact but are time-consuming. This tool helps us optimize our resources.

Conclusion

This online tool adapts our collaborative consultation philosophy and process to a medium that allows instructors—particularly faculty who cannot easily make use of traditional teaching center resources—to find concrete, helpful, contextualized, and research-based solutions to teaching problems and that helps teaching centers use their resources more efficiently to reach a broader audience.

References

Brinko, K. T. (1991). The interactions of teaching improvements. In M. Theall & J. Franklin (Eds.), *New directions for teaching and learning: No. 48. Effective practices for improving teaching* (pp. 39–49). San Francisco: Jossey-Bass.

Cash, W., & Minter, R. (1979). Consulting approaches: Two basic styles. *Training and Development Journal, 33*(9), 26–28.

Knapper, C., & Piccinin, S. (Eds.). (1999). *New directions for teaching and learning: No. 79. Using consultants to improve teaching.* San Francisco: Jossey-Bass.

Nyquist, J., & Wulff, D. (2001). Consultation using a research perspective. In K. Lewis & J. Lunde (Eds.), *Face to face: A sourcebook of individual consultation techniques for faculty/instructional developers* (2nd ed., pp. 45–62). Stillwater, OK: New Forums Press.

Sorcinelli, M. D., Austin, A. E., Eddy, P. L., & Beach, A. L. (2006). *Creating the future of faculty development: Learning from the past, understanding the present.* Bolton, MA: Anker.

Chapter 11

Lessons Learned from Developing a Learning-Focused Classroom Observation Form

Steven K. Jones, Kenneth S. Sagendorf, D. Brent Morris,
David Stockburger, Evelyn T. Patterson
United States Air Force Academy

We thank Bob Noyd for sharing his insights on an early version of the observation form, as well the Academy's Biology, Chemistry, and Physics Departments for assistance and feedback in our initial pilot testing.

At the United States Air Force Academy, we are attempting to go through a cultural transformation, making an overt shift toward a more learning-focused paradigm. In this chapter, we describe the nature of this transformation, as well as why we have chosen to move in this direction. We also describe one specific initiative we have undertaken: the development of a new learning-focused classroom observation form. We conclude by sharing a baker's dozen lessons we have learned about classroom observation, effective teaching, and faculty development in general as a result of having developed this form.

At the United States Air Force Academy (USAFA), we are attempting to go through a cultural transformation, making an overt shift from an instruction-centered paradigm toward a more learning-focused paradigm (Barr & Tagg, 1995; Huba & Freed, 2000; Tagg, 2003). As part of that transformation, we have taken on the ambitious task of operationally defining the learning focus within a classroom observation form. In this chapter, we describe our learning-focused transformation, explain why we have chosen to make it, and introduce readers to our observation form. We conclude with a baker's dozen lessons we've learned about classroom observation, teaching, and faculty development in general by engaging in this effort.

About the Air Force Academy

The mission of USAFA is to "educate, train, and inspire men and women to become officers of character, motivated to lead the United States Air Force in service to our nation." Located in Colorado Springs, Colorado, USAFA is a four-year, undergraduate institution, with an enrollment of approximately 4,400 students. These students (whom we call cadets) participate in a rigorous program consisting of academic courses (both within an academic major and within 102 semester hours of core classes required of all cadets), military training, mandatory athletic participation, and character-development programs. Upon graduation, cadets receive a Bachelor of Science degree and a commission as a Second Lieutenant in the United States Air Force.

One of the unique characteristics of USAFA is the high level of turnover we experience on our faculty. By design, the Academy tries to expose cadets to many different role models from the active duty Air Force. As a result, approximately 75 percent of our faculty members are military officers, almost all of whom have recently served in the operational Air Force. Furthermore, most of the military officers on the faculty are assigned to teach at USAFA for three to four years, after which time they will return to operational duty. The result is a military faculty that turns over very rapidly; we typically welcome approximately 125 new faculty members each year.

This rapid turnover poses a significant faculty development challenge. For the most part, our military faculty are not career educators, and many of them come to USAFA with little or no teaching experience. Furthermore, the short-term nature of their assignment is such that they must get up to speed with regard to their teaching duties very quickly. Obviously, having a robust faculty development program is an absolute must.

As an institution, we have responded to the faculty development challenge by creating a series of intentional learning experiences for faculty. Our Center for Educational Excellence provides an extensive faculty orientation program for new faculty members, as well as follow-on faculty development workshops throughout the academic year. We also use a "course director" system. Faculty members work under an experienced faculty member who is responsible for organizing and guiding a particular course. Therefore, new instructors typically step into existing courses with pre-written syllabi, course materials, and at least some assessment mechanisms. Within individual academic departments, this scaffolding is further supplemented by peer and supervisor mentoring, to include systematic classroom observation programs. Enhancing these classroom observation programs is the focus of this chapter.

Our Move to a Learning-Focused Paradigm

An intentional shift toward a learning focus is certainly not unique to the Air Force Academy. Indeed, nationwide, colleges and universities are engaging in conversations about what they want their students to learn, how they can best facilitate that learning, and how they can use assessment data to improve student learning in the future.

Several significant factors have led to the shift toward a learning focus. One has been an increasing call nationwide for accountability within colleges and universities. Several recent authors (for example, Bok, 2006; Hersh & Merrow, 2005) have provided critical examinations of college practices and have questioned whether colleges are accomplishing everything that they can (or should) be accomplishing. The issue of increased accountability has also gained national political attention, particularly with the release of the Spellings Commission Report, "A Test of Leadership: Charting the Future of U.S. Higher Education" (U.S.

Department of Education, 2006). It is clear that colleges and universities are being called upon as never before to demonstrate that they actually do promote meaningful learning in their students.

The increased emphasis on learning has also appeared in changing accreditation requirements. For example, the Higher Learning Commission of the North Central Association (which accredits USAFA) has recently adopted new accreditation criteria for all of its member schools. These criteria demand that we clearly articulate the learning goals we have for cadets, create systems that allow that learning to take place, and then assess the extent to which those learning goals are met (Higher Learning Commission, 2007).

The national call for accountability has coincided with heightened discussions of what types of learning should take place in college in the first place. In today's information age, the volume of readily available knowledge is growing exponentially. What is "known" today is likely to be very different from what will be "known" even a few years from now. Furthermore, modern technology (the Internet, PDAs, cell phones, and so on) is making the information that is known increasingly easy to access. Therefore, although a college education must still build students' foundational knowledge, it is clear that, by itself, knowledge acquisition is increasingly inadequate. In a national survey commissioned by the Association of American Colleges and Universities (2007), 63 percent of employers reported that recent college graduates lacked the intellectual and practical skills (teamwork, critical thinking skills, and so on) required in our increasingly global economy. Fifty-six percent of the employers also indicated that colleges and universities should do more to promote a sense of integrity and ethics. Clearly, organizing our college classes around acquisition of disciplinary knowledge is not enough. Other types of learning are needed as well.

At the Air Force Academy, we have spent substantial time over the last two years rethinking the desired outcomes of an Academy education. This included considerable consultation with AAC&U, whose recent (2007) publication "College Learning for the New Global Century" spells out the "essential learning outcomes" for students in the twenty-first century. Another major influence on outcomes development has been the United States Air Force, which has released similar guidance about the competencies required of new Air Force officers. The result of this work was the publication of new USAFA outcomes, shown in Table 11.1. These outcomes have been endorsed at all levels of the institution and now provide a target for all faculty, staff, and cadets.

The final factor contributing to the increased emphasis on learning is the burgeoning body of research about the factors that promote learning in college students. For example, educational research is very clear that students are not just passive vessels to be filled with content. Instead, they are active constructors, discoverers, and transformers of knowledge (see Campbell & Smith, 1997; Hake, 1998; for a more comprehensive discussion, see National Research Council, 2000). Therefore, if we at the Air Force

Table 11.1. USAFA Outcomes

Commission leaders of character who embody the Air Force core values are . . .

. . . committed to Societal, Professional, and Individual Responsibilities

    Ethical Reasoning and Action
    Respect for Human Dignity
    Service to the Nation
    Lifelong Development and Contributions
    Intercultural Competence and Involvement

. . . empowered by integrated Intellectual and Warrior Skills

    Quantitative and Information Literacy
    Oral and Written Communication
    Critical Thinking
    Decision Making
    Stamina
    Courage
    Discipline
    Teamwork

. . . grounded in essential Knowledge of the Profession of Arms and the Human and Physical Worlds

    Heritage and Application of Air, Space, and Cyberspace Power
    National Security and Full Spectrum of Joint and Coalition
       Warfare
    Civic, Cultural, and International Environments

Academy have any hope of achieving our lofty institutional outcomes, it is clear that our pedagogy must be one that is intentionally focused on cadet learning. As Biggs (1999, p. 63) points out, we can no longer say, "I taught them, but they didn't learn."

How Our Learning-Focused Paradigm Works

Saying that one is intentionally focused on cadet learning is one thing; actually doing it may be something else. As a result, we have found it necessary to discuss with our faculty what a learning focus really means. The basis of many of our conversations has been what course designers (for example, Fink, 2003; Wiggins, 1998) call "backwards design." That is, when considering a lesson, a course, or even the curriculum as a whole, the faculty member needs to ask, "What is it that I hope a cadet will get from this experience (lesson, course, four-year education) when it is over?" In short, our lessons, courses, and curricula need to be designed with the desired end-point in mind. We then need to use best pedagogical practices to develop learning experiences (in and out of the classroom) that are aligned with those desired learning goals, as well as build in timely, aligned assessment mechanisms to ensure that the desired learning actually took place. The results of those assessments are then fed back to both cadets and faculty to improve learning in the future. Our depiction of this learning-focused cycle is shown in Figure 11.1.

Figure 11.1. USAFA's Learning-Focused Cycle

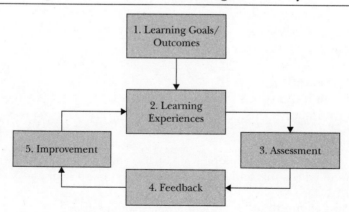

As we have worked with this model, we have discovered the critical importance of alignment between the learning goals, learning experiences, assessments, and feedback. Each component of the cycle must reflect and support the others in order to optimize student learning. Unfortunately, we have discovered that perfect alignment does not always happen. For example, consider a class that is designed to help cadets develop more sophisticated critical thinking skills. To be "in alignment," the learning experiences cadets have in that class should be designed to give them practice honing these skills, not just learning about the content of the discipline. The cadets should be assessed on how well they can think critically, not just on how they answer multiple-choice questions about course readings. The feedback the cadets receive should be aimed toward helping them think more critically, not just aimed at sorting them into piles, based on their grades in the course. And when cadets in the class try to improve, they should focus on improving specific thinking skills for which they are weak, not just focus on "working harder" in the class. *Alignment* means that everything in the class should be in line with the desired learning outcomes for the class.

Development of a Classroom Observation Form

We have spent many hours discussing the learning-focused cycle with faculty members at our institution, and it has been introduced in faculty convocations, regular campuswide e-mails and departmental immersions by our dean, and our internal campus publications. However, our faculty colleagues have said that they want more details. What would it look like to teach in a learning-focused way? How might teaching in this way affect faculty on a day-to-day basis? And what is the research evidence that would suggest that these changes are a good idea anyway? We have also faced tough questions from USAFA leadership, such as How are things going with the learning focus? and Is this having an impact on how faculty are teaching? In order to address each of these challenging questions, we designed a rubric so that our faculty had an instrument to measure the extent to which their teaching was, indeed, learning-focused. The current version of our rubric is included in Appendix A.

This rubric has gone through many, many revisions. When using previous versions, we frequently found ourselves using the rubric in a class, only to discover something we had not previously thought of. Or we had the realization that the rubric did not allow us to provide the best feedback to individual instructors. We even realized that we (members of the Academy's administrative staff) may not even be the best people to use the rubric in classroom observations in the first place. In short, we have learned a great deal. Table 11.2 summarizes the baker's dozen most important lessons we have learned as our rubric has evolved. Each of those lessons is described in more detail later in the chapter.

Table 11.2. Lessons Learned from Developing Our Classroom Observation Form

Our Baker's Dozen

What We Have Learned About Creating an Observation Form

1. Stay true to your educational philosophy.
2. Ensure that the form is grounded in the literature.
3. Highlight those things that are most important.
4. Make the form general enough that it can be used in multiple disciplines.
5. Observe courses multiple times.
6. Focus on the course (rather than the faculty member) as the level of analysis.

What We Have Learned About Effective Teaching

7. Teaching cannot be boiled down to a recipe.
8. Effective course design is critical.

What We Have Learned About the Process of Faculty Development

9. Know (and take advantage of) the institutional context.
10. Be sure to practice what you espouse.
11. Get faculty involved in the process.
12. Seek outside assistance.
13. Be flexible and willing to learn.

What We Have Learned About Creating an Observation Form

1. *Stay true to your educational philosophy.* We intentionally designed our observation form to be an operationalization of the learning-focus cycle, which our institution has endorsed. Therefore, we found it very important that the structure of the form correspond with the steps of the cycle. This is why, in the current form, we created distinct sections for 1) learning goals, 2) learning experiences, 3) assessment, and 4) feedback.

2. *Ensure that the form is grounded in the literature.* Faculty are understandably skeptical about new things, especially when those new things appear to make demands on their time or steer them in directions they are not accustomed to going. As a result, many of our faculty asked us to provide them with the relevant literature dealing with learning goals, learning experiences, assessment, and feedback. We quickly annotated every component of our observation rubric with the most salient research, and these annotations are reflected in our current form.

3. *Highlight those things that are most important.* In earlier versions of our form, we attempted to be as comprehensive as possible. So, in the "learning experiences" section, we tried to identify all of the possible factors that would distinguish effective from ineffective pedagogy. As we pilot tested those early versions, however, we found it very difficult to focus on all dimensions of the form while observing a class. Furthermore, some dimensions defied reliable quantification. We realized that we needed to make the form easier for observers to use.

To do this, we identified two "top-tier" questions for each section of the observation rubric. These top-tier questions, shown at the top of each section of the existing form, reflected those items that our pilot testing suggested were the most important things to look for. We also simplified the structure of the top-tier questions (making them simple YES-NO distinctions) so that we could answer them more reliably. These changes have simplified the task of observing classes tremendously. And although we can still provide informal feedback to instructors on other areas of the form (that is, in those items at the bottom of each section), we have found that the top-tier questions help us home in on our highest-priority area.

4. *Make the form general enough that it can be used in multiple disciplines.* Different disciplines require different ways of thinking (Arons, 1979, 1997; Donald, 2002; Durisen & Pilachowski, 2004), so a teaching technique that is effective in a chemistry course may not necessarily be effective in a history course. Therefore, we were careful to include general principles in our form, rather than more specific techniques. For example, the research (King, 1993; National Research Council, 2000) suggests that cadets will learn more if they do so within a conceptual framework, so we included an item reflecting this finding on our form. However, we did not try to prescribe what those conceptual frameworks should be, how those frameworks should be communicated to cadets, or how the frameworks should be invoked in class.

A significant benefit of having a general-purpose observation form is that instructors from within a particular discipline are able to observe classes in other disciplines. Our hope is that creating a general-purpose form will facilitate conversations about teaching and learning across departmental boundaries. The cross-disciplinary nature of this form is also consistent with other initiatives on our campus (for example, interdisciplinary "outcome teams" responsible for developing the USAFA outcomes across the entire curriculum) that aim to foster greater levels of integration across different functional units.

5. *Observe courses multiple times.* Our original observation form was written to allow a visitor to observe and comment on a single class. During our pilot testing, however, we realized that expecting faculty to be in the "facilitates learning best" category for every entry during every single class was unrealistic. (For example, we know that cadets benefit when they interact with one another in class, but it is probably unrealistic to expect that cadets will interact with one another during every single class session.) Therefore, we feared that our form could be perceived as either setting faculty up for failure or being so unattainable that faculty would simply write it off as unreasonable.

With this in mind, we made an important change. Rather than frame the form in terms of a single classroom observation, we framed it as a frequency measure, to be used over the course of an entire semester. So the data that we ultimately gather would not be whether cadets interacted with each other in a given class session; instead, it would be the percentage of class sessions that cadets interacted with one another. This reframing acknowledged that no instructor would meet all of the criteria for "facilitates learning best" in every class, but it would capture the prevalence of best practices across the semester. Obviously, informal feedback can still be provided to instructors on the basis of any single classroom observation.

6. *Focus on the course (rather than the faculty member) as the level of analysis.* In a similar vein, our original form was designed to focus attention on individual instructors ("Today, we're going to observe Dr. Smith."). However, after only a short time, it became apparent that our faculty were reluctant to endorse an observation form because the results might be used against them. Our original version was perceived as being too threatening.

We tried to make the observation process less threatening by focusing the form on the course ("Today, we're going to observe Physics 110.") rather than on an instructor. The Academy's course director system makes this quite easy to do. For instance, if we observe multiple sections of a core physics course, we could aggregate the data across the entire course before reporting the results to the course director.

What We Have Learned About Effective Teaching

1. *Teaching cannot be boiled down to a recipe.* Especially among our young, inexperienced faculty, it is not uncommon to hear questions about the "right" way to teach a course. However, there is no pedagogical silver bullet. The available research does have much to say about pedagogical best practices, but there is clearly no single best way for faculty members to do things. This truism has become even more apparent as we have observed a variety of courses, instructors, and teaching styles. Our general-purpose form does highlight some of the best practices (recognizing that doing so might encourage people to use them), but our goal is certainly not to prescribe any single teaching method.

2. *Effective course design is critical.* When we began pilot testing our observation rubric, we expected that we would spend most of our time talking about the pedagogies used by individual instructors. Although that has certainly happened to a degree, we have

actually found ourselves talking even more about course design. If a course is not intentionally designed to promote deep learning of meaningful student-learning outcomes, it will not score well on the rubric, no matter how it is taught. Therefore, we are currently planning an extended retreat for the course directors of our core courses, with the goal of helping them design the very best courses possible across the entire institution (for example, by clearly articulating their course learning goals and aligning them with the USAFA outcomes).

What We Have Learned About the Process of Faculty Development

1. *Know (and take advantage) of the institutional context.* The Air Force Academy is a unique institution, and some aspects of what we're doing here might not work successfully at other institutions. However, the same could likely be said about most colleges and universities, as each one has its own unique culture and its own way of doing business. The key is to be aware of the unique aspects of the institutional culture and to take advantage of them.

For instance, consider the unique faculty development challenges that we face at the Air Force Academy. Because of these challenges, our Center for Educational Excellence (which consists of four of the five authors of this chapter) is called on to take a proactive role. Our administration empowers us to promote a culture of learning and development at our institution—a role that involves us in institutional discussions beyond faculty development to include institutional outcomes, curriculum development, and assessment. We recognize that our situation may not be shared by faculty developers at other institutions. However, it is that culture, in part, that has allowed us to make quick progress with our observation form.

Another unique characteristic of the Air Force Academy is that robust classroom observation programs are already in place in departments across our campus. As a result, the idea of faculty members observing one another's classes is not new here. Rather than starting a new observation program, then, we see our efforts as a supplement to the programs that already exist, providing another way to give open, constructive feedback to faculty members about what they are doing in the classroom.

2. *Be sure to practice what you espouse.* Our learning-focused cycle is based largely on the idea of backwards design (Fink, 2003; Wiggins, 1998). That is, we encourage our faculty members to clarify their goals and then act in ways that are well suited to accomplish those goals. As we have proceeded, we have found it valuable to apply the same guidance to ourselves—to clarify the goals for our observation rubric and then behave in ways that are intentionally designed to accomplish them. In our case, we had three goals for our form: 1) to operationalize the learning focus for our faculty, 2) to encourage the use of best educational practices on our campus, and 3) to collect data to measure our improvement. We created our form to accomplish these three goals, and we have assessed, honed, and reassessed it many times to accomplish those goals more effectively. We will continue to do so.

3. *Get faculty involved in the process.* We are all too familiar with the struggle to bridge the gap that can sometimes exist between faculty and administration. Certainly, the faculty will not respond well if an observation form is perceived as something imposed on them from outsiders. Therefore, we have found it helpful to enlist the assistance of faculty members at every step of the way. Our goal is to have faculty take ownership of the learning focus (and consequently of the learning-focused observation rubric), so their engagement in the process, both in designing the form and in performing the observations, is absolutely necessary.

4. *Seek outside assistance.* At AAC&U's 2007 Greater Expectations Institute in Burlington, Vermont, we had the opportunity to share an earlier version of our form with Dee Fink. His 2003 book, *Creating Significant Learning Experiences,* helped us shape our rubric and frame our thinking about what was needed to help our faculty rethink teaching as facilitating student learning. Dr. Fink provided us with encouraging words that assured us we were headed in the right direction. He also suggested some areas that needed to be strengthened and gave us ideas for possible improvements. That external assistance was invaluable.

5. *Be flexible and willing to learn.* In each of our classroom observations, between two and four observers have been in the

classroom using the rubric. After each observation, we have met to gauge our agreement on each item of the form and to brainstorm what improvements to the form could be made. As a result, our form has gone through many modifications, and we have learned a great deal along the way. Despite the difficulties and strains on our patience, our work on the form has been very rewarding, and we are convinced that our persistent efforts have been worth it.

Our Use of the Form Thus Far

To date, we have piloted our form in the introductory classes of three departments: Biology, Chemistry, and Physics. In each department, we observed the instructors of a core course, required for all students on our campus.

One of the core courses we observed has recently gone through a significant redesign in an effort to make it well aligned with the learning focus. In that course, we consistently observed well-constructed learning goals and learning experiences. As a result, our primary contributions were in the areas of assessment and feedback. Following debriefs with faculty of that course, the course director has increased his focus on designing aligned assessment and feedback tools. The department is paying particular attention to course exams and other graded components of the class.

In the other two departments we observed, our experiences were somewhat different. We frequently observed faculty writing outlines on the board about what would be covered in a given class period. However, we rarely saw clearly articulated learning goals that were phrased in terms of what cadets would know or be able to do as a result of that coverage. The lack of clear learning goals made it challenging for us to make reliable judgments about the alignment of learning experiences, assessment, and feedback. For instance, it was difficult to judge whether the learning experiences in a class were well aligned with the learning goals when it was not immediately obvious what the underlying learning goals really were. We shared this dilemma with faculty teaching these courses, and, in one case, the discussion led to the creation of lesson-by-lesson learning goals. We are delighted that, even in its infancy, our use of the observation form has begun to drive instructor behavior toward strategies that improve student learning.

Future Uses of the Form

As we look ahead to the future, we see our observation form as being helpful at multiple levels of the Air Force Academy. At the level of the specific class session, this rubric provides us with a good catalyst for dialogue with individual instructors. By helping faculty become more aware of pedagogical best practices, the observation form can also provide faculty with a platform for their own self-evaluation, reflection, and self-improvement. Ultimately, it will also help faculty determine how well they are reaching and engaging their students.

At a course level, the observation form will enable our course directors to measure the degree to which their courses are learning-focused. This information will be especially helpful in improving courses over time and measuring the impact of specific course changes. For instance, what is the impact of changing (or even clarifying) the specific learning goals for particular lessons or sets of lessons in a course? How do such changes affect the overall "learning focus" of the course as a whole? Consistent use of this rubric would allow course directors to answer these questions.

At an institutional level, the observation form may furnish a different way of collecting and examining data on our educational practices. Although it does not measure student learning directly, the data it generates most likely correlate with direct measures of student learning. For instance, knowing the percentage of courses that have clearly articulated learning goals or offer assessments that are well aligned with those learning goals would probably help us predict, at least to some degree, the amount of meaningful learning that takes place in those courses. In this regard, the form could be used as a complement to the National Survey of Student Engagement (2005), which our cadets take every three years.

Although not our immediate intent, it is even conceivable that some version of this observation rubric could be used across multiple institutions. With the demand for accountability on campuses across the country, colleges and universities are struggling to find ways to measure the quality of their educational processes. Many have expressed concerns about ranking systems used in publications such as *U.S. News & World Report,* but a better solution to the quality controversy is not obvious. As one way to fill the void, perhaps colleges and universities could form consortia that volunteer to use this kind of classroom observation rubric on their campuses. Members of each consortium would share the resulting data and, ideally, their best practices as well.

Beyond classroom observation, our form could also provide the basis of a revised end-of-semester survey for cadets at the end of the semester. Similar to most institutions, our cadets complete surveys at the end of each semester about each of their courses. Currently, we are exploring the possibility of updating our survey so that it more closely reflects the steps of the learning-focused cycle. Our cadets are, arguably, the best observers of what goes on in their classes; aligning the survey with the classroom observation could give our faculty (as well as the institution as a whole) good feedback about the extent to which they are engaged in effective learning practices.

Conclusion

As with anything we work on in our positions, we know that the learning-focused classroom observation form is not a panacea. Fink (2003) describes six critical issues that need to be addressed to support faculty that seek to improve teaching and learning: 1) awareness, 2) encouragement, 3) time, 4) resources, 5) cooperative students, and 6) recognition and reward. Deciding to develop a classroom observation form addresses only a few of these issues. However, we have found doing so to be a valuable investment of our time and energy, and we look forward to implementing it more broadly in the months and years to come. It is our sincere hope that doing so will help move the Air Force Academy forward in its quest to be a truly learning-focused institution.

Appendix A

Learning-Focused Observation Form

(*Note:* The superscripts that follow the heading "Learning Goals" identify the references used to develop that section of the form. Please see "Sources Used in the Development of the Form" at the end of this appendix.)

The following form is designed to provide feedback to instructors, course directors, and senior leadership about the extent to which learning-focused practices are being used in USAFA courses. Data gathered using this form will be summarized by course, rather than by individual instructor.

COURSE BEING OBSERVED: _____

DATE: _____ **Learning Goals**[4, 5, 7, 8, 11, 13]

1. Are there learning goals specific to today's class?   YES   NO
2. Have learning goals been clearly articulated in terms of what cadets will know or be able to do?   YES   NO

If "YES," how did cadets receive feedback?

Follow-on feedback areas:

Criterion	Facilitates Learning Best		In Contrast to . . .
Challenging, yet achievable More than knowledge	LGs are appropriate for cadets' developmental level (challenging, yet achievable) [5, 9, 11, 20]		LGs too lofty or too simplistic for cadets' developmental level
	LGs reflect combination of knowledge, skills, & responsibilities [3, 4, 5, 8, 10, 11, 15, 21]	⟶	LGs reflect only knowledge acquisition

Learning Experiences

1. Are cadets engaged with course material, above and beyond merely being passive recipients of information? [11, 12, 14, 16, 17]   YES   NO

2. Are learning experiences well-aligned with learning goals? [7, 10]   YES   NO

If "YES," how did cadets receive feedback?

Follow-on feedback areas:

Criterion	Facilitates Learning Best		In Contrast to . . .
The role of the instructor	Facilitate cadet learning / accomplishment of learning goals (i.e., help cadets learn, using an appropriate combination and sequence of learning activities) [5, 6, 10, 20]		"Cover" course content
Best practices for creating deep learning	Cadets are motivated to learn (e.g., because they see the relevance of the topic) [5, 7, 15, 18, 19]	⟶	Cadets are not motivated to learn (e.g., because they don't see the relevance of the topic)
	Cadets are given good sources of information and ideas [9, 10]	⟶	Cadets are not given good sources of information and ideas
	Cadets' learning is within a conceptual framework [12, 15]	⟶	Cadets' learning is disorganized, disjointed
	Cadets have opportunities to confront their misconceptions [5, 15]	⟶	Cadets do not have opportunities to confront their misconceptions

(*Continued*)

Follow-on feedback areas: (*Continued*)

Criterion	*Facilitates Learning Best*		*In Contrast to . . .*
	Cadets' tasks are challenging (5, 15)	⟶	Cadets' tasks are too easy / hard
	Cadets spend plentiful time on task (14, 15)	⟶	Cadets spend little time on task
	Cadets interact with instructor (2, 7, 11, 16)	⟶	Cadets do not interact with instructor
	Cadets interact with each other (2, 7, 14, 16, 17)	⟶	Cadets do not interact with each other
	Cadets have opportunity to reflect on what and how they are learning (9. 10, 21)	⟶	Cadets do not have opportunity to reflect on learning

Assessment

1. At some point during class, are cadets required to display what they have learned? (5, 11, 21)   YES   NO

2. Was assessment well aligned with the learning goal(s) (4, 7, 10, 19, 21)   YES   NO

If "YES," how did cadets receive feedback?

Follow-on feedback areas:

Criterion	*Facilitates Learning Best*		*In Contrast to . . .*
Inclusiveness of Display	*All* cadets display their learning [5, 11, 21]		*No* cadets display their learning
Goal/Purpose	Used to facilitate cadet learning (i.e., educative) [1, 5, 10, 20, 21]	⟶	Used exclusively to give cadets a grade (i.e., auditive)
Authenticity	Assessment requires cadets to use their learning to complete a realistic task [10, 21]	⟶	Assessment asks cadets to simply recite their knowledge or follow an established procedure
Criteria and Standards	Cadets are clear on the criteria and standards used to evaluate their work [10, 21]	⟶	Cadets are not clear on the criteria and standards used to evaluate their work

Feedback

1. Do cadets receive feedback (from instructor or other cadets) about what they've learned? [10, 16, 18, 21]   YES   NO
2. Does feedback provide information that will help cadets improve their learning? [1, 5, 19, 21]   YES   NO

If "YES," how did cadets receive feedback?

Follow-on observation areas:

Criterion	Facilitates Learning Best		In Contrast to . . .
Inclusiveness of feedback	All cadets receive feedback on their learning [10, 16, 18, 21]		No cadets receive feedback on their learning
Promptness of feedback	Feedback is provided quickly, so that it can be used to improve [10, 11, 19]	⟶	Feedback is provided slowly, making it difficult to use for improvement
Improvement/ Use of Feedback	Instructor and cadets use feedback to improve learning [1, 5, 10, 21]	⟶	Instructor and cadets do not use feedback to improve learning

Sources Used in the Development of the Form

1. Angelo, T. A., & Cross, K. P. (1993). *Classroom assessment techniques: A handbook for college teachers* (2nd ed.). San Francisco: Jossey-Bass.
2. Astin, A. (1993). *What matters in college? Four critical years revisited.* San Francisco: Jossey-Bass.
3. Association of American Colleges and Universities. (2007). *College learning for the new global century: A report from the National Leadership Council for Liberal Education & America's Promise.* Washington, DC: Author.
4. Association of American Colleges and Universities. (2002). *Greater expectations: A new vision for learning as a nation goes to college.* Washington, DC: Author.
5. Bain, K. (2004). *What the best college teachers do.* Cambridge, MA: Harvard University Press.
6. Barr, R. B., & Tagg, J. (1995). From teaching to learning: A new paradigm for undergraduate education. *Change, 27*(6), 13–25.
7. Biggs, J. (1999). What the student does: Teaching for enhanced learning. *Higher Education Research and Development, 18*(1), 57–75.

8. Bok, D. (2006). *Our underachieving colleges: A candid look at how much students learn and why they should be learning more.* Princeton, NJ: Princeton University Press.

9. Bonwell, C. C., & Eison, J. A. (1991). *Active learning: Creating excitement in the classroom.* San Francisco: Jossey-Bass.

10. Fink, L. D. (2003). *Creating significant learning experiences: An integrated approach to designing college courses.* San Francisco: Jossey-Bass.

11. Gardiner, L. F. (1998, Spring). Why we must change: The research evidence. *Thought & Action, 15,* 71–87.

12. King, A. (1993). From sage on the stage to guide on the side. *College Teaching, 41*(1), 30–35.

13. Kuh, G. D., Kinzie, J., Schuh, J. H., & Whitt, E. J. (2005). *Student success in college: Creating conditions that matter.* San Francisco: Jossey-Bass.

14. McKeachie, W. J., Pintrich, P. R., Lin, Y., & Smith, D. A. F. (1986). *Teaching and learning in the college classroom: A review of the research literature.* Ann Arbor, MI: National Center for Research to Improve Postsecondary Teaching and Learning, University of Michigan.

15. National Research Council. (2000). *How people learn: Brain, mind, experience, and school.* Washington, DC: National Academy Press.

16. Pascarella, E. T., & Terenzini, P. T. (1991). *How college affects students.* San Francisco: Jossey-Bass.

17. Prince, M. (2004). Does active learning work? A review of the research. *Journal of Engineering Education, 93*(3), 223–231.

18. Tagg, J. (2004, May–June). Alignment for learning: Reorganizing classrooms and campuses. *About Campus,* 8–18.

19. Walvoord, B. E., & Anderson, V. J. (1998). *Effective grading: A tool for learning and assessment.* San Francisco: Jossey-Bass.

20. Weimer, M. (2002). *Learner-centered teaching: Five key changes to practice.* San Francisco: Jossey-Bass.

21. Wiggins, G. (1998). *Educative assessment: Designing assessments to inform and improve student performance.* San Francisco: Jossey-Bass.

References

Arons, A. B. (1979). Some thoughts on reasoning capacities implicitly expected of college students. In J. Lochhead & J. Clement (Eds.), *Cognitive process instruction: Research on teaching thinking skills* (pp. 209–216). Philadelphia: The Franklin Institute Press.

Arons, A. B. (1997). *Teaching introductory physics.* New York: Wiley.

Association of American Colleges and Universities. (2007). *College learning for the new global century: A report from the National Leadership Council for Liberal Education and America's Promise.* Washington, DC: Author.

Barr, R., & Tagg, J. (1995, November/December). From teaching to learning—A new paradigm for undergraduate education. *Change, 27*(6), 12–25.

Biggs, J. B. (1999). What the student does: Teaching for enhanced learning. *Higher Education Research and Development,18*(1), 57–75.

Bok, D. (2006). *Our underachieving colleges: A candid look at how much students learn and why they should be learning more.* Princeton, NJ: Princeton University Press.

Campbell, W. E., & Smith, K. A. (Eds.). (1997). *New paradigms for college teaching.* Edina, MN: Interaction Book Company.

Donald, J. G. (2002). *Learning to think: Disciplinary perspectives.* San Francisco: Jossey-Bass.

Durisen, R., & Pilachowski, C. (2004). Decoding astronomical concepts. In D. Pace & J. Middendorf (Eds.), *New directions for teaching and learning: No. 98. Decoding the disciplines: Helping students learn disciplinary ways of thinking* (pp. 33–43). San Francisco: Jossey-Bass.

Fink, L. D. (2003). *Creating significant learning experiences: An integrated approach to designing college courses.* San Francisco: Jossey-Bass.

Hake, R. R. (1998). Interactive-engagement vs. traditional methods: A six-thousand student survey of mechanics test data for introductory physics courses. *American Journal of Physics, 66*(1), 64–74.

Hersh, R. H., & Merrow, J. (Eds.). (2005). *Declining by degrees: Higher education at risk.* New York: Palgrave Macmillan.

Higher Learning Commission. (2007). *Institutional accreditation: An overview.* Retrieved March 7, 2008, from http://hlcommission.org/download/Overview07.pdf

Huba, M. E., & Freed, J. E. (2000). *Learner-centered assessment on college campuses: Shifting the focus from teaching to learning.* Boston: Allyn & Bacon.

King, A. (1993). From sage on the stage to guide on the side. *College Teaching, 41*(1), 30–35.

National Research Council. (2000). *How people learn: Brain, mind, experience, and school.* Washington, DC: National Academy Press.

National Survey of Student Engagement. (2005). *Exploring different dimensions of student engagement.* Retrieved November 17, 2005, from http://nsse.iub.edu/pdf/NSSE2005_annual_ report.pdf

Tagg, J. (2003). *The learning paradigm college.* Bolton, MA: Anker.

U.S. Department of Education. (2006). *A test of leadership: Charting the future of U.S. higher education.* Washington, DC: Author.

Wiggins, G. (1998). *Educative assessment: Designing assessments to inform and improve student performance.* San Francisco: Jossey-Bass.

Chapter 12

Reported Long-Term Value and Effects of Teaching Center Consultations

Wayne Jacobson, Donald H. Wulff, Stacy Grooters,
Phillip M. Edwards, Karen Freisem
University of Washington

The authors would like to acknowledge Jennie Dorman, Kate Dunsmore, Irina Gendelman, Jason Hendryx, Margy Lawrence, Lana Rae Lenz, and Riki Thompson for their assistance in developing the survey and analyzing responses.

We regularly ask clients for feedback on their recent consultations with Center for Instructional Development and Research (CIDR) staff, but in the past we have not systematically assessed our longer-term contributions to the teaching of our clients. We recently surveyed faculty and teaching assistants who consulted with CIDR one to five years ago and found that many former clients highly valued CIDR's contribution to the development of their teaching. However, some of the most highly valued benefits they identified were not limited to what they did each day in class. This chapter identifies benefits of consulting with a teaching center that clients reported valuing one to five years after the consultation.

Since the emergence of teaching and learning centers in the latter half of the twentieth century, scholars increasingly have emphasized the importance of self-assessment as an essential component of faculty development programs (Centra, 1976; Frantz, Beebe, Horvath, Canales, & Swee, 2005; Plank, Kalish, Rohdieck, & Harper, 2005;

Sorcinelli, 2002). Purposes include both summative (such as documenting achievement and justifying the use of resources) and formative (such as improving services and setting examples that can promote institutional accountability). Sorcinelli (2002) suggests that faculty developers can use program assessment not only to demonstrate "that we do what we say we do" (p. 16) but also to satisfy demands for accountability to administrators.

In an effort to understand more about the assessment of faculty development programs, Chism and Szabó (1997–1998) conducted a survey with a sample of two hundred institutions in the United States and Canada. They concluded that faculty developers have begun to heed calls to assess their own services, particularly with the use of participation numbers and satisfaction surveys to assess the success of faculty development events. The researchers noted, though, that fewer than 20 percent of their respondents always or usually evaluated the impact of their services on users' teaching.

Brinko and Menges (1997) note that instructional consultants in centers rarely seek to assess the impact of their consultations. Certainly, there are those who assess consultation services, usually through measures of satisfaction obtained immediately upon completion of the consultation process (Fink & Bauer, 2001) or through occasional assessment of the use of consultations (for example, Wilson, 1986). However, any long-term effects of consultations are rarely assessed.

This chapter describes our attempt to begin addressing this challenge of identifying the long-term effects of our teaching center's consultation services. We designed a client survey that attempts to go beyond user satisfaction by asking former clients to report the value and ongoing effects of their consultations with our staff. We begin with a brief overview of the work of the Center for Instructional Development and Research (CIDR), followed by a description of the survey and a discussion of responses we received from former clients.

CIDR Services, Programs, and Resources

The CIDR has been a resource for teaching and learning at the University of Washington (UW) for nearly twenty-five years. Primarily a consulting center for UW faculty and TAs, CIDR also provides a wide range of additional programs and services for the UW teaching community: we foster campus dialogue on teaching issues through our Quarterly Forum on Teaching and Learning; we play a central role in hosting the Annual Teaching and Learning Symposium, which features scholarship of teaching and learning projects by UW faculty and graduate students. In addition, each fall, we host the Annual TA Conference on Teaching and Learning for 700 to 750 new graduate TAs, as well as work annually with 120 to 150 international graduate students through CIDR's International TA Program. CIDR staff members also play central roles in a number of the UW Graduate School's Preparing Future Faculty initiatives. Finally, we have developed an extensive set of resource materials and Web guides to help faculty and TAs address their teaching and learning questions.

Though we are well known at our institution for these programs and resources, the core of CIDR's work has always remained individual consultations for faculty, TAs, and departments. We annually consult with individuals representing 100–110 different academic units at our institution on a wide range of questions related to teaching, learning, and assessment. During the 2006–2007 academic year, approximately 50 percent of our nearly 700 consultation services were for faculty members, and approximately 35 percent were for graduate TAs. The remaining 15 percent were for administrators and other university leaders. Just over 60 percent of our consultations focused on the individual faculty member or TA's course; 30 percent focused on departmental questions, such as curriculum development or program assessment, and the remaining 10 percent focused on university-wide or off-campus issues.

Because of the central role of consulting in our work, CIDR has made it a regular practice to ask for feedback on our individual consultations each quarter. This practice allows clients to provide anonymous feedback to our staff and provides a valuable client perspective on how we can continue to develop our services for the UW teaching community. Response rates to requests for feedback in the past have typically been 30 to 40 percent and have been as high as 75 percent since we moved the feedback survey form online in 2005.

Faculty and TA responses to these quarterly feedback surveys have given us confidence that many find our consultations highly valuable. Our 2006–2007 rating for the overall value of consultations averaged 4.8 (on a 0 to 5 scale, with 5 = "highly valuable"), and responses to open-ended questions on our quarterly feedback form reveal more specifically what clients value about CIDR's individual consultation services (see Table 12.1).

Though we learn a great deal by regularly asking clients for feedback on their recent work with us, we also realize this feedback is limited. Our hope is that consultations make a lasting contribution to a client's teaching, but other than anecdotal reports from clients who returned to consult with us again, we have little basis for understanding the extent of longer-term contributions we might be making. Thus, to begin identifying these effects, we decided in spring 2007 to survey individuals who had consulted

Table 12.1. Sample 2006–2007 Responses to the Quarterly Feedback Question, "What aspect of your work with CIDR helped you the most?"

A great resource for anyone who is entering unfamiliar territory or needs assistance in actively improving their teaching.

Enormously helpful in working with me and my co-instructor to think through questions of course design, to maximize the integration among the various assignments, and to manage the (sometimes quite complicated) questions of how to assess student work for the class.

Wonderful in getting me to think through my goals for the students, and to consider the best ways to present information. . . . As always, he assisted me in organizing my thinking. He has a talent for presenting options, and letting new ideas emerge from the discussion.

The consultant's wealth of experience is so valuable when trying out something that is new or different for me to use in the classroom. She's an excellent listener and so her suggestions are relevant to the issue at hand.

Learning how to more clearly articulate my learning objectives for the class and how to design the course and assignments with those goals in mind. . . . As a result, I feel students have a much clearer sense of the class and what they should take from it.

You guys rock.

with CIDR during the preceding five years (autumn 2001 through spring 2006) and ask for their current perceptions of the value and effects of their earlier work with us.

Survey and Sample Preparation

CIDR staff worked together to develop a set of survey questions to address our long-term feedback concerns. Our goal was to keep the survey brief and direct, on the assumption that people would be less likely to complete a lengthy survey and more likely to provide a higher level of detail in their responses if they had fewer questions to address.

We limited our questions to topics that could be answered by any of our clients, independent of discipline, academic rank, or CIDR service. We were also careful to develop questions that could be answered meaningfully through retrospective, reflective self-report. For example, we did not ask respondents to rate their own teaching effectiveness (which would require data of other types beyond reflective self-report) but rather, to rate the effects of our services on their teaching (which could be answered based on the client's memory of work done with CIDR).

We chose to request a combination of numerical ratings and open-ended responses. Ratings questions asked respondents to rate the extent to which consulting with CIDR had affected their teaching, the value of their work with CIDR, and the likelihood that they might recommend CIDR to a colleague. Open-ended questions were paired with each of the ratings questions, asking respondents to identify examples of effects on their teaching, specific benefits of their work with CIDR, and both recommendations and further opportunities for CIDR. Finally, since we received significantly higher response rates after moving our quarterly client feedback form online, we chose to administer the survey entirely online (see Appendix A for the printed version). We identified all consultation clients in our database between autumn 2001 and spring 2006. From this group, we removed all clients who were also working with CIDR during the current academic year (2006–2007) in order to avoid confusing effects of current CIDR consultations with effects of consultations in earlier years. We also removed clients who had consulted with CIDR on departmental issues. We are highly interested in the long-term effects of our services to departments, but we determined that a survey with this goal would require different questions, and it was not clear in every case that the contact person for the service in our database would always be the best person to comment on departmentwide effects. Because the survey addressed effects of individual consultation services, we also chose not to address the effects of CIDR events, programs, or resources.

Because clients over the five-year period included graduate students, many of whom had since completed their degrees and left the university, we located current e-mail addresses for all individuals on the survey list. After removing clients from the current academic year, departmental clients, and clients for whom we could not locate current e-mail addresses, we had a list of 784 former individual consultation clients to contact for the survey.

Finally, we created five identical versions of the survey (one for each of the five academic years represented in the sample) and sent each former client a unique e-mail linking them directly to the version of the survey that corresponded to the most recent year they had worked with us. The e-mail invitation to complete the survey was sent out in March 2007, followed by a reminder e-mail request ten days later.

Results

We received a total of 170 responses, giving us an overall response rate of 22 percent. The response rate for the most recent year (2005–2006) was 29 percent and varied from 18 to 22 percent across the four earlier years. Nearly 60 percent of respondents indicated that they had consulted with CIDR one to three times; 20 percent indicated consulting four to six times, and 20 percent indicated seven or more times.

The profile of our respondents represented the full range of academic disciplines and ranks that CIDR typically works with in an academic year. In comparison with the disciplinary distribution of CIDR's individual clients for 2006–2007 (see Table 12.2), humanities clients are underrepresented among the respondents, while clients in the sciences and health sciences are somewhat overrepresented. The proportion of tenure-track faculty is higher than it is among CIDR's individual clients for 2006–2007, while the proportion of graduate students at the time of service is somewhat lower (see Table 12.3).

Table 12.2. Academic Disciplines Represented by Respondents in Comparison to Disciplines Represented by CIDR's 2006–2007 Individual Clients

Discipline	Survey	2006–2007
Engineering	14%	13%
Health sciences	9%	4%
Humanities	8%	24%
Sciences	29%	20%
Social sciences	19%	22%
Other professional schools	14%	16%
Not specified	6%	0%

Table 12.3. Summary of Academic Ranks Represented by Respondents in Comparison to Ranks Represented by CIDR's 2006–2007 Individual Clients

Academic Rank	Survey	2006–2007
Tenure-track faculty	40.0%	29.8%
Non-tenure-track faculty	15.8%	16.3%
Graduate students	38.2%	49.4%
Other	3.0%	4.3%

Ratings

We began analyzing the data by calculating responses to the three ratings questions, shown in Table 12.4. In examining the ratings in relation to different demographic categories, we found no significant difference in overall ratings as a function of discipline, academic rank, or year of service. We identified a high, positive correlation (Kendall's tau = 0.738, $p < 0.01$ [2-tailed]) between the extent to which respondents said their teaching was

Table 12.4. Mean Responses to Ratings Questions
(5 = Highly Valuable, 0 = Not At All Valuable)

Ratings Questions	Mean	Median	Mode
2. To what extent has your teaching (or how you think about teaching) been affected as a result of your work with CIDR?	3.8	4	4
3. Overall, how valuable has your work with CIDR been?	4.1	4	5
6. If a colleague asked for your help or advice about teaching, how likely would you be to mention any of the services offered by CIDR?	4.5	5	5

affected (question 2) and their perception of the value of consultations (question 3). Moderate, positive correlations were observed between the likelihood of referring a colleague (question 6) and the perceived value of consultations (Kendall's tau = 0.492, $p < 0.01$ [2-tailed]), as well as between the likelihood of referral and the extent to which teaching had been affected (Kendall's tau = 0.432, $p < 0.01$ [2-tailed]). The number of times that the respondent met with a consultant exhibited only low, positive correlation with the perceived value of consultations (Kendall's tau = 0.346, $p < 0.01$ [2-tailed]) and the likelihood of referring a colleague (Kendall's tau = 0.210, $p < 0.01$ [2-tailed]). When interpreting the results of these nonparametric statistics, we concluded that characteristics of the consultation itself were far more influential than the client's academic discipline or rank, the number of years since the consultation, or the number of consultations. To begin identifying these qualitative attributes, we turned to an analysis of responses to open-ended survey questions.

Open-Ended Responses

After our preliminary analysis of responses to the ratings questions, we proceeded to code responses to the open-ended questions. We assigned CIDR staff to working groups associated with particular questions. Staff reviewed responses, developed a coding system, individually coded responses, met with working groups to compare coding decisions, and came to a final consensus on codes to assign to each response. The coding system that emerged included fourteen broad categories (for example, "opportunities for reflection" or "services CIDR offers") with three to six specific codes in each. We assigned multiple codes to some individual responses, based on the length and complexity of the response. Then, in order to help us identify the aspects of individual CIDR consultations that were both widely and highly valued, we reviewed both the frequency of responses assigned to each code and the aggregate ratings for responses associated with each code.

In the following paragraphs, we report 1) effects of individual consultations that were the most widely and highly valued, 2) benefits of individual consultations that were the most widely and highly valued, 3) recommendations and opportunities for CIDR that were the most frequently identified, and 4) comments by respondents who gave relatively lower ratings overall.

Effects of Individual Consultations That Were Most Widely and Highly Valued. The first open-ended question asked respondents to provide examples of ways that their teaching had been affected as a result of their work with CIDR. In our analysis of responses to this question, we identified response codes that applied to more than 10 percent of responses, and from among those, identified the codes associated with the highest ratings by respondents. The three most highly and widely valued effects of individual consultations are identified in Table 12.5.

Table 12.5. Most Highly Rated, Frequently Occurring Types of Responses to the Question, "Please give one or more examples of ways that your teaching (or how you think about teaching) has been affected as a result of your work with CIDR."

Type of Response	N	Mean Rating: Effect on Teaching	Mean Rating: Value	Mean Rating: Likely to Recommend
Change in Practices	59	4.0	4.4	4.7
Change in Perspective	38	4.3	4.5	4.6
Student Feedback	34	3.9	4.4	4.8

The most frequent responses to this question were those that indicated a *change in teaching practices.* These were responses that indicated clients had consulted with CIDR on a specific teaching-related question or problem, and as a result, they were able to make constructive changes in their ongoing teaching practices. For example:

- Through my consultation with CIDR I have put more of an emphasis on keeping students apprised of the big picture and how individual lectures and homework assignments support the learning objectives of the course.
- I had a . . . senior seminar in which a student "shut down" the conversation and I couldn't revive it. I contacted CIDR for advice. I now begin every seminar course with a reading and group discussion about "how to seminar" . . . It has made a huge impact on the quantity and quality of the conversations.
- They helped tremendously when I needed to convert my small-class teaching style to serve the needs of a large lecture class. They assisted with assignment design, syllabus design, articulation of learning goals, and test design. They also helped me with ideas for making a large lecture (100+) class interactive with opportunities for active student participation.

The highest ratings were not associated with these changes in teaching practices, however, but with the second most frequent type of response: those indicating a *change in perspective* that has continued to influence their teaching:

- I think more about the student for whom everything is hard. What it might mean to be uncomfortable speaking one's mind in front of a group.
- Considering the student voice . . . began with this work with CIDR and is something I have continued in my tenure-track position at another university.
- I benefited from the sense that I was not teaching "in isolation" and that I was part of a larger community that cared about what was going on in the classroom.

A third type of response that was both frequently occurring and highly rated was the set of responses that described *learning to work constructively with student feedback*:

- I had trouble imagining how to obtain substantial, open-ended feedback from a large class and then make meaningful sense out of the volume of information. Now, I regularly get this kind of feedback and cluster/code it similarly to the way I saw in my CIDR consultations.
- It has helped me understand and use the student ratings in a constructive way, by modifying course content in response to both the midterm interview and final ratings.

Benefits of Individual Consultations That Were Most Widely and Highly Valued. Our second open-ended question asked people to identify the primary benefits they had received from consulting with CIDR. The three most highly and widely valued benefits are identified in Table 12.6. In response to this question, two types of responses occurred with the highest frequency, and the most highly valued of those was the benefit of *CIDR staff expertise*. Examples of responses focusing on staff expertise included the following:

- Their expertise in student learning helps me to view my courses differently.
- Having CIDR experts share the depth of their expertise and their knowledge of what other instructors and programs have done successfully in the past. The CIDR consultants listen to

Table 12.6. Most Highly Rated, Frequently Occurring Types of Responses to the Question, "What were the primary benefits you received from working with CIDR?"

Type of Response	N	Mean Rating: Effect on Teaching	Mean Rating: Value	Mean Rating: Likely to Recommend
CIDR Expertise	31	4.4	4.6	4.8
Change in Practices	31	4.1	4.4	4.7
Change in Perspective	27	3.9	4.1	4.6

individual instructors needs and adapt solutions accordingly, i.e. we don't simply get a "one-size-fits-all" solution.

- CIDR staff was very attentive and knowledgeable. Since they had worked with people in my field before, they knew what common problems were and they could tell me what had worked and what had not. More importantly, they were able to tell me what people in other fields were doing in their classes and how their experiences could help me.

The other most frequently occurring response was the second most highly rated: the benefit of having made lasting *changes in teaching practices*. Examples included the following:

- I create clearer more achievable objectives, I teach more precisely to those objectives. I vary my activities to a greater degree with students, better reaching students with a range of learning styles. I solicit feedback in a variety of ways.
- Assessing student knowledge through classroom discussion (integrating questions in lectures)
- New ideas for lectures, resources to improve style and efficiency for teaching, seeing teaching not as a burden that takes away from research

Although respondents who identified changes in teaching practices as beneficial indicated valuing their consultations with CIDR, some also expressed frustration with challenges they faced in implementing these changes:

- Good teaching means nothing to . . . the faculty chair. Extended efforts are great for students, but counter productive to promotion.
- Lack of departmental support, little concern given to undergrads' needs.

After CIDR expertise and changes in teaching practices, the next most frequently identified benefits were those related to *change in perspective* on teaching:

- The one-to-one post-observation interview with a CIDR representative was a wonderful moment to talk "teaching" . . . It made me realize that—regardless of what research and writing I do—my time in front of a class is a large part of my academic experience and, in order to fully enjoy that time, I can focus on the joy of sharing ideas with my students.

- It was great to talk with someone who'd visited lots of different classes and seen how they worked or didn't work. It made me feel less alone in some of the problems I was having, and also helped me work to improve my teaching.

Recommendations and Opportunities for CIDR That Were Most Frequently Identified by Respondents. Our next open-ended questions asked respondents to identify recommendations for improving CIDR services and future opportunities for CIDR. Our most frequent type of response ($n = 88$) to the request for recommendations was *no recommendation*. The second most frequent type of response ($n = 36$) was a desire for CIDR services to have *more visibility*. For example:

- Most teachers can use some feedback and can stand to improve their teaching. I wonder how many know this resource is available?

Several ($n = 33$) identified recommendations for improvements related to particular *CIDR services*.

- Spend . . . a little more time to help the professor determine what he/she wants from CIDR. All too often, we just come because we know we need help, but we're not always good at identifying what exactly we need help with.
- I found conversations most useful when they were very concrete.

Just as many respondents ($n = 33$) indicated only to *continue what we are doing*:

- Can't think of anything. You're doing a great job.
- Nothing, really. You strike an excellent balance between promoting best practices according to the latest educational research and dealing with real life teaching situations that the literature overlooks.

Our request for recommendations was followed by an invitation to suggest further opportunities for CIDR to assist instructors or departments. Responses to the request for opportunities were similar to responses to the previous question. Our most frequent type of response ($n = 101$) was *no recommendation*. The second most frequent type of response ($n = 44$) was *more visibility* for CIDR services. For example:

- I think just being more present. I don't think that faculty always know just how much benefit can come from talking to people at CIDR. A little bit of time spent with a consultant saves enormous time/energy/sometimes misery (!) later. Maybe sell yourselves more (yucky process, but the product you have is SO good!).

Several respondents ($n = 36$) suggested opportunities related to a variety of different *CIDR services*. Examples included:

- The only thing that I recommend is for CIDR to provide opportunities that are not perceived as too time and energy consuming.
- I would suggest they become advocates for students and somehow get information . . . to department heads and student listservs so that students graduating and entering the job market know what . . . a teaching portfolio is.

Finally, here too we had many respondents ($n = 15$) who indicated that we continue *what we are doing*:

- I think CIDR should continue their work as it is. You guys are doing a fantastic job.
- I have trouble thinking of how you could do more, since your activities are so numerous and varied.

Comments by Respondents Who Gave Relatively Lower Ratings. We identified twenty-seven respondents whose combined score for the three ratings questions was a total of 9 or less. Among those twenty-seven, ten offered no comments indicating dissatisfaction with CIDR, and ten indicated that their relatively lower rating was based on limited contact with CIDR. For example:

- In my limited experience, the service was very helpful.
- If I taught more, I know I'd have used your services more. I have recommended you to other people and spoken highly of you.

Of the remaining seven respondents who gave us relatively lower ratings, four indicated that CIDR did not help them achieve a desired outcome; for one of these four, the perceived lack of help was due to the respondent's time constraints as an adjunct:

- It was my first time teaching, I was very nervous and wanted someone to validate that I was doing the right thing. That's what I got from you guys. But the things suggested were more than I was willing to do as an adjunct.

For three of the four, this perception was based in part on their student ratings; for example,

- CIDR was extremely helpful multiple times in helping me to redesign courses, get feedback from students, and work on improving my teaching. Unfortunately, my issues seemed to be quite intractable. No one could figure out why my student evaluations were relatively low—not colleagues, TAs, or CIDR staff. This is probably a fairly unusual situation.

The last three respondents who gave a composite rating of 9 or less expressed a perception that CIDR is not aware of the needs or challenges faced in their classes or their disciplines:

- I think the person who observed my class missed a lot because she wasn't in my field and therefore couldn't understand the content.
- Be more in touch with the sensitivity of new TAs—there are discipline differences, and sometimes TAs can view CIDR advisers as preachy or basing wide judgments about TAs based on limited evidence.

- CIDR's "one size fits all" approach does not take into account the different needs of students in different majors or the different abilities of students in different majors. CIDR also suffers from this overly liberal assumption that students are always right and the best instructors cater to their whims. Students are almost always going to favor less work and higher grades—when instructors are punished for inflicting standards, in a school with rampant grade inflation and plummeting standards, you know that the system is broken.

We don't want to place inordinate weight on comments made by these seven individuals (4 percent of our total number of respondents). We have many more responses in this survey and in our regular client feedback indicating that faculty and TAs recognize and appreciate our efforts to ground our work in the context of their disciplines, their departments, and their immediate teaching situations. We have received similar positive feedback on our efforts to help clients assess their teaching in more complex and substantive ways than only surveying student opinions at the end of the course. Based on this other feedback we have received, we do not take these respondents' observations as representative of CIDR's work overall.

However, even though these comments seem to represent the exception rather than the rule, we think there are lessons that can be learned from the responses of these seven individuals. First, these comments prompt us to be vigilant in reviewing how consistently our consulting practices reflect our intended approaches to consulting, and also how effectively we train new staff for their roles as consultants. Second, these comments confirm some important features of our work. Much of our work is based on a recognition of disciplinary distinctions and the unique set of contexts each person is negotiating in his or her own teaching. We also regularly inform clients that their ratings won't necessarily improve as a result of their efforts to make changes in their teaching. These comments confirm for us that when clients don't perceive our work in these ways, for whatever reason, they value their work with us much less than when clients perceive it as we intend them to.

Discussion

We found this survey helpful for learning more about the ongoing effects of our services, including both reported effects on our clients' teaching and unanticipated effects that went beyond direct effects to their classroom practices. We found that those who gave CIDR the highest ratings are those who also reported changes in their thinking or in their teaching practices as a result of their work with CIDR, and many of these described the effects of those changes as ongoing: present-tense practices or perceptions are attributed to past-tense work with CIDR. In many ways, these responses confirmed what one might hope to hear from faculty and TAs who came to a teaching center: people who perceived that our services affected their teaching valued their work with us.

However, ratings also raised additional, unexpected questions for us. First, clients rated the value of our services more highly than they rated the effect of our services on their teaching. What, in addition to effect on their teaching, did clients value about our services? Second, clients rated their likelihood to recommend us more highly than the value of our services or the effect on their teaching. What, in addition to value and effect, would motivate them to recommend us? Responses to open-ended questions suggest at least five values added by teaching centers that go beyond direct effects on classroom practices.

First, some respondents noted that they simply didn't teach very much and so had little basis for identifying effects on their teaching. However, they still found it valuable to meet with a consultant, discuss their questions, and gain additional perspective on teaching. For instructors with limited teaching roles, teaching center consultations provide immediate access to information, resources, and support for addressing their questions about teaching.

Second, others found our services valuable for the connections we helped them form—connections both to a community of people who share an interest in teaching and to the work that members of this community are engaged in. Respondents did not always identify direct or immediate effects of these connections, but they reported finding them valuable nonetheless. Through this survey we have learned that one important role for teaching center consultations is to provide faculty and TAs with the opportunity to learn indirectly from the teaching innovations of other faculty and TAs who work with us.

A third value many found was in the additional perspective gained through their work with CIDR. As one client noted, working with CIDR helped make it possible to "focus on the joy of sharing ideas with my students"; for another, it helped make it possible to see teaching "not as a burden that takes away from research." For others, work with CIDR was valuable not necessarily because it solved their problems but because it helped them feel "no longer alone" in trying to solve their problems. This added appreciation of teaching—that it can be enjoyed, that not all problems can be easily solved—was another highly valued contribution of teaching center consultations.

Fourth, even among clients who identified changes in teaching practices as a benefit of their work with CIDR, some expressed the perception that the departmental climate for teaching negatively affected their classroom practices. Clients who see attention to teaching as "counterproductive to promotion," as one of our respondents reported, find value in the opportunity to consult with like-minded colleagues outside their departments, even though they feel the contexts they are working in limit their ability to put changes fully into practice.

A fifth highly valued benefit identified by respondents was the opportunity to consult with experts. In our case at CIDR, we place considerable emphasis on our clients' expertise and ownership of their teaching, and we rarely present ourselves as "experts." And yet, survey results show that respondents highly value our expertise in student learning, our knowledge of what other instructors and programs have done, our understanding of teaching and learning in the disciplines, and our ability to listen and adapt to individual instructors' needs—as one respondent put it, "dealing with real-life teaching situations that the literature overlooks." In the institutional culture of a research university that highly values expertise, clients highly value having a teaching center as a place to consult on questions about teaching that fall outside their own areas of expertise.

This variety of reasons that clients value CIDR consultations raises one important final question for us. Because consultations on teaching are so central to our work, we typically represent ourselves on campus in terms of our contributions to teaching. However, direct effects on teaching are only one thing that clients value about their work with us, and findings from this survey have caused us to question whether we might be underrepresenting our value by focusing primarily on the changes we bring about in classrooms. This wider range of effects is by no means any easier to measure or document than direct effects on teaching, but we would not want to overlook this wider range of effects in communicating what we offer to the teaching community at our university.

Conclusion

Because this was our first attempt to identify long-term effects of our consulting practices, we chose to survey broadly, but future efforts to identify longer-term effects might benefit from a more focused approach. For example, because we wanted survey questions to be relevant to all clients, we did not ask specific questions related to particular CIDR services or instructor needs. A follow-up assessment of particular groups, such as clients who requested a Small Group Instructional Diagnosis (SGID), participants in Preparing Future Faculty (PFF) initiatives, or faculty preparing for tenure review, would allow us to ask more detailed questions related to the specific intents and effects of the consultations. We also chose to ask respondents only for information about academic identities (rank, discipline, institution), not other personal or social identities. What might we learn by looking at consultations in relation to other dimensions of client identity such as race, gender, or age?

Furthermore, we also chose to focus only on the long-term assessment of individual consultations. We would potentially learn a great deal by surveying former clients regarding longer-term effects of other CIDR activities, such as services for departments, materials disseminated through our Web site, and university-wide programs and events.

Finally, this survey raises a number of additional questions for further study that will require additional steps beyond surveying clients for their self-reported reflections on the effects of their work with us, and we conclude by suggesting these as possible next steps for those of us who are interested in examining the roles of teaching and learning centers and the effects we have at our institutions. First, other than the self-reported reflections collected through this survey, we have little documented evidence of the effects of specific CIDR services. For example, how are clients' classroom practices affected by particular services, such as collecting student feedback or consulting on a teaching portfolio?

Second, a number of respondents commented on the influence of departments on individual instructors' teaching efforts. CIDR currently works with departments in a variety of ways, and we may be able to learn a great deal by examining how some of our ongoing departmental collaborations have influenced both the climate for teaching and the awareness and perceptions of CIDR in those departments.

Last of all, what initially motivates faculty and TAs to seek out CIDR? We now have information about what clients found helpful after they came to CIDR, but we have not yet investigated what originally motivated clients to seek us out, or what obstacles might be hindering others from seeking us out. Closer examination of these questions would help all of us at teaching centers to demonstrate and increase both our value and our impact on our campuses.

Appendix A

Feedback Survey

We're interested in learning more about the long-term impact of CIDR services, and we would like to ask your perspective on how your work with CIDR has contributed to your teaching. Please take a few minutes to respond to this brief survey.

Question 1

Approximately how often have you consulted or worked with someone at CIDR?

- ❑ 1–3 times
- ❑ 4–6 times
- ❑ 7 or more times

What has been the primary focus of your work with CIDR? (Please check ALL that apply.)

- ❑ Consult on course, syllabus, or assignment design
- ❑ Discuss teaching issues
- ❑ Diversity and inclusive teaching
- ❑ Feedback from students—written survey
- ❑ Feedback from students—midterm interview (SGID)
- ❑ Observation of my teaching by CIDR
- ❑ Peer/colleague review of teaching
- ❑ Review a video of my teaching
- ❑ Student ratings analysis

❑   Teaching statement or portfolio development
❑   Working with other instructors (faculty or TAs)
❑   Working with student writing
❑   Other: _____

Question 2

To what extent has your teaching (or how you think about teaching) been affected as a result of your work with CIDR?

(Very Much)   (5)   (4)   (3)   (2)   (1)   (0)   (Not at All)

Please give one or more examples of ways that your teaching (or how you think about teaching) has been affected as a result of your work with CIDR:

Question 3

Overall, how valuable has your work with CIDR been?

(Highly Valuable)   (5)   (4)   (3)   (2)   (1)   (0)   (Not at All)

Question 4

What were the primary benefits you received from working with CIDR?

Question 5

What recommendations can you offer for helping CIDR be more effective?

Question 6

If a colleague asked for your help or advice about teaching, how likely would you be to mention any of the services offered by CIDR?

(Very Likely)   (5)   (4)   (3)   (2)   (1)   (0)   (Not at All)

What opportunities do you see for ways that CIDR might be able to assist other instructors or your department in thinking about teaching and learning?

Where do you currently work?

❑   University of Washington

  ❑   Other: _____What is your department?

_____

PLEASE NOTE: We will use this information only to help us analyze survey responses, which are anonymous. If you prefer not to identify your department, please let us know your school, college, or type of academic discipline (for example, engineering, social sciences, humanities, etc.).

What is your current position?

❑   Department Chair
❑   Professor
❑   Associate Professor
❑   Assistant Professor
❑   Senior Lecturer
❑   Lecturer
❑   Lead TA
❑   TA
❑   Graduate Student
❑   Professional Staff
❑   Other: _____What questions or challenges do you currently have regarding teaching?

PLEASE NOTE: We will use this information only to help us plan future CIDR activities. Because your responses are anonymous, we will not be able to respond directly to questions or challenges identified through this survey. If you have an immediate question that you would like to discuss with someone at CIDR, please contact us by sending a message to info@cidr.washington.edu.

Thank you for taking time to give us your feedback!

References

Brinko, K. T., & Menges, R. J. (Eds.). (1997). *Practically speaking: A sourcebook for instructional consultants in higher education.* Stillwater, OK: New Forums Press.

Centra, J. A. (1976). *Faculty development practices in U.S. colleges and universities.* Princeton, NJ: Educational Testing Service.

Chism, N. V. N., & Szabó, B. (1997–98). How faculty development programs evaluate their services. *Journal of Staff, Program, and Organization Development, 15*(2), 55–62.

Fink, L. D., & Bauer, G. (2001). Getting started in one-on-one instructional consulting: Suggestions for new consultants. In K. G. Lewis & J. T. Povlacs Lunde (Eds.), *Face to face: A sourcebook of individual consultation techniques for faculty/instructional developers* (pp. 21–44). Stillwater, OK: New Forums Press.

Frantz, A. C., Beebe, S. A., Horvath, V. S., Canales, J., & Swee, D. E. (2005). The roles of teaching and learning centers. In S. Chadwick-Blossey & D. R. Robertson (Eds.), *To improve the academy: Vol. 23. Resources for faculty, instructional, and organizational development* (pp. 72–90). Bolton, MA: Anker.

Plank, K., Kalish, A., Rohdieck, S., & Harper, K. (2005). A vision beyond measurement: Creating an integrated data system for teaching centers. In S. Chadwick-Blossey & D. R. Robertson (Eds.), *To improve the academy: Vol. 23. Resources for faculty, instructional, and organizational development* (pp. 173–190). Bolton, MA: Anker.

Sorcinelli, M. D. (2002). New conceptions of scholarship for a new generation of faculty members. In K. J. Zahorski (Ed.), *New directions for teaching and learning: No. 90. Scholarship in the postmodern era: New venues, new values, new visions* (pp. 41–48). San Francisco: Jossey-Bass.

Wilson, R. C. (1986). Improving faculty teaching: Effective use of student evaluations and consultants. *Journal of Higher Education, 57*(2), 196–211.

Educational Development by Institutional Type

Chapter 13

Promoting the Scholarship of Teaching and Learning at Community Colleges

Insights from Two Learning Communities

Stanford T. Goto, Andrei Cerqueira Davis
Western Washington University

The Scholarship of Teaching and Learning (SoTL) is a powerful vehicle for professional development. Faculty make their teaching public as they investigate phenomena in their classes. This process encourages sustained discussions of teaching. In conducting SoTL, community college faculty face substantial hurdles: heavy workloads, few institutional supports, no employment rewards, perceived irrelevance, and weak peer networks. Can these challenges be overcome within existing institutional structures? This chapter explores this question by examining how SoTL is pursued in two learning communities. Evidence from these institutional case studies suggests that SoTL programs are viable in community colleges, despite major challenges.

To what extent should community colleges encourage faculty to conduct scholarship? We pose this question, not to challenge the institutional focus on teaching and learning, but rather to explore ways of supporting it. Too often in community college education, scholarship and teaching are viewed in oppositional terms, as if one necessarily distracts from the other. Without a doubt, faculty have their hands full with teaching and administrative work. Few instructors have extra room for a new category of job responsibilities. But what if scholarship could be integrated into one's ongoing professional development? What if there were a substantial overlap between scholarly activities and instructional improvement? In such circumstances, scholarship would be an asset to teaching rather than a distraction. The idea of teaching-related scholarship is gaining traction in community colleges. American Association of Community Colleges president George Boggs (1995–96) and other leaders have called on community colleges to take scholarly approaches to teaching. Meanwhile, increasing numbers of colleges are supporting faculty projects in SoTL (Levinson, 2003; Palmer, 1991).

This chapter analyzes conditions that are likely to promote and sustain teaching-related scholarship in community colleges. We consider commonly articulated challenges to scholarly inquiry, and we identify institutional conditions that help faculty overcome these challenges. Our discussion is informed by a review of research on scholarly practices and professional development activities among community college faculty. Drawing on this body of work, we examine SoTL programs at two colleges: Mesa Community College (MCC) in Arizona and North Seattle Community College (NSCC) in Washington. Not coincidentally, these colleges also have strong learning communities (Cox & Richlin, 2004; Lenning & Ebbers, 1999). These programs illustrate that learning communities can provide a viable infrastructure for SoTL. By identifying structural features that contribute to successful learning communities, one can predict programmatic elements that are likely to support SoTL in community colleges.

Changing Views of Scholarship and Teaching

There are deep historical roots to the assumption that teaching and research are antithetical. Some observers (Block, 1991) suggest that the community college's early ties with secondary schools tended to produce faculties with little desire or training to conduct original scholarship. Another factor is the institution's emphasis on community connections and applied instruction, which has inadvertently fostered ambivalence toward scholarship.

In the late 1940s, the President's Commission on Higher Education affirmed that public two-year colleges should be known as "community colleges" to emphasize how the institution serves local needs (Boggs, 2001). This was a bold departure from the missions of other postsecondary institutions. Research universities focused on basic research which, by definition, was not necessarily tied to particular applications or industries. Liberal arts colleges, like their medieval counterparts in Europe, were devoted to liberal studies that generated knowledge that was not specific to any particular area. It was considered normal, even desirable, for these institutions to maintain some degree of separation from their geographic settings, even if this generated "town and gown" tensions. Community colleges took a much difference stance, deliberately encouraging ties with local constituencies. According to the President's Commission, instruction should prepare community members to lead "a rich and satisfying life, part of which involves earning a living" (1947, p. 6).

The President's Commission left open the possibility that community colleges could engage in research that might enhance instruction. Indeed, the institution was expected to make "frequent surveys of its community so that it can adapt its programs to the educational needs of its full-time students" (p. 6). But this form of needs assessment was considered an administrative function, not a scholarly activity to be conducted by faculty. The role of faculty was to instruct in ways that supported the college's mandate to serve the immediate region.

One presumed implication was that community college instructors should not engage extensively in the types of nonapplied, nonlocalized scholarship found in research universities or liberal arts colleges. This assumption solidified into an unwritten generalization that community college faculty should not engage extensively in original scholarship of any kind. In this way, community colleges came to embrace the term *teaching institution*, which has come to suggest not only that excellent instruction is a top institutional priority (O'Banion, 1997) but also that a commitment to instruction involves a distancing from scholarly pursuits.

Over the years, observers have justifiably questioned the bifurcation of teaching and scholarship (Cross & Angelo, 1989; Cross & Steadman, 1996). In his study of community college faculty,

Seidman argues that this dichotomy is "false and value laden" (1985, p. 254). George Vaughan elaborates: "By accepting the premise that teaching and research are mutually exclusive activities, too many community college faculty members have failed to ask how they should define themselves as scholars as well as teachers, a relationship that is symbiotic for the outstanding teacher" (1991, p. 4).

One approach to bridge this gap has been to broaden the definition of scholarship. Here, Vaughan (1989) and others make a useful distinction between research and scholarship. Research involves inquiry that builds on existing scholarly work and produces empirically verifiable knowledge. Scholarship, on the other hand, more broadly describes the systematic study of a topic, involving precise observation and public dissemination. It's a stretch to imagine community college faculty regularly engaging in research in the university tradition, but it's not unrealistic to imagine them engaging in scholarship, broadly defined. SoTL is built on a variety of activities that instructors regularly pursue: synthesizing literature in one's field, evaluating one's teaching, preparing a conference presentation, analyzing student outcomes, documenting administrative practices, to name a few. This is not to say that teaching-related scholarship is synonymous with effective teaching. Hutchings and Shulman (1999) explain that scholarship of teaching "requires a kind of 'going meta,' in which faculty frame and systematically investigate questions related to student learning . . . and do so with an eye not only to improving their own classroom but to advance practice beyond it" (p. 13).

New categories of institutional inquiry have emerged from broadened notions of scholarship. A report from the American Association for Community and Junior Colleges Commission on the Future of Community Colleges (1988) argues that our understanding of scholarship must include the investigation of knowledge in curriculum development, service, and teaching. Ernest Boyer of the Carnegie Foundation (1990) refined these distinctions, differentiating among scholarship of discovery (generating new areas of knowledge), scholarship of integration (synthesizing knowledge across disciplines), scholarship of application (putting knowledge into action), and scholarship of teaching (analyzing how knowledge is constructed or conveyed in classrooms).

Drawing on this framework, Boggs (2001) challenges community colleges to become "centers for scholarship":

> [T]he work of the professor becomes consequential only as it is understood by others. Further, good teachers must be engaged in scholarship of learning. They must continually learn how to better promote the learning of their students. It is in this form of scholarship that community college faculty excel, reflecting a unique creativeness and innovative spirit. (p. 25)

Challenges to Overcome

Although educators increasingly recognize the value of scholarship in community colleges, they are well aware of considerable obstacles to widespread institutionalization. Commonly articulated challenges include heavy workload, few institutional supports, no employment rewards, perceived irrelevance, and weak peer networks.

Heavy Workload

This is perhaps the most frequently cited barrier to scholarship in community colleges. A survey conducted by the Carnegie Foundation found that, on average, full-time faculty in community colleges spend almost fifteen hours per week engaged in classroom instruction, compared with approximately six hours per week of undergraduate instruction for faculty in research institutions (Huber, 1998). In addition, community college faculty spend four hours per week advising and assisting students. Program structure also influences the administrative load. Compared to universities, community colleges tend to offer a greater diversity of programs. Consequently, there are proportionally more small programs, which increase the proportion of faculty who are engaged in program administration. The administrative load is even greater if programs are self-supporting.

Few Institutional Supports

Another major challenge is a lack of resources. As one dean put it, "Heavy workload with little assistance leaves little time for scholarship" (quoted in Vaughan, 1991, p. 12). This is especially true for part-timers, who often lack the basic tools, such as desk space. Even when funding is available for scholarly activities, faculty still might have difficulty securing that support. It is common for professional development monies to be awarded on a competitive basis, requiring faculty to submit proposals. Typically, colleges give priority to activities that directly benefit an instructor's teaching or subject area knowledge. Proposals for SoTL-related activities may be at a disadvantage in relation to other proposals that provide more direct and immediate benefits.

No Employment Rewards

Presumably, community college faculty spend most of their time working on their teaching, program administration, and professional service. These activities are recognized by the college for purposes of promotion, tenure, or contract renewal. Scholarship is rarely considered as part of the reward system (Vaughan, 1991). Consequently, instructors have little extrinsic incentive to engage in such time-consuming activities.

Perceived Irrelevance

For the most part, community college instructors do not favor increased recognition of scholarship by their institutions. A large majority (82 percent) believe that teaching effectiveness should be the primary criterion for faculty promotion (Huber, 1998). Faculty tend to be favorable (or at least neutral) toward traditional measures of teaching such as peer observations and student evaluations, but, in general, they do not see research output as a valid indicator of good teaching. Huber concludes that most do not want scholarship to be counted for purposes of promotion or retention.

Perceptions of scholarship vary from one discipline to another. Block (1991) notes that instructors who come from professional areas outside universities may view scholarship as unnecessary or disconnected from classroom realities. This is particularly true in vocational or professional and technical fields, where a program's credibility depends on faculty connections with employers. In the eyes of employers, teaching-related scholarship is likely to be seen as a distraction from the central project of preparing students for work. In academic fields, instructors who are trained in research universities are apt to favor discipline-based research as the most valuable form of academic inquiry. Presumably, the study of teaching or program administration would have less cachet in their eyes; consequently, they would be less likely to pursue activities that are not valued in the discipline. Palmer (1991) echoes this concern, noting that community colleges must find a balanced approach to encouraging discipline-based scholarship, as well as pan-disciplinary scholarship of teaching.

Weak Peer Network

A foundational principle of scholarship, as articulated by Boyer (1990) and others, is that inquiry must be made public for critical review by one's peers. This assumes that faculty have regular contact with their colleagues within and across departments and, second, that there is a collective desire to talk about issues of teaching and learning. Multiple studies (Grubb & Associates, 1999; Seidman, 1985) point to pervasive patterns of isolation in community colleges, where instructors oftentimes feel cut off intellectually not only from peers in their department but also from peers in other departments and institutions (Tagg, 2003).

Current Grassroots Interest in Scholarship

Although these challenges seem daunting, studies suggest that scholarship is not uncommon in community colleges. A national survey found that, on average, community college faculty spend over six hours per week on research or comparable scholarly activities (Huber, 1998). More than one-third said they were engaged in a scholarly project that would lead to a publication, exhibit, or performance, and 20 percent reported receiving funding for research in the last three years. A review of faculty curricula vitae found almost half listing at least one publication (Vaughan, 1991). About one-third of sampled instructors published articles in national or regional journals.

Participation in scholarly activities is even greater when judged by a wider definition of scholarship. A strong majority of community college faculty (78 percent) report working with organizations outside their college (for example, industry, educational institutions, government) for purposes of professional service, program administration, or outreach (Huber, 1998). This work sometimes leads instructors to produce technical reports, newspaper articles, or other forms of documentation (Vaughan, 1991). One might infer that those who forge ahead with their own scholarship are strongly motivated by extra-institutional factors such as personal interest, civic engagement, professional pride, or desire for self-betterment. For these individuals, the institutional reward system is not the primary force shaping their scholarly pursuits. The combination of applying and disseminating knowledge clearly fits Boyer's notion of applied scholarship (1990).

These findings illustrate an apparent paradox: On the one hand, instructors generally believe that conducting original research has little relevance to the central project of teaching at a community college (Block, 1991). On the other hand, more than an incidental number of faculty are engaged in scholarly pursuits. What are we to make of this? It is clear that instructors are not categorically opposed to scholarly inquiry. What they oppose, we would argue, are institutional requirements for specific *types* of research. More specifically, they do not want to emulate the university model of "publish or perish." As long as scholarship is not limited to academic publication and not required for promotion or retention, instructors are often quite willing to engage in scholarly activities for personal development or professional service. Indeed, this is common, despite systemic challenges such as heavy workload and lack of employment rewards.

Even the vexing issue of institutional support may be more encouraging than previously assumed. Although community colleges rarely offer direct support for research, they commonly support various forms of professional development that relate (at least potentially) to scholarship. A survey of Southern community colleges found that 69 percent of colleges offer some financial support for presenting papers at conferences—a traditionally recognized form of scholarship (Murray, 2001). In the area of instructional development, almost all surveyed colleges offer workshops conducted by instructors. Workshops on teaching are similar to conference presentations in that they involve systematically generating, synthesizing, and presenting knowledge—activities that Shulman (2000) identifies as hallmarks of scholarship. Community colleges frequently support other forms of faculty development that can be linked to SoTL. For instance, it is relatively common for colleges to provide release time for teaching improvement projects and tuition support for taking university classes (Grant & Keim, 2002; Murray, 1999). These activities, in themselves, do not constitute scholarship, but they can be useful vehicles for pursuing scholarly inquiry. It would be fair to say that many colleges already have at least a basic infrastructure that could support teaching-related scholarship.

Teaching-Related Scholarship in Two Institutions

It is likely that, given at least minimal support, some community college faculty will voluntarily pursue scholarly work, despite the added burden. Consider a hypothetical scenario. An instructor wishes to conduct a workshop at a regional conference on college teaching. The workshop will showcase an innovative curriculum that the instructor has developed for her introductory class. She has tenure, so this work has little if any bearing on her employment status. The only support from the college is reimbursement for registration and travel expenses. Still, the instructor is enthusiastic about this opportunity. She is proud of her curriculum and eager to share it with colleagues who have similar interests. We see two likely factors that would motivate an instructor to pursue this type of teaching-related scholarship. One is that the work is self-determined. Even though there are few institutionally bestowed benefits attached to this project, there are no institutionally imposed expectations or requirements either. Given the freedom to choose topic and purpose, instructors are inclined to focus on things that they find most immediate and interesting in their work. This automatically overcomes the problem of perceived irrelevance of scholarship.

The second factor is that scholarly inquiry often creates opportunities for intellectual exchange with colleagues. Although instructors often work in relative isolation, they generally appreciate opportunities to interface with colleagues (Grubb et al., 1999). It is likely that faculty who conduct teaching-related scholarship are motivated, not only by the prospect of creating a product for dissemination, but also by the opportunity to engage in a collaborative process that stimulates discussions about teaching.

We believe that further development of teaching-related scholarship in community colleges requires the promotion of peer networks and the preservation of self-determined inquiry. Currently, scholarly activities among community college faculty tend to be entrepreneurial, typically with individual faculty designing their own projects and building their own networks, often with peers outside the college. If colleges hope to institutionalize teaching-related scholarship, they must build peer networks within the institution. Specifically, colleges must provide ways for instructors to work with colleagues across disciplines in exploring issues of teaching and learning. We do not wish to imply that community colleges should impose formal requirements or guidelines for scholarship. This undoubtedly would be poisonous to the intrinsic motivation that currently drives scholarly work among community college faculty. The challenge is for colleges to encourage voluntary, self-determined scholarship without creating a new category of work or a new set of employment requirements for instructors.

To illustrate how this can be achieved in community colleges, we look to an established form of faculty development—learning communities. Community colleges have a decades-long history of student learning communities in which multiple courses are linked together and taught collaboratively (Levinson, 2003). Observers (Lenning & Ebbers, 1999) note that student learning communities have the potential, not only to enrich the learning experience of students, but also to stimulate ongoing professional development among faculty. Some community colleges have gone a step further in formalizing this objective, offering faculty learning communities in which groups of instructors participate in professional development activities guided by a formal curriculum (Cox & Richlin, 2004). Both types of learning community foster conditions that are conducive to SoTL. For instance, both create cross-disciplinary networks for faculty to talk to each other about classroom practice. Moreover, both encourage faculty to question their assumptions about teaching. In their study of community college teaching, Grubb and colleagues (1999) found that the promise of immersive professional enrichment was a powerful motivator among faculty participating in learning communities. As one instructor explained:

> It's very, very enriching to see other teachers work, teachers who are already quite adept, quite experienced, veteran teachers with enormous reserves of technique. . . . So there's an enormous kind of fertilization, different sorts of ideas, and also you get a chance to run things up the flagpole, and so there's that kind of enrichment that would never be possible in the normal traditional venue. (p. 265)

As with those conducting SoTL, faculty who facilitate and participate in learning communities are willing to accept a certain amount of additional work if they believe they will gain deep insight into teaching-related issues that they deem important.

Is this potential payoff sufficient to counteract other challenges such as a lack of institutional supports or rewards? Let us consider two colleges that support SoTL, either directly or indirectly, through learning communities. Although they have different administrative configurations, both colleges foster a vibrant institutional culture of scholarly teaching. Our intention is not to advocate one model over another but rather to illustrate that there is more than one way to foster teaching-related scholarship in community colleges.

A Centralized Model: Mesa Community College

The Faculty and Professional Learning Community (FPLC) program at MCC is the college's most recent and significant effort to promote scholarly teaching (Richlin, 2001). Modeled after Miami University's Faculty Learning Community program (Richlin & Essington, 2004), the FPLC encourages participants to "engage in self-selected activities that promote learning, development, community building, and the scholarship of teaching and learning" (CTL Web site, 2007a). The goals, according to program director W. Bradley Kincaid, are to promote connections among faculty, staff, and students and to promote scholarly reflection, which leads to the improvement of teaching and learning (personal communication, December 8, 2006). Interested instructors submit an application to join a learning community, ideally consisting of eight to twelve members. These groups meet every other week for a year to pursue community-defined goals and activities, coordinated and motivated by a facilitator. FPLC members are encouraged to pursue projects related to a common topic:

> Participants usually select a focus course or project in which to implement an innovation or intervention related to the FPLC topic and collaborate to assess impacts on teaching and learning. Local communication about FPLC outcomes is a critical component of the program leading to enhanced campus community and improved teaching and learning. (CTL Web site, 2007b)

Kincaid cites these features of the FPLC program that support scholarly teaching at MCC (personal communication, December 8, 2006):

- Funding reassigned time or special contracts for the director and all facilitators
- Providing a budget for books, printing, travel to present scholarship at national conferences
- Allowing FPLC members to accumulate Faculty Professional Growth credits, which count toward advancement on the salary scale for faculty without a Ph.D.
- Counting FPLC membership as fulfilling the faculty service requirement
- Promoting FPLC membership alternate to completing the required Faculty Evaluation Plan
- Providing support for classroom research design
- Hosting a Conference on Teaching and Learning (supported by the vice chancellor for academic affairs)

In at least two respects, the FPLC program serves as a centralized vehicle promoting SoTL. First, although scholarly inquiries are conducted independently by faculty, they are supported by the facilitator and director, who provide research design consultation. Second, the inquiries are housed in a dedicated program with its own director and budget.

A Decentralized Model: North Seattle Community College

In 2003, NSCC implemented an initiative to promote SoTL across the college. Recognized as a Core Campus by the Carnegie Academy for the Scholarship of Teaching and Learning, NSCC encourages faculty to "engag[e] in scholarly discussions and organiz[e] research projects that explore important questions related to improving teaching and learning in classrooms, at the college, and in the broader field of higher education" (TLC Web site, 2007).

This initiative dovetails comfortably with the Coordinated Studies Program, which offers team-taught courses combining two or more fields of study. Since the 1980s, this program has implemented a model of integrated studies developed at the Evergreen State College and promoted by the Washington Center for the Improvement of Undergraduate Education (Smith, 1993). In these student learning communities, instructors work closely together in planning and administering the course. Also, they observe each other frequently, as they teach together in a common space. There is no formal agenda for professional development within these learning communities, but sustained interaction with colleagues encourages instructors to refine and adapt their teaching methods. This is a fertile environment for teaching-related scholarship. Indeed, some SoTL projects (Lister-Reis, Hamilton, & Nousheen, 2006) have emerged from faculty and student collaboration in Coordinated Studies classes.

These scholarly activities are supported by NSCC's Teaching and Learning Center. According to faculty member and Carnegie Fellow, James Harnish (personal communication, December 12, 2006), the TLC offers an array of workshops and resources on teaching-related topics, including SoTL. In addition, the center provides various forums (both physical and electronic) for faculty to share ideas about instruction. Although the TLC has enthusiastically embraced integrated studies and SoTL, the center historically has tried to avoid imposing models of instructional innovation from the top down. Instead, the center has sought to facilitate faculty collaboration, allowing instructors to develop and disseminate their own innovations. In this respect, NSCC's approach to fostering scholarly teaching is decentralized.

Two Promising Approaches to Teaching-Related Scholarship

There are differences in how the two colleges create scholarly networks across disciplines. At MCC, the locus of scholarly exchange is the faculty learning community—an entity outside the classroom. The ultimate manifestation is the MCC Conference on Teaching and Learning, where faculty present insights into classroom phenomena (Phung, 2006) and instructional best practices (Joshua, 2007). NSCC also holds a campuswide event but, for most of the year, scholarly exchanges happen primarily in their classrooms. This is evident in the administration of Coordinated Studies classes, where faculty often work closely with students. This configuration has influenced NSCC faculty to broaden the definition of peer networks to include students as scholarly partners. In one project, a group of students worked under the supervision of faculty to conduct a survey of student perspectives on the learning environment at NSCC (Allard, Bellomio, Gronbeck, & Wilkin, 2006). We feel that both programmatic configurations (in-class and out-of-class sites) can be fertile environments for teaching-related scholarship. The key, we believe, is for community colleges to institutionalize either or both types and to make them regular components of instruction and professional development.

There is also a difference in levels of funding for SoTL projects at MCC and at NSCC. Mesa's Faculty and Professional Learning Community Program has a larger budget. Participants do not receive direct compensation, but they may be eligible for certain benefits, such as faculty professional growth credit. As a result, the FPLCs attract a larger number of participants (typically about seventy per year). Support for faculty scholarly projects is more limited at North Seattle Community College. Faculty do not receive incentives from the institution to do scholarly projects. Not surprisingly, the number of faculty who pursue teaching-related scholarship is smaller at NSCC. This is not to say that faculty motivation differs categorically between these two programs. Ultimately, at both colleges, faculty report being intrinsically motivated by the opportunity to generate new knowledge while working with colleagues, counteracting the isolation that many feel in a large institution. The difference between the two programs is mainly logistical. Offering faculty supports within a well-funded and well-organized program is likely to widen opportunities for those who want an enriching experience but who otherwise could not afford to devote the time to an extended project. Ultimately, we believe that, if colleges hope to encourage teaching-related scholarship on a widespread and sustainable basis, they must devote funds to such programs and support faculty participation in them. At the same time, we recognize that there may be a silver lining for small-budget programs. Colleges that offer less support for teaching-related scholarship also tend to impose fewer expectations and guidelines. These conditions tend to encourage the entrepreneurialism that typically drives most scholarly work at community colleges.

Beyond these programmatic differences, there are a number of important similarities between MCC and NSCC. Perhaps most significantly, the importance of scholarly teaching is communicated on at least two levels: institutional and programmatic.

At the institutional level, scholarly inquiry is endorsed by executive administration at both colleges. This is evident in the investment that MCC has made in the FPLC Program. At NSCC, the vice president for instruction introduced a collegewide initiative on SoTL. This communicates clearly to the campus community that teaching-related scholarship has a legitimate place in the community college. It is important to note, however, that executive-level endorsement is not sufficient in and of itself to ensure the institutionalization of teaching-related scholarship. Indeed, faculty are likely to react with extreme skepticism if they believe that SoTL is being promoted by administration as a back-door means of evaluating faculty performance (Goto, Kane, Cheung, Hults, & Davis, 2007). For SoTL to gain widespread acceptance at community colleges, the purposes and uses of scholarly inquiry must remain firmly in faculty control. This is the case at MCC and NSCC. As faculty members with administrative duties, the directors of the FPLC (Mesa) or the TLC (North Seattle) are responsible for promoting teaching-related scholarship at the programmatic level. In communicating the purposes of SoTL, the directors tread diplomatically. They let instructors know that they have the option of using their scholarly projects to enhance their professional portfolios. At the same time, they make it clear that teaching-related scholarship is independent of institutionally mandated assessment.

Conclusion

MCC and NSCC demonstrate that teaching-related scholarship at community colleges is not only feasible but also potentially invigorating for purposes of professional development. Although voluntary SoTL programs will never attract all faculty, they are likely to attract at least some enthusiastic participants, as long as faculty see the relevance of teaching-related scholarship and they retain control of the scholarly agenda. This can happen even with heavy workloads and few institutional incentives. Admittedly, SoTL programs have not been around long enough to determine the extent to which they are sustainable. However, learning communities (both faculty and student) provide a programmatic analog that helps us predict conditions in which SoTL is likely to thrive in the long run. The fact that learning communities have spread and diversified in community colleges over the last several decades gives us reason to hope that teaching-related scholarship will likewise gain a sustainable foothold in community colleges.

References

American Association for Community and Junior Colleges. (1988, November). *Building communities: A vision for a new century.* (Commission Report). Washington, DC: Author.

Allard, K., Bellomio, S., Gronbeck, H., & Wilkin, H. (2006, May). *Student voices.* Paper presented at the Pacific Northwest Higher Education Teaching and Learning Conference, Vancouver, WA.

Block, J. (1991). False dichotomies. In G. B. Vaughan & J. C. Palmer (Eds.), *New directions for community colleges: No. 76. Enhancing teaching and administration through scholarship* (pp. 17–26). San Francisco: Jossey-Bass.

Boggs, G. R. (1995–96, December/January). The learning paradigm. *Community College Journal, 66*(3), 24–27.

Boggs, G. R. (2001). The meaning of scholarship in community colleges. *Community College Journal, 72*(1), 23–26.

Boyer, E. L. (1990). *Scholarship reconsidered: Priorities of the professoriate.* Princeton, NJ: Carnegie Foundation for the Advancement of Teaching.

Cox, M. D., & Richlin, L. (Eds.). (2004). *New directions for teaching and learning: No. 97. Building faculty learning communities.* San Francisco: Jossey-Bass.

Cross, K. P., & Angelo, T. A. (1989). Faculty members as classroom researchers. *AACJC Journal, 59*(5), 23–25.

Cross, K. P., & Steadman, M. H. (1996). *Classroom research: Implementing the scholarship of teaching.* San Francisco: Jossey-Bass.

CTL Web site. (2007a). *Center for Teaching and Learning, Mesa Community College: MCC faculty and professional learning communities program.* Retrieved August 22, 2007, from http://ctl.mc.maricopa.edu/_programs/fplc/index.html

CTL Web site. (2007b). *Center for Teaching and Learning, Mesa Community College: CTLpedia.* Retrieved August 22, 2007, from http://ctl.mc.maricopa.edu/wiki/index.php/Main_Page

Goto, S., Kane, C., Cheung, S., Hults, P., & Davis, A. (2007, October). *Scholarship of teaching and learning: Examining your practice in an age of accountability.* Paper presented at the Western Regional Research Conference on the Education of Adults, Western Washington University, Bellingham, WA.

Grant, M. R., & Keim, M. C. (2002). Faculty development in publicly supported two-year colleges. *Community College Journal of Research and Practice, 26,* 793–807.

Grubb, N. W., & Associates. (1999). *Honored but invisible: An inside look at teaching in community colleges.* New York: Routledge.

Huber, M. T. (1998). *Community college faculty attitudes and trends, 1997.* Stanford, CA: National Center for Postsecondary Improvement, Stanford University.

Hutchings, P., & Shulman, L. S. (1999). The scholarship of teaching: New elaborations, new developments. *Change, 31*(5), 10–15.

Joshua, M. (2007, August). *How can students take control of their own learning?* Paper presented at the first annual Mesa Community College Conference on Teaching and Learning, Mesa, AZ.

Lenning, O. T., & Ebbers, L. H. (1999). *The powerful potential of learning communities: Improving education for the future.* (ASHE-ERIC Higher Education Report, Vol. 26, No. 6). Washington, DC: The George Washington University, Graduate School of Education and Human Development.

Levinson, D. J. (Ed.). (2003). Scholarship in the community college [Special issue]. *Community College Journal of Research and Practice, 27*(7).

Lister-Reis, J., Hamilton, C., & Nousheen, F. (2006). *The creation of a "public homeplace" in learning communities: The role of emotional and intellectual safety in student learning.* Retrieved August 27, 2007, from http://webshare.northseattle.edu/tlc/forfaculty_sotl_research1.shtm

Murray, J. P. (1999). Faculty development in a national sample of community colleges. *Community College Review, 27*(3), 47–64.

Murray, J. P. (2001). Faculty development in publicly supported 2-year colleges. *Community College Journal of Research and Practice, 25*(7), 487–502.

O'Banion, T. (1997). *A learning college for the 21st century.* Phoenix, AZ: Oryx Press.

Palmer, J. C. (1991). Nurturing scholarship at community colleges. In G. B. Vaughan & J. C. Palmer (Eds.), *New directions for community colleges: No. 76. Enhancing teaching and administration through scholarship* (pp. 69–77). San Francisco: Jossey-Bass.

Phung, B. (2006). *A contrastive rhetorical study of Chinese and Mexican perspectives of their native writing instruction and its implications for ESL teaching and learning.* Paper presented at the first annual Mesa Community College Conference on Teaching and Learning, Mesa, AZ.

President's Commission on Higher Education. (1947). *Higher education for American democracy.* New York: Harper Brothers.

Richlin, L. (2001). Scholarly teaching and the scholarship of teaching. In C. Kreber (Ed.), *New directions for teaching and learning: No. 86. Scholarship revisited: Perspectives on the scholarship of teaching* (pp. 57–68). San Francisco: Jossey-Bass.

Richlin, L., & Essington, A. (2004). Faculty learning communities to prepare future faculty. In M. Cox & L. Richlin (Eds.), *New directions for teaching and learning: No. 97. Building faculty learning communities* (pp. 149–157). San Francisco: Jossey-Bass.

Seidman, E. (1985). *In the words of the faculty: Perspectives on improving teaching and educational quality in community colleges.* San Francisco: Jossey-Bass.

Shulman, L. S. (2000, October). *Fostering a scholarship of teaching and learning.* Paper presented at the 12th annual Louise McBee Lecture, Athens, GA.

Smith, B. L. (1993). Creating learning communities. *Liberal Education, 79*(4), 32–39.

Tagg, J. (2003). *The learning paradigm college.* Bolton, MA: Anker.

TLC Web site. (2007). *Teaching and Learning Center, North Seattle Community College: NSCC scholarship of teaching and learning initiative.* Retrieved August 22, 2007, from http://webshare.northseattle.edu/tlc/forfaculty_sotl.shtm

Vaughan, G. B. (1989). *Scholarship: The community college's Achilles' heel.* Virginia Community College's Association Occasional Paper Series, No. 1. (Eric Document Reproduction Service No. ED 313 081)

Vaughan, G. B. (1991). Scholarship and the community college professional: Focusing the debate. In G. B. Vaughan & J. C. Palmer (Eds.), *New directions for community colleges: No. 76. Enhancing teaching and administration through scholarship* (pp. 3–15). San Francisco: Jossey-Bass.

Chapter 14

Starting and Sustaining Successful Faculty Development Programs at Small Colleges

Michael Reder
Connecticut College

Kim M. Mooney
St. Lawrence University

Richard A. Holmgren
Allegheny College

Paul J. Kuerbis
Colorado College

This chapter complements a recent chapter in To Improve the Academy by Mooney and Reder (2008) that discusses the distinctive features and challenges of faculty development at small and liberal arts colleges. As a continuation and expansion of that more conceptual discussion, we aim to convey practical strategies for relatively new faculty developers at small institutions with incipient programs. The suggestions offered in this chapter are grounded in our experiences as faculty developers at liberal arts colleges and developed through numerous national conference presentations and conversations with colleagues in the field over the past decade. Although our recommendations are particularly salient for faculty developers working in a small college setting, our ideas should be applicable across institutional types.

Over the past decade, we have been involved with the implementation and evolution of faculty development programs now rapidly taking place at small colleges. Since 2001, we have facilitated conference sessions focused on small college faculty development work at the annual Professional and Organizational Development (POD) Network meetings, at numerous Association of American Colleges and Universities (AAC&U) conferences, and at a variety of other higher education gatherings, both national and regional. In various forums—primarily workshops, but also on panels, through roundtable discussions, and at organizational meetings—we have begun to identify and theorize about the tenets for starting and sustaining successful teaching and learning programs in the small college environment. In an earlier *To Improve the Academy* chapter (Mooney & Reder, 2008), we discuss from a conceptual perspective the distinct features and challenges of faculty development at small and liberal arts colleges. This chapter complements that work with a discussion of thirteen specific strategies for small college faculty development. Some of these strategies were originally generated for a workshop (Reder & Mooney, 2004) and have since been expanded and refined through conversations with faculty developers at a wide variety of small institutions. It is important to note that although our recommendations are tailored specifically for practitioners at small colleges, most of our ideas are applicable to a variety of institutional types.

As is true of our workshops, this chapter has several goals. First, we identify the distinctive challenges of small college faculty development and describe the general work of program directors on small campuses. Next, we offer some basic strategies for starting and sustaining successful faculty development programs at small colleges. Finally, we pose questions to encourage some self-reflection and help with the identification of the next steps needed to develop or improve an institution's programs.

Challenges for the Small College Faculty Developer

Starting and sustaining a successful faculty development program at a small college presents challenges distinctive from those at larger institutions. Because these challenges are covered elsewhere in some detail (Mooney & Reder, 2008), we address only two: 1) those related to faculty culture at small institutions and 2) those related to the multiple roles often played by small college faculty developers.

There is an implicit assumption that small and liberal arts institutions value excellent teaching and therefore only hire faculty who "already know how to teach" (Reder & Gallagher, 2007). Faculty at small colleges report experiencing greater stress from the demands of their teaching (Lindholm, Szeleny, Hurtado, & Korn, 2005), and when they already feel confident in their teaching, they may hesitate to allocate their time to improving an activity in which they are considered to be proficient. Although faculty across a wide range of institutions, from two-year colleges to research-intensive universities, may report feeling over-taxed and stressed, the competing demands of teaching, advising, conducting research, and doing committee work may be felt more keenly by small college faculty than by their peers at larger institutions (see Gibson, 1992).

Small college faculty developers also face competing and compelling demands on their time. Unlike their counterparts at larger institutions, who often have positions that focus primarily on supporting teaching and learning, small college faculty developers often devote only a small fraction of their total time to their faculty development work. Like many faculty developers at larger institutions, virtually all faculty developers at small schools teach at least one course per year, often more. Such teaching is not only important for legitimacy in the eyes of the faculty with whom they work, but it also gives faculty developers experiences with the current student population from which to draw on and allows for their own ongoing pedagogical development. However, in addition to their teaching duties, many small college faculty developers have other administrative responsibilities as an associate dean, department chair, or director of programs such as first-year seminars or a writing center. In addition, most have multiple committee assignments (sometimes as part of their regular faculty duties, sometimes specifically because of their involvement in faculty development), and they frequently continue their ongoing advising or other responsibilities to students.

These multiple roles are further complicated by the broad range of faculty development activities for which small college faculty developers may be responsible. In contrast to faculty developers at larger institutions, many of whom have positions devoted specifically to supporting faculty in their teaching, sometimes even to a specific aspect of teaching and learning (for example, instructional design, working with teaching assistants, teaching with technology, or working within a specific discipline), faculty developers at small colleges are required to be generalists, responsible for supporting all areas of faculty work. Not only are they often the one-stop shop for everything having to do with teaching and learning, but they may also be expected to coordinate mentoring to new and early-career faculty (including scholarship, promotion, and tenure), to run programs that address institutional priorities (such as diversity, writing, quantitative literacy, assessment, accreditation), or to support departmentally based curricular initiatives and revision. In our roles on our campuses, for example, we have been called on to do the following:

- Help individual faculty with course design, including incorporating technology, writing, speaking, and research assignments
- Lead departmental curriculum revision
- Assist in the development of department chairs
- Facilitate groups for early-career faculty and experienced faculty
- Run campuswide discussions on issues such as general education, diversity, and assessment
- Support the institution's accreditation review process, including chairing the college's accreditation review committee in the case of two authors
- Host events where faculty and students talk about teaching and learning
- Assist individual faculty, departments, and programs in designing tools for assessing teaching and learning

Thirteen Principles of Small College Faculty Development

Although many principles are important to successful faculty development (Sorcinelli, 2002), we believe the ideas we offer here are particularly relevant to small colleges. As with all such recommendations, we affirm that what defines "best practices" is almost always dependent on the local conditions at your particular institution, and we caution the reader to bear in mind your own faculty culture as you use these principles to guide your program development. In our experience, the majority of small college faculty developers are drawn from the ranks of the faculty at the institution they serve, and they often retain significant teaching, research, and service responsibilities; therefore, the following principles, although readily transferable to a variety of institutional types and situations, are designed for the small college faculty developer for whom faculty development is only one part of a larger set of responsibilities.

1. *Seek guidance from stakeholders.* It is impossible to overstate the importance of connecting small college faculty development to the needs and interests of the faculty and the institution as a whole (Sorcinelli, Austin, Eddy, & Beach, 2006). Given the limited size of the faculty community at small colleges, what might be isolated incidents at a larger institution can dramatically change the general climate and openness to faculty development at a smaller institution. For example, on the positive side, a school notes that a few of the promising new faculty (all come from doctoral programs at large, research-intensive universities) may struggle to adjust to a new teaching climate that is heavy on small seminars or courses outside their area of expertise. The difficulties of a few of these new faculty may prompt department chairs or the academic administration to seek assistance from the faculty developer. Conversely, any perception that candidates who receive a negative tenure decision spent too much time on their teaching to the detriment of their research can poison the water for faculty development efforts. Perhaps more maddening for those working in such a climate is that the small college faculty community is small enough that faculty opinion can swing

rapidly from position to position, sometimes controlled by only one influential voice. In such an environment, keeping an ear to the ground is absolutely essential to success.

If you are charged with launching a formal faculty development program or expanding the programming currently offered, it is good to have the go-ahead from the chief academic officer and even better to have a direct charge from some formal entity within the faculty governance structure. A good first step is to start discussing new programming with faculty colleagues, including a few "*un*usual suspects." An effective developer will meet with a broad sample of the college faculty. Indeed, it is possible and can be very valuable for a single person to meet individually with every member of the faculty over the course of a few months (Holmgren, 2005).

2. *Create an advisory board.* Any such information gathering can be the first step to creating an advisory board. Advisory boards or other formal advisory structures are necessary to keep a one-person operation connected to the diverse faculty community. Having a reliable, engaged committee to evaluate ideas and provide the leadership for some programs is critical to your productivity and mental health. An advisory group can serve as eyes and ears around campus, act as a sounding board for ideas and programming, and support the director or coordinator in making important decisions.

An ideal advisory board member should be known for teaching, scholarship, and leadership. The board should contain individuals who represent diverse disciplines and levels of experience. Reaching out to a few faculty who initially may not appear to be interested in faculty development efforts might broaden your audience and expand your own thinking. On a small college campus where teaching is already assumed to be important and faculty may be hesitant to devote extra time to improving their pedagogy, advisory board members can also serve as role models to other faculty. If campus leaders are willing to devote time and energy to programming to improve teaching, these activities will be seen by others as valuable. As political allies and advocates who understand your work and programmatic goals, the advisory board itself can play an invaluable role in the (not always popular) decisions you will make. For example, such a board is particularly important when the center for teaching and learning (CTL) offers—or denies—funding for faculty development initiatives proposed by individuals or departments.

One critical issue that should be addressed by the advisory board of any new program is the question of the program's or center's relationship to the tenure and promotion process. This issue is salient at small institutions because there may be implicit expectations about the information a faculty developer or faculty affiliated with the program can provide about candidates for promotion and tenure; such expectations are at odds with good faculty development and the creation of a "safe space" in which faculty can learn. An active faculty development program may draw on the skills of many faculty over a period of a few years, and any number of senior faculty might work mentoring untenured faculty. If all those senior faculty were to recuse themselves from addressing tenure cases, it would dramatically skew the available pool of those able to weigh in on such decisions. Unfortunately, there is no easy answer to this challenge because the faculty community is so small, and it is therefore important to address this issue openly and early on in the program development.

The advisory board can let you know how frequently it needs to meet. Once programs are established, monthly meetings may suffice. You may wish to establish an advisory board listserv for contact, advice, and input between meetings.

3. *Make your program or center a place of excellence.* Your program or center should be the place where good teachers talk about good teaching. Make every effort to get the best teachers and leaders involved in running programs: invite faculty who have won teaching awards, who are known by students and other faculty as excellent teachers, and who have the respect of faculty across the campus. Their participation will help facilitate topical conversations that bridge disciplinary and pedagogical differences.

At small and liberal arts colleges, the idea of the scholar-teacher should come to fruition: ideally, faculty teaching and scholarship should support each other. Boyer's idea of the scholarship of teaching should be particularly appealing in these small institutions that emphasize faculty commitment to being both teachers and scholars (Boyer, 1990). One way to incorporate a scholarly approach to faculty conversations and programs is to "assign" a common reading in advance of a session or workshop. In addition to facilitating a discussion, this approach signals to colleagues that this workshop, this conversation, this endeavor is grounded in theory, practice, and previous scholarly applications of ideas. These conversations about pedagogy and class assignments are not about remediation; they are about teaching excellence and critical practice—ideas well suited to small college faculty culture.

4. *Start with one program and do it very well.* Doing too many things at once not only can dilute your program's effectiveness, it can also sabotage its success. On a small college campus there is an interesting multiplier effect: faculty know each other, and they talk. An event attended by 20 faculty at a large institution with 700 faculty accounts for fewer than 3 percent of the faculty; at a small college with 140 faculty, that workshop represents almost 15 percent of the total faculty. Because each and every event is high stakes, quality matters more than quantity. If faculty find your programming worthwhile, they will spread the word, demand for your services will increase, and your programming will expand naturally. If they find it a waste of time, they will also tell others, and faculty will start avoiding your events. An ill-considered abundance of faculty development opportunities can quickly deplete the limited pool of available faculty development hours, but one well-considered and strategically targeted program can create an ongoing demand for additional programming.

5. *A good place to start: working with incoming faculty.* The first program you develop should be for new faculty. A liberal arts or other small college needs to do more than merely inform new faculty that teaching is important; it needs to explicitly support this claim if new faculty, who often have little experience teaching at small colleges, are to be successful. Such programming sends the message to faculty from the start that teaching is valued at the college, talked about, and shared (Reder & Gallagher, 2007). Evidence suggests that after several years, a school's entire teaching culture can be transformed, as subsequent

classes of entering faculty not only share the same vocabulary around teaching but treat it as a public act that can be examined and improved (Frederick, 2007; Holmgren, 2005; Reder & Gallagher, 2007).

In addition, programs for first- and second-year faculty are "safe" programs for faculty at all levels to support, because these programs play into the false and somewhat paternalistic idea that newer faculty will most benefit from faculty development programming. Finally, incoming and early-career faculty need support, not only for their teaching but to ensure a successful transition into their new lives. Targeted programming helps new faculty connect with other faculty across the disciplines, introduces them to the different expectations of teaching in a small college setting, and facilitates their understanding of institutional values, expectations, and cultures.

6. *Make careful and deliberate choices about expanding programming.* An effective teaching and learning program will offer at least two types of programming: 1) a year-long experience designed specifically to meet the needs of incoming faculty and 2) ongoing programming open to faculty of all ranks. Among the varieties of programming for experienced faculty, two types often have the most impact: 1) a year-long exploration of some aspect of teaching and learning or 2) a series of one-off events that faculty can attend according to their interests and needs. Programs such as Colorado College's "Thinking Inside and Outside the Block Box" series (www.colora docollege.edu/learningcommons/tlc/programs_luncheons.asp) and Connecticut College's "Talking Teaching" series (http://ctl. conncoll.edu/programs.html#talking) offer faculty the opportunity to discuss specific teaching issues with colleagues in an informal setting.

More structured, year-long seminars (sometimes called learning communities) invite a group of faculty to meet regularly to discuss specific pedagogical issues. Examples of successful year-long programs at liberal arts colleges include Allegheny College's Teaching Partners (Holmgren, 2005), Macalester College's mid-career faculty seminar (www.macalester.edu/cstMid%20Career% 20Seminar/ Index.htm), St. Lawrence University's Oral Communication Institute (Mooney, Fordham, & Lehr, 2005), and St. Olaf

College's Center for Innovation in the Liberal Arts associates program that focuses on the scholarship of teaching and learning (Peters, Schodt, & Walczak, 2008).

Once you have established two well-running programs, we encourage you think about expanding your activities using these four guidelines:

1. Consider the balance between events for both occasional participants (for example, using Excel gradebook or active learning in large classes) and ongoing users (for example, a learning community focused on cognition and learning or a multiple-workshop series in various dimensions of teaching using an online course management system).
2. Select topics of both general interest (for example, "how students learn") and focused on specific issues (for example, "teaching science labs" or "grading student presentations").
3. Offer programming options that appeal to a variety of faculty at different points in their careers, full-time or part-time, across disciplines and teaching styles.
4. Align specific programs with the time of the semester (for example, a pre-semester syllabus workshop or a discussion of grading at the end of the semester).

7. *Use the talent pool on your own campus.* At its most basic level, our job is to provide the impetus for faculty to get together and talk about their teaching. Lee Shulman, president of the Carnegie Foundation for the Advancement of Teaching, talks about the "pedagogical solitude" that most faculty face; our job is to overcome this isolation and make teaching, again in Shulman's terms, "community property." Recognizing the depth of expertise and excellence already present on our campuses by asking our faculty to share their ideas with other colleagues builds community and collegiality. As an added benefit, your faculty best know your college's distinctive culture, along with its students and curriculum, and will be seen as credible sources of ideas by their colleagues. To make these conversations possible, it is important that you keep abreast of who is doing what in terms of their teaching. Because of the small size of our campuses, simply maintaining an ongoing conversation with colleagues and students about what is

happening in their classrooms allows you to identify who is up to something interesting.

One additional facet of small college culture makes focused but informal faculty-facilitated conversations particularly important. There is a strange intimacy among the faculty of a small college that is at once immediate but distant: they work in close confines, yet even those who may see each other every day for a year or have offices next to each other may know little about the other's work and even less about the other's teaching. Those with offices at opposite ends of the campus may rarely see each other unless they share a committee assignment. Because of the campus's small size, faculty feel that they should know each other, but often they do not. We have experienced moments at our events, when we realize that a recently tenured faculty member who has been on campus for six years is unknown to a more senior colleague. Although two tenured colleagues meeting for the first time is not an unusual scenario at a large university with multiple colleges, a large physical plant, and thousands of faculty, on a residential campus with fewer than two hundred faculty, it surprises us that this scenario recurs several times each year. Faculty events centered around teaching are an opportunity to draw in diverse participants from across the disciplines.

As a final benefit of using local talent, when we ask faculty to get involved in the leadership of our programming, we also offer them an opportunity to develop their ideas about teaching into something that can be shared with a wider audience. For many faculty, the next natural step is to present at a teaching conference or, for some, to write an article on their teaching or pedagogical research. For example, one of our faculty led a successful lunchtime discussion about his approach to teaching critical thinking skills; his discussion led to a request from his colleagues that he offer a more developed workshop. His materials and ideas from that workshop were subsequently turned into an article that was then published in a national periodical.

8. *Generate grassroots interest in your programs before announcing them.* We have all found that extending conversations about potential programming beyond the advisory board is quite helpful and

elicits useful feedback before programs are announced. We recommend taking the time to describe to at least five colleagues from across the disciplines what you are planning. By engaging their interest early and incorporating their feedback before you commit additional time and resources to a new project, you not only have started building your participant base, you have also ensured its attractiveness to colleagues from multiple disciplines.

By taking this principle even further and asking for faculty commitments to attend an event before it is officially announced, you can dramatically increase participation. For example, by inviting several faculty to be featured discussants on the session's topic, Connecticut College's "Talking Teaching" Series of lunchtime pedagogical discussions more than doubled in attendance, going from an average of eight to ten faculty participants to an average of over twenty (http://ctl.conncoll.edu/programs. html#talking). These discussants, who represent a variety of disciplines, teaching styles, and career stages, do not run the discussion or workshop, but their presence draws in diverse participants eager to learn about their colleagues' teaching.

9. *Collaborate widely within your own institution.* At small colleges, even those without formal teaching and learning programs, faculty learn about teaching in a variety of decentralized locations: first-year experience programs, community learning projects, general education, information fluency initiatives, the writing program, instructional technology, and departmental discussions (P. Frederick in Mooney & Reder, 2008; Sorcinelli, Austin, Eddy, & Beach, 2006). Because the faculty developer has limited time, forging strategic partnerships with other campus groups with similar aims allows a teaching center to expand its programming, increase its influence on the college's teaching culture, and best use both time and the school's resources.

Because teaching and learning programs are focused on supporting faculty teaching and improving student learning, they are often viewed as neutral entities that are able to address charged campus political issues. Our programs have been asked to sponsor discussions on topics such as changes in general education, diversity, accountability, grade inflation, and policies (final exams, course enrollment limits) that affect teaching and learning. Faculty teaching and learning centers can be thought of as the center of a nexus of opportunities for faculty learning—helping shape events and cosponsoring events with a diverse variety of campus offices and connecting faculty to these initiatives.

10. *Build your program's visibility by making it the "center" of faculty learning.* We are often asked how important it is to have a physical center, and the answer is, "It depends." Certainly, the wrong space—an ill-maintained house on the edge of campus or a nice suite of rooms that is hard to find or inconveniently located—might be worse than no space. Similarly, space that has been "liberated" from a department whose members hold grudges and have a lot of influence may hinder rather than help your cause. What is most important is that your *program* be felt as a presence on campus, and the right space may help with that. At Colorado College, for example, the Crown Faculty Center was established within some unused basement space in the main library. Several years later, with a gift and matching funds provided by the College itself, the faculty center became part of a cluster of "centers," each with a focus on learning for both students and faculty. A collaboration among the directors of the library, instructional technology, and the faculty center led to The Learning Commons at Tutt Library (Dickerson, Kuerbis, & Stiles, 2007). What constitutes the right space will depend on the institutional culture. At some schools, space in the central administration building near the chief academic officer or president communicates importance and influence that enhance the program and its effectiveness. At others, such close association with "the administration" is the kiss of death.

But physical space is not the only way to gain visibility. At Connecticut College, the faculty development program does not have a physical space, but centers are important. Consequently, faculty development is housed in the Center for Teaching & Learning, which exists as the metaphorical center of opportunities for faculty development (see Frederick, 2007; Mooney & Reder, 2008). Given the Connecticut College culture, creating a clear presence with extensive programming for faculty is more important than physical space (Reder & Gallagher, 2007).

As another example, early on in the formation of Allegheny College's faculty development program, the associate dean charged with developing the program was struggling with creating a presence for the program in the absence of both effective space and a name on which to hang the program. At the suggestion of a small college faculty development colleague, the associate dean catalogued the existing programs housed in the dean's office—travel support, workshops for new faculty, the sabbatical leave program, research mini-grants managed by a faculty committee, a small endowment for curricular development grants—and created a tri-fold brochure that was distributed to all faculty. In that single act, which required relatively little time and few resources, a faculty development program was born. Many faculty contacted the dean and the associate dean to say how surprised and pleased they were to see how many faculty development programs were available. The irony is that none of the programs were new, but many were not well known or understood as part of faculty development.

11. *Reward faculty for participating.* Two responses typically emerge early on in any discussion of how one builds participation in faculty development programs: pay them or threaten them. Although rats will run through mazes to get treats or avoid shocks, deep learning of the kind that leads to the pedagogical growth we seek in faculty development programs is unlikely to derive from simplistic approaches such as blatant rewards or coercion. Clearly, to be effective we need to provide faculty with a different type of impetus. Wergin (2003) asserts that faculty are motivated by four underlying desires: autonomy, community, recognition, and efficacy. In our experience, most effective programs attend to at least three of these four motivators.

Mandatory faculty development, which might be perceived as forced remediation, is rarely effective, and we suggest all faculty development programs honor faculty autonomy by being voluntary in nature. In addition, to the extent possible while respecting the program's integrity, participants will appreciate and respond well if they have wide latitude in helping to shape the program or the activities therein. Most faculty development programs build community by incorporating common attendance at a workshop, by creating shared experiences, and by offering regular opportunities for substantive conversation about teaching. Community development is another reason to offer meals or refreshments in conjunction with faculty development activities. Any program that fosters increased teaching skill and confidence enhances participants' sense of efficacy. Providing participants opportunities to reflect on and discuss practical issues they face in their classrooms (for example, by grounding a discussion of human learning in classroom experiences common at the college) can help realize benefits in ways that are immediately apparent and motivating for participants. Recognition can come in a variety of ways, including thanks or acknowledgment from the president or provost; an invitation to a faculty member to share experiences, lead a session, or serve as a mentor; and, when handled well, a stipend.

12. *Details matter. Communicate quality in the setting and food that you provide.* Attending to faculty needs and the physical space demonstrates that you value faculty time enough to pay attention to the details. Whenever possible and whatever the budget allows for, providing refreshments sends the right welcoming message. Being careful to acknowledge dietary restrictions communicates that you care about the participants as individuals. Providing a comfortable setting that is conducive to conversation and the task at hand supports the informal exchanges that sustain and inform community and faculty development on small campuses. Because time is a faculty member's most precious resource, events during the breakfast or lunch hour are often the most convenient and best attended. At our institutions, we typically build time for informal conversation over food into faculty development opportunities. By publicizing when the gathering begins (for example, "lunch is served at noon") and when the formal program starts ("Professor Black will begin with introductory comments at 12:25"), we also allow faculty the autonomy to decide whether they will come for the meal (most do) or just the structured sessions. Providing delicious meals—the best possible given your funding—is a wonderful way to draw faculty in and

let them know that their participation is appreciated. It also meets a very practical need: if no food is provided, faculty may need to choose between either getting sustenance or participating in faculty development. The symbolism and power of sharing good food together, coupled with good conversation and learning, can make a discussion or workshop all the more enjoyable and effective.

13. *Attend to your own needs and development.* Whereas centers for teaching and learning at large institutions often have multiple staff members, those of us involved in faculty development work at small colleges often do our planning in relative professional isolation and without mentors. It is essential for our own professional development to reach out to colleagues, not only at similar institutions but also at a variety of colleges and universities. The exchange of energy and ideas at conferences focused on teaching, learning, and curricular issues, be they regional (for example, the New England Faculty Development Consortium, the Collaboration for the Advancement of Teaching and Learning, the Lilly conferences) or national (for example, the annual POD, AAC&U, and Teaching Professor conferences), is invaluable for your current and future work. Although you work in a distinctive context, learning about faculty programming at a variety of schools can help enrich your programming back on your home campus. Equally important, small colleges, particularly private colleges, can sometimes feel cut off from the larger world of higher education. It is important to understand your work and your institution in a larger context, including the many forces, both positive and negative, that are shaping the future of teaching and learning: the shifting nature of faculty work, technology and its effect on learning, assessment and accountability, the changing demographics of the college-age population, and the financial pressures on colleges and universities.

At the end of the workshops we run for faculty developers, we always ask participants to assess their own distinctive situations and those of their college, consider what they have learned, and then begin to plan their next steps. We end this chapter with an invitation to engage in similar reflections through a set of overarching questions we have found useful in focusing our own work and advancing our faculty development programs. We pose these questions within two frames: 1) the mission and context of faculty development programs or centers and 2) the challenges and goals specific to one's faculty and institutional culture. Asking yourself these questions is important, particularly because reflection—practicing meta-cognition within our profession—is a key to sustaining our work and refining it.

Conclusion

We propose the following questions to guide your reflective process for this frame: 1) What is the purpose, the mission, the philosophy behind the work you do? 2) Does your philosophical purpose always drive your programming? 3) Can you identify two situational challenges relevant to your work that you can address in the next two semesters?

These questions can guide your reflective process for this frame: 1) If you could only design (or redesign) one program, what one teaching and learning issue or practice would it address? 2) What would its goal be? 3) What possible ideas or programming are you familiar with that might help you address this goal? 4) What first step(s) will you take on your campus? 5) Whom will you contact? 6) What will you propose? 7) What might be the questions they ask? 8) What response do you want?

Although we have emphasized in this chapter a set of practical principles derived from best practices, our own engagement in reflective practice leads us to suggest that small-college faculty developers might also consider recent work in cognitive science and how people learn as we think about how teachers learn about teaching. Because the parallels between human learning and teacher (faculty) learning are striking, they provide one such lens through which to view our work. The seminal book *How People Learn* (Bransford, Brown, & Cocking, 1999) provides us with three related areas of inquiry regarding faculty growth and learning. First, we need to recognize that faculty bring to our sessions and programmatic events a highly personal set of experiences and beliefs. How do we recognize that prior knowledge, and how do we activate and build on it with new ideas about teaching and learning? Second, faculty development over one's lifespan consists of moving from novices as learners of teaching to more expert status. How do we account for this growth and development over one's career as we plan sessions and programmatic events? Third, how do we encourage colleagues to engage in critical reflection on their teaching practices so that the impact on student learning is enhanced?

Each of us has found through our individual experiences that faculty development opportunities at small colleges, especially workshops and ongoing seminars, are usually highly collaborative, rewarding, and fun. Generally speaking, our faculty colleagues at small and liberal arts colleges understand teaching to be a primary responsibility and genuinely care about teaching well; they know one another and value opportunities to exchange ideas with faculty outside their disciplines. Programs that encourage and instruct in developing substantive courses with engaging assignments that address multiple aspects of student learning have a strong pull for faculty if these faculty development opportunities are offered with sensitivity to faculty culture and needs. Although we have noted more than once that our colleagues' time is a precious commodity and that integrating faculty development programs into their priorities on any given day is a faculty developer's persistent challenge, there are some very powerful forces working in our favor. First among them is the genuine and deep commitment to excellence in teaching and deep student learning that the majority of our colleagues bring to each and every course they teach.

References

Boyer, E. L. (1990). *Scholarship reconsidered: Priorities of the professoriate*. Princeton, NJ: Carnegie Foundation for the Advancement of Teaching.

Bransford, J. D., Brown, A. L., & Cocking, R. R. (Eds.). (2000). *How people learn: Brain, mind, experience, and school* (Expanded ed.). Washington, DC: National Academy Press.

Dickerson, C., Kuerbis, P., & Stiles, R. (2007, February). Learning centers, libraries, and IT: Providing integrated support services in a learning commons. In *Research Bulletin* (issue 5). Retrieved April 5, 2007, from http://connect.educause.edu/Library/ECAR/LearningCentersLibrariesa/40161

Frederick, P. (2007, October). *Sixteen reflections from 30 years of faculty development*. Paper presented at the 32nd annual meeting of the Professional and Organizational Development Network in Higher Education, Pittsburgh, PA. Retrieved March 5, 2008, from http://ctl.conncoll.edu/smallcollege/index.html

Gibson, G. W. (1992). *Good start: A guidebook for new faculty in liberal arts colleges*. Bolton, MA: Anker.

Holmgren, R. A. (2005). Teaching partners: Improving teaching and learning by cultivating a community of practice. In S. Chadwick-Blossey & D. R. Robertson (Eds.), *To improve the academy: Vol. 23. Resources for faculty, instructional, and organizational development* (pp. 211–219). Bolton, MA: Anker.

Lindholm, J. A., Szelenyi, K., Hurtado, S., & Korn, W. S. (2005). *The American college teacher: National norms for the 2004–2005 HERI Faculty Survey*. Los Angeles, CA: Higher Education Research Institute, University of California.

Mooney, K. M., & Reder, M. (2008). Faculty development at small and liberal arts colleges. In D. R. Robertson & L. B. Nilson (Eds.), *To improve the academy: Vol. 26. Resources for faculty, instructional, and organizational development* (pp. 158–172). San Francisco: Jossey-Bass.

Mooney, K. M., Fordham, T., & Lehr, V. (2005). A faculty development program to promote engaged classroom dialogue: The oral communication institute. In S. Chadwick-Blossey & D. R. Robertson (Eds.), *To improve the academy: Vol. 23. Resources for faculty, instructional, and organizational development* (pp. 219–235). Bolton, MA: Anker.

Peters, D., Schodt, D., & Walczak, M. (2008). Supporting the scholarship of teaching and learning at liberal arts colleges. In D. R. Robertson & L. B. Nilson (Eds.), *To improve the academy: Vol. 26. Resources for faculty, instructional, and organizational development* (pp. 68–84). San Francisco: Jossey-Bass.

Reder, M., & Gallagher, E. V. (2007). Transforming a teaching culture through peer mentoring: Connecticut College's Johnson Teaching Seminar for Incoming Faculty. In D. R. Robertson & L. B. Nilson (Eds.), *To improve the academy: Vol. 25. Resources for faculty, instructional, and organizational development* (pp. 327–344). Bolton, MA: Anker.

Reder, M., & Mooney, K. (2004, November). *Getting started in small college faculty development*. Roundtable at the 29th annual meeting of the Professional and Organizational Development Network in Higher Education, Montreal, Quebec, Canada.

Sorcinelli, M. D. (2002). Ten principles of good practice in creating and sustaining teaching and learning centers. In K. H. Gillespie (Ed.), *A guide to faculty development: Practical advice, examples, and resources* (pp. 9–23). Bolton, MA: Anker.

Sorcinelli, M. D., Austin, A. E., Eddy, P. L., & Beach, A. L. (2006). *Creating the future of faculty development: Learning from the past, understanding the present.* Bolton, MA: Anker.

Wergin, J. F. (2003). *Departments that work: Building and sustaining cultures of excellence in academic programs.* Bolton, MA: Anker.

Chapter 15

Essential Faculty Development Programs for Teaching and Learning Centers in Research-Extensive Universities

Larissa Pchenitchnaia, Bryan R. Cole
Texas A&M University

This research highlights the imperative nature of designing programs to address the full range of faculty development needs. It presents a framework for essential faculty development programs for teaching and learning centers in research-extensive universities for introducing, enhancing, and improving faculty development offerings. The nationwide Delphi study of faculty development programs identified eighteen currently essential and twenty-eight future essential faculty development programs for teaching and learning centers in research-extensive universities. This list of programs may serve as a baseline for evaluating existing faculty development programming and guiding the expansion of established programs and the planning of new ones.

Now is a time of high expectations and demands for colleges and universities. The university of the twenty-first century has to deal with significant reductions in financial resources, increasing accountability for student learning outcomes, a shift in emphasis toward the learner, rising public expectations for institutional involvement in economic development, expanding faculty workloads, and intense competition among numerous providers of education (Altbach, 2005; Brancato, 2003; Levine, 2001; Lieberman & Guskin, 2003; Morris, 2004; Ruben, 2004; Sorcinelli, Austin, Eddy, & Beach, 2006; Tice, 2005; Wulff & Austin, 2004). The quality of higher education and the ability of colleges and universities to perform their missions are inextricably linked to the quality and commitment of the faculty (Schuster & Wheeler, 1990). Boyer (1990), in *Scholarship Reconsidered,* began the search for a new paradigm of faculty work that could meet the diverse and changing needs of our society. According to Shulman (2004),

> [T]he intellectual and political message of *Scholarship Reconsidered* is that we need a broader conception of scholarship—one that points to the power of scholarship to discover and invent, to make sense and connect, to engage with the world, and to teach what we have learned to others. . . . Boyer and his colleagues wanted these different scholarly activities to be seen as of equal value to the broader community. (p. 165)

Gaff and Simpson (1994) noted that faculty work includes teaching and advising, designing curricula, serving the community, and participating in the governance of their institutions. All these roles are proper foci for development. Brancato (2003) commented that increased attention is being given to faculty development programs that address today's demands on higher education. Faculty members are being encouraged to transform their roles and responsibilities in order to enhance student learning, and faculty development initiatives can offer them strategies for a successful transition.

In a recent work Sorcinelli and colleagues (2006) proffered that faculty development has, from its inception, proven its capacity to anticipate and respond to changes and to act as a lever of change in higher education. It has evolved from individual to collective development, from singular to multidimensional purposes, from largely uncoordinated activities to centralized units, from "soft" funding to foundation, association, government, and institutional support, and from a small network of developers in the United States to a global faculty development profession.

Millis (1994) contended that faculty development programs are essential if campuses are to respond to complex changes in 1) expectations about the quality of undergraduate education, 2) views regarding the nature and value of assessment, 3) societal needs, 4) technology and its impact on education, 5) the diverse student populations, and 6) paradigms in teaching and learning (p. 458). Because such changes are ongoing, faculty development programs should never remain static. They must adjust creatively and responsively to meet changing student, faculty, institutional, and societal needs.

Some researchers argued for expanding the role of faculty developers to that of institutional change agents (Eckel, 2002; Diamond, 2005; Zahorski, 2002). Eckel (2002) maintained that a central role for faculty developers is to help the institution decide how much change is needed and to develop appropriate strategies to affect the level and breadth of change. Faculty developers have an important institution-wide perspective on the complexity of problems, opportunities, and constraints. They can create opportunities for facilitated, institution-wide conversations about key elements of change and what they mean for faculty and staff.

Today, an identifiable, centralized unit with professional staff typically coordinates faculty development programming (Millis, 1994; Singer, 2002; Sorcinelli et al., 2006; Wright, 2000, 2002). According to Wright (2002), the activities of campuswide teaching and learning centers take a variety of approaches to serving a large audience. Program offerings are numerous and may include varying combinations of activities (Eble & McKeachie, 1985; Frantz, Beebe, Horvath, Canales, & Swee, 2005; Millis, 1994; Schuster & Wheeler, 1990; Sorcinelli et al., 2006; Wright, 2002). Recent studies endorse comprehensive faculty development programs (Schuster & Wheeler, 1990) and holistic faculty development (Zahorski, 2002) that supports a faculty member's growth into a "complete scholar" (Rice, 1996). In Zahorski's (2002) view, a holistic approach assumes that "whereas individual program components do help foster and support scholarship, even more powerful is the synergy resulting from components working together and interacting with other institutional agencies" (pp. 29–30).

Research Purpose

This research highlights the importance of designing programs that address the full range of faculty development needs. According to Wright (2000) and Frantz and colleagues (2005), only a handful of studies have examined the functions and resources of teaching and learning centers and other faculty development units (Centra, 1976; Crawley, 1995; Diamond, 2002; Erickson, 1986; Frantz et al., 2005; Gullatt & Weaver, 1997; Sorcinelli et al., 2006; Wright, 2002). This study seeks to identify a list of current and future essential faculty development programs for teaching and learning centers from the viewpoint of the current center directors in selected research-extensive universities. It is the first Delphi study with a panel of knowledgeable members—center directors—that reached consensus on the essential programs for teaching and learning centers in research-extensive universities.

The Delphi Methodology

Linstone and Turoff (1975) defined the Delphi technique as "a method for structuring a group communication process so that the process is effective in allowing a group of individuals, as a whole, to deal with a complex problem" (p. 3). Delbecq, Van de Ven, and Gustafson (1975, as cited in Murry and Hammons, 1995, p. 423) characterize it as "a method for the systematic solicitation and collection of judgments on a particular topic through a set of carefully designed sequential questionnaires interspersed with summarized information and feedback of opinions derived from earlier responses." Originally developed by Dalkey and Helmer (1963) to technologically forecast future events, this technique is now considered a reliable qualitative research method for use in problem solving, decision making, and group consensus–reaching in many areas (Eggers & Jones, 1998; Linstone & Turoff, 1975; Murry & Hammons, 1995; Wilhelm, 2001). In higher education, the Delphi method has been used primarily in four areas: 1) developing educational goals and objectives, 2) improving curriculum, 3) assisting in strategic planning, and 4) developing criteria for evaluation (Judd, 1972, as cited in Eggers & Jones, 1998; Murry & Hammons, 1995). In this study, we apply it to the identification of current and future essential faculty development programs for teaching and learning centers in research-extensive universities.

The Delphi data collection approach offers the benefit of being participant led. It is an iterative process that shows respondents how their ideas and opinions are influencing the research process and shaping the results, which usually creates goodwill between the participants and research team (Garavalia & Gredler, 2004). According to Ziglio (1996), the Delphi method is intended to structure information for which there is some evidence in a way that achieves informed judgment and decision making.

In a Delphi study, the research population must be a panel of experts (Linstone & Turoff, 1975; Wilhelm, 2001). Panel size depends on the purpose and complexity of the study and the expertise required, not statistical issues (Clayton, 1997; Ziglio, 1996). Unlike other research designs, randomization is neither warranted nor needed (Stone Fish, & Busby, 1996). Respondents may represent a random or nonbiased sample of various types of expertise (Clayton, 1997). According to Linstone and Turoff (1975) and Ziglio (1996), a homogeneous panel of experts required only ten to fifteen individuals. For this study an appropriate Delphi panel is a national sample of twelve to fifteen faculty development experts who know the theory and practice of faculty professional development in a research-extensive university setting.

The Study Population

We identified 102 public research-extensive universities from the year 2000 Carnegie Classification of Institutions of Higher Education and matched them against those in the 2005 Professional and Organizational Development Network in Higher Education (POD) Membership Directory and Networking Guide, yielding 70 public research-extensive universities with formal faculty development programs. A research-extensive university is an institution that typically offers a wide range of baccalaureate programs and is committed to graduate education through the doctorate. We limited this study to this type of institution to ensure that the expert panel members brought comparable perspectives on faculty development to the table. We also anticipated that teaching and learning centers in research-extensive universities would have the most comprehensive faculty development programming and thus could serve as a reference point, not only for research-extensive universities but for other institutional types as well. From this list of 70, we chose 22 teaching and learning centers for this study on these criteria: 1) a centrally located unit with an administrative staff managed by a director, 2) a minimum of five years in existence, 3) geographically dispersed locations, 4) the variety of faculty development programs (from the center Web site), and 5) the identification of teaching and learning centers with a national reputation made by a past POD president. Each of the 22 center directors was professionally competent and actively involved in faculty development initiatives at the national level. These panel member nominees were asked to participate by e-mail and received a description of the study emphasizing the importance of their contribution to the study. Fifteen of the 22 directors agreed to participate and completed all four rounds of the Delphi study.

The Data-Collection Questionnaires

We collected data through a series of four questionnaires. The first round of program items was derived from the faculty development literature, then evaluated by a review panel of experts. A pilot instrument review panel included three experts in the area of faculty development: a past POD president, an associate director of a teaching and learning center in a research-extensive university, and a research professor working in a teaching and learning center in a research-extensive university. This pilot evaluation by an expert panel and the Delphi experts' rankings of the programs during the survey rounds established the content validity of the survey instrument. After we made all the revisions suggested by the reviewers, we sent the first questionnaire to the study participants requesting them to rank various faculty development programs by how essential they were. The programs fell into seven categories: consultations; university-wide orientations; university-wide workshops; intensive programs; grants, awards, and exchange programs; resources and publications; and other services.

Appendix A shows an example of a page from the first-round questionnaire. The tables provided checkboxes for ranking the essentiality (current and future) of the programs listed on a four-level scale. We defined an "essential" program as one that a director thought any research-extensive university should have. During this first round, each expert was free to add any missing essential programs they believed should be included, and the panel of fifteen added a total of thirty-two new programs.

For each survey round, we computed the descriptive statistics (mean scores and standard deviations) for each program item, then prepared the next individual survey instrument for each panel member with his or her rankings and the descriptive statistics on each program, allowing each member to compare his or her responses to the aggregate responses. We then invited the panel members to change any rankings they wished. The Delphi procedure ended when the panel achieved consensus or panel member responses stabilized. Scheibe, Skutsch, and Schofer (1975) reasoned that opinion stability—stability of the respondents' vote distribution curve over successive rounds of the Delphi—serves as a measure of consensus. Using the 15 percent change level to represent a state of equilibrium, any two distributions showing marginal changes of less than 15 percent have reached stability. Items with successive distributions showing more than 15 percent change are included in later rounds of the Delphi, as they have not reached equilibrium.

Findings

In interpreting the results, we defined faculty development programs with a consensus group mean between 1.49 and 1.00 as "unimportant and should not be included" for teaching and learning centers in research-extensive universities. We considered programs with a consensus group mean between 1.50 and 2.49 as "helpful but not very important" for centers in research-extensive universities. We defined programs with a consensus group mean between 2.50 and 3.49 as "important but not essential," and only those with a consensus group mean between 3.50 and 4.00 as "essential."

The Delphi panel members considered eighteen faculty development programs in five program categories as "essential" for teaching and learning centers: consultations, university-wide orientations, university-wide workshops, resources and publications, and other services. None of the programs in the remaining two categories—Intensive Programs and Grants, Awards, and Exchange Programs—emerged as essential. The findings are presented in Table 15.1.

Table 15.1. Essential Faculty Development Programs,
Final Framework

Program Category	Program	Consensus Mean	Consensus SD
1. Consultations	**1.1.** classroom videotaping, observations and critique of classroom instruction for individual faculty	3.53	0.52
	1.2. consultation on enhancing teaching practices for individual faculty	4.00	0.00
	1.5. individual consultations for TAs	3.80	0.41
	1.11. consultation with campus groups or departmental units on teaching related issues	3.93	0.26
	1.12. consulting with departments on TA programs	3.60	0.63
2. University-wide Orientations	**2.1.** organized, campus-wide programs for new TAs	3.67	0.49
	2.3. organized, campus-wide programs for new faculty	3.60	0.63

**Table 15.1. Essential Faculty Development Programs,
Final Framework (*Continued*)**

Program Category	Program	Consensus Mean	Consensus SD
3. University-wide Workshops	**3.1.** enhancing teaching strategies	3.87	0.35
	3.2. course and syllabus design	3.80	0.41
	3.3. testing, test construction and evaluating student performance	3.67	0.49
	3.5. assessing student learning outcomes	3.80	0.41
	3.16. college teaching for TAs	3.53	0.64
	3.17. developing teaching strategies and methods of active and cooperative learning	3.87	0.35
	3.20. teaching for student-centered learning	3.87	0.35
	3.37. teaching large classes	3.80	0.41
6. Resources and Publications	**6.3.** updated Web site (with resources to download and links to other Web-based resources)	3.87	0.35
7. Other Services	**7.14.** service on university, college, and departmental committees in support of teaching and learning	3.53	0.64
	7.17. faculty-facilitated sessions for colleagues on issues of teaching and teaching methods	3.60	0.63

As far as the future is concerned, the Delphi panel forecasted that twenty-eight faculty development programs in five program categories would be "essential": Consultations, University-wide Orientations, University-wide Workshops, Resources and Publications, and Other Services. Again, no program within Intensive Programs or Grants, Awards, and Exchange Programs emerged as essential for centers in the future. Table 15.2 displays these results,

Table 15.2. Future Essential Faculty Development Programs, Final Framework

Program Category	Program	Consensus Mean	Consensus SD
1. Consultations	**1.1.f.** classroom videotaping, observations and critique of classroom instruction for individual faculty	3.60	0.51
	1.2.f. consultation on enhancing teaching practices for individual faculty	4.00	0.00
	1.5.f. individual consultations for TAs	3.87	0.35
	1.11.f. consultation with campus groups or departmental units on teaching related issues	3.93	0.26
	1.12.f. consulting with departments on TA programs	3.53	0.64
2. University-wide Orientations	**2.1.f.** organized, campus-wide programs for new TAs	3.60	0.51
	2.2.f. organized, campus-wide programs for international TAs	3.53	0.52
	2.3.f. organized, campus-wide programs for new faculty	3.73	0.46

Table 15.2. Future Essential Faculty Development Programs, Final Framework (*Continued*)

Program Category	Program	Consensus Mean	Consensus SD
3. University-wide Workshops	**3.1.f.** enhancing teaching strategies	3.80	0.56
	3.2.f. course and syllabus design	3.87	0.35
	3.3.f. testing, test construction, and evaluating student performance	3.67	0.82
	3.4.f. developing effective writing assignments	3.53	0.64
	3.5.f. assessing student learning outcomes	3.87	0.52
	3.7.f. understanding college students (learning styles, developmental patterns, diversity)	3.67	0.49
	3.11.f. multicultural teaching and learning; infusing multiculturalism into a course	3.67	0.49
	3.12.f. application of instructional technology; teaching with technology; using various multimedia software	3.73	0.46
	3.16.f. college teaching for TAs	3.53	0.74
	3.17.f. developing teaching strategies and methods of active and cooperative learning	3.87	0.35
	3.20.f. teaching for student-centered learning	3.87	0.35

(*Continued*)

**Table 15.2. Future Essential Faculty Development
Programs, Final Framework (*Continued*)**

Program Category	Program	Consensus Mean	Consensus SD
	3.30.f. part-time/adjunct faculty development	3.60	0.74
	3.36.f. developing faculty in the scholarship of teaching	3.73	0.46
	3.37.f. teaching large classes	3.87	0.35
	3.38.f. peer review as a form of assessment; training faculty and TAs in the peer review process	3.53	0.74
	3.40.f. critical thinking and inquiry	3.60	0.51
6. Resources and Publications	**6.3.f.** updated Web site (with resources to download and links to other Web-based resources)	4.00	0.00
7. Other Services	**7.3.f. customized programs on instructional issues for individual academic departments**	3.60	0.63
	7.14.f. service on university, college, and departmental committees in support of teaching and learning	3.87	0.35
	7.17.f. faculty-facilitated sessions for colleagues on issues of teaching and teaching methods	3.73	0.46

where "f" designates "future." The panel ranked ten more programs as essential for the future than they did for the past, and these are bolded in the table.

Table 15.3 compares the consensus group means for the current and the future essential programs for teaching and learning centers. Again, the ten programs deemed essential in the future

Table 15.3. Comparison Between Consensus Group Means for Current and Future Essential Faculty Development Programs

Program Category	Program	Consensus Mean Current	Consensus SD Current	Consensus Mean Future	Consensus SD Future
1. Consultations	**1.1.** classroom video-taping, observations, and critique of classroom instruction for individual faculty	3.53	0.52	3.60	0.51
	1.2. consultation on enhancing teaching practices for individual faculty	4.00	0.00	4.00	0.00
	1.5. individual consultations for TAs	3.80	0.41	3.87	0.35
	1.11. consultation with campus groups or departmental units on teaching related issues	3.93	0.26	3.93	0.26
	1.12. consulting with departments on TA programs	3.60	0.63	3.53	0.64
2. University-wide Orientations	**2.1.** organized, campus-wide programs for new TAs	3.67	0.49	3.60	0.51
	2.2. organized, campus-wide programs for international TAs	**3.47**	**0.52**	**3.53**	**0.52**
	2.3. organized, campus-wide programs for new faculty	3.60	0.63	3.73	0.46

(*Continued*)

**Table 15.3. Comparison Between Consensus Group
Means for Current and Future Essential Faculty
Development Programs (*Continued*)**

Program Category	Program	Consensus Mean Current	Consensus SD Current	Consensus Mean Future	Consensus SD Future
3. University-wide Workshops	**3.1.** enhancing teaching strategies	3.87	0.35	3.80	0.56
	3.2. course and syllabus design	3.80	0.41	3.87	0.35
	3.3. testing, test construction, and evaluating student performance	3.67	0.49	3.67	0.82
3. University-wide Workshops	**3.4. developing effective writing assignments**	**3.47**	**0.64**	**3.53**	**0.64**
	3.5. assessing student learning outcomes	3.80	0.41	3.87	0.52
	3.7. understanding college students (learning styles, developmental patterns, diversity)	**3.40**	**0.51**	**3.67**	**0.49**
	3.11. multicultural teaching and learning; infusing multiculturalism into a course	**3.33**	**0.72**	**3.67**	**0.49**
	3.12. application of instructional technology; teaching with technology; using various multimedia software	**3.33**	**0.62**	**3.73**	**0.46**
	3.16. college teaching for TAs	3.53	0.64	3.53	0.74
	3.17. developing teaching strategies and methods of active and cooperative learning	3.87	0.35	3.87	0.35

Table 15.3. Comparison Between Consensus Group Means for Current and Future Essential Faculty Development Programs (*Continued*)

Program Category	Program	Consensus Mean Current	Consensus SD Current	Consensus Mean Future	Consensus SD Future
	3.20. teaching for student-centered learning	3.87	0.35	3.87	0.35
	3.30. part-time/adjunct faculty development	**3.13**	**0.83**	**3.60**	**0.74**
	3.36. developing faculty in the scholarship of teaching	**3.40**	**0.63**	**3.73**	**0.46**
	3.37. teaching large classes	**3.80**	**0.41**	**3.87**	**0.35**
	3.38. peer review as a form of assessment; training faculty and TAs in the peer review process	**3.20**	**0.68**	**3.53**	**0.74**
	3.40. critical thinking and inquiry	**3.40**	**0.51**	**3.60**	**0.51**
6. Resources and Publications	**6.3.** updated Web site (with resources to download and links to other Web-based resources)	3.87	0.35	4.00	0.00
7. Other Services	**7.3. customized programs on instructional issues for individual academic departments**	**3.47**	**0.52**	**3.60**	**0.63**
	7.14. service on university, college, and departmental committees in support of teaching and learning	3.53	0.64	3.87	0.35
	7.17. faculty-facilitated sessions for colleagues on issues of teaching and teaching methods	3.60	0.63	3.73	0.46

but not currently are bolded in the table. We see dramatic differences between current and future group consensus means for most of these programs:

- Understanding college students (learning styles, developmental patterns, diversity)
- Multicultural teaching and learning; infusing multiculturalism into a course
- Application of instructional technology; teaching with technology; using various multimedia software
- Part-time/adjunct faculty development
- Developing faculty in the scholarship of teaching
- Peer review as a form of assessment; training faculty and TAs in the peer-review process
- Critical thinking and inquiry
- Customized programs on instructional issues for individual academic departments

Conclusion

According to center directors themselves, some types of faculty development programming are essential in fulfilling their mission. The Delphi panel identified individual consultations, whether simple discussions on teaching strategies or follow-ups of classroom videotapings and observations of individual faculty, as essential programs. These consultations may extend to advising with other units and groups on campus. Another critical type of program is the university-wide orientation for new faculty and TAs. Directors expect such orientations for international TAs to become essential in time. Also considered essential, both now and in the future, are university-wide workshops on topics important to faculty. For the present, the essential topics are these: enhancing teaching strategies; course and syllabus design; testing, test construction, and evaluating student performance; assessing student learning outcomes; college teaching for TAs; developing teaching strategies and methods of active and cooperative learning; teaching for student-centered learning; and teaching large classes. But in the future, the directors anticipate that a changing educational environment will require workshops on different topics, such as developing effective writing assignments, understanding college students (learning styles, developmental patterns, diversity), introducing multiculturalism into a course, teaching with technology, developing part-time and adjunct faculty, developing faculty in the scholarship of teaching, using peer review as a form of assessment, and developing critical thinking and inquiry. In addition, directors see their centers as information, research, and resource centers, making an updated, library-like Web site essential.

Finally, as Sorcinelli and colleagues (2006) have argued, faculty development has recently entered a new age—the Age of the Network. In support of this claim, directors consider designing customized instructional programs for individual academic departments an essential mode of faculty development; so is recruiting faculty to facilitate instructional sessions for their colleagues and using committee service at all levels in support of teaching and learning, which may also involve planning and coordinating faculty development activities with other campus units on institutional initiatives (for example, assessing student learning outcomes, multiculturalism, diversity, changing faculty roles).

The inventory of essential faculty development programs that we have assembled for both the present and the future can serve as a yardstick for evaluating existing faculty development programming and guiding both the expansion of established programs and the planning of new ones, at least at research-extensive universities. Our results suggest that teaching and learning centers need to respond flexibly to the changing needs of faculty and to offer a variety of programs to serve a large and diverse university community. They must stay current with research on faculty careers, adult learning, organizational change, educational reform, and faculty development. They must also assess their program offerings regularly, as the roles and the needs of faculty and institutions continue to change.

Appendix A

Example Page from First-Round Questionnaire

Ranking: "4" represents a program that is "essential"; "3" represents a program that is "important but not essential"; "2" represents a program that maybe "helpful but not very important;" "1" represents a program that is "unimportant and should not be included." Please CLICK the ranking that best represents your view of the essentiality of these programs for teaching and learning centers at research extensive universities.

Program Category	Program	Rank Current Essentiality	Rank Future Essentiality
1. Consultations	classroom videotaping, observations and critique of classroom instruction for individual faculty	☐4 ☐3 ☐2 ☐1	☐4 ☐3 ☐2 ☐1
	consultation on enhancing teaching practices for individual faculty	☐4 ☐3 ☐2 ☐1	☐4 ☐3 ☐2 ☐1
	consultation on career goals and other personal questions for individual faculty	☐4 ☐3 ☐2 ☐1	☐4 ☐3 ☐2 ☐1
	consultations on ethical conduct and teacher-student relationships for individual faculty	☐4 ☐3 ☐2 ☐1	☐4 ☐3 ☐2 ☐1

(Continued)

Program Category	Program	Rank Current Essentiality			Rank Future Essentiality		
	individual consultations for TAs	☐4	☐3	☐2 ☐1	☐4	☐3	☐2 ☐1
	mentoring services for TAs	☐4	☐3	☐2 ☐1	☐4	☐3	☐2 ☐1
	mentoring services for new faculty members	☐4	☐3	☐2 ☐1	☐4	☐3	☐2 ☐1
	pre-tenure review support for individual faculty	☐4	☐3	☐2 ☐1	☐4	☐3	☐2 ☐1
	post-tenure review support for individual faculty	☐4	☐3	☐2 ☐1	☐4	☐3	☐2 ☐1
	consultation on preparing teaching and course portfolios for individual faculty	☐4	☐3	☐2 ☐1	☐4	☐3	☐2 ☐1

References

Altbach, P. (2005). Academic challenges: The American professoriate in comparative perspective. In A. Welch (Ed.), *The professoriate: Profile of a profession* (pp. 147–165). New York: Springer.

Boyer, E. L. (1990). *Scholarship reconsidered: Priorities of the professoriate.* Princeton, NJ: Carnegie Foundation for the Advancement of Teaching.

Brancato, V. C. (2003, Summer). Professional development in higher education. *New Directions for Adult and Continuing Education, 98,* 59–65.

Centra, J. A. (1976). *Faculty development practices in U.S. colleges and universities.* Princeton, NJ: Educational Testing Service.

Clayton, M. J. (1997). Delphi: A technique to harness expert opinion for critical decision-making tasks in education. *Educational Psychology, 17*(4), 373–386.

Crawley, A. (1995). Faculty development programs at research universities: Implications for senior faculty renewal. In E. Neal & L. Richlin (Eds.), *To improve the academy: Vol. 14. Resources for faculty, instructional, and organizational development* (pp. 65–90). Stillwater, OK: New Forums Press.

Dalkey, N. C., & Helmer, O. (1963). An experimental application of the Delphi method to the use of experts. *Management Science, 9,* 458–467.

Diamond, R. M. (2002). Faculty, instructional, and organizational development: Options and choices. In K. H. Gillespie (Ed.), *A guide to faculty development: Practical advice, examples, and resources* (pp. 2–8). Bolton, MA: Anker.

Diamond, R. M. (2005). The institutional change agency: The expanding role of academic support centers. In S. Chadwick-Blossey & D. R. Robertson (Eds.), *To improve the academy: Vol. 23. Resources for faculty, instructional, and organizational development* (pp. 24–37). Bolton, MA: Anker.

Eble, K. E., & McKeachie, W. J. (1985). *Improving undergraduate education through faculty development: An analysis of effective programs and practices.* San Francisco: Jossey-Bass.

Eckel, P. D. (2002). Institutional transformation and change: Insights for faculty developers. In D. Lieberman & C. Wehlburg (Eds.), *To improve the academy: Vol. 20. Resources for faculty, instructional, and organizational development* (pp. 3–19). Bolton, MA: Anker.

Eggers, R. M., & Jones, C. M. (1998). Practical considerations for conducting Delphi studies: The oracle enters a new age. *Educational Research Quarterly, 21*(3), 53–66.

Erickson, G. (1986). A survey of faculty development practices. In M. Svinicki (Ed.), *To improve the academy: Vol. 5. Resources for student, faculty, and institutional development* (pp. 182–196). Stillwater, OK: New Forums Press.

Frantz, A. C., Beebe, S. A., Horvath, V. S., Canales, J., & Swee, D. E. (2005). The roles of teaching and learning centers. In S. Chadwick-Blossey & D. R. Robertson (Eds.), *To improve the academy: Vol. 23. Resources for faculty, instructional, and organizational development* (pp. 72–90). Bolton, MA: Anker.

Gaff, J. G., & Simpson, R. D. (1994, Spring). Faculty development in the United States. *Innovative Higher Education, 18*(3), 167–176.

Garavalia, L., & Gredler, M. (2004). Teaching evaluation through modeling: Using the Delphi technique to assess problems in academic programs. *American Journal of Evaluation, 25*(3), 375–380.

Gullatt, D. E., & Weaver, S. W. (1997, October). *Use of faculty development activities to improve the effectiveness of U.S. institutions of higher education.* Paper presented at the 22nd annual meeting of the Professional and Organizational Development Network in Higher Education, Hines City, FL. (ERIC Document Reproduction Service No. ED 414 796)

Levine, A. (2001). The remaking of the American university. *Innovative Higher Education, 25*(4), 253–267.

Lieberman, D. A., & Guskin, A. E. (2003). The essential role of faculty development in new higher education models. In C. M. Wehlburg & S. Chadwick-Blossey (Eds.), *To improve the academy: Vol. 21. Resources for faculty, instructional, and organizational development* (pp. 257–272). Bolton, MA: Anker.

Linstone, H. A., & Turoff, M. (Eds.). (1975). *The Delphi method: Techniques and applications.* Reading, MA: Addison-Wesley.

Millis, B. J. (1994). Faculty development in the 1990s: What it is and why we can't wait. *Journal of Counseling and Development, 72*, 454–464.

Morris, L. V. (2004). Changing institutions and changing faculty. *Innovative Higher Education, 29*(1), 3–6.

Murry, J. W., & Hammons, J. O. (1995). Delphi: A versatile methodology for conducting qualitative research. *The Review of Higher Education, 18*(4), 423–436.

Rice, R. E. (1996). *Making a place for the new American scholar: Inquiry #1.* Washington, DC: American Association for Higher Education.

Ruben, B. D. (2004). *Pursuing excellence in higher education.* San Francisco: Jossey-Bass.

Scheibe, M., Skutsch, M., & Schofer, J. (1975). Experiments in Delphi methodology. In H. A. Linstone & M. Turoff (Eds.), *The Delphi method: Techniques and applications* (pp. 262–287). Reading, MA: Addison-Wesley.

Shulman, L. S. (2004). *Teaching as community property: Essays on higher education.* San Francisco: Jossey-Bass.

Singer, S. R. (2002, Fall). Learning and teaching centers: Hubs of educational reform. In J. L. Narum & K. Conover (Eds.), *New directions for higher education: No. 119. Building robust learning environments in undergraduate science, technology, engineering, and mathematics* (pp. 59–64). San Francisco: Jossey-Bass.

Sorcinelli, M. D., Austin, A. E., Eddy, P. L., & Beach, A. L. (2006). *Creating the future of faculty development: Learning from the past, understanding the present.* Bolton, MA: Anker.

Stone Fish, L. S., & Busby, D. M. (1996). The Delphi method. In D. H. Sprenkle & S. M. Moon (Eds.), *Research methods in family therapy* (pp. 469–482). New York: Guilford Press.

Tice, S. L. (2005). Preface. In S. L. Tice, N. Jackson, L. M. Lambert, & P. Englot (Eds.), *University teaching: A reference guide for graduate students and faculty* (pp. xi–xii). Syracuse, NY: Syracuse University Press.

Wilhelm, W. J. (2001). Alchemy of the oracle: The Delphi technique. *Delta Pi Epsilon Journal, 43*(1), 6–26.

Wright, D. L. (2000). Faculty development centers in research universities: A study of resources and programs. In M. Kaplan & D. Lieberman (Eds.), *To improve the academy: Vol. 18. Resources for faculty, instructional, and organizational development* (pp. 291–301). Bolton, MA: Anker.

Wright, D. L. (2002). Program types and prototypes. In K. H. Gillespie (Ed.), *A guide to faculty development: Practical advice, examples, and resources* (pp. 24–34). Bolton, MA: Anker.

Wulff, D. H., & Austin, A. E. (Eds.). (2004). *Paths to the professoriate: Strategies for enriching the preparation of future faculty.* San Francisco: Jossey-Bass.

Zahorski, K. J. (2002). Nurturing scholarship through holistic faculty development: A synergistic approach. In K. J. Zahorski (Ed.), *New directions for teaching and learning: No. 90. Scholarship in the postmodern era* (pp. 29–37). San Francisco: Jossey-Bass.

Ziglio, E. (1996). The Delphi method and its contribution to decision-making. In M. Adler & E. Ziglio (Eds.), *Gazing into the oracle: The Delphi method and its application to social policy and public health* (pp. 3–33). London: Jessica Kingsley Publishers.

Faculty Evaluation

Establishing External, Blind Peer Review of Scholarship of Teaching and Learning Within the Disciplines

Cheryl A. Stevens
East Carolina University

Erik Rosegard
San Francisco State University

Colleges and universities face growing pressure to reward multiple forms of scholarship in order to align their missions with faculty roles and rewards. This chapter proposes that disciplinary societies develop templates, processes, and criteria for external, blind peer review of the scholarship of teaching and learning (SoTL) in order to provide a reliable and valid way to judge the quality of faculty SoTL work. Although SoTL requires support from faculty development programs and other interdisciplinary SoTL forums, it will continue to be viewed as evidence of teaching excellence rather than scholarship until discipline-based external, blind peer-review processes are established.

In the novel, *Catch-22,*

> Yossarian lay in the hospital with . . . a pain in his liver that fell just short of being jaundice. The doctors were puzzled by the fact that it wasn't quite jaundice. If it became jaundice they could treat it.

> If it didn't become jaundice and went away they could discharge
> him. But this just being short of jaundice all the time confused
> them. (Heller, 1961, p. 7)

Like Yossarian, colleges and universities are caught in a Catch-22
with regard to the scholarship of teaching and learning (SoTL)
because they do not yet have a reliable way to judge its quality.
On the one hand, SoTL is increasingly supported as valuable and
important to the mission of colleges and universities. On the
other hand, because colleges and universities do not know how
to reliably determine whether or not SoTL is *good* scholarship
(that is, judged as on par with peer-reviewed research), they are
unable to integrate SoTL in meaningful ways into the most
important faculty reward system—tenure and promotion. By
necessity, faculty faced with full plates focus their energies on
those activities they know will be rewarded (Rice, 2005a, 2005b).
As Weimer (2006) pointed out, it is reasonable to believe that
many faculty do not pursue SoTL because they do not see the
work as being rewarded or recognized, and "they do not view it
as a viable path to professional advancement" (p. 6). Faculty
know it is important to be good teachers with strong service
records, but when the day of reckoning comes, it is still research
publications that count. However, if colleges and universities are
to successfully address growing concerns about their institution's
relevance to society, they need to embrace transformative change
in tenure and promotion criteria. At present, reward structures
recognize discovery research as evidence of scholarship, and they
need to explicitly recognize all forms of scholarship identified by
Boyer (1990): discovery, integration, application, and teaching.
Indeed, when Boyer set forth this paradigm, his intent was to
make it possible for colleges and universities to tap the full range
of faculty talents in order to align missions with reward systems,
thus allowing educational institutions to better meet their commitments to students (teaching), communities (service), and discovery (research) (Glassick, Huber, & Maeroff, 1997).

Shulman (2000b, p. 105) predicted that by 2005 "there will
be a fundamental recognition at colleges and universities that
good teaching requires serious investigation and learning," and
its inclusion in the expected repertoire of scholarly practices will

replace SoTL's present status as an add-on. Although SoTL has certainly received much of the support Shulman predicted in the form of teaching academies and faculty development programs, little progress has been made regarding changes in reward structures governing tenure and promotion (Lueddeke, 2008). As was the case prior to Boyer's (1990) reconceptualization of scholarship, the majority of colleges and universities still apply scholarship standards that primarily value discovery research. Thus, SoTL is still viewed primarily as an add-on in the sense that it counts more as evidence of excellent teaching than of scholarship. The authors posit that once colleges and universities have reliable and valid methods for judging the quality of SoTL, they will be empowered to revise reward structures governing tenure and promotion in order to count SoTL as scholarship. This chapter proposes that disciplinary societies develop templates, processes, and criteria for external, blind peer review of SoTL in order to accomplish this goal.

Definition of SoTL and Related Terms

The terms *excellent teaching, scholarly teaching, scholarship of teaching,* and *SoTL* must be clearly defined in order to establish context for this proposal. First, it is necessary to understand that excellent teaching is not the same as scholarly teaching or SoTL. Excellent teaching, or teaching effectiveness, has long been a valued faculty role and is usually defined and measured via presentation of course materials, student evaluations, peer-classroom observations, and other supportive documentation. Faculty collect evidence of their teaching effectiveness and place it in teaching portfolios and personnel action documents. Excellent teachers often give presentations and publish articles (both peer reviewed and otherwise) that provide teaching tips and advice based on personal experience (Witman & Richlin, 2007). Witman and Richlin point out that although this advice is often useful, it is not the same thing as SoTL because there is no way for a reader to judge the quality of the advice. Scholarship of teaching, first conceptualized by Boyer (1990), is defined by Glassick and colleagues (1997) as "teaching [that] initiates students into the best values of the academy, enabling them to comprehend better and participate more fully in the larger culture" (p. 9). Further, these researchers identify six criteria that exemplify scholarship of teaching: 1) clear goals, 2) adequate preparation, 3) appropriate methods, 4) significant results, 5) reflective critique, and 6) effective presentation. Therefore, teaching is scholarship when a teacher frames a problem related to student learning, reviews related literature, devises a suitable method to investigate the effect of teaching strategies, gathers and analyzes evidence, and reflects on what he or she learned about teaching and student learning.

Over time, it has become apparent that an understanding of scholarship of teaching required further clarification. Witman and Richlin (2007) point out that the scholarship of teaching "contains within it two separate systems: *scholarly teaching* and the resulting *scholarship* that reports its results" (p. 2). The scholarly teacher analyzes evidence of student learning, reflects on his or her teaching, and subsequently invites peer collaboration and review (Trigwell, Martin, Benjamin, & Prosser, 2000). Scholarly teaching becomes scholarship when it is made public. Shulman (2000a) explains it this way: "We develop a scholarship of teaching when our work as teachers becomes public, peer-reviewed and critiqued, and exchanged with other members of our professional communities, so they, in turn, can build on our work. These are the qualities of all scholarship" (p. 49).

The addition of *learning* to the oft-used phrase *scholarship of teaching* denotes that the focus of SoTL is not just on teaching, but it also carries an implied focus on discovering more about how teaching methods relate to students' acquisition of learning outcomes. This chapter focuses specifically on SoTL because it represents the product of scholarly teaching that can be evaluated by peers.

An overview of a faculty member's evolution from scholarly teaching to SoTL presents the reader with a frame of reference. Consider that a line of SoTL, much like discovery research, develops over time. Also recognize that a faculty member's SoTL starts small, with general questions about how to improve teaching effectiveness and student learning. For teaching to become scholarly, the faculty member follows four steps: 1) conducts a thorough examination of the literature related to disciplinary teaching and student learning, 2) develops methodology and investigates the question(s), 3) analyzes results related to student learning outcomes, and 4) engages in reflection. SoTL requires two steps beyond scholarly teaching—"putting the results into the context of what others have done (the literature) and dissemination through presentation and publication" (Witman & Richlin, 2007, p. 2). SoTL can be critiqued using the criteria for scholarship described by Glassick and colleagues (1997).

The Problems of Relevance and Time

Times have changed, and institutions of higher education can no longer afford to remain unresponsive to public demand for high-quality, relevant education. The Kellogg Commission (1999) made a strong case that the work of universities today is quickly becoming irrelevant, as specialized disciplines increasingly fail to respond to real-world problems. The Commission argued that by becoming "engaged institutions," universities can "redesign their teaching, research, extension and service functions" (p. 9). However, faculty are already stretched to the limit and asking them to do more is becoming problematic. Former Cornell University president Frank Rhodes (2001) points out that it is not surprising faculty cannot do everything they are being asked, and that it is still research, not great teaching, mentoring, or service that is receiving reward and recognition. He concludes that "perhaps the greatest surprise is that, given these competing distractions, so many faculty members continue to exhibit such devotion to their students" (p. 25). Recently, a number of experts have argued that embracing SoTL as scholarship is increasingly imperative and no longer a choice (Huber & Hutchings, 2005; Lueddeke, 2008; O'Meara & Rice, 2005; Weimer, 2006).

Shulman (2000a) presents the rationale for embracing SoTL from three perspectives: professional, pragmatic, and policy. The most important reason for engaging in SoTL is that it is part of faculty professional responsibility. Although professors are obligated to add to the core of disciplinary knowledge, "we also assume the responsibility for passing on what we learn through teaching, social action, and through exchanging our insights" (Shulman, p. 49). Although not all faculty need to be engaged in SoTL in order for a discipline to develop a better understanding of effective and relevant educational methods, as more faculty do engage in SoTL, quality of teaching and student learning will continue to improve. Responsive, effective teaching is not a simplistic, intuitive process—understanding what works requires serious scholarship, the same as discovery research. Yet many professors have had little, if any, training in effective teaching methods, and few find they have adequate time to address their teaching in a scholarly manner. However, the Kellogg Commission (1999) report states, higher education "can and must do better" (p. 3), and we "must be organized to respond to the needs of today's students and tomorrow's, not yesterday's" (p. 10).

SoTL is also pragmatic. It allows a faculty member to integrate teaching and scholarship roles in interesting, relevant, and efficient ways (Stevens, 2007). Undertaking a SoTL research agenda can help faculty address the full plate syndrome by allowing them to strategically integrate the roles of teaching and scholarship. For example, a new assistant professor with a strong interest in excellent teaching could plan a SoTL research agenda early in his career if he had confidence that his work would count as scholarship when he applies for tenure and promotion. At present, new faculty are often well advised not to spend too much time on teaching or service because it will be research publications that count—they are told SoTL can wait until after tenure (Stevens & Wellman, 2007).

SoTL provides policy benefits to educational institutions as well. For example, accreditation bodies now insist on audits that include evidence of student learning outcomes and continual curricular improvement in order to ensure that students are receiving a high-quality, relevant education (Shulman, 2000a). Shulman points out that quick-and-dirty, off-the-shelf approaches to learning outcomes assessment are rapidly becoming unacceptable. He notes that "this kind of work cries out for a vigorous scholarship of teaching and learning engaged by discipline and field-specific scholars of teaching" (p. 51). In addition, Shulman contends that the viability of colleges and universities is threatened if they do not provide the type of education students need. Unless colleges and universities hold themselves accountable to quality, relevant education, they will find themselves less competitive in a free market economy that provides increasing opportunities for students to enroll in distance learning via for-profit providers.

In sum, we argue that SoTL is important to institutions of higher education, but until faculty are sufficiently rewarded for SoTL, they will not have resources to do it adequately. As O'Meara and Rice (2005) point out:

> Colleges and universities will not be able to genuinely recognize and reward multiple forms of scholarly work unless faculty have confidence in the integrity of the institution's mission, aspiration and goals, and values. The definition of scholarship, accordingly, must be aligned with the basic institutional mission and the various forms of scholarship—whether discovery, teaching, integration, or engagement, must be rewarded in ways that encourage faculty members to contribute to the fulfillment of institutional goals as well as their own disciplinary aspirations. (pp. 11–12)

Some have expressed concern that rewarding multiple forms of scholarship will diminish the value of discovery research, but as Rice (2005b) points out, while campuses have been debating ways to support and reward multiple forms of scholarship, there has been a concurrent increased emphasis on scholarship of discovery; its prestige remains unthreatened and undiminished. Therefore, those who worry that discovery research will have less support have little to worry about. The authors contend that the time is right to look at SoTL in a new way that will enable colleges and universities to regard it as scholarship.

The Proposed Solution

Dialogue has produced numerous documents, articles, models, and active scholarly teaching communities built on Boyer's (1990) concept of SoTL (Glassick et al., 1997; Healy, 2000; Hutchings, 1996, 1998; Kreber, 2002; Lueddeke, 2008; Quinlan, 2002; Shulman, 1993; Theall & Centra, 2001; Trigwell et al., 2000). Several colleges and universities (Indiana University at Purdue University Indianapolis, Texas A&M University, University of Wisconsin-La Crosse) and foundations (Carnegie Foundation, Pew Charitable Trusts, William and Flora Hewlett Foundation) are currently conducting SoTL projects. Some disciplines accept and publish SoTL (for example, natural sciences and professional studies), and in "others it is not yet broadly accepted" (for example, social sciences and humanities) (Witman & Richlin, 2007, p. 14). There are also several multidisciplinary journals that publish SoTL, including the *International Journal for the Scholarship of Teaching and Learning* (IJ-SoTL), *The Journal of the Scholarship of Teaching and Learning* (JoSoTL), and the *Journal on Excellence in College Teaching* (JECT). Further, the Carnegie Academy for the Scholarship of Teaching and Learning (CASTL) is an initiative of the Carnegie Foundation, designed to develop and support SoTL (Carnegie Foundation, 2007). However, although many colleges and universities already count SoTL to the degree these scholarly efforts result in peer-reviewed journal publications, most of these journals have low citation rates (Braxton, Luckey, & Helland, 2002), and their value to faculty varies substantially by discipline and university.

All of these efforts are essential for the development and dissemination of SoTL, but something else is needed for SoTL to be considered solid enough for faculty to stake their tenure and promotion on it. Because there is little question that the external, blind peer-review process used for discovery research plays a critical role in tenure and promotion decisions, the authors believe that external, blind peer review of SoTL can provide the impetus educational institutions need to count SoTL as scholarship.

Discipline-Based External, Blind Peer Review

One way to validate the quality of SoTL is to establish external, blind peer-review processes specific to SoTL within the disciplines. According to Shapiro and Coleman (2000), "peer review is the bedrock of the evaluative process and can best ensure that the quality and standards of the scholarship meet the standards of the academic community" (p. 987). Blind peer review is standard practice in the majority of scholarly journals when reviewing manuscripts. This review system involves reviewers from outside one's institution but within one's discipline, allowing reviewers to be drawn from a pool of individuals with recognized expertise in the areas most closely related to one's scholarship. Given that good scholarship must demonstrate adequate preparation (that is, understanding of the relevant literature) and significant results, it takes a reviewer intimately familiar with the discipline to make a qualified judgment.

The significance of peer review of SoTL is gaining increasing recognition. In 1991, the University of California strongly advocated for a peer-review process of teaching scholarship and stated that "if the scholarship of teaching is to be restored to its proper place, it follows directly that peer evaluation of teaching must be pursued with the same level of enthusiasm and dedication now afforded peer evaluation of research" (p. 11). Several accreditation bodies have followed suit by adopting broader definitions of discipline-based scholarship in order to capture teaching and service as viable fields of research. For example, the American Association of Colleges of Nursing (1999) has defined *scholarship* in nursing as "those activities that systematically advance the teaching, research, and practice of nursing through rigorous inquiry" (p. 6). Also, the Association to Advance Collegiate Schools of Business (2005) provided specific language to include SoTL in their revision of accreditation standards: "A generalized categorization of intellectual contributions includes contributions to learning and pedagogical research, contributions to practice, and discipline-based scholarship" (p. 23).

However, the use of an external, blind peer-review process for SoTL is virtually absent in the literature, and the majority of dialogue has been limited to examining internal review processes. An external peer review that is discipline-based and blind minimizes issues related to confidentiality, anonymity, and reciprocity (Malik, 1996). External peer review has the advantages of increasing the number and quality of reviewers and allowing greater range of expertise. Although the Clearinghouse and National Review Board (2002) provides an avenue for faculty to pursue external review of scholarship of engagement, which can be integrative across teaching, research, and service, these reviews are not blind and results are not made public. Recognizing that blind peer review has long been the standard for judging the quality of research, and because the question of judging the credibility and quality of SoTL is at the heart of the debate concerning whether SoTL is evidence of excellent teaching or scholarship, external, blind peer review of SoTL is needed.

External, blind peer review of SoTL should be housed within the disciplines (Braxton et al., 2002; Healy, 2000; Huber, Hutchings, & Schulman, 2005; Malik, 1996; O'Meara & Rice, 2005). Healy provides two reasons: 1) most academic staff have a

primary allegiance to their subject or profession and their allegiance to the university is secondary, and 2) there is a strong perception among academic staff that there are significant differences
among disciplines in what academics do and how activities are
valued. Weimer (2008) counters the argument to positioning
SoTL within the disciplines with two points: 1) placing scholarship within the disciplines narrows the potential audience, and
2) a good deal of reinvention occurs because many instructional
issues and teaching methods transcend disciplines. The authors
concur with Healy and others, that discipline-based review is the
best approach and suggest that Weimer's concerns can be
addressed by ensuring reviewers' expertise and use of electronic
publication venues. Although it would be up to each discipline to
determine portfolio content, evaluation standards, review procedures, and a public forum in which to share SoTL, the following
sections elaborate on existing practices and present a template
that disciplines can build on for developing an external, blind
peer-review process for SoTL. The questions one might ask at
this point include, What would the discipline-based peer reviewers evaluate? If not a journal article, then what?

The SoTL Portfolio

A SoTL portfolio provides one viable answer. A portfolio is, arguably, the most useful format because SoTL requires a kind of
"going meta" in which faculty frame and systematically investigate
questions related to student learning—the conditions under which
it occurs, what it looks like, how to deepen it, and so forth—and to
do so with an eye not only to improving their own classroom but
to advancing practice beyond it (Shulman & Hutchings, as cited in
Huber et al., 2005, p. 37).

SoTL, like scholarship of engagement, involves a kind of action
research, extended into a faculty member's classroom practice,
which is made available to peers in order to invite dialogue, as well
as innovation in practices (Huber et al., 2005). Thus, SoTL differs
from scholarship of discovery, and a SoTL portfolio provides a suitable format for its presentation. Notably, those working on establishing peer review for scholarship of engagement reached similar
conclusions (Diamond & Adam, 1995, 2000; Driscoll & Lynton,
1999).

Faculty development programs and other SoTL forums have important roles to play in facilitating the development of faculty members' scholarly teaching by providing needed resources, support, and formative feedback. The scholarly teacher would be a candidate to compile a SoTL portfolio and submit it for discipline-based external, blind peer review once he or she has completed one or more SoTL projects. The review, tenure, and promotion process could incorporate the resulting evaluation as evidence of scholarship, the quality of which has been judged by peers. Using this model, discipline-based external, blind peer review of SoTL can be designed to complement (not duplicate) educational institutions' existing tenure and promotion criteria.

Bernstein (1998) argues that while a teaching portfolio focuses on teaching, a course portfolio involves both teaching and learning. Hutchings (1998) echoes this argument stating, "the course is a powerful unit of analysis for documenting teaching because it is within the course that knowledge of the field intersects with knowledge about particular students and their learning" (p. 14). Cerbin (1996) explains that course portfolios are . . . intended to be a coherent explanation about the nature and quality of teaching—explaining what the instructor intends to accomplish with students; the methods used; and the results of the experience in terms of students' learning, thinking, and development. The course portfolio establishes connections between goals, methods, and outcomes (p. 5).

Alternatively, a SoTL portfolio could systematically assess student learning outcomes in a disciplinary degree program. In this case, the scholar would investigate what the students should be learning within the discipline and subsequently investigate how well they are learning it. Curricular modifications based on student learning outcomes assessment would be implemented and evaluated over time to determine how to deliver the best possible education.

Although Cerbin (1996) states that the course portfolio is equivalent to a "scholarly manuscript . . . a draft, of ongoing inquiry" (p. 53), the presentation and format of the portfolio is as diverse as the number of disciplines within higher education (Huber, 1998). This wide range of formatting possibilities poses a potential concern regarding consistency of SoTL evaluation. Given that most disciplines are familiar with the five sections of a thesis (that is, introduction, literature review, methodology, results, and discussion), this format provides a recognizable template for disciplines evaluating SoTL and can accommodate many possible portfolio design approaches. Although the format of a course portfolio is important for communicating with a disciplinary audience, the identification of criteria from which to assess the course portfolio is the critical element of validating SoTL.

Glassick and colleagues (1997) articulated questions for each of the six evaluation criteria (see Table 16.1). These questions are being used as evaluation criteria for proposal submissions in refereed journals and other venues (for example, *International Journal for the Scholarship of Teaching and Learning* and the Clearinghouse & National Review Board for The Scholarship of Engagement). The first five evaluation criteria parallel the five sections of a thesis, and the sixth criterion (effective presentation) suggests, among other venues, the preparation of a portfolio. Thus, adoption of Glassick and colleagues' framework provides a reliable evaluation scheme for evaluating SoTL.

We propose that each disciplinary group establish portfolio and evaluation guidelines. Based on the criteria in Table 16.1 and existing portfolio models, it seems probable that a SoTL portfolio could be compiled and presented using submission guidelines from a scholarly journal (that is, twenty pages following the American Psychological Association guidelines). The references in this and other SoTL articles (Bernstein, 1998; Cerbin, 1996; Diamond & Adam, 1995, 2000; Huber & Hutchings, 2005; Hutchings, 1998; Kreber, 2002; Quinlan, 2002; Shulman, 1999; Trigwell et al., 2000; Weimer, 2006) include many resources to assist discipline-based groups in this process.

Issues in Developing a Discipline-Based, Blind Peer-Review Process

In addition to issues of portfolio design, the peer review of SoTL is not devoid of issues related to the reviewee, reviewer, and the review itself (Hutchings, 1996; Kreber, 2002; Paulsen, 2002). Hutchings (1996) identified five issues regarding peer review. In discussing these issues, the viewpoint of a discipline-based, external, blind peer review will be used. The notion of external review is not intended to replace internal peer review, which provides an important formative role in SoTL, but to build onto existing supports in order to conceptualize an external review process for judging the quality of SoTL.

The first issue concerns the individual being reviewed. Traditionally, teaching has been a private exchange between an individual faculty member and students. Going public with one's teaching can be unsettling to a junior faculty going up for tenure and promotion. One strategy to minimize this apprehension is to institute an external, blind peer review. This process ensures anonymity, which reduces the potential for negative feelings between colleagues. In addition, faculty seeking a review should understand that the SoTL external, blind peer-review process focuses on the scholarship, not the individual's teaching; this may lessen feelings of vulnerability related to opening the door to one's teaching.

A second issue involves establishing standards and operationalizing the concepts of SoTL. In the years since Boyer's (1990) publication, much progress has been made regarding definitions and evaluation criteria (Glassick et al., 1997; Huber & Hutchings, 2005; Trigwell et al., 2000; Weimer, 2006; Witman & Richlin, 2007). Implementing a discipline-based external, blind peer review for SoTL will allow for consideration of ways that student learning differs by discipline (for example, studio arts, sociology, and medicine). Even with the wealth of information currently available, members of each disciplinary group will want to familiarize themselves with a broad base of SoTL literature (both within and outside the discipline) in order to draw on best practices and codify the criteria to be used in their review process. Thus, a discipline-based approach will allow for emphasis on evaluation of the most relevant teaching methods and assessment of student learning outcomes as they relate to each particular discipline.

Identifying qualified peers to evaluate SoTL is a third issue that affects the review process. The authors propose that the lead individual (serving in a capacity like that of a peer-reviewed journal editor) would select reviewers for a particular SoTL portfolio based on their expertise in the discipline and teaching literature used in the SoTL project. The authors further suggest that a SoTL review team should have representative expertise in three areas:

1) an understanding of SoTL (in general), 2) disciplinary content expertise, and 3) teaching and student learning literature. Although housing the review process within the discipline follows the accepted model for peer review of discovery research, thus ensuring content expertise, disciplinary review boards may want to recruit reviewers with expertise in teaching and student learning literature from outside the discipline. Other issues related to reviewers concern confidentiality, anonymity, potential conflict of interest, bias, and reciprocity (Centra, 1993; Chism, 1999; Hutchings, 1996). Basing external peer review within the discipline can broaden the pool of reviewers beyond the educational institution to a national (and even international) scope. Selecting peers to do the external review from a larger pool decreases the likelihood of reviewers recognizing an individual's work, even when it is presented anonymously. The use of reviewers external to the university also keeps the focus on the scholarship and not instructional delivery. Anonymity would be ensured using similar processes to those used for journal submissions.

Hutchings (1996) notes a fourth issue—evaluation methods. What artifacts are included? How do you organize and communicate the evidence? What criteria will the evidence be evaluated against? Is there a limit to the volume of evidence that may be submitted? The answers to each question will have a resounding "it depends," as each discipline will have to determine the content and evaluative criteria for SoTL portfolios. Ideally, a discipline would want an external, blind peer-review process that limits evaluations to specific format, criteria, and documentation while maintaining flexibility that allows for a wide range of SoTL to be assessed. A proposed portfolio format using Glassick and colleagues' (1997) scholarship framework provides guidance for all disciplines (see Table 16.1). As soon as one discipline establishes an external, blind peer review of SoTL, others will be able to draw on their model. In 2007, the Society of Park and Recreation Educators (SPRE) established a two-year pilot program to design and implement a blind peer-review process for SoTL (Stevens & Wellman, 2007; Stevens, Wellman, DeGraaf, Dustin, Paisley, & Ross, 2007). Other disciplines can benefit from the results of this pilot, which is scheduled to begin soliciting SoTL portfolios in 2009.

Table 16.1. Scholarship Evaluation Questions

Clear Goals

1. Does the scholar state the basic purposes of his or her work clearly?
2. Does the scholar define objectives that are realistic and achievable?
3. Does the scholar identify important questions in the field?

Adequate Preparation

1. Does the scholar show an understanding of existing scholarship in the field?
2. Does the scholar bring the necessary skills to her or his work?
3. Does the scholar bring together the resources necessary to move the project forward?

Appropriate Methods

1. Does the scholar use methods appropriate to the goals?
2. Does the scholar apply effectively the methods selected?
3. Does the scholar modify procedures in response to changing circumstances?

Significant Results

1. Does the scholar achieve the goals?
2. Does the scholar's work add consequentially to the field?
3. Does the scholar's work open additional areas for further exploration?

Effective Presentation

1. Does the scholar use a suitable style and effective organization to present his or her work?
2. Does the scholar use appropriate forums for communicating work to its intended audiences?
3. Does the scholar present her or his message with clarity and integrity?

Reflective Critique

1. Does the scholar critically evaluate his or her own work?
2. Does the scholar bring an appropriate breadth of evidence to her or his critique?
3. Does the scholar use evaluation to improve the quality of future work?

Source: Reprinted from "Scholarship Assessed: Evaluation of the Professoriate" by C. Glassick, M. Huber, and G. Maeroff. San Francisco: Jossey-Bass. Copyright 1997 by Jossey-Bass. Adapted with permission.

A fifth issue related to peer review is time. Although Hutchings (1996) identified time as the greatest obstacle to advancing SoTL and implementing a peer-review system, the authors contend that external, blind peer review of SoTL will help resolve the time issue. At institutions where reward structures value primarily discovery research, faculty have to make time to labor over research, often at the expense of other responsibilities, such as teaching and service. Once SoTL can be externally blind peer reviewed, it will be easier for institutions to recognize SoTL as scholarship, and then faculty will have incentive to pursue SoTL research agendas. Institutions of higher education will benefit as well; when more faculty find time to engage in SoTL, institutional missions will be realized to a fuller extent. Thus, external, blind peer review of SoTL will help, not exacerbate, the full-plate problem.

Weimer (2008) brings up a sixth issue by raising concerns about positioning SoTL within the disciplines. Specifically, she notes that "lessons learned in one field are relearned in another and that collective information never becomes a coherent knowledge base," and "also lost are unique research designs and forms of inquiry developed within the disciplines" (Weimer, p. 2). Thus, there are two seemingly conflicting needs: 1) the need to house the evaluation of SoTL within the disciplines (for reasons previously mentioned) and 2) the need to share SoTL among disciplines. We present the following thoughts for further discussion of this concern. Electronic venues for SoTL publications are increasingly popular (for example, IJ-SoTL, JoSoTL, and JECT), and disciplinary associations implementing external, blind peer review of SoTL will likely be selecting electronic venues for publicizing quality SoTL portfolios (that is, those that meet preestablished criteria). Search engines, such as Google Scholar, will provide easier access to SoTL housed within the disciplines. The Carnegie electronic venues have the potential to facilitate interdisciplinary access as well.

Conclusion

Although there are valid concerns for a discipline-based external, blind peer review of SoTL, "submitting work . . . for anonymous refereeing by unknown peers is still one of the best tests of scholarly credibility in the academic world" (Roberts, 1999, p. 15). We have already addressed a number of challenges and concerns related to SoTL: faculty do not have time for SoTL because they are already overloaded; SoTL cannot be evaluated in a rigorous, credible manner; SoTL is not going to be adequately supported or rewarded; and, valuing SoTL as scholarship would diminish the value of discovery research. One might then ask, Would implementing discipline-based external, blind peer-review processes for SoTL be a case of putting the cart before the horse? Should the disciplines wait until more colleges and universities include SoTL in scholarship criteria for tenure and promotion? The authors contend the time to act is now. All the pieces are in place. There is wide recognition of the need to reward multiple forms of scholarship, models for external, blind peer review of discovery research can be adapted for SoTL, and many examples for portfolio content and evaluation criteria have been developed and tested. What remains is to put the pieces together. Once disciplinary associations provide leadership by implementing external, blind peer-review processes for SoTL, colleges and universities will be able to take the next steps. Together, we can embrace this opportunity to take a transformative look at faculty roles and rewards to the benefit of students, faculty, and educational institutions. The consequences of failing to do so will become greater, not less, over time. The concerns raised by the Kellogg Commission (1999) about the work of universities today quickly becoming irrelevant need to be taken seriously. Perhaps it is time to remember that a crisis foretells both danger and opportunity. The opportunity is upon us to correct "the growing mismatch between the responsibilities that most colleges and university faculty members undertake on a daily basis" (Shulman, 2000b, p. 5) by instituting external, blind peer-review processes for SoTL within the disciplines.

References

American Association of Colleges of Nursing. (1999). *Position statement on defining scholarship for the discipline of nursing.* Retrieved May 19, 2008, from www.aacn.nche.edu/publications/positions/scholar.htm

Association to Advance Collegiate Schools of Business. (2005). *Eligibility procedures and accreditation standards for business accreditation.* Retrieved December 2, 2007, from www.aacsb.edu/accreditation/standards.asp

Bernstein, D. (1998). Putting the focus on student learning. In P. Hutchings (Ed.), *The course portfolio: How faculty can examine their teaching to advance practice and improve student learning* (pp. 77–83). Sterling, VA: Stylus.

Boyer, E. L. (1990). *Scholarship reconsidered: Priorities of the professoriate.* Princeton, NJ: Carnegie Foundation for the Advancement of Teaching.

Braxton, J. M., Luckey, W., & Helland, P. (2002). *Institutionalizing a broader view of scholarship through Boyer's four domains.* San Francisco: Jossey-Bass.

Carnegie Foundation. (2007). *Carnegie Academy for the Scholarship of Teaching and Learning.* Retrieved January 2, 2008, from www.carnegiefoundation .org/programs/index.asp?key=21

Cerbin, W. (1996). Inventing a new genre: The course portfolio at the University of Wisconsin–La Crosse. In P. Hutchings (Ed.), *Making teaching community property: A menu for peer collaboration and peer review* (pp. 52–56). Washington, DC: American Association for Higher Education.

Centra, J. A. (1993). *Reflective faculty evaluation: Enhancing teaching and determining faculty effectiveness.* San Francisco: Jossey-Bass.

Chism, N. V. N. (1999). *Peer review of teaching: A sourcebook.* Bolton, MA: Anker.

Clearinghouse and National Review Board for the Scholarship of Engagement. (2002). *Evaluation criteria for the scholarship of engagement.* Retrieved February 21, 2008, from http://scholarshipofengagement .org/

Diamond, R. M., & Adam, B. E. (Eds.). (1995). *The disciplines speak: Rewarding the scholarly, professional, and creative work of faculty.* Washington, DC: American Association for Higher Education.

Diamond, R. M., & Adam, B. E. (Eds.). (2000). *The disciplines speak II: More statements on rewarding the scholarly, professional, and creative work of faculty.* Washington, DC: American Association for Higher Education.

Driscoll, A., & Lynton, E. A. (1999). *Making outreach visible: A guide to documenting professional service and outreach.* Washington, DC: American Association for Higher Education.

Glassick, C. E., Huber, M. T., & Maeroff, G. I. (1997). *Scholarship assessed: Evaluation of the professoriate.* San Francisco: Jossey-Bass.

Healy, M. (2000). Developing the scholarship of teaching in higher education: A discipline-based approach. *Higher Education Research and Development, 19*(2), 169–188.

Heller, J. (1961). *Catch-22.* New York: Simon & Schuster.

Huber, M. T. (1998). Why now? Course portfolios in context. In P. Hutchings (Ed.), *The course portfolio: How faculty can examine their teaching to advance practice and improve student learning.* Washington, DC: American Association for Higher Education.

Huber, M. T., & Hutchings, P. (2005). *The advancement of learning: Building the teaching commons.* San Francisco: Jossey-Bass.

Huber, M. T., Hutchings, P., & Schulman, L. (2005). The scholarship of teaching and learning. In K. O'Meara & R. E. Rice, *Faculty priorities reconsidered* (pp. 34–42). San Francisco: Jossey-Bass.

Hutchings, P. (1996). The peer review of teaching: Progress, issues and prospects. *Innovative Higher Education, 20*(4), 221–234.

Hutchings, P. (Ed.). (1998). *The course portfolio: How faculty can examine their teaching to advance practice and improve student learning.* Washington, DC: American Association for Higher Education.

Kellogg Commission on the Future of State and Land-Grant Universities. (1999). *Public higher education reform five years after the Kellogg Commission on the Future of State and Land-Grant Universities.* Washington, DC: National Association of State Universities and Land-Grant Colleges.

Kreber, C. (2002). Controversy and consensus on the scholarship of teaching. *Studies in Higher Education, 27*(2), 151–167.

Lueddeke, G. R. (2008). Reconciling research, teaching and scholarship in higher education: An examination of disciplinary variation, the curriculum and learning. *International Journal for the Scholarship of Teaching and Learning, 2*(1), 1–16. Retrieved January 15, 2008, from www.georgiasouthern.edu/ijsotl/issue_v2n1.htm

Malik, D. (1996). Peer review of teaching: External review of course content. *Innovative Higher Education, 20,* 277–286.

O'Meara, K., & Rice, R. E. (2005). *Faculty priorities reconsidered.* San Francisco: Jossey-Bass.

Paulsen, M. B. (2002). Evaluating teaching performance. In C. L. Colbeck (Ed.), *New directions for institutional research: No. 114. Evaluating faculty performance* (pp. 5–18). San Francisco: Jossey-Bass.

Quinlan, K. M. (2002). Inside the peer review process: How academics review a colleague's teaching portfolio. *Teaching and Teacher Education, 18*(8), 1035–1049.

Rhodes, F. H. T. (2001). *The creation of the future: The role of the American university.* Ithaca, NY: Cornell University Press.

Rice, R. E. (2005a). It all started in the sixties: Movements for change across the decade—A personal journey. In D. R. Robertson & L. B. Nilson (Eds.), *To improve the academy: Vol. 25. Resources for faculty, instructional, and organizational development* (pp. 3–17). Bolton, MA: Anker.

Rice, R. E. (2005b). The future of the scholarly work of faculty. In K. O'Meara & R. E. Rice, *Faculty priorities reconsidered* (pp. 303–312). San Francisco: Jossey-Bass.

Roberts, P. (1999). Scholarly publishing, peer review and the Internet. *First Monday, 4*(4–5). Retrieved December 10, 2007, from www.uic .edu/htbin/cgiwrap/bin/ojs/index.php/fm/issue/view/104

Shapiro, E. D., & Coleman, D. L. (2000). The scholarship of application. *Faculty Medicine, 75,* 895–898.

Shulman, L. S. (1993, November/December). Teaching as community property: Putting an end to pedagogical solitude. *Change, 25*(6), 6–7.

Shulman, L. S. (1999). Professing educational scholarship. In E. Lagemann & L. S. Shulman (Eds.), *Issues in education research: Problems and possibilities* (pp. 159–165). San Francisco: Jossey-Bass.

Shulman, L. S. (2000a). From Minsk to Pinsk: Why a scholarship of teaching and learning? *Journal of the Scholarship of Teaching and Learning, 1*(1), 48–52. Retrieved December 3, 2007, from www .iupui.edu/~josotl/VOL_1/NO_1/SHULMAN.PDF

Shulman, L. S. (2000b). Inventing the future. In P. Hutchings (Ed.), *Opening lines: Approaches to the scholarship of teaching and learning* (pp. 95–105). Menlo Park, CA: Carnegie Foundation for the Advancement of Teaching.

Stevens, C. A. (2007, January). *Do more with less: The well-rounded faculty's guide to integration of teaching, service and scholarship.* Paper presented at the Society of Park and Recreation Educators Teaching Institute, Clemson, SC.

Stevens, C. A., & Wellman, J. D. (2007). Establishing a national board for the peer review of scholarly teaching: A proposal for the Society of Park and Recreation Educators. *Schole: A Journal of Leisure Studies and Recreation Education, 22,* 1–16.

Stevens, C. A., Wellman, J. D., DeGraaf, D., Dustin, D., Paisley, K., & Ross, C. (2007). Proposal to establish blind peer review of scholarly teaching for park and recreation educators. *SPRE Teaching Professor: Issues and Innovations*, 7–9.

Theall, M., & Centra, J. A. (2001). Assessing the scholarship of teaching: Valid decisions from valid evidence. In C. Kreber (Ed.), *New directions for teaching and learning: No. 86. Scholarship revisited: Perspectives on the scholarship of teaching* (pp. 31–43). San Francisco: Jossey-Bass.

Trigwell, K., Martin, E., Benjamin, J., & Prosser, M. (2000). Scholarship of teaching: A model. *Higher Education Research and Development, 19*, 155–168.

University of California. (1991). *The university-wide task force on faculty awards*. Retrieved January 26, 2008, from www.universityofcalifornia .edu/senate/reports/pisterreport1991.pdf

Weimer, M. (2006). *Enhancing scholarly work on teaching and learning: Professional literature that makes a difference*. San Francisco: Jossey-Bass.

Weimer, M. (2008). Positioning scholarly work on teaching and learning. *International Journal for the Scholarship of Teaching and Learning, 2*(1), 1–6. Retrieved January 15, 2008, from www.georgiasouthern .edu/ijsotl/v2n1/invited_essays/Weimer/index.htm

Witman, P. D., & Richlin, L. (2007). The status of the scholarship of teaching and learning in the disciplines. *International Journal for the Scholarship of Teaching and Learning, 1*(1), 1–17. Retrieved January 14, 2008, from www.georgiasouthern.edu/ijsotl/v1n1/essays/witman/ IJ_witman.pdf

Chapter 17

Learning-Centered Evaluation of Teaching

Trav D. Johnson
Brigham Young University

Over the past decade, institutions of higher education have placed increased emphasis on promoting student learning. This emphasis has influenced thinking about teaching, course design, and faculty development, but it has had little effect on the evaluation of teaching. In other words, the evaluation of teaching remains focused on instruction (that is, teacher performance and course characteristics) rather than on student learning. Learning-centered evaluation of teaching provides a viable way to emphasize student learning in the evaluation process. This approach uses principles of program evaluation and emphasizes learning goals, learning activities, learning assessments, and learning outcomes in the evaluation of teaching.

In 1995 Robert Barr and John Tagg authored a seminal article in *Change* titled, "From Teaching to Learning: A New Paradigm for Undergraduate Education." The authors explain that the dominant paradigm in higher education had focused on teaching, where institutions assumed that providing instruction was an end in itself. They argue for a paradigm shift from a focus on teaching to a focus on learning. In other words, the mission of colleges and universities should not be to provide instruction but rather to bring about student learning. They maintain that

> [W]e are beginning to recognize that our dominant paradigm
> mistakes a means for an end. It takes means or method—called
> "instruction" or "teaching"—and makes it the college's end or

purpose. To say that the purpose of colleges is to provide instruction is like saying that General Motors' business is to operate assembly lines or that the purpose of medical care is to fill hospital beds. We now see that our mission is not instruction but rather that of producing *learning* with every student by *whatever* means work best. (p. 13)

This shift to the learning paradigm requires changes in how educators think about course design, the teacher's role, and criteria for success, as illustrated by the contrasting questions in Table 17.1.

The Barr and Tagg article is one of the most cited articles in the literature on teaching and learning in higher education. Along with other articles and books with similar premises, it has influenced current thinking and writing about teaching, course design, faculty development, and organizational development in higher education (for example, Association of American Colleges & Universities, 2004; Barr, 1998; Boggs, 1995–96; Fink, 2003; Huba & Freed, 2000; Tagg, 2003; Weimer, 2002). On the other hand, this paradigm shift has had very little impact on the *evaluation* of teaching. More than a decade after the Barr and Tagg article, the evaluation of teaching still centers on instruction (that is, teacher performance and course characteristics) rather than on student learning.

Table 17.1. Shift in Focus from Instruction to Learning

	Instruction/Teacher Focus	*Learning/Learner Focus*
Course Design	What do *I* want to teach?	What do *students* need to learn?
	How can the quality of *instruction* be improved?	How can the quality of *student learning* be improved?
Teacher's Role	What will *I do* to teach?	What will *students do* to learn?
	What is the best way to *present* this material?	What are the best ways for students to *construct* new understanding and *develop* new skills?
Success Criteria	What evidence demonstrates *my teaching* ability?	What evidence demonstrates *student learning?*
	How well do *I perform* in the classroom?	How well do *students perform* in and out of the classroom now and in the future?

Alignment of Evaluation and Desired Teaching Practices

Colleges and universities will find it very difficult to promote the learning paradigm if their evaluation practices emphasize the instructional paradigm. People tend to focus on what is evaluated. For example, faculty members pay particular attention to what they need to do to gain promotion and tenure. If institutions fail to emphasize student learning in their evaluations, they are sending the wrong message to faculty and other constituencies. They are supporting the instructional paradigm through their actions, regardless of what they may say in support of the learning paradigm. In order for the learning paradigm to become firmly rooted in higher education, institutions must align their evaluation practices with their desired teaching practices.

Barr and Tagg (1995) emphasize the importance of changing institutional structures to support the learning paradigm. Institutional structures are features of an organization "that form the framework within which activities and processes occur and through which the purposes of the organization are achieved" (p.18). For example, institutional structures include communication channels, roles and reward structures, decision-making processes, feedback loops, and funding arrangements. Barr and Tagg explain that, in supporting the learning paradigm, institutional restructuring

> offers the greatest hope for increasing organizational efficiency
> and effectiveness. Structure is leverage. If you change the structure
> in which people work, you increase or decrease leverage applied to
> their efforts. A change in structure can either increase productivity
> or change the nature of organizational outcomes. . . . [S]tructure is
> the concrete manifestation of the abstract principles of the organiza-
> tion's governing paradigm. Structures reflecting an old paradigm
> can frustrate the best ideas and innovations of new-paradigm
> thinkers. As the governing paradigm changes, so likewise must the
> organization's structures. (p. 18)

A fundamental aspect of institutional restructuring is aligning faculty and course evaluation with the learning paradigm. Evaluation and related activities (for example, feedback loops, decision-making processes, reward systems) are some of the most influential structures institutions have to support (or to undermine) a focus on student learning. These structures convey to faculty and others what is important to the institution. Thus, learning-centered evaluation approaches and processes are essential to establishing and sustaining the learning paradigm.

Evaluation and Measurement

Despite compelling reasons to align the evaluation of teaching with the learning paradigm, higher education has generally not achieved this alignment. Why is this the case? One of the more significant reasons is the tendency for educators to equate student learning with exam scores. In other words, understanding student learning is considered a *measurement* issue, and tests are the primary instrument by which learning is measured. But administrators and faculty are often uncomfortable using exam scores as the primary measure of teaching. Concerns about this approach center on the fact that exam scores may be affected by a number of variables other than learning that results from teaching in a course. For example, test scores may be influenced by student learning and ability *prior* to entering a course (Bernstein, 1998; Haertel, 1986). Tests may not be good measures of student learning because test items are poorly written (Jacobs & Chase, 1992). Test scores are affected by the difficulty of exams and the degree to which exams are aligned with what was actually taught in the course (Cohen, 1987; Koretz, 2002). In addition, tests may reflect only surface rather than deep learning (Pearlman & Tannenbaum, 2003); they may not include what is *most* important or valuable for students to learn (Jacobs & Chase, 1992; Ory & Ryan, 1993). And often, exams do not address the transfer of learning to future situations, including whether students know when, where, and how to use their knowledge (Pellegrino, Chudowsky, & Glaser, 2001).

Although measurement is often an important part of evaluation, it is not synonymous with evaluation. In educational settings, measurement and evaluation are defined as follows:

- *Measurement* is "the process of assigning numbers or categories to performance according to specified rules" (Joint Committee, 2003, p. 230).
  Example: scores on an exam

- *Evaluation* is "the systematic process of determining the merit, value, and worth of someone . . . such as a teacher, student, or employee . . . or something . . . such as a product, program, policy, procedure, or process" (Wheeler, Haertel, & Scriven, 1993, p. 13).

    Example: determining the value of an educational program in meeting the needs of students, faculty, and the institution

It is important to remember that evaluating teaching is in fact an *evaluation* activity, which may include measurement, but it is broader than measurement in its scope and purpose. Whereas measurement focuses on assigning meaningful numbers to performance, evaluation centers on determining the value or worth of something in a given context.

The Process of Evaluating Teaching

The evaluation of teaching can successfully focus on student learning if those involved in the evaluation process agree on two premises:

1. The purpose of evaluating teaching is to determine the effectiveness of teaching in *increasing student learning*.
2. The appropriate approach for evaluating teaching is to focus on *evaluation* rather than on measurement.

These two premises provide the foundation for a learning-centered evaluation of teaching.

Although evaluation processes vary somewhat, depending on specific contexts and approaches, the general evaluation process may be described in the following steps (see Fink, 1995; Killion, 2003; LeTendre, 2000; Worthen, Sanders, & Fitzpatrick, 1997):

1. Identify the purpose or focus of the evaluation.
2. Develop appropriate evaluation questions.
3. Determine which data sources can provide information to answer the evaluation questions.
4. Collect the needed information from the data sources.
5. Analyze the data and make informed decisions based on the results.

A learning-centered approach to the evaluation of teaching influences each of these steps, as we discuss in the next sections.

1. *Identify the purpose or focus of the evaluation.* In a learning-centered evaluation of teaching, the primary purpose of evaluation is to determine the effectiveness of instruction in *increasing learning;* the focus is on student learning. For learning-centered evaluation to be successful, the primary stakeholders in the evaluation—usually faculty, students, and administrators—must agree to focus on student learning. Therefore, the first task is for these groups to shift their thinking from the typical focus on teacher performance and course characteristics to a focus on what students learn in a course. In order to effectively evaluate teaching based on student learning, all stakeholders must work together to support the learning paradigm.

2. *Develop appropriate evaluation questions.* Well-designed evaluation questions are a critical element of the evaluation process because they guide all aspects of the evaluation. Following a learning-centered approach to teaching, stakeholders develop evaluation questions that focus on student learning. Various student learning outcomes may be identified in different courses. Nevertheless, the focus must remain on what and how much students learn from their experiences in a course. Obviously, if an evaluation of teaching is based on student learning, the evaluation will include questions about learning outcomes. Based on Fink's (2003) work on significant student learning, evaluations should also include questions about learning goals, learning activities, and learning assessments (also see Anderson & Krathwohl, 2001). For example:

Learning Goals

- What are students expected to learn?
- Are these the most valuable/important learning goals for students in this course?

Learning Activities

- What learning activities are students expected to engage in?
- Are learning activities designed to maximize student achievement of the learning goals?
- Does the teacher interact with students in ways that support students in their learning?

Learning Assessments

- How is student learning assessed in this course?
- Are assessments aligned with the learning goals and learning activities of this course?
- Are assessments accurate measures of student learning?

Learning Outcomes

- What evidence can demonstrate that students learned what was expected?
- Have students achieved the learning goals?

Other evaluation questions may be used in these four areas, depending on context and needs, as long as these questions focus on student learning.

3. *Determine which data sources can provide information to answer the evaluation questions.* The next step is to identify data sources that can answer each of the evaluation questions. Obtaining data for evaluating teaching typically draws from three primary sources: teachers, students, and peers (see Braskamp & Ory, 1994; Centra, 1993). These groups have different but complementary perspectives on student learning. None of these groups by themselves can provide sufficient information to evaluate teaching based on student learning, but combined, they can. Each source can furnish important information about learning goals, activities, assessment, and outcomes:

Learning Goals

- Teachers can identify their goals for student learning and explain the value of these goals.
- Students can provide information on whether what they were expected to learn seems relevant to their personal and professional goals and circumstances.
- Peers are in a good position to assess the importance of the learning goals in the context of students' further study and professional endeavors.

Learning Activities

- Teachers can describe the learning activities used in a course and explain why they chose these activities to help students achieve the learning goals.

- Students are in the best position to provide information on learning activities. Specifically, they can give feedback on how well the learning activities helped them achieve course learning goals and the extent to which interactions with the teacher were helpful to their learning.
- Peers can provide information on the value of assignments and other learning activities in achieving learning goals.

Learning Assessments

- Teachers can provide valuable information on how learning was assessed, why they believe assessments were accurate measures of student learning, and how the assessments were linked to learning goals and activities.
- Students can give feedback on whether assessments were aligned with learning goals and activities and served as good measures of their learning.
- Peers can assess the extent to which exams and assignments were good measures of student learning and the alignment of assessments, goals, and activities.

Learning Outcomes

- Teachers are in a good position to provide evidence of student learning and explain why student work demonstrates high levels of learning and achievement.
- Students can give valuable feedback on what and how much they learned in a course.
- Peers are in a good position to assess the extent to which students achieved course learning goals by reviewing student work and the results of learning assessments.

Each of these groups can provide relevant information about the four areas of learning-centered evaluation (learning goals, learning activities, learning assessments, and learning outcomes), but some groups are better suited than others for answering individual evaluation questions. Table 17.2 includes sample evaluation questions and the groups that are best suited to answer each question.

4. *Collect the needed information from the data sources.* Evaluators must decide the best ways to collect the needed information. Notice that evaluators do not start with existing instruments (for

Table 17.2. Data Sources to Answer Each Evaluation Question

Areas	Questions	Teachers	Students	Peers
Learning Goals	What are students expected to learn?	✓		
	Are these the most valuable/important learning goals for students in this course?	✓	✓	✓
Learning Activities	What learning activities are students expected to engage in?	✓		
	Are learning activities designed to maximize student achievement of the learning goals?	✓	✓	✓
	Does the teacher interact with students in ways that support students in their learning?		✓	
Learning Assessments	How is student learning assessed in this course?	✓		
	Are assessments aligned with the learning goals and learning activities of this course?	✓	✓	✓
	Are assessments accurate measures of student learning?	✓	✓	✓
Learning Outcomes	What evidence can demonstrate that students have learned what was expected?	✓		
	Have students achieved the learning goals?	✓	✓	✓

example, student ratings of instruction) and let these determine what data are collected. Rather, they begin with what they want to know (that is, evaluation questions) and what sources can provide this information (for example, teachers, students, peers). Then they decide what methods and instruments will work best to collect the needed information from these sources. Thus, student ratings can be a useful tool to collect information from one important data source (that is, students) if items on the rating form are learning-focused. But student ratings by themselves are not sufficient; additional methods and sources are needed. For example, teachers can provide course materials and statements that identify and provide a rationale for course learning goals, learning activities, and learning assessments. They can also provide evidence for the achievement of learning outcomes. Peers can examine course materials to determine the quality and value of learning goals, learning activities, and learning assessments. To assess learning outcomes, peers may review assessment results and samples of student work (for example, assignments, projects, portfolios, performances).

Two principles guide data collection in learning-centered evaluation of teaching: 1) focus on student learning, and 2) ask each data source only for information that it is well suited to provide. In other words, decide what is most important to know about student learning, and identify the most efficient ways to gather this information from the groups that can best provide it. For example, peer classroom observations are resource-intensive and difficult to standardize (Arreola, 2007; Centra, 1993; Chism, 1999; Weimer, 1990), and they may duplicate what students can easily answer because students experience class instruction throughout the semester. Therefore, peer observations may not be the most efficient way to gather information on classroom instruction. On the other hand, peer review of course materials and student work can answer important evaluation questions for which students are not qualified to answer (for example, the quality of student work, the content and design of class materials).

Table 17.3 displays the four types of documents to be gathered from the data sources relative to each evaluation question:

1. Course materials and sample student work
2. Instructor statements on learning goals, activities, assessments, and outcomes

Table 17.3. Evaluation Questions and Data-Collection Documents

Areas	Questions	Teachers	Students	Peers
Learning Goals	What are students expected to learn?	Course syllabus		
	Are these the most valuable/important learning goals for students in this course?	Statement on the value/importance of learning goals	Student questionnaire reports	Reviews of syllabus and teacher statements
Learning Activities	What learning activities are students expected to engage in?	Course syllabus and materials		
	Are learning activities designed to maximize student achievement of the learning goals?	Statement on the design of learning activities	Student questionnaire reports	Reviews of syllabus, course materials, and teacher statements
	Does the teacher interact with students in ways that support students in their learning?		Student questionnaire reports	
Learning Assessments	How is student learning assessed in this course?	Course syllabus and assessments		

**Table 17.3. Evaluation Questions and
Data-Collection Documents (*Continued*)**

Areas	Questions	Teachers	Students	Peers
	Are assessments aligned with the learning goals and learning activities of this course?	Statement on the alignment of assessments with goals and activities	Student questionnaire reports	Reviews of assessments, materials, and teacher statements
	Are assessments accurate measures of student learning?	Statement on the accuracy of assessments	Student questionnaire reports	Reviews of assessments and teacher statements
Learning Outcomes	What evidence can demonstrate that students have learned what was expected?	Course assessment results and sample student work		
	Have students achieved the learning goals?	Statement explaining student achievement of learning goals	Student questionnaire reports	Reviews of assessment results, student work, & teacher statements

3. Student questionnaire reports
4. Peer reviews of course materials and student work

Additional data may add to the overall picture of student learning in a course, but these document types alone can answer the evaluation questions addressing student learning.

Teachers are responsible for providing pertinent course materials and sample student work. They also provide statements, based on evidence and rationale, of the value of learning goals, the design of learning activities, the alignment and accuracy of learning assessments, and the achievement of learning outcomes. This self-assessment process has parallels to the scholarship of teaching, where faculty members study their own teaching and share their findings with others (see Boyer, 1990; Hutchings & Shulman, 1999), and to the benchmark portfolio used at the University of Nebraska-Lincoln (Bernstein, Burnett, Goodburn, & Savory, 2006). It also supports the idea of teaching as community property, as described by Shulman (1993).

Students provide feedback on teaching primarily through student rating questionnaires and, when possible and appropriate, through senior or alumni questionnaires (see Braskamp & Ory, 1994). These questionnaires should focus on student learning, with items querying students about what they learned, how much they learned, and what contributed most to their learning (or to the lack thereof). For many institutions, implementing learning-centered evaluation of teaching requires redesign of their student rating forms.

Peers review relevant course materials, samples of student work, and teacher statements about learning goals, activities, assessments, and outcomes. Their reviews should focus on answering the evaluation questions, thus narrowing the scope of their assessments to what matters most in teaching: student learning.

5. *Analyze the data and make informed decisions based on the results.* Table 17.4 summarizes the documents and reports that administrators and review committees should use for evaluating learning goals, activities, assessments, and outcomes. These evaluators are also responsible for verifying the integrity of the data collection processes and for establishing criteria for evaluating the four areas—criteria that should align with the specific program or department, college, and institutional learning goals. Then the reviewing parties can analyze the documents and reports and come to an overall evaluation of the teaching under review.

Learning-centered evaluation of teaching can be equally valuable to teachers, program directors, departments, and other units in their efforts to improve teaching and learning. It requires all involved to think seriously about student learning and to analyze how teaching can best facilitate learning. It can be especially helpful

Table 17.4. Documents and Reports Used for Evaluation

Areas	Documents and Reports
Learning Goals	Program/department, college, and institutional learning goals Course syllabi Teacher statements on the value/importance of learning goals Student questionnaire reports Peer-review reports
Learning Activities	Course syllabi Teacher statements on the effectiveness of learning activities Student questionnaire reports Peer-review reports
Learning Assessments	Program/department, college, and institutional learning goals Teacher statements on the alignment and accuracy of assessments Student questionnaire reports Peer-review reports
Learning Outcomes	Teacher statements explaining student achievement of learning goals Student questionnaire reports Peer-review reports

to teachers as they work to understand and successfully promote student learning in their classes.

Conclusion

If the shift from the instructional to the learning paradigm is to have a lasting impact on education, it must influence not only how people think about teaching but also how teaching is evaluated. Evaluation is one of the primary means by which an institution conveys what is valuable and important to its members. If institutions fail to emphasize student learning in their evaluation practices, they will find it very difficult to promote a focus on student learning. Evaluation practices must be aligned with and support the learning paradigm.

Learning-centered evaluation of teaching offers an effective way to focus course and faculty evaluation on student learning. It centers on specific evaluation questions. Evaluators and other stakeholders need to be clear about what questions they want answered and how the answers relate to student learning. With the appropriate questions in place, it is a relatively straightforward process to determine who can best answer these questions and how data can be gathered from these sources.

When evaluation questions and processes focus on student learning, administrators, review committees, and teachers can interpret the evaluation results from a learning-centered perspective. A clear picture of student learning emerges as students, teachers, and peers describe and provide evidence for the quality of learning goals, learning activities, learning assessments, and learning outcomes. This requires changes in thinking, changes in methods, and changes in analysis and use of evaluation results. But as Barr and Tagg (1995) emphasize, the most difficult change is the fundamental paradigm shift from a focus on teaching to a focus on learning.

References

Anderson, L. W., & Krathwohl, D. R. (2001). *A taxonomy for learning, teaching, and assessing: A revision of Bloom's taxonomy of educational objectives.* New York: Longman.

Arreola, R. A. (2007). *Developing a comprehensive faculty evaluation system: A guide to designing, building, and operating large-scale faculty evaluation systems* (3rd ed.). Bolton, MA: Anker.

Association of American Colleges and Universities. (2004). *Taking responsibility for the quality of the baccalaureate degree: A report from the greater expectations project on accreditation and assessment.* Washington, DC: Author.

Barr, R. (1998, September/October). Obstacles to implementing the learning paradigm—What it takes to overcome them. *About Campus, 3*(4), 18–25.

Barr, R., & Tagg, J. (1995, November/December). From teaching to learning—A new paradigm for undergraduate education. *Change, 27*(6), 12–25.

Bernstein, D. (1998). Putting the focus on student learning. In P. Hutchings (Ed.), *The course portfolio: How faculty can examine their teaching to advance practice and improve student learning* (pp. 77–83). Sterling, VA: Stylus.

Bernstein, D., Burnett, A. N., Goodburn, A., & Savory, P. (2006). *Making teaching and learning visible: Course portfolios and the peer review of teaching.* Bolton, MA: Anker.

Boggs, G. R. (1995–96, December/January). The learning paradigm. *Community College Journal, 66*(3), 24–27.

Boyer, E. L. (1990). *Scholarship reconsidered: Priorities of the professoriate.* Princeton, NJ: Carnegie Foundation for the Advancement of Teaching.

Braskamp, L. A., & Ory, J. C. (1994). *Assessing faculty work: Enhancing individual and institutional performance.* San Francisco: Jossey-Bass.

Centra, J. A. (1993). *Reflective faculty evaluation: Enhancing teaching and determining faculty effectiveness.* San Francisco: Jossey-Bass.

Chism, N. V. N. (1999). *Peer review of teaching: A sourcebook.* Bolton, MA: Anker.

Cohen, S. A. (1987, November). Instructional alignment: Searching for a magic bullet. *Educational Researcher, 16*(8), 16–20.

Fink, A. (1995). *Evaluation for education and psychology.* Thousand Oaks, CA: Sage.

Fink, L. D. (2003). *Creating significant learning experiences: An integrated approach to designing college courses.* San Francisco: Jossey-Bass.

Haertel, E. (1986). The valid use of student performance measures for teacher evaluation. *Educational Evaluation and Policy Analysis, 8*(1), 45–60.

Huba, M. E., & Freed, J. E. (2000). *Learner-centered assessment on college campuses: Shifting the focus from teaching to learning.* Boston: Allyn & Bacon.

Hutchings, P., & Shulman, L. S. (1999). The scholarship of teaching: New elaborations, new developments. *Change, 31*(5), 10–15.

Jacobs, L. S., & Chase, C. I. (1992). *Developing and using tests effectively: A guide for faculty.* San Francisco: Jossey-Bass.

Joint Committee on Standards for Educational Evaluation. (2003). *The student evaluation standards.* Thousand Oaks, CA: Corwin Press.

Killion, J. (2003). Eight smooth steps: Solid footwork makes evaluation of staff development programs a song. *Journal of Staff Development, 24*(4), 14–26.

Koretz, D. M. (2002). Limitations in the use of achievement tests as measures of educators' productivity. *Journal of Human Resources, 37*(4), 752–777.

LeTendre, B. G. (2000). Six steps to a solution: Guide can help educators reach an answer. *Journal of Staff Development, 21*(1), 20–25.

Ory, J. C., & Ryan, K. E. (1993). *Tips for improving testing and grading.* Newbury Park, CA: Sage.

Pearlman, M., & Tannenbaum, R. (2003). Teacher evaluation practices in the accountability era. In T. Kellaghan & D. L. Stufflebeam (Eds.), *International handbook of educational evaluation* (pp. 609–642). Norwell, MA: Kluwer.

Pellegrino, J. W., Chudowsky, N., & Glaser, R. (2001). *Knowing what students know: The science and design of educational assessments.* Washington, DC: National Academy Press.

Shulman, L. S. (1993, November/December). Teaching as community property: Putting an end to pedagogical solitude. *Change, 25*(6), 6–7.

Tagg, J. (2003). *The learning paradigm college.* Bolton, MA: Anker.

Weimer, M. (1990). *Improving college teaching: Strategies for developing instructional effectiveness.* San Francisco: Jossey-Bass.

Weimer, M. (2002). *Learner-centered teaching.* San Francisco: Jossey-Bass.

Wheeler, P., Haertel, G. D., & Scriven, M. (1993). *Teacher evaluation glossary.* Kalamazoo, MI: Center for Research in Educational Accountability and Teacher Evaluation.

Worthen, B. R., Sanders, J. R., & Fitzpatrick, J. L. (1997). *Program evaluation: Alternative approaches and practical guidelines.* New York: Longman.

For the Next Generation

Chapter 18

Meeting New Faculty at the Intersection

Personal and Professional Support Points the Way

Ann Riley
University of Oklahoma

Faculty developers can play a significant role in increasing the retention of new faculty. This chapter presents a study conducted at a public research university that reveals that first-year faculty need personal, relational, and professional support. However, the importance of each type of support shifts during this first year, suggesting that faculty development efforts aimed toward new faculty should adjust accordingly. This study uses a sequential mixed-method design and is grounded in adult development theory, which views new faculty as adult learners in a career-life transition and faculty developers as adult educators.

Stakes for the development and retention of new faculty are high. A costly investment of both money and time is required to acclimate these new employees to their roles, and the impact they have on both curriculum and student learning can be profound. Faculty developers have a responsibility to understand new faculty's early adjustment needs and to establish a productive helping relationship. By focusing on their personal and professional needs for support, faculty development practice broadens to encompass the *intra*personal and *inter*personal needs of these faculty as adult learners as they go through a major career adjustment. Programming should address their career development with a holistic approach to their adult learning needs. This chapter presents an empirical study that suggests a model for such practice.

Over twenty-five years ago, Baldwin and Blackburn (1981) urged higher education leaders to "broaden their focus to include the professional, organizational, and personal development of faculty" (p. 608). Although the primary aim of most faculty development programs has been to provide faculty with instructional skills and knowledge about teaching and learning (Eble & McKeachie, 1985; Gaff, 1976), some scholars have called for more comprehensive, holistic programming (Schuster, 1989; Watson & Grossman, 1994). Still, few faculty development centers have responded to this call. We need to consider whether it is simply innocuous or potentially harmful to continue to ignore the personal needs of our faculty. Adult development theory, as well as these study findings, indicates that the basis for such programming efforts exists.

Research on New Faculty Support

This study focused on the first-year experiences of the new-faculty cohort hired for the 2005–06 academic year at the University of Oklahoma. It aims to identify the felt needs of new faculty for both personal and professional support as they begin their career.

Theoretical Basis

Adult development theory anchors this inquiry in the support needs of new faculty. Viewing these faculty as adult learners, the faculty developer plays the role of an adult educator responsible for the growth and needs of these learners. Theoretical perspectives from adult development include life structure theory (Levinson, 1978, 1986), which emphasizes the internal and external management of the adult self in the world, and transitions theory (Bridges, 1980), which highlights the importance of adapting to new roles, particularly involving a career change. With new faculty in the midst of both personal life and career adjustment, career development theory addresses the multiple personal development issues inherent in occupational adjustment (Hansen, 1997; Super, 1990).

Research Setting

The University of Oklahoma is a flagship public research institution that includes campuses in Norman, Oklahoma City, and Tulsa. It employs over twenty-two hundred faculty, enrolls approximately thirty thousand students, and houses nineteen colleges offering a wide variety of degrees through the Ph.D. (University of Oklahoma, n.d.). The annual New Faculty Seminar Orientation, coordinated by the Program for Instructional Innovation, consists of fourteen weekly luncheon meetings during the fall semester. These sessions give new faculty the chance to meet, eat, and talk with one another, as well as to hear informative presentations by various campus speakers on campus resources and services. Of the sixty-eight new faculty hired in 2005–06, forty-eight regularly attended the luncheon meetings that fall semester, representing a typically heterogeneous cohort: twenty-nine men and nineteen women, ranging in ages from their twenties to their sixties, from thirty-five programs in ten colleges. Although most were Caucasian Americans, two were African Americans; one-third of the group were natives of other countries.

Methodology

Although the literature on new faculty uses both survey and qualitative approaches to gather data (Boice, 1992, 2000; Fink, 1984, 1992; Sorcinelli, 1994, 2002; Sorcinelli & Austin, 1992), no study to date takes a mixed-method approach that sequentially addresses the new-faculty career transition. Because the project was conducted as a phenomenological investigation and approached through faculty development practice, it was important that the participants benefited from being in the study. All faculty involved in the interview and group sessions indicated they did receive some personal benefit from their participation. One faculty member was overheard commenting to a peer:

> At first I thought I would be nice (to participate). After the interview was over, though, I realized I enjoyed the opportunity for reflection. No one ever asks you about these things, you know. It was useful to have someone listen, and it helped me think about things.

The participants were recruited from those attending the fall 2005 New Faculty Orientation Seminar. This researcher acted as a participant observer at the lunch tables each week, taking notes on their conversations about their adjustment. By the time the survey was administered late in the semester, those attending regularly had thinned to half ($n = 24$) the original number ($n = 48$). All of the twenty-four completed the survey, and 75 percent agreed to participate further ($n = 16$): ten men and six women from fifteen departments and eight colleges.

The data were collected in three phases during the participants' first year through three means: 1) a first-semester survey questionnaire ($n = 24$), 2) midyear individual interviews ($n = 16$), and 3) end-of-spring-semester focus group sessions ($n = 13$). Although the survey data came from a relatively small sample in relation to the entire cohort of new faculty hires, they represent half of those in regular attendance and all of those in attendance that day. Most of the active new faculty (a demographically representative group) also participated in the interviews, providing a wealth of qualitative data.

The survey used a twenty-seven-item questionnaire adapted for this study from Boice's (1992) survey of new faculty. Almost all of the nondemographic items addressed support needs and stress level and were scored on Likert-scales ranging 1 (Low) to 10 (High).

Further data collection was sequentially planned to offer both individual (interview) and collective (focus group) opportunities for reflection during the second semester. The individual interviews were sixty- to ninety-minute audiotaped sessions conducted in each faculty member's office early in the spring semester. Naturalistic and nondirective, they followed a process called *clustering*, adapted from Karpiak (1996, 1997) in her study of midcareer faculty. Items asked participants to report the first-year support they received both personally and professionally by completing the sentence, "My support needs in this new position are, or have been. . . " Given a blank piece of paper, they were asked to mind-map their thoughts on the page and elaborate on them in the interviews.

Finally, at the end of the second semester, four ninety-minute focus groups were conducted and videotaped to gain a collective understanding of new-faculty support needs. Such groups allow participants to express multiple perspectives on a similar experience (Glesne, 2006). This researcher guided the discussions in a semi-structured way, asking the participants to share whether, how, and by whom their support needs were met. No two faculty represented any one program, department, or college, and the cross-disciplinary interaction among the participants seemed to reinforce a sense of anonymity among them while promoting a general, nondetailed exchange of their experiences.

Data Analysis

Questionnaire responses were analyzed using SPSS. Of the respondents ($n = 24$), sixteen were male and eight female, eighteen had Ph.D.s and six master's, 75 percent were in a significant relationship, and 50 percent had family (some with children). Their ages ranged from the midtwenties to over sixty, with 58 percent in their thirties. They spanned the Colleges of Arts and Sciences (botany, chemistry, economics, health and exercise science, mathematics, modern languages, social work, and sociology), architecture, business, education, engineering, fine arts, geosciences, and the university library.

Survey Findings

Table 18.1 highlights the findings on seven items. At the time of the survey, the respondents indicated their mean stress level to be in the medium range (5.54), reflecting an adequate potential for successful adjustment. A certain amount of stress is normal for new employees in transition, whereas a high stress rating would be of concern. Sense of department fit (7.58), campus identification (7.71), and the degree to which the new position meets career expectations (8.25) averaged in the moderate range. These scores suggested good potential for successful adjustment, as professional connections had begun to be established. Items scoring in the high range included their felt need for collegiality (8.25), the collegial support they perceived to be receiving (8.54), and direct support they saw from their chair (9.08). These items indicated a strong need for belonging and for getting feedback from their department chair. These findings are consistent with Fink's (1984) study, which he conducted on this same campus twenty years earlier.

**Table 18.1. Survey Results: Mean Ratings on Items
(Low = 1 to High = 10)**

Mean Rating: Medium	Mean Rating: Moderate	Mean Rating: High
Perceived Stress Level (5.54)	Sense of Dept. Fit (7.58)	Need for Collegiality (8.25)
	Campus Identification (7.71)	Collegial Support (8.54)
	Career Expectations (8.21)	Chair Support (9.08)
(Adjustment potential)	*(Connection established)*	*(Belonging needs strong)*

Among the teaching-related items, the perceived quality of student interaction and perceived teaching effectiveness were predictably highly correlated (.729). But an unexpected correlation was found between teaching effectiveness and faculty's need for collegiality (.794). Why would this relationship exist? Further investigation revealed that many of those from the College of Arts & Sciences (half of the faculty surveyed, $n = 12$) had recently attended meetings on faculty matters with their college dean and chairs. Perhaps the additional support they received increased this correlation.

Overall, this group seemed satisfied with their first semester and hopeful about the prospects for their new position—a typical honeymoon reaction. Although the new faculty arrived with a diverse range of experience (the newly degreed with limited experience, those with some-to-plenty of academic experience, and those from professional arenas with no academic experience), most considered their job decision to have been voluntary and within their control (Bridges, 2002), thereby enhancing their initial attitudes toward their new job and life transition.

Interviews

The sixteen participants interviewed early in the spring semester were demographically similar to those of the survey group: 75 percent were in a significant relationship, 60 percent had family or children, and half were in their thirties. In addition, they came from a broad cross-section of departments and colleges. Interviews were transcribed and analyzed through coded thematic interpretation using NVivo (a qualitative software for coding narrative data), member checking, literature triangulation, and audit review with a project consultant (Glesne, 2006).

Six themes of support needs emerged from the qualitative data, reflecting both personal and professional needs: personal impact, professional roles, relationship dynamics, employment, the higher education system, and campuswide issues. Table 18.2 displays the frequencies.

Table 18.2. Interview Results: Coded Reference Tallies of Six Support Themes

Personal Impact Issues	338
Professional Roles	241
Relationship Dynamics	234
Employment Issues	160
Higher Education System	120
Campuswide Issues	84
TOTAL	1,177

Throughout the interviews, new faculty discussed their need for personal support and the impact of their career transition on their life significantly more frequently than other matters. Personal impact issues included job satisfaction, feelings about being a new faculty member, discovery of the local community, personal adjustment, family adjustment, religious or spiritual issues, and general social needs. For example, one experienced new-faculty hire described his feelings as a new faculty member like "drowning in a whirlpool" and now felt relieved not to have "that big gorilla on my back." Some mentioned religious or spiritual factors relevant to their personal adjustment. One said his daily meditation practice was crucial to managing the pressure; another found a church community that gave her needed support; still another discovered a new sense of meaning and purpose through teaching. Some first-year faculty credited community support and social interaction as being essential to their own and their family's adjustment. Several prized having the flexibility to meet family needs, from medical appointments for a special-needs child to a child's sports event. Regarding the personal pressures of being a professor, one participant said "it pays to be selfish" and just "crank out your research," but he also found this hard to do. He said that it took finding "some kind of . . . place in your skin . . . that you're happy with being."

Professional roles included grant and financial issues, professional development, program issues, research agendas, scholarship plans, service obligations, teaching matters, and time management. Particularly important to the new faculty were the logistics of teaching—"the resources, classrooms, who sets it up, how it's set up." One female faculty said, "So that was number one for me, to understand teaching here, the culture." Most said time management was a problem, and many appreciated having reduced teaching loads during their first year. Of the conflict between teaching and research roles, one male faculty said, "The problem is, I've been too busy with teaching and don't have time to travel. The important thing is to keep hot in your area with people [by] going to conferences." Another participant, one with additional administrative duties, spoke of needing information about the "nuts and bolts" of her job. She said this is what "scared her the most" and admitted that being responsible for a large budget was "anxiety-producing."

Relationship dynamics included support needs related to colleagues, mentoring, staff, students, and supervision interactions. Some departments had sophisticated mentoring programs in place, and new faculty were securely involved, while other departments provided no formal mentoring channels. The new faculty valued the staff support they received, and departmental secretaries were often cited as invaluable sources for knowing "how to get things." Regarding his departmental colleagues, one dual-hire faculty said,

> There seems to be a bit more of a tradition here of colleagues
> not really interacting much with one another. It's definitely
> different from (our previous university) and it's hard to develop a
> community if you're not really interacting with your colleagues in
> some form or other.

Focus Groups

The focus-group data collected at the end of the spring semester, just three months later, revealed an interesting change in the new faculty's support need priorities. Relationship dynamics rose to the top, followed by professional roles, and then personal issues, and the discussions focused less on higher education system, campuswide, and employment issues. The data yielded a total of 439 coded references from thirteen participants (eight males and five females), each from a different department (see Table 18.3).

In these small group sessions, the participants responded to three prompts on their needs and support over their first two semesters: what needs they had, who had and had not been helpful, and how their needs had or had not been met. They expressed appreciation for this group interaction and the exchange of their varied experiences, as well as the confidential nature of the group. One member said, "It really drives it home that there are other people out here who are fighting the same issues, but somehow that sense of community helps."

Participants spoke more extensively than previously about the importance of student relationships, both as a source of support and an energy drain. One participant reported that he learned a lot about his department from students who had been around longer than he had, "giving me knowledge, their knowledge, of procedures and history of what we do in our department, what they think has worked in the past, what needs they feel needs

Table 18.3. Focus Group Results: Coded Reference Tallies of Six Support Themes

Relationship Dynamics	121
Professional Roles	110
Personal Impact Issues	73
Higher Education System	64
Campuswide Issues	44
Employment Issues	27
TOTAL	439

changing." Another called the university "a fountain of youth," as he described how teaching invigorated him. Others honed in on the challenges of student interaction, and one explained,

> Students do come and bother us a lot more. I never remember when I was an undergrad going to my professors all the time—I have this problem, I have that problem, you know, both personal and academic . . . I just want to shut the door sometimes. It's like "figure it out for yourself, that's why you're here."

Participants also discussed the crucial support they received from mentors. As one faculty member recalled:

> But the biggest thing I've had and found very helpful was the colleagues and friends that I can go to. Just somebody you can kind of bounce thoughts off of and get input, somebody that's been through the same thing before, since this is my first time teaching. It was a person that I felt comfortable speaking with, a friend and colleague of mine.

Another faculty member, hired from the professional arena and new to academe, related his experience with more formal mentoring:

> I was lucky enough to be assigned a faculty mentor, and that person was invaluable, along with other faculty members in my department. Knowledge of the department on the street . . . dealing with students, you know, different situations you come in contact with—how should I handle this or that type of thing?

Four additional issues not mentioned in their individual interviews emerged in the focus-group discussions. These fit within the six themes of support needs: community outreach (professional roles), interdisciplinary faculty relations (relationship dynamics), being junior faculty (employment issues), and tacit knowledge (higher education issues). Like the proverbial light bulb, they glowed with excitement when the issue they called "tacit knowledge awareness" surfaced. They shared the realization that they had to discover, informally and on their own, information deemed necessary to their adjustment that no formal channel supplied.

Interpretation of Findings

These new faculty appeared to be learning new things and transitioning through their career adjustment at such a pace that their needs changed priority within just a few months. Brammer (1991) examined the importance of learning to cope with change and finding meaning in life transitions. He contended that people need time and space to reflect and take hold of the new possibilities ahead: "We need to reflect on what the transition means to us, to let the pain or discomfort subside, and to prepare for new experiences" (p. 35). Ultimately, all transitions are opportunities for positive change toward growth and development. Career development theorists address the complexity of multiple aspects of personal development within occupational development (Hansen, 1997; Super, 1990) and call on "career professionals to become genuine agents of change to improve the human condition" (Hansen, 1997, p. 49).

At midyear, the three top core concerns for these new faculty reflected, in order of frequency, personal, professional, and relational themes. By the end of the year, their three top core concerns were relational, professional, and personal. Their professional support needs—issues related to teaching, research, and service—remained a second-ranked priority through both semesters, while personal issues progressively faded from first place to third and relational needs rose from third to first. Even though the group's mean self-rated stress was only in the medium range (from the first-semester survey), personal support was their top concern in the interviews. Perhaps the new faculty achieved some personal stability after the first semester, freeing them to shift their focus to the relational dynamics of securing their place and fit with colleagues, staff, and students. Lindholm's (2003, 2004) research on the adaptive importance of fit within the academic environment lends validity to this interpretation.

These findings mirror those in counseling research in that, in working with adult learners, the adult educator needs to consider whether the learner is *moving into* a new situation, *moving through* it, or *moving on* from it (Schlossberg, Lynch, & Chickering, 1989). The importance of an individual's stage of adjustment supports the choice of the sequential methodological design used here to identify the support needs of first-year faculty.

Conclusion

If faculty development represents a specialized form of adult education, and our faculty clients are themselves adult learners going through life and career transitions, then it is time well spent figuring out how best to support and retain first-year faculty. The results presented here suggest that new faculty need much more substantial and enduring support than just an orientation. This study invites replication on other new-faculty cohorts during their first year, starting with an early faculty survey, followed by individual meetings on the personal and professional support faculty are getting, and, finally, cross-disciplinary discussion groups for sharing first-year experiences. Whether or not different patterns of needs and priorities emerge, new faculty benefit from opportunities for individual reflection and collective exchanges and from their institution's expressed interest in their well-being. Obviously, this kind of programming requires intensive staff time and energy, but from a relational point of view, where better to invest our efforts than in our faculty of the future?

Faculty developers can benefit as well. Building a helping relationship with new faculty from the beginning shows them we understand their needs and care about their adjustment and their long-term success. This initial programming can establish strong social and professional bonds that will ensure new hires will take advantage of other faculty development programming throughout their career. We may find our own programs enriched in other ways as well. The information that new faculty can provide may inform us, not only of their changing needs but also of various departmental dynamics—knowledge that can help us understand and meet the needs of the broader faculty.

References

Baldwin, R. G., & Blackburn, R. T. (1981). The academic career as a developmental process: Implications for higher education. *Journal of Higher Education, 52*(6), 598–614.

Boice, R. (1992). *The new faculty member: Supporting and fostering professional development.* San Francisco: Jossey-Bass.

Boice, R. (2000). *Advice for new faculty members: Nihil nimus.* Needham Heights, MA: Allyn & Bacon.

Brammer, L. M. (1991). *How to cope with life transitions: The challenge of personal change.* New York: Hemisphere.

Bridges, W. (1980). *Transitions: Making sense of life's changes.* Boston: Addison-Wesley.

Bridges, W. (2002). *Managing transitions: Making the most of change.* London: Nicholas Brealey.

Eble, K. E., & McKeachie, W. J. (1985). *Improving undergraduate education through faculty development: An analysis of effective programs and practices.* San Francisco: Jossey-Bass.

Fink, L. D. (1984). The first year of college teaching. In K. E. Eble (Ed.), *New directions for teaching and learning: No. 17. The first year of college teaching* (pp. 11–15). San Francisco: Jossey-Bass.

Fink, L. D. (1992). Orientation programs for new faculty. In M. D. Sorcinelli & A. E. Austin (Eds.), *New directions for teaching and learning: No. 50. Developing new and junior faculty* (pp. 39–49). San Francisco: Jossey-Bass.

Gaff, J. G. (1976). *Toward faculty renewal.* San Francisco: Jossey-Bass.

Glesne, C. (2006). *Becoming qualitative researchers: An introduction* (3rd ed.). Boston: Pearson.

Hansen, L. S. (1997). *Integrative life planning: Critical tasks for career development and changing life patterns.* San Francisco: Jossey-Bass.

Karpiak, I. E. (1996). Ghosts in a wilderness: Problems and priorities of faculty at mid-career and mid-life. *Canadian Journal of Higher Education, 26*(3), 49–78.

Karpiak, I. E. (1997). University professors at mid-life: Being a part of . . . but feeling apart. In D. DeZure (Ed.), *To improve the academy: Vol. 16. Resources for faculty, instructional, and organizational development* (pp. 21–40). Stillwater, OK: New Forums Press.

Levinson, D. J. (1978). *The seasons of a man's life.* New York: Knopf.

Levinson, D. J. (1986). A conception of adult development. *American Psychologist, 41*(1), 3–13.

Lindholm, J. A. (2003). Perceived organizational fit: Nurturing the minds, hearts, and personal ambitions of university faculty. *Review of Higher Education, 27*(1), 125–149.

Lindholm, J. A. (2004). Pathways to the professoriate: The role of self, others, and environment in shaping academic career aspirations. *Journal of Higher Education, 75*(6), 603.

Schuster, J. H. (1989). The personal dimension: Faculty development. *Thought and Action, 5*(1), 61–62.

Schlossberg, N., Lynch, A., & Chickering, A. (1989). *Improving higher education environments for adults: Responsive programs and services from entry to departure.* San Francisco: Jossey-Bass.

Sorcinelli, M. D. (1994). Effective approaches to new faculty development. *Journal of Counseling and Development, 72,* 474–479.

Sorcinelli, M. D. (2002). New conceptions of scholarship for a new
generation of faculty members. In K. J. Zahorski (Ed.), *New directions for teaching and learning: No. 90. Scholarship in the postmodern
era: New venues, new values, new visions* (pp. 41–48). San Francisco:
Jossey-Bass.

Sorcinelli, M. D., & Austin, A. E. (Eds.). (1992). *New directions for teaching and learning: No. 50. Developing new and junior faculty.* San
Francisco: Jossey-Bass.

Super, D. E. (1990). A life-span, life-space approach to career development. In D. Brown, L. Brooks, & Associates, *Career choice and
development: Applying contemporary theories to practice* (2nd ed., pp.
197–261). San Francisco: Jossey-Bass.

University of Oklahoma. (n.d.) *Campus profile 2007–2008.* Retrieved March
11, 2008, from http://go2.ou.edu/documents/07CampusProfile.pdf

Watson, G., & Grossman, L. H. (1994). Pursuing a comprehensive faculty development program: Making fragmentation work. *Journal
of Counseling and Development, 72,* 465–473.

Chapter 19

When Mentoring Is the Medium

Lessons Learned from a Faculty Development Initiative

Jung H. Yun, Mary Deane Sorcinelli
University of Massachusetts Amherst

Campuses across the country are investing considerable time, effort, and expense to replenish their faculty ranks with a new generation of scholars. How can mentoring help these new faculty juggle the many demands of surviving and thriving in academia? And how can institutions frame mentoring as a broader faculty development initiative in which faculty at all stages of the academic career can teach and learn from each other? This chapter addresses these questions by sharing the goals, design, and lessons learned from the Mutual Mentoring Initiative at the University of Massachusetts Amherst.

Efforts to build, diversify, and better prepare the future professoriate have increased significantly during the past two decades. Programs for talented undergraduate and graduate students, such as the Institute for the Recruitment of Teachers, the Mellon Mays Undergraduate Fellowship Program, the Leadership Alliance, the National Science Foundation's Alliance for Graduate Education and the Professoriate, and the Preparing Future Faculty program, have greatly enriched and diversified the pool of candidates electing graduate studies and careers in academia.

Despite these advances, however, the success of individual candidates as new faculty depends largely on the level of support they receive at their hiring institutions, which can vary dramatically (Ashburn, 2007). Since the mid-1980s, research on new faculty has been conducted across a variety of disciplines and institutional types, using a range of methodological approaches (Boice, 1992; Fink, 1984; Menges, 1999; Olsen & Crawford, 1998; Olsen & Sorcinelli, 1992; Reynolds, 1992; Rice, Sorcinelli, & Austin, 2000; Solem & Foote, 2004; Sorcinelli, 1988; Tierney and Bensimon, 1996; Trower, 2005; Whitt, 1991). Findings consistently indicate that many new faculty members (commonly defined in the literature as faculty in their pre-tenure years) experience a number of significant stressors as they seek to establish themselves. Women and faculty of color, in particular, encounter many barriers that can negatively affect their productivity and career advancement. These barriers include managing expectations for performance, particularly the tenure process, finding collegiality and community, and creating balance between professional roles, particularly teaching and research, and also between work and family life.

Like many institutions of higher education, the University of Massachusetts Amherst (UMass Amherst) is actively recruiting new and underrepresented faculty with the goal of enlarging its faculty ranks to better meet the needs of its growing student population. In 2006, the provost and senior vice chancellor of academic affairs charged our unit—the Office of Faculty Development (OFD)—with creating a campuswide mentoring program to better support, develop, and retain these new hires. This chapter describes what we experienced and learned during the needs assessment and pilot phase of this program and how it came to evolve into a broader faculty development initiative.

The Needs Assessment

In response to the provost's charge, we decided to undertake a comprehensive needs assessment in order to better understand "the state of mentoring" on our campus. The goals of this needs analysis were threefold:

1. To build a knowledge database of the campus's existing mentoring activities and programs

2. To solicit feedback on the challenges experienced by our new and underrepresented faculty from individuals in a wide variety of departmental, school or college, interdisciplinary, and administrative contexts

3. To encourage faculty, administrators, and staff to imagine the "ideal" features of a campuswide mentoring program designed to help address these challenges

During the six-month needs assessment period, we conducted one-on-one, small-group, and focus-group interviews of over 150 new and underrepresented faculty, mid- to senior-career faculty, department chairs, deans, campus service providers, and all major councils and committees of the Faculty Senate and faculty union. We also conducted an online survey of pre-tenure faculty, which yielded responses from 177 participants (for a return rate of approximately 73 percent). One of the key things that we learned from the needs assessment was that our pre-tenure faculty—with minimal variances across gender, race or ethnicity, and discipline—experienced a number of common challenges, which fell into the following categories:

1. *Getting started:* understanding the academic culture of departments, schools or colleges, and the institution; identifying resources to support research and teaching; creating a trusted network of junior and senior colleagues

2. *Excelling at teaching and research:* learning about best practices and resources for course design, assignments, grading, technology, and teaching strategies; finding support for developing a research and writing plan; identifying sources of internal and external funding; soliciting feedback on manuscripts and grant proposals

3. *Navigating the tenure track:* developing a better understanding of the specific steps of the tenure process; learning about the criteria for evaluating research and teaching performance; finding support for developing the tenure dossier; soliciting feedback from department chairs and other relevant administrators on the quality and quantity of work through the annual faculty review

4. *Creating work-life balance:* prioritizing and balancing teaching, research, and service; finding support for goal setting;

developing time management skills; attending to quality-of-life issues such as dual careers, child care, and affordable housing

5. *Developing professional networks:* establishing substantive, career-enhancing relationships with faculty who share similar interests in research and teaching, both on campus and off

Given the range of challenges experienced by our new and underrepresented faculty, which closely mirrored those found in the literature, we knew that the structure of our program, as well as the form of mentoring that it encouraged, had to be flexible, responsive, and faculty-driven in order to accommodate the many unique cultural and disciplinary differences among our university's sixty-one departments and ten schools and colleges.

The Pilot Phase

From our research, we were aware that mentoring had long been acknowledged as one of the few common characteristics of a successful faculty career, particularly for women and faculty of color. Yet the most common form of mentoring that we discovered in the literature was a "traditional model," which was defined by a top-down, one-on-one relationship between an experienced faculty member who guided and supported the career development of a new or underrepresented faculty member (see Figure 19.1).

Figure 19.1. Traditional Mentoring Model

Senior Faculty

New and underrepresented faculty

Recent literature, however, documents the emergence of new, more flexible approaches to mentoring in which new and early-career faculty worked with "multiple mentors" (de Janasz & Sullivan, 2004), "constellations" of mentors (van Emmerik, 2004), "networks" of mentors (Girves, Zepeda, & Gwathmey, 2005), or a "portfolio" of mentors who addressed a variety of career competencies (Baugh & Scandura, 1999; Higgins & Kram, 2001). We opted for, and optimized, a network-based model of support titled Mutual Mentoring, which encourages new and underrepresented faculty to develop networks of "mentoring partners" in nonhierarchical, collaborative, and cross-cultural partnerships. The Mutual Mentoring model features five key characteristics (Sorcinelli & Yun, 2007; Yun & Sorcinelli, 2007):

1. Mentoring partnerships with a wide variety of individuals, including peers, near peers, tenured faculty, chairs, administrators, librarians, and students
2. Mentoring approaches that accommodate the partners' personal, cultural, and professional preferences for contact (for example, one-on-one, small group, group, or online)
3. Partnerships that focus on specific areas(s) of experience and expertise, rather than generalized, "one-size-fits-all" knowledge
4. Benefits to not only the person traditionally known as the "protégé" or "mentee" but also the person traditionally known as the "mentor" (as the bi-directional arrows in Figure 19.2 illustrate)
5. Perhaps most important, a sense of empowerment in which new and underrepresented faculty are not seen or treated solely as the recipients of mentoring but as agents in their own career development

Having arrived at this model and its key characteristics in consultation with our needs assessment participants, our challenge was to determine a programmatic structure that would encourage its adoption across the campus. Given our concern that mentoring based on hierarchies would not meet the needs of our diverse faculty, it seemed incongruous to impose Mutual Mentoring "from above." Therefore, we turned to the idea of

Figure 19.2. Mutual Mentoring Model

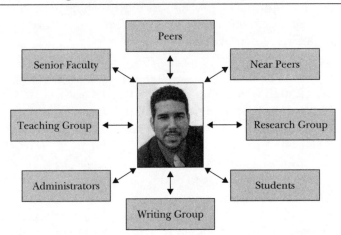

competitively awarding mentoring grants to encourage faculty to develop Mutual Mentoring-based projects that addressed their unique departmental, interdisciplinary, or school-college contexts. In doing so, we were "mentored" by colleagues from the Center for Excellence in Teaching at the University of Southern California, who had created a mentoring grant program two years earlier for undergraduates, graduate students, and faculty. We also drew on our own experiences in planning and implementing departmental and interdisciplinary faculty development programs (List & Sorcinelli, 2007; Ouellett & Sorcinelli, 1995; Shih and Sorcinelli, 2007; Sorcinelli, 2004).

During the nine-month pilot phase, we awarded five Mutual Mentoring pilot grants to the following departmental and interdisciplinary teams: the Anthropology Department, "Blacklist" (a self-named interdisciplinary network for female faculty of color), the History Department, the Psychology Department, and the Women's Studies Department. The members of these pilot grant teams designed their own Mutual Mentoring-based projects to address specific areas of interest and concern for their new and underrepresented faculty. Seventy-three faculty members participated in these projects (60 percent faculty of color and 82 percent women), and the range of structures, priorities, and topics addressed, as outlined next and in Table 19.1, attests to the flexibility of the Mutual Mentoring model.

Table 19.1. Summary of Mutual Mentoring Pilot Grant Projects

Department or Pilot Project Name	Pilot Project Leader(s)	Key Highlights of the Pilot Project	Funds Primarily Spent on	Number of Participants	Number of Faculty of Color Participants	Number of Female Participants
Anthropology Department	Department Chair	One-on-one mentoring with department chair; group mentoring (including Five Colleges) organized by junior faculty; alumnae and alumni mentoring initiative at professional association conference	Travel grants for junior faculty to attend national conference, reception costs, regular meetings throughout the semester	8	2	4
Blacklist	1 Assistant Professor & 1 Associate Professor	Interdisciplinary mentoring among female faculty of color at various stages of the academic career, including faculty from UMass Amherst and the Five Colleges	Regular meetings throughout the semester, travel grants to present research, post-conference debriefing meetings to discuss effective techniques for professional networking	26	26	26

(Continued)

Table 19.1. Summary of Mutual Mentoring Pilot Grant Projects (*Continued*)

Department or Pilot Project Name	Pilot Project Leader(s)	Key Highlights of the Pilot Project	Funds Primarily Spent on	Number of Participants	Number of Faculty of Color Participants	Number of Female Participants
History Department	Department Chair	Group mentoring initiative featuring two specialization field-based mentoring partners for each new faculty member (one in the same field, the other with similar research methods) plus one "go-to" person for issues not covered by the field-based partners	Regular meetings throughout the semester, modest stipends for mentoring partners	17	3	10

Psychology Department	Tenured Faculty Member/ Associate Dean of the College	Group mentoring initiative featuring two mentoring partners at different stages of the academic career for each new faculty member (one early career and one tenured)	Regular meetings throughout the semester, stipends for mentoring partners to meet independently and in small mentoring groups	10	2	8
Women's Studies Department at UMass Amherst & Bennett College	Department Chairs (2)	Cross-institutional mentoring initiative focused on creating shared research and teaching projects between the Women's Studies Departments at UMass Amherst and Bennett College	Travel to/from Washington, D.C. and accommodations for planning conference participants; long-distance communication during the semester (postage, telephone)	12	9	11
			Totals:	73	42 (58%)	59 (81%)

Source: Retrieved November 24, 2007, from www.umass.edu/ofd/guide.

Anthropology Department

The Anthropology Department assigned one formal mentoring partner to each of its new faculty members. These partners met one-on-one on an as-needed basis. In addition, the new faculty came together as a peer cohort five times a year for discussion-based lunch meetings, the topics of which were chosen by the new faculty. The department also used its pilot grant to offset a portion of the travel costs for the new faculty to attend the national conference of the American Anthropological Association, where they hosted a Mutual Mentoring reception for all alums of the department, thereby establishing important mentoring partnerships with alumnae and alumni anthropologists in related fields.

Blacklist

The members of Blacklist organized themselves as an interdisciplinary mentoring network for female faculty of color at a variety of career levels (assistant, associate, and full professors). The goal of this group was to support and retain female faculty of color through regular meetings of the network. The members brainstormed ways to overcome challenges in and outside of the classroom, created a travel grant program for members to present their scholarly work at conferences and return to the group to discuss tips and strategies for networking, and served as an important source of professional and social support for each other.

History Department

The History Department assigned two mentoring partners to all pre-tenure faculty (one mentoring partner in a similar geographical or subject field and another with a similar methodological or theoretical research approach). The mentoring partners met four times over the course of the pilot period in meetings organized around issues of orientation, research, teaching, and preparing for tenure. The department provided modest stipends for the mentoring partners and also conducted two needs assessments to ensure that the mentoring efforts were responsive to the needs and concerns of early career faculty.

Psychology Department

The Psychology Department implemented a Group Mentoring Initiative (GMI) in which all new psychology faculty were paired with two mentoring partners, one at the early or midcareer stage and one at a later career stage. The GMI met formally six times over the course of the pilot period in facilitated, topically driven group meetings on issues of research, teaching, and tenure. In addition, the new faculty met individually or in small groups with their mentoring partners to discuss issues of specialized interest and were provided with modest stipends to offset the costs of getting together.

Women's Studies Department

The Department of Women's Studies created an inter-institutional Mutual Mentoring project with the Department of Africana Women's Studies at Bennett College in Greensboro, North Carolina. The purpose of doing so was to create a supportive and productive alliance between an established women's studies program at a large public university in the Northeast and a new program at a small, religiously affiliated historically black college in the South. The departments organized a planning conference in Washington, D.C., where they developed teaching modules and team-taught courses and other programs to help build on the teaching and research strengths of their respective faculty.

Mentoring as Faculty Development

At the outset of the pilot phase, our intent was to develop a single program that competitively awarded grants to support faculty-driven mentoring projects based on the Mutual Mentoring model. However, based on the many lessons learned from our faculty, pilot phase participants, and external consultants, what evolved was a significantly broader faculty development initiative, characterized by a multitiered, multiprogram framework with self-selected points of entry at four key levels (individual, department/school/college/interdisciplinary, campuswide, and inter-institutional). With a three-year grant from the Andrew W. Mellon Foundation and additional support from our provost's office, this initiative (now known as the Mellon Mutual Mentoring Initiative) formally launched in the fall of 2007. It is now made up of the following:

The Mellon Mutual Mentoring (M^3) Grant Program

Similar to the grants that we distributed during the pilot phase, M^3 Grants are *team mentoring grants* that support faculty-driven, context-sensitive Mutual Mentoring projects based at the departmental, school-college, or interdisciplinary levels. In recognition of the many new and underrepresented faculty who mentored us about the areas in which they most needed support, we designated their top five categories of challenges as Priority Mentoring Areas. All applications for the M^3 Grant Program must clearly indicate how the proposed project will help new and underrepresented faculty address one or more Priority Mentoring Areas, which include 1) getting started, 2) excelling in research and teaching, 3) preparing for tenure, 4) balancing work-life, and 5) building professional networks.

In addition to the types of mentoring projects developed during the pilot phase, other examples of M^3 Grant-eligible activities include creating an interdisciplinary mentoring network within a particular school or college, establishing a research mentoring program that connects new and early career faculty with peers or senior faculty off-campus as mentoring partners, building a special interest roundtable of faculty across the Five Colleges, and organizing a work-life mentoring series for dual-career couples. Currently, the OFD awards up to ten M^3 Grants per academic year.

The Mellon Mutual Mentoring Micro-Grant (M^4) Program

M^4 Grants are *individual mentoring grants,* designed to encourage new and underrepresented faculty to identify desirable areas for professional growth and opportunity, and to develop the necessary mentoring relationships to make such changes possible.

Initially, we did not envision creating a program of small seed grants awarded directly to individual faculty; however, during the needs assessment and pilot phase, the only consistently negative feedback that we received about the team grant program was that it might "shut out" faculty who wished to develop a mentoring network, but whose departments, schools or colleges, or interdisciplinary groups did not apply for or receive a grant. This was particularly troubling feedback, as it related to women and faculty of color, especially those who belonged to departments or schools or colleges that did not recognize a need for mentoring.

The M^4 Program encourages new and underrepresented pretenure faculty members to build mentoring networks around self-selected topics of interest, such as teaching, research, tenure, or work-life balance. Examples of M^4 Grant-eligible activities include organizing on-campus meetings of faculty to come together around a particular issue, such as research interests, effective teaching, tenure prep, work-life balance; creating a faculty writing group to peer review manuscripts or tenure dossier components; sharing travel expenses to copresent with a mentoring partner (or partners) at a professional conference; and developing faculty colloquia on or off campus.

One of our key considerations in designing this micro-grant program was to encourage new and underrepresented faculty to be proactive and intentional about their professional development—two factors that research has proven to be necessary to achieve successful faculty mentoring (Haring, 2006). The M^4 Program also eliminated the department or school or college as the only point of entry to a Mutual Mentoring grant. Currently, the OFD awards up to fifteen M^4 Grants per academic year.

The Mellon Five College (M^5) Network

UMass Amherst is part of a local consortium of colleges and universities called the Five Colleges, which includes Amherst College, Hampshire College, Mount Holyoke College, and Smith College. Given the physical proximity of these institutions, as well as our faculty's desire to network with their peers at nearby campuses, we created a vehicle for bringing them together socially, as well as around shared topics of professional interest. This proved to be particularly important for new and underrepresented faculty from departments at UMass Amherst who lacked peers at the same career stage or peers with similar disciplinary specialization or research methods.

The M^5 Network now hosts several Five College-wide events to encourage the development of social connections, scholarly networks, and Mutual Mentoring partnerships among faculty across the Five Colleges, especially new and underrepresented faculty and joint appointees, who teach at two or more participating schools within the consortium. Networking events include an autumn welcoming reception for new faculty from the five campuses, as well as workshops on topics of interest across campuses, such as time management for pre-tenure faculty.

Mutual Mentoring-Based Programs Sponsored by the Office of Faculty Development

The needs assessment indicated that most of our faculty had very clear opinions about mentoring. The majority of pre-tenure respondents to our online survey believed that mentoring others was an important part of their responsibility as a faculty member (approximately 64 percent of the respondents "agreed strongly" with this statement). Furthermore, approximately 43 percent "agreed strongly" with the idea that being mentored was integral to their future success as a faculty member. However, when asked to characterize their previous experiences as recipients of mentoring in graduate school, nearly 44 percent of the respondents described their experiences as "negative" or "neutral," thus indicating a possible reticence to engage in such activities again.

Given these figures, we recognized a need to give faculty a variety of low-risk, self-selected, and topically driven entry points into mentoring activities that best suited their unique personalities, schedules, departmental cultures, and preferences. One of the most logical ways for us to do so was to restructure the OFD's campuswide programming as Mutual Mentoring-based events. This required us to reexamine all of our existing programs and move away from anything resembling a top-down exchange, "talking head" or "lecture" that simply communicated information rather than encouraged faculty to create knowledge interactively. An equally valuable step was to expand our own network of support by inviting a wide range of campus partners to serve as cosponsors or contributors to our programs (for example, the Center for Teaching, UMass Amherst Libraries, Office of Information Technology, Office of Research Affairs, Provost's Office, and the Writing Program).

Our office now sponsors nine programs per year, all of which have been reorganized around the Mutual Mentoring model and serve as regular reminders of the value of bringing together faculty at all career stages to share their experiences and expertise. These programs, which rely on a wide variety of dialogue-driven formats such as panels, roundtables, and peer or near-peer advisory groups, include the following:

1. New Faculty Orientation
2. Welcoming Reception for New Faculty and Their Families
3. Tenure Preparation Seminar
4. Time Management Workshops
5. Monthly Mini-Retreats for Writing
6. Annual Faculty Writing Retreat
7. Local Writing Coach and Editor Program
8. Online Summer Writing Group
9. In-Person Summer Writing Group

Preliminary Assessment

Prior to releasing funds to our pilot grant recipients, we stressed the importance of collecting evaluation data to assess each project in relation to its stated goals. We also provided informational materials on key performance indicators and evaluation rubrics. However, due to the differences in project design and subjects addressed, we initially did not require project teams to use a standardized assessment instrument. Late in the pilot phase, after consulting with grant recipients who were having difficulties creating their own assessment instruments, we decided to intervene and assist. This proved to be an important decision because the variability among the projects, as well as certain disciplinary preferences for qualitative or quantitative data, would have resulted in data that could not be compared with each other, or with data from grant-funded projects in subsequent years. After consulting with our Office of Academic Planning and Assessment (OAPA), we distributed a standardized assessment to all members of the five pilot teams.

Although it is too early to evaluate whether the Mellon Mutual Mentoring Initiative will have an impact on our ability to retain our new and underrepresented faculty over the long term, we are encouraged by several promising early indicators. Approximately 78 percent of the participants in the pilot projects described their Mutual Mentoring experiences as "excellent" or "very good." Open-ended feedback also indicated that the participants appreciated how the pilot grants allowed them to "create a project that really worked for US. This definitely wasn't mentoring as dictated from above. It was 'grass roots,' ground-up mentoring around the issues that hit closest to home for those of us trying to succeed in this department."

To date, our faculty have created twenty-four unique Mutual Mentoring projects (five pilot projects in 2006–07, nine team projects in 2007–08, and ten micro-grant projects in 2007–08). Over two hundred faculty at all career stages have participated in or are currently participating in these projects, which represents approximately 20 percent of the total number of pre-tenure and tenured faculty on our campus. Of this figure, approximately 68 percent are women and 44 percent are faculty of color, and these mentoring networks are growing every day.

In addition, every OFD program based on the Mutual Mentoring model has received a minimum satisfaction rating of 4.5 (out of 5.0). Qualitative feedback indicates that faculty participants appreciate the way these programs are structured because "Mutual Mentoring emphasizes faculty at all career stages coming together and talking *with* each other, instead of younger faculty coming to be talked *to*." Also, faculty participants describe Mutual Mentoring as "such a commonsense approach to learning . . . it mirrors the academic mission itself in that it encourages discourse and values the experiences of everyone in the room, no matter their rank."

Although these early indicators are very positive and encouraging, there are other areas where additional work and refinement will be necessary as the initiative moves forward. For example, the pilot phase projects demonstrated an excellent range of faculty participants (23 percent chairs and full professors, 19 percent associate professors, and 51 percent assistant professors). However, only 7 percent of the pilot project participants were nonfaculty (librarians, students, and campuswide administrators). In addition, only two of the five projects featured interdisciplinary or inter-institutional mentoring (such as mentoring projects that included faculty from one or more of the Five Colleges).

Currently, we are exploring ways in which faculty can more easily engage in mentoring partnerships with academic leaders, professional staff, and students, all of whom bring different types of valuable expertise and experience to the table. To better inform future grant applicants about the wide range of mentoring partners and possibilities available to them, we have developed a list of exemplars from the pilot phase, outlining the various types of mentoring that occurred in each project, as well as the range of mentoring partners involved. This list is now available online at www.umass.edu/ofd/initiative.htm.

A final note on assessment: to ensure that future data from every grant-funded project will not only be consistently collected but comparable enough to see the "big picture" of the Mellon Mutual Mentoring Initiative, we have continued our collaboration with OAPA to determine key indicators of success, as well as the most appropriate methods of collecting regular, consistent, and comparable formative and summative data. All M^3 and M^4 Grant recipients are now required to complete both standardized midterm and end-of-year assessments designed by staff from OAPA and OFD.

Conclusion

The Mellon Mutual Mentoring Initiative is currently in its first year of full implementation. What began as a single campuswide program that promoted mentoring as the medium to support new and underrepresented faculty has since grown into a broad-based faculty development initiative. The guiding principles of the initiative mirror many of the evidence-based "good practices" for creating and sustaining faculty development programs, which include building stakeholders by listening to all perspectives, ensuring effective program leadership, emphasizing faculty ownership, cultivating administrative commitment, developing clear goals and assessment procedures, offering a range of opportunities and multiple points of entry, encouraging collegiality and community, creating collaborations with campus partners, and providing measures of recognition and rewards (Sorcinelli, 2002).

Perhaps what distinguishes the Mellon Mutual Mentoring Initiative most is its organic evolution from a single program into a multicomponent, multitiered offering of faculty development opportunities at the individual, department/school/college/interdisciplinary, campuswide, and inter-institutional levels. Much like our visual model of Mutual Mentoring, the initiative's guiding principles, structure, and programs are all designed to create opportunities for faculty and other constituencies to connect, network, teach, and learn from each other. Equally important is the active role played by new and underrepresented faculty, senior faculty, chairs and academic leaders in the design and implementation of the Mellon Mutual Mentoring Initiative, which contributes to a strong sense of campuswide ownership in the past, present, and future of faculty mentoring at UMass Amherst.

References

Ashburn, E. (2007). Survey identifies colleges that know how to keep junior faculty members happy. *The Chronicle of Higher Education, 53*(22), A6.

Baugh, S. G., & Scandura, T. A. (1999). The effect of multiple mentors on protégé attitudes toward the work setting. *Journal of Social Behavior and Personality, 14,* 503–522.

Boice, R. (1992). *The new faculty member: Supporting and fostering professional development.* San Francisco: Jossey-Bass.

de Janasz, S. C., & Sullivan, S. E. (2004). Multiple mentoring in academe: Developing the professional network. *Journal of Vocational Behavior, 64*(2), 263–283.

Fink, L. D. (1984). The first year of college teaching. In K. E. Eble (Ed.), *New directions for teaching and learning: No. 17. The first year of college teaching* (pp. 11–15). San Francisco: Jossey-Bass.

Girves, J. E., Zepeda, Y., & Gwathmey, J. K. (2005). Mentoring in a post-affirmative action world. *Journal of Social Issues, 61*(3), 449–479.

Haring, M. (2006, November). *Networking mentoring.* Paper presented at the meeting of the Mentoring in the Academy Conference, Providence, RI.

Higgins, M. C., & Kram, K. E. (2001). Reconceptualizing mentoring at work: A developmental network perspective. *Academy of Management Review, 26,* 264–288.

List, K., & Sorcinelli, M. D. (2007). Staying alive. *Journal of Faculty Development, 21*(3), 173–178.

Menges, R. J. (1999). *Faculty in new jobs.* San Francisco: Jossey-Bass.

Olsen, D., & Crawford, L. (1998). A five-year study of junior faculty expectations about their work. *Review of Higher Education, 22*(1), 39–54.

Olsen, D., & Sorcinelli, M. D. (1992). The pretenure years: A longitudinal perspective. In M. D. Sorcinelli & A. E. Austin (Eds.), *New directions for teaching and learning: No. 50. Developing new and junior faculty* (pp. 15–25). San Francisco: Jossey-Bass.

Ouellett, M. L., & Sorcinelli, M. D. (1995). Teaching and learning in the diverse classroom: A faculty and TA partnership program. In E. Neal & L. Richlin (Eds.), *To improve the academy: Vol. 14. Resources for faculty, instructional, and organizational development* (pp. 205–217). Stillwater, OK: New Forums Press.

Reynolds, A. (1992). Charting the changes in junior faculty: Relationships among socialization, acculturation, and gender. *Journal of Higher Education, 63,* 637–652.

Rice, R. E., Sorcinelli, M. D., & Austin, A. E. (2000). *Heeding new voices: Academic careers for a new generation.* Washington, DC: American Association for Higher Education.

Shih, M., & Sorcinelli, M. D. (2007). Technology as a catalyst for senior faculty development. *Journal of Faculty Development, 21*(1), 23–31.

Solem, M. N., & Foote, K. E. (2004). Concerns, attitudes, and abilities of early career geography faculty. *Annals of the Association of American Geographers, 1*(4), 889–912.

Sorcinelli, M. D. (2002). Ten principles of good practice in creating and sustaining teaching and learning centers. In K. H. Gillespie (Ed.), *A guide to faculty development: Practical advice, examples, and resources* (pp. 9–23). Bolton, MA: Anker.

Sorcinelli, M. D., & Yun, J. H. (2007). From mentors to mentoring networks: Mentoring in the new academy. *Change, 39*(6), 58–61.

Tierney, W. G., & Bensimon, E. M. (1996). *Promotion and tenure: Community and socialization in academe.* Albany, NY: State University of New York Press.

Trower, C. (2005). How do junior faculty feel about your campus as a work place? *Harvard Institutes for Higher Education: Alumni Bulletin.* Cambridge, MA: Harvard Institutes for Higher Education.

van Emmerik, I. J. H. (2004). The more you can get the better: Mentoring constellations and intrinsic career success. *Career Development International, 9*(6/7), 578.

Whitt, E. (1991). Hit the ground running: Experiences of new faculty in a school of education. *Review of Higher Education, 14*(2), 177–197.

Yun, J. H., & Sorcinelli, M. D. (2007). *Mellon Mutual Mentoring program guide.* Retrieved November 24, 2007, from www.umass.edu/ofd/guide

Preparing Advocates for Faculty Development

Expanding the Meaning of "Growing Our Own"

Deborah S. Meizlish, Mary C. Wright
University of Michigan

Discussions about preparing newcomers for faculty development focus almost exclusively on the staffing needs of teaching centers. Unfortunately, this emphasis significantly narrows what it means to prepare people for the field. Instead, we suggest that successful preparation has two elements: preparation of talented individuals for formal positions in the field and preparation of knowledgeable advocates or allies. As evidence, we present results from a survey of our center's graduate teaching consultants, documenting how their work shaped their future connections to faculty development. Our results challenge centers to consider how their programming can "grow" both professionals in and advocates for faculty development.

Since the early 1990s, POD members have discussed how best to attract and prepare newcomers for work in faculty development (Chism 1998, 2007; Chism, Palmer, & Stanley, 2006; Gillespie, 2001; Sell & Chism, 1991; Sorcinelli, Austin, Eddy, & Beach, 2006). This conversation has focused almost exclusively on the staffing needs of administrative units devoted to faculty development. Unfortunately, this emphasis significantly narrows what it means to attract people to and prepare them for work in the field.

Instead, we suggest that successful preparation has two elements: 1) direct preparation of talented individuals for formal positions in faculty development *and* 2) preparation of knowledgeable advocates or allies who are prepared to weave connections with faculty development into their own faculty roles. To explore this issue more fully, we present here the results of a survey of the individuals who have served in our center's Graduate Teaching Consultant (GTC) program. One purpose of the survey was to discern how their work as GTCs shaped their future connections to the field of faculty development. We believe the results challenge all teaching centers to examine how their programming, especially their programming for graduate students, can be used to "grow" both professionals in and advocates for faculty development.

Context

Faculty development has grown and institutionalized substantially since the early 1960s (Sorcinelli et al., 2006). With that growth have come discussions about how best to attract talented and diverse individuals to the field. Understandably, much of that attention has focused on issues particular to staffing administrative units devoted to faculty development. For example, some authors describe the characteristics or qualifications of ideal faculty developers (Chism, 1998, 2007; Gillespie, 2001; Porter, Lewis, Kristensen, Stanley, & Weiss, 1993). Others provide advice for those seeking to hire new faculty developers (Cook, Kalish, & Pingree, 2004; Sell & Chism, 1991). Because of the diverse paths to faculty development, identifying pools of recruits is a challenge in itself, necessitating institutionalized teaching centers to play a major role in "growing our own" (Sell & Chism, p. 27).

Cook and Sorcinelli (2002, p. B21) describe how this path to the profession unfolds: "Many instructional developers enter the profession by serving apprenticeships with a teaching center. There they get practical experience, learn about best practices, and access the rich body of literature on student learning." Yet this focus on the staffing needs of centers overlooks several other realities. First, a significant amount of faculty development is conducted by individuals who do not define themselves as professionals in the field (Sorcinelli et al., 2006). For example, faculty at many liberal arts or comprehensive institutions may rotate on and off professional development committees. In addition, administrators in other types of units may find themselves exploring or responding to issues of faculty development. Second, the work of those in faculty development units rests on the ability to build connections with allies in many roles and settings in higher education. As we focus on ways to attract people to the field, we must consider our ability to influence those located throughout a college or university, such as administrators, faculty, and lecturers.

Despite these realities, little work has documented how established centers use their resources to help "seed" an appreciation for faculty development among future faculty or administrators. For example, despite the attention Cook and Sorcinelli (2002) and Sell and Chism (1991) pay to teaching center apprenticeships, they do so only in the context of growing future professional staff. Any additional benefits of these apprenticeships are to the graduate students' own future careers—equipping them to be more effective teachers—rather than to the field of faculty development.

Yet there is fragmentary evidence that teaching center programs can prepare both professionals in and advocates for the field of faculty development. For example, in assessing the impact of the POD Diversity Internship Grant, Ouellett and Stanley (2004) document how center apprenticeships can attract talented individuals to the field. In describing the paths of the POD interns they interviewed, they note the following:

> The eight past interns were split equally between those specifically interested in a career in faculty and instructional development and those who viewed their internship experiences as contributing to different career goals in higher education (e.g., tenure-track faculty lines). At the time of this study, one past intern now served as chair of her college's faculty development committee, one intern was hired by her center as a permanent instructional development consultant, and one intern has a full-time position in student affairs with significant responsibilities related to faculty and instructor development. (p. 215)

Although they do not use these results to highlight the dual meaning of "preparation" that we posit, the Ouellett and Stanley data are clear evidence of the value of doing so.

In the pages that follow, we first provide a brief overview of the Graduate Teaching Consultant program at the Center for Research on Learning and Teaching (CRLT), University of Michigan. We then describe our evaluation methodology and present our findings. We end with some final thoughts about the implications of this work for faculty development.

Program Overview

CRLT's Graduate Teaching Consultant (GTC) program was created in 1997 in order to enhance the center's ability to meet the individualized consulting needs of teaching assistants at the University of Michigan. Each year, between six and twelve advanced graduate students participate in the program. Overall, forty-eight students have served as GTCs. GTCs typically work with the center for one to three years, though some have served longer. Many interact with the center beyond the confines of the GTC program itself, working with us on TA orientations and workshops or attending our Preparing Future Faculty programs.

In recruiting GTCs, deliberate efforts have been made to construct demographically diverse groups. The GTC population is about evenly divided among the humanities (31 percent), social sciences (40 percent), and science, mathematics, and engineering disciplines (29 percent), and most GTCs are female (65 percent). In spite of outreach to organizations serving graduate students of color, most GTCs are white (77 percent), which is probably due to the underrepresentation of minorities in many graduate programs on campus.

The GTC program has two main components: 1) a teaching circle that meets weekly or biweekly and 2) the individual consultations conducted by each GTC. The teaching circle, led by an experienced center consultant, serves as the primary training seminar for the group. Meetings are facilitated both by center staff and by GTCs, who often take the lead by presenting consulting case studies or topical training sessions. Content reflects both center needs and participant interest, with sessions focusing on effective consulting techniques, multicultural learning and teaching, and general teaching strategies. As the GTC program evolved, we added content to introduce graduate students to the field of faculty development, complementing their exposure to the methods and literature of the field. Varying from year to year, the program generally includes readings and class discussions about teaching centers, center staff postings, the POD Network, as well as interaction with guest speakers from the field. Most recently, two GTCs attended the POD Conference and shared resources gathered and experiences gained with the rest of the group.

Method

To assess the long-term impact of the GTC program, we posed two focal questions to guide our evaluation. Specifically, we asked whether the GTC program situates the work of GTCs in the larger field of faculty development in a way that, first, seeds future connections to teaching and learning centers and, second, encourages interactions with colleagues around instructional and professional development issues. We asked all GTCs who had been through the program, from its inception (1997–98 academic year) through the 2006–07 academic year, to respond to an online survey distributed through SurveyMonkey. Of these forty-eight GTCs, forty-two responded to the survey, resulting in an 88 percent response rate.

The survey instrument asked GTCs about their current positions, their interface with a teaching and learning center (if any) on their campus, their networking with colleagues around pedagogical and professional development issues, and the influences they perceived the program had on their careers. The survey, a copy of which appears in Appendix A, collected both quantitative and qualitative information. For this study, the quantitative findings were primary. We report these in descriptive statistics, complemented by illustrative quotes.

We asked the former GTCs to report on their current careers and institutional contexts. Given that recent cohorts were included in the survey, it is not surprising that a third (fourteen, or 33 percent) of respondents are still in graduate school at the University of Michigan (see Table 20.1). A minority (five, or 12 percent) are now employed in nonacademic positions for government, industry, or nonprofits, or they are looking for work.

Table 20.1. Current Employment of Former GTCs

Current Position	Number (%)
Tenure-Track Faculty	17 (41%)
Graduate Student	14 (33%)
Nonacademic Position	5 (12%)
Faculty/TA Development	3 (7%)
Lecturer	2 (5%)
Higher Education Administration (not faculty/ TA development-related)	1 (2%)

However, a majority (twenty-three, or 55 percent) of respondents have their doctorates and now work in higher education. A few former GTCs (three) have entered into faculty development careers, confirming the observations of Cook and Sorcinelli (2002) and Sell and Chism (1991) that some instructional developers enter the field through apprenticeships at teaching centers. However, most are now working in tenure-track faculty positions (seventeen), as lecturers (two), or in nonfaculty development higher education administration positions (one). Given the teaching focus of the GTC program, it is interesting that nearly half of the respondents (eleven) in higher education positions were located in research university contexts. Others worked in master's universities (six), liberal arts colleges (four), or specialized institutions (two).

Findings and Discussion

In this section, we explore two key ways that the faculty and graduate students in our study describe the impact of the GTC program. First, we focus on the twenty-three respondents who now work in higher education, and we document the new connections that they have made with teaching and learning centers on their campuses. Second, we look at both graduate students and faculty and administrators, and we examine their instructional and organizational development initiatives. We also note our hypotheses about why the GTC program may have helped foster these activities.

**Table 20.2. Number and Percent of Respondents
Reporting Interactions with Teaching Centers
and Colleagues, by Current Position**

Type of Interaction	Faculty and Administrators	Graduate Students
Worked in/with teaching center	10 (71%)[a]	NA[b]
Mentored	21 (91%)	13 (93%)
Provided resources	15 (65%)	11 (79%)
N	23	14

[a]Percent indicates the proportion of those who have worked with the teaching center (ten), out of those who have a teaching center on campus (fourteen).
[b]Not asked of graduate students because as a GTC, they have worked with CRLT.

Connections with Teaching Centers

Of the twenty-three respondents in higher education faculty and administrative positions, most (fourteen) report that their campuses host a teaching center. Of those with a teaching center, a majority (ten) have, at some time, worked in or with these units (see Table 20.2). (Current graduate students were not asked this question, because by definition, they have worked with CRLT on their home campus.) As mentioned earlier, three former GTCs have careers in faculty development. However, most past GTC participants work not within but in partnership with their teaching centers. Many report attending programs or facilitating workshops. For example, one current faculty member at a large research university notes that she has "attended programs and participated in a summer fellowship that included facilitating two workshops."

Even more significantly, respondents say that their GTC experience has encouraged them to value and make connections with teaching centers on their current campuses. An award-winning professor at a research university notes:

> The experience I gained as a GTC, both training and an awareness of how important and valuable it is to talk about teaching with peers, made me seek out the [teaching center] here at [my research university] right away.

Even those without teaching centers report a similar impact. A faculty member at a Hispanic-serving institution describes a drive to create a teaching and learning unit on his campus, using the connections made in the GTC program, this way: "The staff at CRLT continues to be a valuable resource for me. My recent correspondence with them has helped me formulate ideas to start a similar center on our campus."

What aspects of the GTC program foster these connections? We believe there are two. First, the program teaches processes for continual instructional improvement, which enables GTCs to see critical student feedback as constructive, rather than as attributable to poor students or to immutable personal failures. For example, a professor in the humanities notes, "Based on the evaluations I participated in, I tend to think of things I am doing WELL and ways that I would like to IMPROVE, rather than in more negative terms (e.g., framing as failures)." Another respondent—a student affairs administrator who continues to teach—also describes how the program has helped him significantly reframe student feedback:

> CRLT opened my eyes. It changed my life. I was one of those graduate students on the way to blaming students for the shortcomings of his own courses. . . . I began to see that there were alternatives to "blaming the students," specifically ways . . . to promote "significant learning experiences."

Because instructional improvement is framed positively, GTCs may be likely to seek out resources that can help interpret and gather student feedback. Second, by providing an explicit introduction to the field of faculty development, the program provides GTCs with the information needed to locate instructional resources available on other campuses.

Connections with Colleagues

The GTC program also appears to facilitate the development of social networks around teaching. Among former GTCs, a significant majority of both the graduate students and faculty and higher education administrators report mentoring peers (thirteen and twenty-one, respectively) and sharing resources around instructional issues (fifteen and eleven) in the past year (see Table 20.2). These pedagogical interactions took two forms. First, particularly among graduate students, respondents describe how they developed one-to-one relationships to support others' instructional and professional development. In addition, graduate students report "increased communication with other instructors" and regular "mentoring around professional development issues."

Second, while those in faculty roles have also connected individually with their colleagues around teaching, some also have undertaken broader educational development initiatives. For example, one engineering faculty member describes creating pedagogical discussion groups on her campus: "Even though my university does not have a teaching and learning center, the experiences I had with the GTC teaching circle led me to find others with similar priorities and create our own informal teaching circle." Another professor in the humanities recounts how he serves as a bridge between his unit and the broader pedagogical community: "I . . . take faculty to the annual Lilly Conference at Miami. I also attend national workshops, and I present on those workshops when I return."

In explaining why they develop these connections, some GTCs explicitly cite the consultation approaches they learned in their GTC group, which stress collaborative problem solving. For example, one liberal arts faculty member reports:

> I spend more time talking with other faculty about their teaching methods and listening to and learning from their approaches. . . . I think my CRLT experience has especially helped me to get other faculty to open up and share their teaching techniques without feeling competitive or judged, so I get more/better information.

A lecturer states that through her GTC group experience she "became a much better collaborator and developed skills to talk about teaching with people that make the conversations more egalitarian and productive."

Conclusion

Much research documents that postsecondary teaching can be "a private affair" (Seldin, 1990, p. 5) in which faculty tend not to discuss their teaching with colleagues (Shulman, 2004; Wright, 2005). In contrast, many former GTCs indicate that they are connected to—and building—teaching exchanges and resources on their campuses and that their involvement with the GTC program has helped them see teaching as "community property" (Shulman, 2004).

The implications for faculty development are threefold. First, our research calls for a greater attentiveness to the ways that allies and advocates create connections to the field of faculty development. Others have examined paths into professional faculty development positions (for example, Pathways to the Profession of Educational Development, n.d.; Sorcinelli et al., 2006). We suggest a similar focus on those drawn into the "orbit" of faculty development work. Such a focus would document the path of faculty and administrators who do instructional and organizational development but do not have appointments in teaching centers.

Second, the evaluation model presented here may be useful to investigate the long-term impact of other GTC programs. Although they are not common, other examples of such models include the University of Virginia's Teaching Fellows program and the University of North Carolina Graduate Teaching Consultants program, as well as teaching consultant programs at Brown University and Northwestern University.

Finally, the positive impact of the University of Michigan GTC program suggests that it may be helpful to expand opportunities for such training beyond the limited number of universities offering GTC programs. There may be a role for the POD Network to create cross-institutional opportunities for graduate student or postdoctoral apprenticeships in teaching centers. Furthermore, it would be useful to explore how faculty development issues can be woven into the extensive network of Preparing Future Faculty programs and even TA preparation programs. How can we better prepare prospective faculty and higher education administrators to see the rich possibilities of engagement with faculty development programs and resources? Features of our GTC program, such as discussions of POD and teaching centers, student feedback models, and the introduction of faculty development as a career path may be useful enhancements applicable to many programs for tomorrow's professoriate.

One can never have too many allies, and better examining how we attract advocates to faculty development would serve us all.

Appendix A

GTC Survey

Consent

The Center for Research on Learning and Teaching (CRLT) is exploring the impact of the Graduate Teaching Consultant (GTC) Program. Your participation in this short survey is confidential and voluntary. You may choose not to respond to the survey. You should understand that your participation will have no impact on current or future employment with CRLT.

Responding to the survey should take you fewer than ten minutes.

Moving on to complete the survey indicates your consent to participate in this research.

If you have questions about the study or this survey, please contact one of the co-investigators:

1. Mary Wright, CRLT, 1071 Palmer Commons, Ann Arbor, MI. 48109, Email: mcwright@umich.edu
2. Deborah Meizlish, CRLT, 1071 Palmer Commons, Ann Arbor, MI. 48109, E-mail: debmeiz@umich.edu, Phone: 734-763-2396.

Should you have questions regarding your rights as a participant in research, please contact: Institutional Review Board, 540 E. Liberty Street, Suite 202, Ann Arbor, MI 48104-2210, (734) 936-0933, e-mail: irbhsbs@umich.edu.

1. Do you wish to go on to complete the survey?

   ❏ I consent to move on to this survey. I understand that I may skip any question I do not wish to answer.
   ❏ I do not consent.

Your Background

2. Please describe your current career: (Choose the *one* that best applies, but feel free to write additional clarification in the Other box.)

   ❑ Graduate student
   ❑ Lecturer
   ❑ Tenured or tenure-track faculty
   ❑ Faculty or graduate student development professional (working in a teaching center)
   ❑ Higher education administrator (other than faculty/graduate student development)
   ❑ I am not working in higher education (please describe your position in the Other box below)
   ❑ Other: (please describe)

Teaching Center

3. [*If respondent is not a graduate student and is working in higher education*] Does your campus have a teaching center? (Here, a teaching center is defined as a designated individual or an organizational unit that works with instructors and administrators on teaching and learning-related issues.)

   ❑ Yes
   ❑ No

4. [*If yes*] In any capacity, have you worked with this teaching center on your campus?

   ❑ Yes
   ❑ No

5. In what capacity have you worked with the teaching center on your campus? Please describe (e.g., facilitated workshops, attended programs, directed the center, served as a faculty liaison).

Higher Education Context

6. [*If respondent is working in higher education*] In what type of institution do you work?

   ❑ Research university

❑ Comprehensive/master's university
❑ Liberal arts college
❑ Community/two-year college
❑ Other (please specify)

Teaching

7. Please choose the response that best applies to your teaching at the postsecondary level.

   ❑ I currently teach at the postsecondary level.
   ❑ In the past year, I taught at the postsecondary level.
   ❑ It's been 1–2 years since I taught at the postsecondary level.
   ❑ It's been over 2 years since I taught at the postsecondary level.

8. [*If respondent has taught in the past 2 years*] Has your experience in the GTC program influenced your teaching practice?

   ❑ Yes
   ❑ No

9. Please give examples of the way your experience in the GTC program has influenced your teaching practice.

Mentoring

10. In the past year, have you formally or informally mentored, advised, or consulted with other graduate students or faculty around instructional or professional development issues?

    ❑ Yes
    ❑ No

11. [*If yes*] Please give some examples of how you have mentored other graduate students or faculty around instructional or professional development issues. (e.g., the type of assistance you were able to provide)

Resources

12. In the past year, have you provided resources on teaching, learning, or higher education to other graduate students or faculty?

    ❑ Yes
    ❑ No

13. [*If yes*] Please give examples of the types of resources you have provided on topics pertaining to teaching, learning, and higher education. Also, please note if there were any resources that you originally learned about from the GTC program.

Career Path

14. Did your involvement in the GTC program influence your career path (i.e., your intended or current choice of career type or setting)?
    ❑ Yes
    ❑ No
15. [*If yes*] In what ways did your involvement with the GTC program influence the direction of your career?
16. Please describe any other influence of the GTC Program on you personally that you feel is significant.

Thank you very much for your participation.

References

Chism, N. V. N. (1998). The role of educational developers in institutional change: From the basement office to the front office. In M. Kaplan & D. Lieberman (Eds.), *To improve the academy: Vol. 17. Resources for faculty, instructional, and organizational development* (pp. 141–154). Stillwater, OK: New Forums Press.

Chism, N. V. N (2007, October). *A professional priority: Preparing future developers.* Session presented at the 32nd annual meeting of the Professional and Organizational Development Network in Higher Education, Pittsburgh, PA.

Chism, N. V. N, Palmer, M., & Stanley, C. (2006, October). *If there's a scholarship of professional development, why don't we educate for it?* Workshop presented at the 31st annual meeting of the Professional and Organizational Development Network in Higher Education, Portland, OR.

Cook, C. E., & Sorcinelli, M. D. (2002, April 26). The importance of teaching centers. *Chronicle of Higher Education,* p. B21.

Cook, C. E., Kalish, A., & Pingree, A. (2004, November). *Finding great faculty developers: Best practices in the search process.* Workshop presented at the 29th annual meeting of the Professional and Organizational Development Network in Higher Education, Montreal, Quebec, Canada.

Gillespie, K. (2001, October). *Marketplace reality and our dreams of the profession.* Workshop presented at the 26th annual meeting of the Professional and Organizational Development Network in Higher Education, St. Louis, MO.

Ouellett, M. L., & Stanley, C. A. (2004). Fostering diversity in a faculty development organization. In C. M. Wehlburg & S. Chadwick-Blossey (Eds.), *To improve the academy: Vol. 22. Resources for faculty, instructional, and organizational development* (pp. 206–225). Bolton, MA: Anker.

Pathways to the profession of educational development. (n.d.). *About the project.* Retrieved November 28, 2007, from www.iathe.org/pathways/eng/about.asp

Porter, E., Lewis, K., Kristensen, E. W., Stanley, C. A., & Weiss, C. A. (1993). Applying for a faculty development position: What can our colleagues tell us? In D. L. Wright & J. P. Lunde (Eds.), *To improve the academy: Vol. 12. Resources for faculty, instructional, and organizational development* (pp. 261–272). Stillwater, OK: New Forums Press.

Seldin, P. (1990). Academic environments and teaching effectiveness. In P. Seldin (Ed.), *How administrators can improve teaching: Moving from talk to action in higher education* (pp. 3–22). San Francisco: Jossey-Bass.

Sell, G. R., & Chism, N. V. N. (1991). Finding the right match: Staffing faculty development centers. In K. J. Zahorski (Ed.), *To improve the academy: Vol. 10. Resources for faculty, instructional, and organizational development* (pp. 19–32). Stillwater, OK: New Forums Press.

Sorcinelli, M. D., Austin, A. E., Eddy, P. L., & Beach, A. L. (2006). *Creating the future of faculty development: Learning from the past, understanding the present.* Bolton, MA: Anker.

Wright, M. C. (2005). Always at odds? Congruence in faculty beliefs about teaching at a research university. *Journal of Higher Education, 76*(3), 331–353.

Chapter 21

Teaching Learning Processes—to Students and Teachers

Pamela E. Barnett, Linda C. Hodges
Princeton University

Our teaching and learning center serves faculty and graduate students as teachers and undergraduates as learners. Here we share the experiences of graduate student facilitators whom we trained to lead problem-solving skills workshops for undergraduates. Our aim was to help these graduate students see themselves as teachers of disciplinary thinking as much as of disciplinary content. However, they also began to reexamine their teaching beliefs and practices, recognize and respond to the needs of novice learners, and become more conscious of the demands of learning their disciplines. We offer this program as a model for developing future faculty.

As educational consultants in the McGraw Center for Teaching and Learning at Princeton University, we often work with graduate students and faculty as instructors, asking them to think about student learning as the purpose of their teaching. This process requires that instructors become more aware of how students learn. However, as experts in their disciplines, instructors are often unconscious of the processes that they themselves use to learn in their field and the differences between their approaches as experts and those of novice learners. We describe here a program that helped make instructors more aware of these processes and the necessity of teaching them directly. Even though this program began with the aim of teaching undergraduates about learning processes, it resulted in shifts in instructors' beliefs about learning and teaching.

Our teaching and learning center, like some others, serves faculty and graduate students as teachers, as well as undergraduates as learners, and we have found that our work with the one constituency is informed and improved by our work with the other. In an attempt to promote greater interest in and relevance for our undergraduate academic skills workshops, we began offering a few sessions specifically for quantitative classes, using content from those classes to model the processes of problem solving in those disciplines. We enlisted the help of graduate student teachers of biology, economics, and engineering to provide content expertise for the workshops, but we trained them to lead sessions focused on student learning processes, rather than the content per se.

During that training, we discovered that in most cases we were asking these experienced instructors to adopt a different model of teaching in a discipline. We were asking them to dig deeper into processes of learning than they were generally accustomed to. Our aim was to help graduate students see themselves as teachers of disciplinary thinking and ways of learning as much as of disciplinary content. After participating in our program, graduate student facilitators were more likely to consider their students as learners and become more conscious of the demands of learning their disciplines. This change in thinking was not easy to elicit, however, even for reflective young teachers. When graduate students worked with a peer group of graduate students across science and engineering disciplines, they were more likely to examine and reconsider their beliefs about learning and teaching than when they worked with us alone.

Our experience has implications for training graduate students as future faculty. This initiative illustrates the importance of collaboration between teaching and learning center staff who work primarily with instructors and those who provide academic support services to undergraduates. When graduate students lead workshops designed explicitly to teach academic skills rather than content, they must focus on the processes required to learn in the discipline—a new approach for them. This new situation opens great possibilities for their development as teachers. We argue that the combination of reflection and practice that these graduate student facilitators experience leads to promising shifts in teaching beliefs that may lead to changes in their own teaching practice.

The Nature of the Problem

Instructors face a number of unperceived challenges as they seek to facilitate student learning. For example, they rarely recognize the implicit knowledge required for successful learning, and thus they seldom explicitly teach academic skills. Expert scholars have so developed the learning strategies and habits of mind required by the discipline that they can mobilize them largely unconsciously. Think, for instance, of the expert problem solver who intuitively asks conceptual questions about a problem and its relationship to other, similar problems before embarking on computation. Or the social science scholar who writes questions and criticisms in the margins of texts or tables while reading. Although this unconscious mobilization of processes is the hallmark of expert scholars, these processes are often unfamiliar and invisible to the students they teach (Bransford, Brown, & Cocking, 2000; Schoenfeld, 1985; Simon & Simon, 1978). Instructors in science or quantitative courses commonly require students to solve many problems for homework and may even demonstrate solutions in class on the board. It is less common for college instructors, including graduate student assistants leading problem-solving sessions, to break down the process through verbal or written annotation methods (Leonard, Dufresne, & Mestre, 1996).

Instructors may also fail to realize when the teaching goals they articulate do not match the teaching approach they routinely use. This lack of coherence arises when the teaching theories that instructors profess are not the theories guiding their actual practice (Argyris, Putnam, & McLain Smith, 1985). For example, most instructors wish to promote student learning. Specifically, many aim to help undergraduates develop as *deep learners* (Biggs, 1987; Entwistle & Ramsden, 1983): learning for understanding and developing the capacity for independent learning. Instructors who seek to help students not only acquire content but also a deeper understanding of disciplinary ways of knowing must be explicit about the cognitive processes embedded in academic work. We have found that in practice, however, students and teachers alike frequently focus on the specificity of the content to be learned, even though their espoused goals for student learning are those recognized as higher-order thinking skills: analysis, synthesis, evaluation (Bloom, 1956), and creation of knowledge. Often the ideas about teaching that instructors use in everyday practice are a form of *tacit knowledge*—understandings shaped by experience, beliefs, and context that they often cannot explain (Argyris & Schön, 1974; Polanyi, 1966). Before any change in practice is possible, instructors must recognize the implicit theories they are using in practice and willfully examine them to bring them into coherence with their explicit goals of teaching.

Graduate student teachers face these dual challenges. They are likely to assume that the learning processes and academic skills needed for learning in the discipline are obvious. In addition, their theories-in-action may not match their professed theories of teaching. The invisibility of the expert's learning processes contributes to this lack of coherence between professor goals and teaching practices. As we set about to train experienced graduate student instructors to lead the academic skills workshops, we uncovered unexpected resistance and difficulties. As part of our training process, then, we had to find ways to make their assumptions about learning and teaching explicit. Only then could they effectively examine and reassess their teaching beliefs.

Descriptions of the Programs and the Methodology

The seven graduate student facilitators we write about here all participated in our program for either one or two semesters, each offering two to eight academic skills workshops during that time. We found that our facilitators' experience and reflections constituted a rich case study that could provide insight into qualitative questions about what occurred in our program, the implications of those occurrences for the individuals involved, and the relationships linking those occurrences (Honigmann, 1982). These kinds of characteristics describe what may be called a "found" research study.

In retrospect, we identify ours as a purposive and unique sample (Merriam, 1998); we only recruited and hired graduate students who were recommended as good teachers and whom we found, in interviews, to be reflective about their teaching. Our sample was also unique in that each facilitator was attracted to teach in the program, expressing an interest in teaching about process, as much as content. As teaching and learning center professionals, we conducted the training for our sample of graduate student teachers. We also conducted the interviews. Thus, the interviewed graduate student facilitators were being asked to share their beliefs and assumptions with their own teaching mentors, knowing fully our assumptions about the importance of teaching learning processes.

Each facilitator provided workshops for a specific class in his discipline. We wanted the workshops to be designed with the research on novice versus expert problem solvers in mind. This research shows that in addition to disciplinary knowledge, effective problem solving requires a knowledge of strategies, the ability to use what one knows, and effective beliefs about the process of problem solving. Novice problem solvers, such as college students, typically rush to computation, believing that the process is quick and as simple as finding an equation that fits the problem. Expert problem solvers, on the other hand, explore, adapt, and reject various paths as part of thinking through the process (Schoenfeld, 1985). We thus trained workshop facilitators to guide students into thinking consciously about problem-solving processes. For example, a workshop—Problem Solving for Physics 101—taught students to begin their problem-solving process with techniques for fully comprehending a given physics problem: restating a problem in their own words, writing down all givens and constraints, and drawing and labeling a picture that represented the problem visually.

As is often the case when developing new programs, we began the process of training these graduate students with one kind of plan, but as we assessed the effectiveness of our training process, we made changes to the approach we took. In the pilot semester of the program, each of our three graduate facilitators had an initial meeting with a staff member of our center to discuss students' learning challenges, their own learning and problem-solving processes, and the aims of the program they would lead. Either before or after this meeting, facilitators were given a problem-solving strategies tip-sheet to study (see Appendix A), as well as a model lesson plan to work from. They were instructed to draft their own workshop lesson plan, including opportunities for students to practice the strategies to be taught. After attempting to draft a plan, each facilitator again met with a staff member for feedback. Their plans were essentially review sessions, focused on solving a specific problem rather than on teaching a problem-solving process.

Recognizing the graduate students' difficulty in understanding and isolating their processes, we attempted one-on-one training conversations with the three facilitators from our pilot cohort. This conversation worked well in the one case where we paired an economics graduate student, "Mary," with one of our staff who was a chemist. It was not as successful when the graduate facilitators had follow-up conversations with a staff member who was a humanist by training or with the center's senior graduate fellow, who was a molecular biologist and peer.

Having learned from our experience with the pilot cohort, we designed a different approach for the other four facilitators who led sessions during the second and third semesters of the program. They met instead with their cohort to discuss their processes and to "workshop" lesson plans together. This method was more successful in clarifying beliefs and promoting change. We held a total of three such meetings throughout the academic year. As they compared their processes, these four facilitators were able to isolate the specific, transferable skills and strategies, while articulating some differences as well. They also read each others' lesson plans, getting and giving ideas for building in opportunities for interaction and practice.

We interviewed five graduate students who participated in the program for one year and collected their thoughts and actions as evidence of changes in their teaching beliefs. Four were from the second cohort, but one facilitator from the pilot cohort (Mary) was interviewed for the study. Though we engaged in a long-term observation, talking with members of our sample over the course of a year, we report here on responses to a formal interview occurring on one occasion, at the end of the year of service. Each interviewee was asked the same questions, though not always in the same order. Three of the interviews were conducted like a focus group, with members of the group answering the questions and discussing their answers with each other. Two of the interviews were conducted with the interviewer alone. Each interviewee's comments were written down as well as videotaped, allowing for confirmation of what was heard. We also enhanced internal validity through "member checks," giving each interviewee the opportunity to review the data we had collected and our interpretations of those data (Merriam, 1998). Finally, to triangulate our findings, one or both of us observed each facilitator teaching the workshop in question on at least one occasion. These observations indicated that some of the professed teaching beliefs were reflected in teaching practice. Our aim here is not validity, however, but what Wolcott (1994) calls understanding: "something else, a quality that points more to identifying critical elements and wringing plausible interpretations from them" (p. 366).

As we summarize the findings in the next section, we note the contrast between the graduate students who met together to discuss plans and two facilitators from the pilot cohort who never came to understand our conception of learning processes. We speculate on the role that the group conversations might have played in the development of these graduate students as teachers. Here we outline five of the promising differences in teaching beliefs effected by this program.

Observed Attitude Changes

We noted some changes in facilitators' attitudes as the result of having gone through the program. We found that facilitators

1. Became more aware of the processes they use to learn their disciplines
2. Revised their perspectives on novice learners
3. Examined their beliefs about students as recipients and constructors of knowledge
4. Recognized the need for instructors to teach learning processes
5. Experienced the value of a "teaching commons"

1. *Facilitators became more aware of the processes they use to learn their disciplines.* When they were first asked to lead these sessions focusing on process rather than content, several of the graduate student facilitators were unsure about what we were asking of them. They did not think of their processes as the core of how and what they learned in their disciplines. What did it mean to teach physics problem-solving strategies rather than a specific physics problem? What were the actual steps they took or the questions they asked themselves? We found that almost all of our facilitators used their processes intuitively and unconsciously and needed some time to reflect before they could articulate them. Some facilitators found it more challenging than others.

Though Mary (economics), "Vince" (physics), and "Amy" (chemistry) each had a tip-sheet outlining some problem-solving steps for students and instructions to teach those, their first draft workshop plans were for review sessions in which students were led through solutions to particular problems. Per our suggestion, the facilitators had included interactive segments, but they were discussions of particular steps in the problem or particular concepts involved, not discussions or activities designed to help them understand or practice their processes. (For instance, they might have included a segment in which students were asked to draw a picture of the problem, then compare their representations with peers in the room.) We speculate that our graduate student facilitators were wrestling with their prior knowledge of teaching, and it was difficult for them to imagine a teaching task so different from the models they had been exposed to as students themselves. We also believe that we were confronting powerful prior conceptualizations about learning. Our disciplinary experts were more aware of their disciplinary knowledge than of their disciplinary habits of mind. They thus reverted to a content-transmission model of teaching, which is commonly modeled in quantitative disciplines. Conversations with a center staff member who was a chemist, and more study of the tip-sheet, led to greater understanding for Mary. As we noted earlier, however, neither Vince nor Amy ever came to our understanding of the goals of the workshops.

The other facilitators more quickly understood the teaching goal, but they had not reflected on their own learning process and would have been hard-pressed to describe them before this experience. As "Nick" (engineering) expressed it, "I hadn't thought about problem solving in an abstract way." Once he did think about it, however, he quickly realized the system behind what he had been doing "unsystematically." He was able to write out a list of techniques and "put them in order." Since teaching the workshop and after discussing it with the course head for an introductory physics class, he realized other aspects of his process, which he added to the workshop program.

Similarly, "Lachelle" (molecular biology) revealed that before the workshops, "[she] had not thought of biology as a problem-solving field." On reflection, she realized that these content-heavy courses also required application of that content through problem solving. It turned out that this skill was essential to learning in the discipline, but the teaching conventions so emphasized content coverage that she had failed to see how necessary problem-solving skills were to success. Nor had she recognized the sophistication of her own processes.

Perhaps the most interesting development was with "Susan" (engineering), who led calculus workshops and was inspired to better understand her own process once asked to teach it. She started by studying the tip-sheet and found that even though she did take many of the steps outlined, her process was not quite captured. She reported having so "internalized [her] process" that she had to view herself with a different question in mind. Instead of trying to get the answer, she wanted to study *how* she got the answer. She set to work on some unfamiliar problems, monitoring her own processes as she went. She realized that she questioned herself at every step of the way: "I was like my own teacher, asking myself questions that tested my ideas or clarified my understanding."

She was so interested in what she was discovering about her own processes that she decided to read further about others' problem-solving processes, discovering Polya's 1957 book *How to Solve It*. Combining her own self-reflexive process with some "phases of problem solving" described by Polya, Susan created her own tip-sheet for the Center called "Questions to Ask Yourself When Problem Solving" (Appendix B). It broke down the process into four phases, each with an attendant set of questions. For example, "Phase I: Understanding the Problem" included such questions as, What information have I been given and what information do I need to find? Can I draw a picture depicting the given information? Have I seen a similar problem before?

All of the facilitators affirmed that becoming more aware of their own processes was necessary for teaching strategies to students. As Nick put it, "When you teach it, you have to learn it, and you have to know it." The facilitators' heightened awareness of their own academic processes is consistent with the academic benefits accrued by leaders of supplemental instructions sessions (Stone, Jacobs, & Hayes, 2006).

2. *Facilitators revised their perspectives on novice learners.* The expert who teaches is challenged to recognize what is obvious versus what is familiar (Leamnson, 1999). We have found that novice teachers are more likely to conflate the two, mistakenly thinking that students are as familiar as they are with certain disciplinary habits and ways of thinking. As Mary (economics) became more certain of the workshop's aims and the focus on process, she decided she was unsure about the value. Did not students already do these things—such as drawing graphs and considering the concepts involved—intuitively, as she did? Would they be insulted by such instruction? Could we not avoid that by just inviting the students who were doing poorly to attend?

Mary's conception of the obvious, as opposed to the familiar, was not atypical of her cohort. Vince, for instance, did not articulate these concerns verbally, but they were manifest in his actual leading of the physics problem-solving workshop. Despite a carefully designed lesson, he abandoned the plan as soon as he began the session, reverting to his "review session" approach. One telling detail was that Vince did not bring a copy of the problem to the workshop as planned, electing instead to read it aloud to the students and then start solving on the board. Center staff intervened to make copies and otherwise maintain the emphasis on the process. In a post-session debrief, Vince seemed surprised by our assessment that it had not gone as planned. When asked why he did not bring copies of the problem as planned, he said that students could do some of the steps, such as restating the problem in their own words, "in their heads." He also thought these things were "easy" and "could be done relatively quickly," as this was his own experience.

For most of the facilitators, leading academic skills workshops and getting some student feedback shifted these misconceptions. For instance, about a week after an economics problem-solving workshop, the center solicited candid feedback from workshop participants, and Mary was surprised by the overwhelmingly positive responses:

> This workshop helped me clarify my thought process when solving Econ problems. Also, it was good being told how important thinking is when solving a problem. They gave us some steps to follow when doing the problem and made sure to remind us to think intuitively. That gave me more confidence when tackling the problem sets and has resulted in my getting very high scores on the problem sets without too much stress.

Other students' comments included, "I think I'll approach my problems with the 'is that reasonable?' conjecture," and, "It was also helpful when you discussed the need to separate the givens from the constraints." Things that Mary thought basic were new and worth learning for a novice. Mary tried to understand the feedback by imagining herself in the situation of the novice. She realized that she was herself "more deliberate in this way when the problem is very unfamiliar or elusive." She recognized that for novice students, *most* problems are unfamiliar or elusive.

Lachelle (molecular biology) claimed that her newfound understanding of the novice student had been profound: "It is easy to lose track of what it is like at that stage. It has been a long time since I approached problem solving as a novice." Working with students on these workshops was "an eye opener." She had expectations about what students knew and how they conceptualized "what it means to be a student." For instance, reflecting on her teaching of a writing seminar about science, she realized students had different definitions of "reading." What a student might call "reading a text" would be merely "glancing over a text" to this graduate student teacher. As she reflected on teaching both the writing seminar and the academic skills workshop for molecular biology, she mused that "we get disconnected from what it means to be an introductory student" and speculated that this gap widens with increasing expertise, specialization, and years away from the novice learner experience. Susan similarly argued that the most experienced professors may be the most challenged to see the novice's point of view.

Susan was equally surprised at how "different my study process was from others' processes." For one, she "never memorized anything." Her process was much more about understanding a theorem by engaging it in some way, preferably by drawing a picture, which led to remembering it for far longer. In addition, she was truly puzzled by the fact that the undergraduates initially found this to be a "strange suggestion." She came to realize that they were treating problem solving as "a recipe," trying to memorize the steps needed to solve *this* problem. They spent less time actually trying to learn the theorem and were more likely to see each problem as unique. She never knew there was such a big division between her processes and theirs. As she put it, "the surprise went both ways." She was surprised by what students did not know, and the students were surprised by what the problem-solving process demanded of them.

The most experienced teacher in the group was not surprised. Allie (economics), a former high school teacher, was prepared to find a lot of variety in students' skill levels and expected many students to be unfamiliar with aspects of her discipline. She expected them to need this instruction. By facilitating these academic skills workshops, the other teachers were able to make up, at least in part, for their lack of experience and began to acquire Allie's more seasoned perspective—one more likely to recognize the students' level and the difference between the obvious and the familiar.

3. *Facilitators examined their beliefs about students as recipients and constructors of knowledge.* For many facilitators, recognizing the value of teaching process as well as content led to a reevaluation of traditional modes of instruction. Some articulated a relationship between overvaluing content and the pedagogical strategy of transmitting content to students, predicated on the assumption that the mind is a receptacle for information. After the workshops, the facilitators were more likely to think of students as

needing instruction and practice if they are to be coconstructors of knowledge and, thus, learn deeply.

Lachelle said that without this experience it would have "taken [her] a couple of semesters" to realize what some of the learning challenges were for students. Introductory biology is a "content-driven class," but leading these workshops led her to see the discipline anew. For one, she noted that we often ask students to memorize information, then "give it back," and then "apply it" to solve a problem. If this exercise is what we are going to ask students to do to demonstrate that they have learned the material, then they need some practice doing it. She believed that it is important to highlight processes if the goal is to help students learn to think like scientists rather that to regurgitate information. One way to emphasize process is by solving problems in class. As she put it, "More chalk equals more process." She wants to get students actually watching the process or participating in it. She found it hard to imagine how to do this, given "inherited models" of content transmission in a lecture based on slides: "That's how I was taught, and probably how my professors were taught." She said that this experience has given her some ideas about making students constructors of knowledge, rather than recipients.

Lachelle was already thinking about the content-driven nature of the introductory class in her discipline, and this reflection led her to the "less is more" determination. She decided that in trying to cover too much material, she lost opportunities for deeper learning. She had not realized before that what was missing was not just time to linger on a topic but a *way of engaging* the topic. She told a story about encountering what seemed to be new material in graduate school. "I was certain I had never seen this stuff before." Upon reviewing old class notes, however, she recognized that she had, in fact, studied and learned some of these things. She earned an "A," but the material just did not stick. She knew one problem was the rush to coverage, but part of the explanation for her memory loss was that she "was not taught a process." She learned the material in a particular way, and she had to learn it again, in a more engaged way, to build on it for her future as a molecular biologist. She said that, as a teacher, she wants to promote those more engaged processes.

Susan (engineering) talked about the difference between grappling with a concept versus grappling with a problem-solving process. She gave an example from her work as a teaching assistant: "A student comes to my office confused about a concept, so I ask questions, trying to guide them to understand the thing that is in the way. But I never thought about needing to teach them how to do this on their own, how to ask their own questions." Now she is concerned that, without the proper instruction, many students are "not equipped to study on their own." In this case, part of her job as a teacher is to teach them how to study and thus construct their own knowledge.

Allie (economics) defined "the magic of the classroom" as a space for the active construction of knowledge. She stated her intention to create a space where "we are here in a room figuring something out together." As the most experienced teacher, this experience only solidified previous conceptions. Deep learning requires active engagement and the discussion of problem solving as a process, and this engagement is the antithesis, she said, of teaching with PowerPoint. She argued, "PowerPoint kills class participation." By simply transmitting knowledge, instructors allow students to miss out on the experience of solving a problem and thinking it through together.

4. *Facilitators recognized the need for instructors to teach learning processes.* As they have critiqued traditional lecture or "chalk and talk" pedagogy, they have also considered how these ideas might affect their future teaching. What would it look like to teach problem-solving processes in an introductory math, economics, or physics class? Would one offer a full class period focused entirely on the process, similar to the center's workshop? Or could the processes be tied to the content and incorporated throughout the course? The facilitators uniformly agreed that the instruction of process should not be relegated entirely to an external unit, such as a teaching and learning center. It was the instructor's responsibility.

Lachelle imagined that a workshop on problem solving could be "the first precept or discussion section" of the year. At this point, students are less focused on the grade and more likely to be open to strategies for learning. She also maintained that teachers should be explicit about the fact that the strategies are transferable to other disciplines. She noted that she was teaching a writing class—obviously about process versus content—and yet students had a hard time seeing writing as a transferable skill. They wondered how they will now learn to write "an economics paper" or a "literature paper." Lachelle recognized how difficult they found it to think about writing as similar across the disciplines, as the task of constructing and supporting an argument. Given her experience teaching writing, she came to believe that students may need direct instruction to recognize problem-solving strategies learned in molecular biology as transferable to other disciplines such as math and physics.

What might a course look like if such instruction were incorporated throughout the semester rather than relegated to a session? Nick (engineering) imagined incorporating problem-solving instruction throughout the term, wedding it to the content: "Since there are problems with diving into problem solving before any content has been covered, I would probably try to distribute the techniques or break the lecture into five-minute "mini lectures" to be given through the term—perhaps a short discourse on a technique followed by desk or pair work on a problem which illustrates its utility, handed in after the first five minutes of lecture. It would also be an easy way of taking attendance!"

Allie (economics) agreed with this approach philosophically, arguing that by engaging in the process of doing economics, students would learn that these questions and strategies are part of working in the discipline. Problem solving would not be a separate class to be taught. She imagined having students work on problems, then present to the class what they did. Each group would be pressed to answer such questions as these: How did you approach this? How was it like what you did before? Her experience with the center made her consider exactly how she would teach the processes, but it was not the key factor in her beliefs. She knew the importance of focusing the class on process from her own experience as a learner and from her previous experience teaching K–12, even if she did not articulate this idea aloud.

Allie also felt strongly that process instruction would be more effective if done by the course instructor rather than by the kind of supplemental program that the Center for Teaching and Learning designed. For one, the course instructor knows students' needs, whereas "by design, the workshop facilitator can't know the students." Susan also talked about the need for the course instructor to accept this responsibility. Now that she knew that even highly prepared and successful students do not have the strategies, she argued "it would be irresponsible" for a course instructor not to teach these processes.

Susan recounted her taking a class as a college student where the problem-solving process was taught explicitly. It was an excellent course for her and the kind she intends to run as a faculty member. She criticized the model in which the professor works the problem and delivers a totally clean package with "no wrong turns." Susan argued that this model does not represent the nature of learning in the field and that we should ask more of our own problem-solving questions aloud and "show the messy process." In other words, teachers should allow for the fact that before they use an equation, they face uncertainty. Students should see what experts do to take things apart. In Susan's view, instructors should first articulate their own questions about a problem out loud, then have students add their own questions and thought, and finally have them work on the problems in class, with the instructor's guidance.

Lachelle used an opportunity to get students practicing an academic skill in a writing seminar she was teaching on science and media. "[She] was always sold on the idea [of study skills instruction] for students," but then she saw how it affected her own teaching. As the writing seminar progressed, she realized that her definition and expectation of "reading" in the discipline were different from those of her students. To make her processes and expectations transparent, she handed out a tip-sheet on active reading skills and devoted ten minutes of class time to actively reading an article. Students practiced posing questions and writing notes in the margins. This activity led to the most engaging and thoughtful discussion of a text for the semester. She speculated that her students were more likely to recall and use this reading process than if she had simply passed out the tip-sheet and suggested they try some of these strategies at home.

5. *Facilitators experienced the value of a "teaching commons."* All who had the opportunity to meet and talk with the facilitator cohort found it valuable. For one, they solidified their understanding of

their own processes by talking with others using similar cognitive strategies to tackle different disciplinary questions and problems. They also felt that they were able to develop better workshop lesson plans by reading each others' plan drafts and discussing the benefits of particular approaches and workshop activities. Finally, with a supportive, thoughtful sounding board, they could discuss a broad range of pedagogical issues: new teaching goals, new ways of teaching, and the challenges encountered in teaching.

Lachelle found it easier to see her own discipline of molecular biology as a "problem-solving discipline" once she compared notes and recognized similarities with her fellow teachers in more obvious problem-solving disciplines such as math and physics. She came to deeper understanding of her own process but also more conviction about the value of learning this process, given the transferability to other disciplines. She said it would be easier to sell to students and that teachers should be direct about how the skills can be used in other contexts, thus eliciting more student motivation to learn them. Lachelle also argued that when considering or trying out a new teaching model, instructors "need a quorum" and some "support" from others.

She talked about fellow teachers as tremendous resources for understanding and addressing "student roadblocks." These difficulties are "roadblocks that they [students] have in common" and other teachers are likely to have encountered them. She imagined turning to more experienced teachers in the future, learning what they have observed from teaching the same course over time and thus getting some advice about "what to anticipate." Lachelle also imagined the benefits of novice and experienced teachers discussing roadblocks together, coming up with potential solutions, experimenting with them, and sharing appropriate strategies and methods.

Conclusion

Before leading these workshops, the graduate students all had the explicit goal of promoting their students' learning of content. Each of them believed that students showed their understanding of content through their ability to solve problems, but their teaching-in-action illustrated their tacit belief that the processes required for students to solve problems—a higher-order skill—were obvious. Their own problem-solving approaches were invisible to them, thus supporting this belief. Most of the graduate students were challenged to recognize the need to teach processes of thinking in the discipline in order to encourage deep learning. The graduate students who worked with their peers as they developed these workshops confronted these inconsistencies between their goals for teaching and their teaching practice. They also showed greater willingness to try other teaching approaches that made the processes of problem solving more explicit.

As they imagine designing and teaching their own courses, most of the graduate student facilitators say that they will incorporate academic skills instruction into class time or that they see the value in it, even if they are not sure how, exactly, to implement it. They agree that students cannot pick up this kind of learning in a one-time workshop. The facilitators also address the formidable goal of teaching transferable skills. As the molecular biologist put it: "Transfer is the challenge. I'm still struggling with how to teach them 'the skill' and how to use it, and recognize the need for it, in another context."

This comment brings us to the hopes we have for these future faculty and their own transfer of knowledge and skills. In addition to bringing academic skills instruction to their future classes, we also hope they will recall the value of talking about teaching with a group of fellow instructors. Perhaps their experience in this program will encourage them to extend their involvement to participating in teaching and learning center programming, joining face-to-face and online pedagogy discussion groups, or starting their own formal or informal networks with fellow faculty. Such activities constitute a kind of "teaching commons"—opportunities for an exchange of ideas among a "community of educators committed to pedagogical inquiry and innovation" (Huber & Hutchings, 2005, p. x). These kinds of meetings provide faculty with support and resources that will better enable them to meet the challenges of teaching for deep learning and transfer.

Appendix A

Successful Strategies for Solving Problems on Assignments

Solving complex problems is a challenging task and warrants ongoing effort throughout your career. A number of approaches that expert problem solvers find useful are summarized next, and you may find these strategies helpful in your own work. Any quantitative problem, whether in economics, science, or engineering, requires a two-step approach: analyze, then compute. Jumping directly to "number-crunching" without thinking through the logic of the problem is counterproductive. Conversely, analyzing a problem and then computing carelessly will not result in the right answer either. So, think first, calculate, and always check your results. And remember, attitude matters. Approach solving a problem as something that you know you can do, rather than something you think that you can't do. Very few of us can see the answer to a problem without working through various approaches first.

Analysis Stage

- Read the problem carefully at least twice, aloud if possible, then **restate the problem in your own words.**
- **Write down all the information** that you know in the problem and separate, if necessary, the "givens" from the "constraints."
- **Think about what can be done with the information that is given.** What are some relationships within the information given? What does this particular problem have in common conceptually with course material or other questions that you have solved?

- **Draw pictures or graphs** to help you sort through what's really going on in the problem. These will help you recall related course material that will help you solve the problem. However, be sure to check that the assumptions underlying the picture or graph you have drawn are the same as the assumptions made in the problem. If they are not, you will need to take this into consideration when setting up your approach.

Computing Stage

- If the actual numbers involved in the problem are too large, small, or abstract and seem to be getting in the way of your thinking, **substitute simple numbers and plan your approach.** Then, once you get an understanding of the concepts in the problem, you can go back to the numbers given.
- **Once you have a plan, do the necessary calculations.** If you think of a simpler or more elegant approach, you can try it afterwards and use it as a check of your logic. Be careful about changing your approach in the middle of a problem. You can inadvertently include some incorrect or inapplicable assumptions from the prior plan.
- Throughout the computing stage, pause periodically to **be sure that you understand the intuition behind each concept in the problem.** Doing this will not only strengthen your understanding of the material, but it will also help you in solving other problems that also focus on those concepts.
- **Resist the temptation to consult the answer key** before you have finished the problem. Problems often look logical when someone else does them; that recognition does not require the same knowledge as solving the problem yourself. Likewise, when soliciting help from the AI or course head, ask for direction or a helpful tip only—avoid having them work the problem for you. This approach will help ensure that you really understand the problem—an essential prerequisite for successfully solving problems on exams and quizzes where no outside help is available.
- **Check your results.** Does the answer make sense given the information you have and the concepts involved? Does the answer make sense in the real world? Are the units reasonable?

Are the units the ones specified in the problem? If you substitute your answer for the unknown in the problem, does it fit the criteria given? Does your answer fit within the range of an estimate that you made prior to calculating the result? One especially effective way to check your results is to work with a study partner or group. Discussing various options for a problem can help you uncover both computational errors and errors in your thinking about the problem. Before doing this, of course, make sure that working with someone else is acceptable to your course instructor.

- **Ask yourself why this question is important.** Lectures, precepts, problem sets, and exams are all intended to increase your knowledge of the subject. Thinking about the connection between a problem and the rest of the course material will strengthen your overall understanding.

If you get stuck, take a break. Research has shown that the brain works very productively on problems while we sleep—so plan your problem-solving sessions in such a way that you do a "first pass." Then, get a night's rest, return to the problem set the next day, and think about approaching the problem in an entirely different way.

Source: Adapted in part from Walter Pauk. *How to Study in College,* 7th ed., Houghton Mifflin, 2001.

Appendix B

Questions to Ask Yourself When Problem Solving

Phase I: Understanding the Problem

What information have I been given? What information do I need to find? Can I draw a picture depicting the given information? How would I restate the problem in my own words? What type of problem is this? Have I seen a similar problem before? Is there a similar problem in the textbook? What characteristics of the given information jump out as potentially important? Why might they be important? Do I fully understand the set-up and what is required of me? If not, what can I do that would help me better understand this?

Do not move on to Phase II until you feel sure you understand the problem!

Phase II: Devising a Plan

- **Initial ideas:** Do I have any initial ideas as to how I might possibly solve this problem? What other information can I derive from the given information? How have I solved a similar problem in the past?
- **Following up on initial ideas:** Where would this idea get me? How would it help me get closer to the answer? What would I do next after this idea? Does the idea make sense?
- **Troubleshooting:** Can I think of a simpler version of this problem that is easier to solve? How would I solve the simpler

problem? Can I break this problem into smaller parts that are easier to solve? Have I considered *all* pieces of given information? What other ways might I approach this problem?

Phase III: Carrying Out the Plan

- **Have I achieved what I intended to in this step?** Is the result of this step correct?

Phase IV: Checking Your Answer

- **Verifying your answer:** Does my answer make sense? Is it plausible? Can I substitute my answer for the unknown in the problem? Does my answer match up with the given information? Does my answer have the right units?
- **Learning from your solution:** Can I look back and see a simpler way to solve this problem? Can I succinctly summarize the approach I used to solve this problem?
- **Why was I asked this to solve this problem?**

References

Argyris, C., & Schön, D. (1974). *Theory in practice: Increasing professional effectiveness.* San Francisco: Jossey-Bass.

Biggs, J. B. (1987). *Student approaches to learning and studying.* Hawthorne, Victoria: Australian Council for Educational Research.

Bloom, B. S. (1956). *Taxonomy of educational objectives: The classification of educational goals, by a committee of college and university examiners. Handbook 1: Cognitive domain.* New York: Longmans.

Bransford, J. D., Brown, A. L., & Cocking, R. R. (Eds.). (2000). *How people learn: Brain, mind, experience, and school* (Expanded ed.). Washington, DC: National Academy Press.

Entwistle, N. J., & Ramsden, P. (1983). *Understanding student learning.* London: Croom Helm.

Honigmann, J. J. (1982). Sampling in ethnographic fieldwork. In R. G. Burgess (Ed.), *Field research: A sourcebook and field manual* (pp. 121–139). London: Allen & Unwin.

Huber, M. T., & Hutchings, P. (2005). *The advancement of learning: Building the teaching commons.* San Francisco: Jossey-Bass.

Leamnson, R. (1999). *Thinking about teaching and learning: Developing habits of mind with first year college and university students.* Sterling, VA: Stylus.

Leonard, W. J., Dufresne, R. J., & Mestre, J. (1996). Using conceptual problem-solving strategies to highlight the role of conceptual knowledge in solving problems. *American Journal of Physics, 64*(12), 1495–1503.

Merriam, S. B. (1998). *Qualitative research and case study applications in education.* San Francisco: Jossey-Bass.

Polanyi, M. (1966). *The tacit dimension.* New York: Doubleday.

Polya, G. (1957). *How to solve it* (2nd ed.). Princeton, NJ: Princeton University Press.

Schoenfeld, A. H. (1985). *Mathematical problem solving.* New York: Academic Press.

Simon, D. P., & Simon, H. A. (1978). Individual differences in solving physics problems. In R. S. Siegler (Ed.), *Children's thinking: What develops?* (pp. 325–348). Hillsdale, NJ: Erlbaum.

Stone, M. E., Jacobs, G., & Hayes, H. (2006). Supplemental instruction: Student perspectives in the 21st century. *Student standpoints about access programs in higher education. Center for Research in Developmental Education and Urban Literacy Monographs, 6,* 129–141.

Wolcott, H. F. (1994). *Transforming qualitative data: Description, analysis, and interpretation.* Thousand Oaks, CA: Sage.

Bibliography

Alasuutari, P. (1995). *Researching culture: Qualitative method and cultural studies.* Thousand Oaks, CA: Sage.

Alexander, P., & Murphy, P. (2000). The research base for APA's learner-centered psychological principles. In N. Lambert & B. McCombs (Eds.), *How students learn* (pp. 25–60). Washington, DC: American Psychological Association.

Allard, K., Bellomio, S., Gronbeck, H., & Wilkin, H. (2006, May). *Student voices.* Paper presented at the Pacific Northwest Higher Education Teaching and Learning Conference, Vancouver, WA.

Altbach, P. (2005). Academic challenges: The American professoriate in comparative perspective. In A. Welch (Ed.), *The professoriate: Profile of a profession* (pp. 147–165). New York: Springer.

Alvesson, M. (2002). *Understanding organizational culture.* Thousand Oaks, CA: Sage.

Ambrose, D. (1987). *Managing complex change.* Pittsburgh, PA: The Enterprise Group, Ltd.

American Association for Community and Junior Colleges. (1988, November). *Building communities: A vision for a new century.* (Commission Report). Washington, DC: Author.

American Association of Colleges of Nursing. (1999). *Position statement on defining scholarship for the discipline of nursing.* Retrieved May 19, 2008, from www.aacn.nche.edu/publications/positions/scholar.htm

American Association of University Professors. (2005–06). *Annual report of the economic status of the profession.* Washington, DC: Author.

American Institutes for Research. (2006). *The literacy of America's college students.* Washington, DC: Author.

Anderson, L. W., & Krathwohl, D. R. (2001). *A taxonomy for learning, teaching, and assessing: A revision of Bloom's taxonomy of educational objectives.* New York: Longman.

Argyris, C. (1976). Single-loop and double-loop models in research on decision making. *Administrative Science Quarterly, 21,* 363–375.

Argyris, C. (1982). *Reasoning, learning, and action.* San Francisco: Jossey-Bass.

Argyris, C., & Schön, D. (1974). *Theory in practice: Increasing professional effectiveness.* San Francisco: Jossey-Bass.

Argyris, C., Putnam, R., & McLain Smith, D. (1985). *Action science.* San Francisco: Jossey-Bass.

Arons, A. B. (1979). Some thoughts on reasoning capacities implicitly expected of college students. In J. Lochhead & J. Clement (Eds.), *Cognitive process instruction: Research on teaching thinking skills* (pp. 209–216). Philadelphia: The Franklin Institute Press.

Arons, A. B. (1997). *Teaching introductory physics.* New York: Wiley.

Arreola, R. A. (2007). *Developing a comprehensive faculty evaluation system: A guide to designing, building, and operating large-scale faculty evaluation systems* (3rd ed.). Bolton, MA: Anker.

Ashburn, E. (2007). Survey identifies colleges that know how to keep junior faculty members happy. *The Chronicle of Higher Education, 53*(22), A6.

Association of American Colleges and Universities. (2002). *Greater expectations: A new vision for learning as a nation goes to college.* Washington, DC: Author.

Association of American Colleges and Universities. (2004). *Taking responsibility for the quality of the baccalaureate degree: A report from the greater expectations project on accreditation and assessment.* Washington, DC: Author.

Association of American Colleges and Universities. (2007). *College learning for the new global century: A report from the National Leadership Council for Liberal Education and America's Promise.* Washington, DC: Author.

Association of College and Research Libraries. (2004). *Information literacy competency standards for higher education.* Retrieved October 5, 2004, from www.ala.org/ala/acrl/acrlstandards/information-literacycompetency.htm

Association to Advance Collegiate Schools of Business. (2005). *Eligibility procedures and accreditation standards for business accreditation.* Retrieved December 2, 2007, from www.aacsb.edu/accreditation/standards.asp

Astin, A. W., & Astin, H. S. (1999). *Meaning and spirituality in the lives of college faculty: A study of values, authenticity, and stress.* Los Angeles: Higher Education Research Institute, University of California at Los Angeles.

Astin, A. W., & Astin, H. S. (2000). *Leadership reconsidered: Engaging higher education in social change.* Washington, DC: Kellogg Foundation.

Astin, A. W., Astin, H. S., Chambers, L., Chambers, T., Chickering, A., Elsner, P., et al. (2002, April). *A position statement from the initiative for authenticity and spirituality in higher education.* Retrieved August 15, 2007, from www.collegevalues.org/spirit.cfm?id=982&a=1

Auster, C. J., & MacRone, M. (1994). The classroom as a negotiated social setting: An empirical study of the effects of faculty members' behavior on students' participation. *Teaching Sociology, 22,* 289–300.

Austin, A. E. (1990). Faculty cultures, faculty values. In W. G. Tierney (Ed.), *New directions for institutional research: No. 68. Assessing academic climates and cultures* (pp. 61–73). San Francisco: Jossey-Bass.

Austin, A. E. (1994). Understanding and assessing faculty cultures and climates. In M. K. Kinnick (Ed.), *New directions for institutional research: No. 84. Providing useful information for deans and department chairs* (pp. 47–63). San Francisco: Jossey-Bass.

Baird, L. L. (1990). Campus climate: Using surveys for policy-making and understanding. In W. G. Tierney (Ed.), *New directions for institutional research: No. 68. Assessing academic climates and cultures* (pp. 35–45). San Francisco: Jossey-Bass.

Baker, G. A. (1998). *Managing change: A model for community college leaders.* Washington, DC: Community College Press.

Baldwin, R. G., & Blackburn, R. T. (1981). The academic career as a developmental process: Implications for higher education. *Journal of Higher Education, 52*(6), 598–614.

Baron, L. (2006). The advantages of a reciprocal relationship between faculty development and organizational development in higher education. In S. Chadwick-Blossey & D. R. Robertson (Eds.), *To improve the academy: Vol. 24. Resources for faculty, instructional, and organizational development* (pp. 29–43). Bolton, MA: Anker.

Barr, R. (1998, September/October). Obstacles to implementing the learning paradigm—What it takes to overcome them. *About Campus, 3*(4), 18–25.

Barr, R., & Tagg, J. (1995, November/December). From teaching to learning—A new paradigm for undergraduate education. *Change, 27*(6), 12–25.

Bartlett, T. (2002, March 22). The unkindest cut. *The Chronicle of Higher Education,* p. A10.

Bartunek, J. M., & Moch, M. K. (1987). First-order, second-order, and third-order change and organization development interventions: A cognitive approach. *Journal of Applied Behavioral Science, 23*(4), 483–500.

Bate, P. (1990). Using the culture concept in an organization development setting. *Journal of Applied Behavioral Science, 26*(1), 83–106.

Bate, P., Khan, R., & Pye, A. (2000). Towards a culturally sensitive approach to organization structuring: Where organization design meets organization development. *Organization Science, 11*(2), 197–211.

Baugh, S. G., & Scandura, T. A. (1999). The effect of multiple mentors on protégé attitudes toward the work setting. *Journal of Social Behavior and Personality, 14,* 503–522.

Beer, M., & Nohria, N. (2002). *Breaking the code of change.* Boston: Harvard Business School Press.

Bennis, W. G. (1969). *Organization development: Its nature, origins, and prospects.* Reading, MA: Addison-Wesley.

Bensimon, E. M. (1990). The new president and understanding the campus as a culture. In W. G. Tierney (Ed.), *New directions for institutional research: No. 68. Assessing academic climates and cultures* (pp. 75–86). San Francisco: Jossey-Bass.

Bergquist, W. (1992). *The four cultures of the academy.* San Francisco: Jossey-Bass.

Bergquist, W. (2006). *The six cultures of the academy.* San Francisco: Jossey-Bass.

Bernstein, D. (1998). Putting the focus on student learning. In P. Hutchings (Ed.), *The course portfolio: How faculty can examine their teaching to advance practice and improve student learning* (pp. 77–83). Sterling, VA: Stylus.

Bernstein, D., Burnett, A. N., Goodburn, A., & Savory, P. (2006). *Making teaching and learning visible: Course portfolios and the peer review of teaching.* Bolton, MA: Anker.

Biggs, J. B. (1987). *Student approaches to learning and studying.* Hawthorne, Victoria: Australian Council for Educational Research.

Biggs, J. B. (1999). What the student does: Teaching for enhanced learning. *Higher Education Research and Development, 18*(1), 57–75.

Biggs, J. B. (2003). *Teaching for quality learning at university* (2nd ed.). Berkshire, UK: Society for Research into Higher Education and Open University Press.

Birnbaum, R. (1988). *How colleges work: The cybernetics of academic organization and leadership.* San Francisco: Jossey-Bass.

Birnbaum, R. (1989). The implicit leadership theories of college and university presidents. *Review of Higher Education, 12*(2), 125–136.

Blackwell, R., & Blackmore, P. (2003). *Towards strategic staff development in higher education.* London: Society for Research into Higher Education and Open University Press.

Block, J. (1991). False dichotomies. In G. B. Vaughan & J. C. Palmer (Eds.), *New directions for community colleges: No. 76. Enhancing teaching and administration through scholarship* (pp. 17–26). San Francisco: Jossey-Bass.

Bloom, B. S. (1956). *Taxonomy of educational objectives: The classification of educational goals, by a committee of college and university examiners. Handbook 1: Cognitive domain.* New York: Longmans.

Bloom, L. (1985). Anxious writers in context: Graduate school and beyond. In M. Rose (Ed.), *When a writer can't write: Studies in writer's block and other composing-process problems* (pp. 119–133). New York: Guilford Press.

Blumberg, P. (2004). Beginning journey toward a culture of learning centered teaching. *Journal of Student Centered Learning, 2*(1), 68–80.

Blumberg, P. (2008). *Developing learner-centered teaching: A practical guide for faculty.* San Francisco: Jossey-Bass.

Blumberg, P., & Everett, J. (2005). Achieving a campus consensus on learning-centered teaching: Process and outcomes. In S. Chadwick-Blossey & D. R. Robertson (Eds.), *To improve the academy: Vol. 23. Resources for faculty, instructional, and organizational development* (pp. 191–210). Bolton, MA: Anker.

Boggs, G. R. (1995–96, December/January). The learning paradigm. *Community College Journal, 66*(3), 24–27.

Boggs, G. R. (2001). The meaning of scholarship in community colleges. *Community College Journal, 72*(1), 23–26.

Boice, R. (1990). *Professors as writers: A self-help guide to productive writing.* Stillwater, OK: New Forums Press.

Boice, R. (1992). *The new faculty member: Supporting and fostering professional development.* San Francisco: Jossey-Bass.

Boice, R. (1994). *How writers journey to comfort and fluency: A psychological adventure.* Westport, CT: Praeger.

Boice, R. (2000). *Advice for new faculty members: Nihil nimus.* Needham Heights, MA: Allyn & Bacon.

Bok, D. (2006). *Our underachieving colleges: A candid look at how much students learn and why they should be learning more.* Princeton, NJ: Princeton University Press.

Bolman, L. G., & Deal, T. E. (1991). *Reframing organizations: Artistry, choice, and leadership.* San Francisco: Jossey-Bass.

Bolman, L. G., & Deal, T. E. (1992, Autumn). What makes a team work? *Organizational Dynamics,* 34–44. Retrieved October 18, 2006, from www.fromccl.org/leadership

Boyer, E. L. (1990). *Scholarship reconsidered: Priorities of the professoriate.* Princeton, NJ: Carnegie Foundation for the Advancement of Teaching.

Brabrand, C. (Co-Producer/Writer/Director), & Andersen, J. (Co-Producer). (2006). *Teaching teaching and understanding understanding* [DVD]. Denmark: University of Aarhus and Daimi Edutainment.

Brammer, L. M. (1991). *How to cope with life transitions: The challenge of personal change.* New York: Hemisphere.

Brancato, V. C. (2003, Summer). Professional development in higher education. *New Directions for Adult and Continuing Education, 98,* 59–65.

Bransford, J. D., Brown, A. L., & Cocking, R. R. (Eds.). (2000). *How people learn: Brain, mind, experience, and school* (expanded ed.). Washington, DC: National Academy Press.

Braskamp, L. A., & Ory, J. C. (1994). *Assessing faculty work: Enhancing individual and institutional performance.* San Francisco: Jossey-Bass.

Braxton, J. M., Luckey, W., & Helland, P. (2002). *Institutionalizing a broader view of scholarship through Boyer's four domains.* San Francisco: Jossey-Bass.

Bridges, W. (1980). *Transitions: Making sense of life's changes.* Boston: Addison-Wesley.

Bridges, W. (2002). *Managing transitions: Making the most of change.* London: Nicholas Brealey.

Brinko, K. T. (1991). The interactions of teaching improvements. In M. Theall & J. Franklin (Eds.), *New directions for teaching and learning: No. 48. Effective practices for improving teaching* (pp. 39–49). San Francisco: Jossey-Bass.

Brinko, K. T., & Menges, R. J. (Eds.). (1997). *Practically speaking: A sourcebook for instructional consultants in higher education.* Stillwater, OK: New Forums Press.

Brown, R. (1999, January). The teacher as contemplative observer. *Educational Leadership, 56*(4), 70–73.

Bruner, J. (1966). *Toward a theory of instruction.* Cambridge, MA: Harvard University Press.

Bunch, K. J. (2007). Training failure as a consequence of organizational culture. *Human Resource Development Review, 6,* 142–163.

Burke, W. W. (2002). *Organization change: Theory and practice.* Thousand Oaks, CA: Sage.

Burke, W. W., & Litwin, G. H. (1992). A causal model of organizational performance and change. *Journal of Management, 18*(3), 532–545.

Campbell, R., & Seigel, B. N. (1967). The demand for higher education in the United States, 1919–1964. *American Economic Review, 57*(3), 482–494.

Campbell, W. E., & Smith, K. A. (Eds.). (1997). *New paradigms for college teaching.* Edina, MN: Interaction Book Company.

Carey, K. (2007, September/October). Truth without action: The myth of higher-education accountability. *Change, 39*(5), 24–29.

Carnegie Foundation. (2007). *Carnegie Academy for the Scholarship of Teaching and Learning.* Retrieved January 2, 2008, from www .carnegiefoundation.org/programs/index.asp?key=21

Cash, W., & Minter, R. (1979). Consulting approaches: Two basic styles. *Training and Development Journal, 33*(9), 26–28.

Centra, J. A. (1976). *Faculty development practices in U.S. colleges and universities.* Princeton, NJ: Educational Testing Service.

Centra, J. A. (1993). *Reflective faculty evaluation: Enhancing teaching and determining faculty effectiveness.* San Francisco: Jossey-Bass.

Cerbin, W. (1996). Inventing a new genre: The course portfolio at the University of Wisconsin–La Crosse. In P. Hutchings (Ed.), *Making teaching community property: A menu for peer collaboration and peer review* (pp. 52–56). Washington, DC: American Association for Higher Education.

Chavez, A. F. (2001). Spirit and nature in everyday life: Reflections of a mestiza in higher education. In M. A. Jablonski (Ed.), *New directions for student services: No. 95. The implications of student spirituality for student affairs practice* (pp. 69–80). San Francisco: Jossey-Bass.

Chesler, M. A. (1998). Planning multicultural audits in higher education. In M. Kaplan & D. Lieberman (Eds.), *To improve the academy: Vol. 17. Resources for faculty, instructional, and organizational development* (pp. 171–201). Stillwater, OK: New Forums Press.

Chism, N. V. N. (1998). The role of educational developers in institutional change: From the basement office to the front office. In M. Kaplan & D. Lieberman (Eds.), *To improve the academy: Vol 17. Resources for faculty, instructional, and organizational development* (pp. 141–154). Stillwater, OK: New Forums Press.

Chism, N. V. N. (1999). *Peer review of teaching: A sourcebook.* Bolton, MA: Anker.

Chism, N. V. N. (2003). *How professional development units keep track of their services (based on responses to an e-mail inquiry on the POD listserv, December 30, 2002).* Unpublished manuscript, Indiana University–Purdue University Indianapolis.

Chism, N. V. N. (2006, October). *If there's a scholarship of professional development, why don't we educate for it?* Concurrent session at the 31st annual meeting of the Professional and Organizational Development Network in Higher Education, Portland, OR.

Chism, N. V. N. (2007, October). *A professional priority: Preparing future developers.* Session presented at the 32nd annual meeting of the Professional and Organizational Development Network in Higher Education, Pittsburgh, PA.

Chism, N. V. N., & Szabó, B. (1996). Who uses faculty development services? In L. Richlin (Ed.), *To improve the academy: Vol. 15. Resources for student, faculty, and institutional development* (pp. 115–128). Stillwater, OK: New Forums Press.

Chism, N. V. N., & Szabó, B. (1997–98). How faculty development programs evaluate their services. *Journal of Staff, Program, and Organization Development, 15*(2), 55–62.

Chism, N. V. N., Palmer, M., & Stanley, C. (2006, October). *If there's a scholarship of professional development, why don't we educate for it?* Workshop presented at the 31st annual meeting of the Professional and Organizational Development Network in Higher Education, Portland, OR.

Clayton, M. J. (1997). Delphi: A technique to harness expert opinion for critical decision-making tasks in education. *Educational Psychology, 17*(4), 373–386.

Clearinghouse and National Review Board for the Scholarship of Engagement. (2002). *Evaluation criteria for the scholarship of engagement.* Retrieved February 21, 2008, from http://scholarshipofengagement .org/

Cohen, S. A. (1987, November). Instructional alignment: Searching for a magic bullet. *Educational Researcher, 16*(8), 16–20.

Cook, C. E., & Sorcinelli, M. D. (2002). *The value of a teaching center.* Retrieved September 25, 2007, from www.podnetwork.org/faculty_development/values.htm

Cook, C. E., & Sorcinelli, M. D. (2002, April 26). The importance of teaching centers. *Chronicle of Higher Education,* p. B21.

Cook, C. E., Kalish, A., & Pingree, A. (2004, November). *Finding great faculty developers: Best practices in the search process.* Workshop presented at the 29th annual meeting of the Professional and Organizational Development Network in Higher Education, Montreal, Quebec, Canada.

Cox, M. D. (2001). Faculty learning communities: Change agents for transforming institutions into learning organizations. In D. Lieberman & C. Wehlburg (Eds.), *To improve the academy: Vol. 19. Resources for faculty, instructional, and organizational development* (pp. 69–93). Bolton, MA: Anker.

Cox, M. D., & Richlin, L. (Eds.). (2004). *New directions for teaching and learning: No. 97. Building faculty learning communities.* San Francisco: Jossey-Bass.

Crawley, A. (1995). Faculty development programs at research universities: Implications for senior faculty renewal. In E. Neal & L. Richlin (Eds.), *To improve the academy: Vol. 14. Resources for faculty, instructional, and organizational development* (pp. 65–90). Stillwater, OK: New Forums Press.

Creswell, J. W. (2008). *Educational research: Planning, conducting, and evaluating quantitative and qualitative research* (3rd ed.). Upper Saddle River, NJ: Prentice Hall.

Cross, K. P., & Angelo, T. A. (1989). Faculty members as classroom researchers. *AACJC Journal, 59*(5), 23–25.

Cross, K. P., & Steadman, M. H. (1996). *Classroom research: Implementing the scholarship of teaching.* San Francisco: Jossey-Bass.

CTL Web site. (2007a). *Center for Teaching and Learning, Mesa Community College: MCC faculty and professional learning communities program.* Retrieved August 22, 2007, from http://ctl.mc.maricopa.edu/ _programs/fplc/index.html

CTL Web site. (2007b). *Center for Teaching and Learning, Mesa Community College: CTLpedia.* Retrieved August 22, 2007, from http://ctl .mc.maricopa.edu/wiki/index.php/Main_Page

Cummings, T. G., & Worley, C. G. (2000). *Organization development and change* (7th ed.). Mason, OH: South-Western College Publishing.

Curry, B. K. (1992). *Instituting enduring innovations: Achieving continuity of change in higher education.* (Report No. 7), ASHE-ERIC Higher Education. Washington, DC: George Washington University.

Cuseo, J. (2004). *The empirical case against large class size: Adverse effects on teaching, learning, and retention of first-year students.* Retrieved August 6, 2007, from www.ulster.ac.uk/star/curriculum_development/cuseo_ class_size.pdf

Dalkey, N. C., & Helmer, O. (1963). An experimental application of the Delphi method to the use of experts. *Management Science, 9,* 458–467.

Deal, T. E., & Kennedy, A. A. (2000). *Corporate cultures.* New York: Perseus.

de Janasz, S. C., & Sullivan, S. E. (2004). Multiple mentoring in academe: Developing the professional network. *Journal of Vocational Behavior, 64*(2), 263–283.

Diamond, R. M. (2002). Faculty, instructional, and organizational development: Options and choices. In K. H. Gillespie (Ed.), *A guide to faculty development: Practical advice, examples, and resources* (pp. 2–8). Bolton, MA: Anker.

Diamond, R. M. (2005). The institutional change agency: The expanding role of academic support centers. In S. Chadwick-Blossey & D. R. Robertson (Eds.), *To improve the academy: Vol. 23. Resources for faculty, instructional, and organizational development* (pp. 24–37). Bolton, MA: Anker.

Diamond, R. M., & Adam, B. E. (Eds.). (1995). *The disciplines speak: Rewarding the scholarly, professional, and creative work of faculty.* Washington, DC: American Association for Higher Education.

Diamond, R. M., & Adam, B. E. (Eds.). (2000). *The disciplines speak II: More statements on rewarding the scholarly, professional, and creative work of faculty.* Washington, DC: American Association for Higher Education.

Dickerson, C., Kuerbis, P., & Stiles, R. (2007, February). Learning centers, libraries, and IT: Providing integrated support services in a learning commons. In *Research Bulletin* (issue 5). Retrieved April 5, 2007, from http://connect.educause.edu/Library/ECAR/LearningCentersLibrariesa/40161

Donald, J. G. (2002). *Learning to think: Disciplinary perspectives.* San Francisco: Jossey-Bass.

Driscoll, A., & Lynton, E. A. (1999). *Making outreach visible: A guide to documenting professional service and outreach.* Washington, DC: American Association for Higher Education.

Driskell, G. W., & Brenton, A. L. (2005). *Organizational culture in action: A cultural analysis workbook.* Thousand Oaks, CA: Sage.

Durisen, R., & Pilachowski, C. (2004). Decoding astronomical concepts. In D. Pace & J. Middendorf (Eds.), *New directions for teaching and learning: No. 98. Decoding the disciplines: Helping students learn disciplinary ways of thinking* (pp. 33–43). San Francisco: Jossey-Bass.

Dwyer, P. M. (2005). Leading change: Creating a culture of assessment. In S. Chadwick-Blossey & D. R. Robertson (Eds.), *To improve the academy: Vol. 23. Resources for faculty, instructional, and organizational development* (pp. 38–46). Bolton, MA: Anker.

Eaton, J. (2007, September/October). Institutions, accreditors, and the federal government: Redefining their "appropriate relationship." *Change, 39*(5), 16–23.

Eble, K. E., & McKeachie, W. J. (1985). *Improving undergraduate education through faculty development: An analysis of effective programs and practices.* San Francisco: Jossey-Bass.

Eckel, P. D. (2002). Institutional transformation and change: Insights for faculty developers. In D. Lieberman & C. Wehlburg (Eds.), *To improve the academy: Vol. 20. Resources for faculty, instructional, and organizational development* (pp. 3–19). Bolton, MA: Anker.

Eckel, P. D., & Kezar, A. (2003). *Taking the reins: Institutional transformation in higher education.* Westport, CT: Praeger.

Eckel, P. D., Hill, B., Green, M., & Mallon, B. (1999). Reports from the road: Insights on institutional change. *On Change,* No. 2. Washington, DC: American Council on Education.

Eggers, R. M., & Jones, C. M. (1998). Practical considerations for conducting Delphi studies: The oracle enters a new age. *Educational Research Quarterly, 21*(3), 53–66.

Entwistle, N. J., & Ramsden, P. (1983). *Understanding student learning.* London: Croom Helm.

Eodice, M., & Cramer, S. (2001). Write on! A model for enhancing faculty publication. *Journal of Faculty Development, 18,* 113–120.

Erickson, G. (1986). A survey of faculty development practices. In M. Svinicki (Ed.), *To improve the academy: Vol. 5. Resources for student, faculty, and institutional development* (pp. 182–196). Stillwater, OK: New Forums Press.

Ewell, P. (2001). Editorial: Listening up. *Change, 33*(3), 4.

Eynon, J., & Chism, N. V. N. (2007, October). *Tracking purpose and priorities: Database systems for monitoring our work.* Paper presented at the 32nd annual meeting of the Professional and Organizational Development Network in Higher Education, Pittsburgh, PA.

Faculty Development Council. (2007, February). *Defining the field: The CSU faculty development center survey 2006.* Summary report, p. 3. Faculty Development Council (January 2000). Report on a discussion of center director burnout.

Fenwick, T. (2006). Toward enriched conceptions of work learning: Participation, expansion, and translation among individuals with/in activity. *Human Resource Development Review, 5*(3), 285–302.

Fetterman, D. M. (1990). Ethnographic auditing: A new approach to evaluating management. In W. G. Tierney (Ed.), *New directions for institutional research: No. 68. Assessing academic climates and cultures* (pp. 19–34). San Francisco: Jossey-Bass.

Fetterman, D. M. (1998). *Ethnography* (2nd ed.). Thousand Oaks, CA: Sage.

Fink, A. (1995). *Evaluation for education and psychology.* Thousand Oaks, CA: Sage.

Fink, L. D. (1984). The first year of college teaching. In K. E. Eble (Ed.), *New directions for teaching and learning: No. 17. The first year of college teaching* (pp. 11–15). San Francisco: Jossey-Bass.

Fink, L. D. (1992). Orientation programs for new faculty. In M. D. Sorcinelli & A. E. Austin (Eds.), *New directions for teaching and learning: No. 50. Developing new and junior faculty* (pp. 39–49). San Francisco: Jossey-Bass.

Fink, L. D. (2003). *Creating significant learning experiences: An integrated approach to designing college courses.* San Francisco: Jossey-Bass.

Fink, L. D., & Bauer, G. (2001). Getting started in one-on-one instructional consulting: Suggestions for new consultants. In K. G. Lewis & J. T. Povlacs Lunde (Eds.), *Face to face: A sourcebook of individual consultation techniques for faculty/instructional developers* (pp. 21–44). Stillwater, OK: New Forums Press.

Fish, S. (2003, May 16). Aim low. *The Chronicle of Higher Education,* p. C5.

Fox, M. F. F. (1992). Research, teaching, and publication productivity: Mutuality versus competition in academia. *Sociology of Education, 65,* 293–305.

Frantz, A. C., Beebe, S. A., Horvath, V. S., Canales, J., & Swee, D. E. (2005). The roles of teaching and learning centers. In S. Chadwick-Blossey & D. R. Robertson (Eds.), *To improve the academy: Vol. 23. Resources for faculty, instructional, and organizational development* (pp. 72–90). Bolton, MA: Anker.

Frederick, P. (2007, October). *Sixteen reflections from 30 years of faculty development.* Paper presented at the 32nd annual meeting of the Professional and Organizational Development Network in Higher Education, Pittsburgh, PA. Retrieved March 5, 2008, from http://ctl.conncoll.edu/smallcollege/index.html

French, W. L., & Bell, C. H. (1999). *Organizational development* (6th ed.). Upper Saddle River, NJ: Prentice Hall.

Fullan, M., & Miles, M. (1992, June). Getting reforms first: What works and what doesn't. *Phi Delta Kappan,* 745–752.

Gaff, J. G. (1976). *Toward faculty renewal.* San Francisco: Jossey-Bass.

Gaff, J. G. (2007). What if the faculty really do assume responsibility for the educational program? *Liberal Education, 93*(4), 6–13.

Gaff, J. G., & Simpson, R. D. (1994, Spring). Faculty development in the United States. *Innovative Higher Education, 18*(3), 167–176.

Garavalia, L., & Gredler, M. (2004). Teaching evaluation through modeling: Using the Delphi technique to assess problems in academic programs. *American Journal of Evaluation, 25*(3), 375–380.

Gardiner, L. F. (1994). *Redesigning higher education: Producing dramatic gains in student learning.* Washington, DC: The George Washington University, Graduate School of Education and Human Development.

Gardiner, L. F. (2005). Transforming the environment for learning: A crisis of quality. In S. Chadwick-Blossey & D. R. Robertson (Eds.), *To improve the academy: Vol. 23. Resources for faculty, instructional, and organizational development* (pp. 3–23). Bolton, MA: Anker.

Gardner, H., Csikszentmihalyi, M., & Damon, W. (2001). *Good work: When excellence and ethics meet.* New York: Basic Books.

Gayle, D. J., Tewarie, B., & White, A. Q. (2003). *Governance in the twenty-first century university: Approaches to effective leadership and strategic management.* (ASHE-ERIC Higher Education Report, Vol. 30, No. 1). San Francisco: Jossey-Bass.

Geertz, C. (1973). *The interpretation of cultures.* New York: Basic Books.

Gere, A. R. (1987). *Writing groups: History, theory, and implications.* Carbondale, IL: Southern Illinois University Press.

Gibson, G. W. (1992). *Good start: A guidebook for new faculty in liberal arts colleges.* Bolton, MA: Anker.

Gillespie, K. (2001, October). *Marketplace reality and our dreams of the profession.* Workshop presented at the 26th annual meeting of the Professional and Organizational Development Network in Higher Education, St. Louis, MO.

Gillespie, K., Hilsen, L., & Wadsworth, E. (Eds.). (1997). *A guide to faculty development: Practical advice, examples, and resources.* Bolton, MA: Anker.

Gilley, J. W., Eggland, S. A., & Gilley, A. M. (2002). *Principles of human resource development* (2nd ed.). New York: Basic Books.

Gilley, J. W., & Maycunich, A. (1998). *Strategically integrated HRD: Partnering to maximize organizational performance.* Reading, MA: Addison-Wesley.

Girves, J. E., Zepeda, Y., & Gwathmey, J. K. (2005). Mentoring in a post-affirmative action world. *Journal of Social Issues, 61*(3), 449–479.

Gladwell, M. (2005). *Blink: The power of thinking without thinking.* New York: Little, Brown.

Glassick, C. E., Huber, M. T., & Maeroff, G. I. (1997). *Scholarship assessed: Evaluation of the professoriate.* San Francisco: Jossey-Bass.

Glesne, C. (2006). *Becoming qualitative researchers: An introduction* (3rd ed.). Boston: Pearson.

Golembiewski, R. T., Billingsley, K. R., & Yeager, S. (1976). Measuring change and persistence in human affairs: Types of change generated by OD designs. *Journal of Applied Behavioral Science, 12,* 133–157.

Goto, S., Kane, C., Cheung, S., Hults, P., & Davis, A. (2007, October). *Scholarship of teaching and learning: Examining your practice in an age of accountability.* Paper presented at the Western Regional Research Conference on the Education of Adults, Western Washington University, Bellingham, WA.

Grant, M. R., & Keim, M. C. (2002). Faculty development in publicly supported two-year colleges. *Community College Journal of Research and Practice, 26,* 793–807.

Gray, T., & Conway, E. (2007). Build it [right] and they will come: Boosting attendance at your teaching center by building community. *Journal of Faculty Development, 12*(3), 179–184.

Greene, J. P., & Forster, G. (2003, September). *Public high school gradua-tion and college readiness rates in the United States* (Education work-ing paper No. 3). Retrieved August 6, 2007, from Manhattan Institute for Policy Research Web site: www.manhattan-institute. org/html/ewp_03.htm

Grubb, N. W., & Associates. (1999). *Honored but invisible: An inside look at teaching in community colleges.* New York: Routledge.

Gullatt, D. E., & Weaver, S. W. (1997, October). *Use of faculty develop-ment activities to improve the effectiveness of U.S. institutions of higher education.* Paper presented at the 22nd annual meeting of the Professional and Organizational Development Network in Higher Education, Hines City, FL. (ERIC Document Reproduction Service No. ED 414 796)

Haertel, E. (1986). The valid use of student performance measures for teacher evaluation. *Educational Evaluation and Policy Analysis, 8*(1), 45–60.

Hake, R. R. (1998). Interactive-engagement vs. traditional methods: A six-thousand student survey of mechanics test data for introductory physics courses. *American Journal of Physics, 66*(1), 64–74.

Hansen, L. S. (1997). *Integrative life planning: Critical tasks for career devel-opment and changing life patterns.* San Francisco: Jossey-Bass.

Haring, M. (2006, November). *Networking mentoring.* Paper presented at the meeting of the Mentoring in the Academy Conference, Providence, RI.

Hatala, J., & Fleming, P. R. (2007). Making transfer climate visible: Utilizing social network analysis to facilitate the transfer of train-ing. *Human Resource Development Review, 6*(1), 33–63.

Hatch, M. J. (1997). *Organization theory: Modern, symbolic, and postmodern perspectives.* New York: Oxford University Press.

Healy, M. (2000). Developing the scholarship of teaching in higher education: A discipline-based approach. *Higher Education Research and Development, 19*(2), 169–188.

Heller, J. (1961). *Catch-22.* New York: Simon & Schuster.

Heracleous, L. (2001). An ethnographic study of culture in the context of organizational change. *Journal of Applied Behavioral Science, 37,* 426–446.

Hersh, R. H., & Merrow, J. (Eds.). (2005). *Declining by degrees: Higher edu-cation at risk.* New York: Palgrave Macmillan.

Higgins, M. C., & Kram, K. E. (2001). Reconceptualizing mentor-ing at work: A developmental network perspective. *Academy of Management Review, 26,* 264–288.

Higher Learning Commission. (2007). *Institutional accreditation: An over-view.* Retrieved March 7, 2008, from http://hlcommission.org/download/Overview07.pdf

Hilsen, L. R., & Wadsworth, E. C. (2002). Staging successful workshops. In K. H. Gillespie (Ed.), *A guide to faculty development: Practical advice, examples, and resources* (pp. 108–122). Bolton, MA: Anker.

Hjortshoj, K. (2001). *Understanding writing blocks.* New York: Oxford University Press.

Holmgren, R. A. (2005). Teaching partners: Improving teaching and learning by cultivating a community of practice. In S. Chadwick-Blossey & D. R. Robertson (Eds.), *To improve the academy: Vol. 23. Resources for faculty, instructional, and organizational development* (pp. 211–219). Bolton, MA: Anker.

Holton, S. A. (2002). Promoting your professional development program. In K. H. Gillespie (Ed.), *A guide to faculty development: Practical advice, examples, and resources* (pp. 100–107). Bolton, MA: Anker.

Honigmann, J. J. (1982). Sampling in ethnographic fieldwork. In R. G. Burgess (Ed.), *Field research: A sourcebook and field manual* (pp. 121–139). London: Allen & Unwin.

Howard-Grenville, J. A. (2006). Inside the "black box": How organizational culture and subculture inform interpretations and actions on environmental issues. *Organization Environment, 19,* 46–73.

Huba, M. E., & Freed, J. E. (2000). *Learner-centered assessment on college campuses: Shifting the focus from teaching to learning.* Boston: Allyn & Bacon.

Huber, M. T. (1998). *Community college faculty attitudes and trends, 1997.* Stanford, CA: National Center for Postsecondary Improvement, Stanford University.

Huber, M. T. (1998). Why now? Course portfolios in context. In P. Hutchings (Ed.), *The course portfolio: How faculty can examine their teaching to advance practice and improve student learning.* Washington, DC: American Association for Higher Education.

Huber, M. T., & Hutchings, P. (2005). *The advancement of learning: Building the teaching commons.* San Francisco: Jossey-Bass.

Huber, M. T., Hutchings, P., & Schulman, L. (2005). The scholarship of teaching and learning. In K. O'Meara & R. E. Rice, *Faculty priorities reconsidered* (pp. 34–42). San Francisco: Jossey-Bass.

Hurley, J. J. P. (1990). Organizational development in universities. *Journal of Managerial Psychology, 5*(1), 17–22.

Hutchings, P. (1996). The peer review of teaching: Progress, issues and prospects. *Innovative Higher Education, 20*(4), 221–234.

Hutchings, P. (Ed.). (1998). *The course portfolio: How faculty can examine their teaching to advance practice and improve student learning.* Washington, DC: American Association for Higher Education.

Hutchings, P., & Huber, M. (2007). *Building the teaching commons.* Retrieved August 15, 2007, from www.carnegiefoundation.org/perspectives/sub.asp?key=245&subkey=800

Hutchings, P., & Shulman, L. S. (1999). The scholarship of teaching: New elaborations, new developments. *Change, 31*(5), 10–15.

Institute for Teaching and Learning. (1994, October). Summary of the October 7, 1994, discussion on the future direction of the ITL.

Jacobs, L. S., & Chase, C. I. (1992). *Developing and using tests effectively: A guide for faculty.* San Francisco: Jossey-Bass.

Johnson, G. (1987). *Strategic change and the management process.* Oxford: Blackwell.

Johnson, V. E. (2003). *Grade inflation: A crisis in college education.* New York: Springer-Verlag.

Johnson, W. D. (1991). Student-student interaction: The neglected variable in education. *Educational Research, 10*(1), 5–10.

Joint Committee on Standards for Educational Evaluation. (2003). *The student evaluation standards.* Thousand Oaks, CA: Corwin Press.

Joshua, M. (2007, August). *How can students take control of their own learning?* Paper presented at the first annual Mesa Community College Conference on Teaching and Learning, Mesa, AZ.

Kafai, Y., & Resnick, L. M. (1996). *Constructionism in practice.* Mahwah, NJ: Erlbaum.

Kanter, R. M. (1983). *The change masters.* London: Thomson Business Press.

Kanter, R. M., Stein, B. A., & Jick, T. D. (1992). *The challenge of organizational change: How companies experience it and leaders guide it.* New York: Free Press.

Karpiak, I. E. (1996). Ghosts in a wilderness: Problems and priorities of faculty at mid-career and mid-life. *Canadian Journal of Higher Education, 26*(3), 49–78.

Karpiak, I. E. (1997). University professors at mid-life: Being a part of . . . but feeling apart. In D. DeZure (Ed.), *To improve the academy: Vol. 16. Resources for faculty, instructional, and organizational development* (pp. 21–40). Stillwater, OK: New Forums Press.

Kegan, R. (1982). *The evolving self.* Cambridge, MA: Harvard University Press.

Kegan, R. (1994). *In over our heads.* Cambridge, MA: Harvard University Press.

Kegan, R., & Lahey, L. L. (2001). *Seven languages for transformation.* San Francisco: Jossey-Bass.

Kellogg Commission on the Future of State and Land Grant Universities (1999). *Returning to our roots: The engaged institution.* Washington, DC: National Association of State Universities and Land-Grant Colleges.

Kellogg Commission on the Future of State and Land-Grant Universities. (2006). *Public higher education reform five years after the Kellogg Commission on the Future of State and Land-Grant Universities.* Washington, DC: National Association of State Universities and Land-Grant Colleges.

Kezar, A. (2001). *Understanding and facilitating organizational change in the 21st century: Recent research and conceptualizations.* (ASHE-ERIC Higher Education Report, Vol. 28, No. 4.) San Francisco: Jossey-Bass.

Kezar, A., & Eckel, P. D. (2002). The effect of institutional culture on change strategies in higher education. *Journal of Higher Education, 73*(4), 435–459.

Kezar, A., Lester, J., Carducci, R., Gallant, T. B., & McGavin, M. C. (2007). Where are the faculty leaders? *Liberal Education, 93*(4), 14–21.

Killion, J. (2003). Eight smooth steps: Solid footwork makes evaluation of staff development programs a song. *Journal of Staff Development, 24*(4), 14–26.

King, A. (1993). From sage on the stage to guide on the side. *College Teaching, 41*(1), 30–35.

Knapper, C., & Piccinin, S. (Eds.). (1999). *New directions for teaching and learning: No. 79. Using consultants to improve teaching.* San Francisco: Jossey-Bass.

Koretz, D. M. (2002). Limitations in the use of achievement tests as measures of educators' productivity. *Journal of Human Resources, 37*(4), 752–777.

Kotter, J. P. (1996). *Leading change.* Boston: Harvard Business School Press.

Kouzes, J. M., & Posner, B. Z. (2002). *Leadership challenge.* San Francisco: Jossey-Bass.

Kreber, C. (2002). Controversy and consensus on the scholarship of teaching. *Studies in Higher Education, 27*(2), 151–167.

Kreber, C., & Cranton, P. (2000). Fragmentation versus integration of faculty work. In M. Kaplan & D. Lieberman (Eds.), *To improve the academy: Vol. 18. Resources for faculty, instructional, and organizational development* (pp. 217–230). Bolton, MA: Anker.

Kuh, G. D., & Umbach, P. (2004). College and character: Insight from the national survey of student engagement. In J. C. Dalton, T. R. Russell, & S. Kline (Eds.), *New directions for institutional research: No. 122. Assessing character outcomes in college* (pp. 37–53). San Francisco: Jossey-Bass.

Kuh, G. D., & Whitt, E. J. (1988). *The invisible tapestry: Culture in American colleges and universities.* (ASHE-ERIC Higher Education Report, Vol. 17, No. 1.) Washington, DC: The George Washington University, Graduate School of Education and Human Development.

Lambert, N., & McCombs, B. (2000). Introduction: Learner-centered schools and classrooms as a direction for school reform. In N. Lambert & B. McCombs (Eds.), *How students learn* (pp. 1–15). Washington, DC: American Psychological Association.

Latta, G. F. (2006). *Understanding organizational change in cultural context: Chief academic officers' acquisition and utilization of cultural knowledge in implementing institutional change.* Unpublished doctoral dissertation, University of Nebraska–Lincoln.

Latta, G. F., & Myers, N. F. (2005). The impact of unexpected leadership changes and budget crisis on change initiatives at a land-grant university. *Advances in Developing Human Resources, 7*(3), 351–367.

Leamnson, R. (1999). *Thinking about teaching and learning: Developing habits of mind with first year college and university students.* Sterling, VA: Stylus.

Lenning, O. T., & Ebbers, L. H. (1999). *The powerful potential of learning communities: Improving education for the future.* (ASHE-ERIC Higher Education Report, Vol. 26, No. 6). Washington, DC: The George Washington University, Graduate School of Education and Human Development.

Leonard, W. J., Dufresne, R. J., & Mestre, J. (1996). Using conceptual problem-solving strategies to highlight the role of conceptual knowledge in solving problems. *American Journal of Physics, 64*(12), 1495–1503.

LeTendre, B. G. (2000). Six steps to a solution: Guide can help educators reach an answer. *Journal of Staff Development, 21*(1), 20–25.

Levine, A. (2001). The remaking of the American university. *Innovative Higher Education, 25*(4), 253–267.

Levinson, D. J. (Ed.). (2003). Scholarship in the community college [Special issue]. *Community College Journal of Research and Practice, 27*(7).

Levinson, D. J. (1978). *The seasons of a man's life.* New York: Knopf.

Levinson, D. J. (1986). A conception of adult development. *American Psychologist, 41*(1), 3–13.

Lévi-Strauss, C. (1969). *The elementary structures of kinship.* Boston: Beacon Press.

Lewin, K. (1947). *Field theory in social science.* New York: Harper & Brothers.

Lewis, K., & Povlacs Lunde, J. (Eds.). (2001). *Face to face: A sourcebook of individual consultation techniques for faculty/instructional developers.* Stillwater, OK: New Forums Press.

Lieberman, D. A., & Guskin, A. E. (2003). The essential role of faculty development in new higher education models. In C. M. Wehlburg & S. Chadwick-Blossey (Eds.), *To improve the academy: Vol. 21.*

Resources for faculty, instructional, and organizational development (pp. 257–272). Bolton, MA: Anker.

Lindholm, J. A. (2003). Perceived organizational fit: Nurturing the minds, hearts, and personal ambitions of university faculty. *Review of Higher Education, 27*(1), 125–149.

Lindholm, J. A. (2004). Pathways to the professoriate: The role of self, others, and environment in shaping academic career aspirations. *Journal of Higher Education, 75*(6), 603.

Lindholm, J. A., & Astin, H. S. (2006). Understanding the "interior" life of faculty: How important is spirituality? *Religion and Education, 33*(2), 64–90.

Lindholm, J. A., Szelenyi, K., Hurtado, S., & Korn, W. S. (2005). *The American college teacher: National norms for the 2004–2005 HERI Faculty Survey.* Los Angeles, CA: Higher Education Research Institute, University of California.

Linstone, H. A., & Turoff, M. (Eds.). (1975). *The Delphi method: Techniques and applications.* Reading, MA: Addison-Wesley.

List, K., & Sorcinelli, M. D. (2007). Staying alive. *Journal of Faculty Development, 21*(3), 173–178.

Lister-Reis, J., Hamilton, C., & Nousheen, F. (2006). *The creation of a "public homeplace" in learning communities: The role of emotional and intellectual safety in student learning.* Retrieved August 27, 2007, from webshare.northseattle.edu/tlc/forfaculty_sotl_research1.shtm

Lueddeke, G. R. (1999). Toward a constructivist framework for guiding change and innovation in higher education. *Journal of Higher Education, 70*(3), 235–260.

Lueddeke, G. R. (2008). Reconciling research, teaching and scholarship in higher education: An examination of disciplinary variation, the curriculum and learning. *International Journal for the Scholarship of Teaching and Learning, 2*(1), 1–16. Retrieved January 15, 2008, from www.georgiasouthern.edu/ijsotl/issue_v2n1.htm

Maki, P. L. (2004). *Assessing for learning: Building a sustainable commitment across the institution.* Sterling, VA: Stylus.

Malik, D. (1996). Peer review of teaching: External review of course content. *Innovative Higher Education, 20,* 277–286.

Martin, J. (1992). *Cultures in organizations: Three perspectives.* New York: Oxford University Press.

Martin, J. (2002). *Organizational culture: Mapping the terrain.* Thousand Oaks, CA: Sage.

Maslow, A. (1943). A theory of human motivation. In J. M. Shafritz, J. S. Ott, & Y. S. Jang (Eds.), *Classics of organization theory* (pp. 159–173). New York: Wadsworth Press.

Matlin, M. W. (2002). Cognitive psychology and college-level pedagogy: Two siblings that rarely communicate. In D. F. Halpern & M. D. Hakel (Eds.), *Applying the science of learning to university teaching and beyond* (pp. 87–103). San Francisco: Jossey-Bass.

Maxwell, W. E. (1998, Fall). Supplemental instruction, learning communities and students studying together. *Community College Review.* Retrieved December 20, 2005, from www.findarticles.com

McLean, G. N. (2005). Doing organization development in complex systems: The case at a large U.S. research, land-grant university. *Advances in Developing Human Resources, 7*(3), 311–323.

Meisinger, S. (2007, October). Job satisfaction: A key to engagement and retention. *HR Magazine, 45*(10), 8.

Menges, R. J. (1999). *Faculty in new jobs.* San Francisco: Jossey-Bass.

Merriam, S. B. (1998). *Qualitative research and case study applications in education.* San Francisco: Jossey-Bass.

Merriam-Webster's Online Dictionary. Definition of *burnout.* Retrieved October 16, 2007, from www.m-w.com/dictionary/burnout

Michael, J. (2007). Faculty perceptions about barriers to active learning. *College Teaching, 55*(2), 42–47.

Middendorf, J. K. (1998). A case study in getting faculty to change. In M. Kaplan & D. Lieberman (Eds.), *To improve the academy: Vol. 17. Resources for faculty, instructional, and organizational development* (pp. 203–223). Stillwater, OK: New Forums Press.

Middle States Commission on Higher Education. (2003). *Student learning assessment.* Retrieved July 18, 2008, from www.msche.org/publications/SLABook07070925104757.pdf

Miller, M. A., & Murray, C. (2005). *Advising academically underprepared students.* Retrieved November 12, 2007, from NACADA Clearinghouse of Academic Advising Resources Web site: www.nacada.ksu.edu/Clearinghouse/AdvisingIssues/Academically-Underprepared.htm

Miller, V. (2001). Transforming campus life: Conclusions and other questions. In V. Miller & M. Ryan (Eds.), *Studies in education and spirituality* (pp. 299–312). New York: Peter Lang.

Millis, B. J. (1994). Faculty development in the 1990s: What it is and why we can't wait. *Journal of Counseling and Development, 72,* 454–464.

Mooney, K. M., & Reder, M. (2008). Faculty development at small and liberal arts colleges. In D. R. Robertson & L. B. Nilson (Eds.), *To improve the academy: Vol. 26. Resources for faculty, instructional, and organizational development* (pp. 158–172). San Francisco: Jossey-Bass.

Mooney, K. M., Fordham, T., & Lehr, V. (2005). A faculty development program to promote engaged classroom dialogue: The oral communication institute. In S. Chadwick-Blossey & D. R. Robertson (Eds.), *To improve the academy: Vol. 23. Resources for faculty, instructional, and organizational development* (pp. 219–235). Bolton, MA: Anker.

Morris, L. V. (2004). Changing institutions and changing faculty. *Innovative Higher Education, 29*(1), 3–6.

Mullinix, B. B. (2006). Building it for them: Faculty-centered program development and eManagement. In S. Chadwick-Blossey & D. R. Robertson (Eds.), *To improve the academy: Vol. 24. Resources for faculty, instructional, and organizational development* (pp. 183–200). Bolton, MA: Anker.

Mullinix, B. B. (2008). Credibility and effectiveness in context: An exploration of the importance of faculty status for faculty developers. In D. R. Robertson & L. B. Nilson (Eds.), *To improve the academy: Vol. 26. Resources for faculty, instructional, and organizational development* (pp. 173–195). Bolton, MA: Anker.

Murray, J. P. (1999). Faculty development in a national sample of community colleges. *Community College Review, 27*(3), 47–64.

Murray, J. P. (2001). Faculty development in publicly supported 2-year colleges. *Community College Journal of Research and Practice, 25*(7), 487–502.

Murry, J. W., & Hammons, J. O. (1995). Delphi: A versatile methodology for conducting qualitative research. *The Review of Higher Education, 18*(4), 423–436.

National Center for Educational Statistics. (1996). *Remedial education at higher education institutions in fall 1995* (Report No. NCES 97–584). Washington, DC. Summary retrieved November 12, 2007, from www.ecs.org/clearinghouse/25/33/2533.htm

National Center for Higher Education Management. (2007). *The emerging policy triangle: Economic development, workforce development, and education.* Boulder, CO: Western Interstate Commission for Higher Education.

National Center for Public Policy and Higher Education. (2006). *Measuring up: The national report card on higher education.* San Jose, CA: Author.

National Research Council. (2000). *How people learn: Brain, mind, experience, and school.* Washington, DC: National Academy Press.

National Survey of Student Engagement. (2005). *Exploring different dimensions of student engagement.* Retrieved November 17, 2005, from http://nsse.iub.edu/pdf/NSSE2005_annual_ report.pdf

National Survey of Student Engagement. (n.d.). Retrieved March 7, 2008, from http://nsse.iub.edu/index.cfm

Nelson, G. (1988). Organizational development: Working with change agents. In E. Wadsworth (Ed.), *A handbook for new practitioners* (pp. 175–180). Stillwater, OK: New Forums Press.

Neumann, A. (1995). Context, cognition and culture: A case analysis of collegiate leadership and cultural change. *American Educational Research Journal, 32*(2), 251–279.

Neumann, A., & Bensimon, E. M. (1990). Constructing the presidency: College presidents' images of their leadership roles, a comparative study. *Journal of Higher Education, 61*(6), 678–701.

Nilson, L. B. (2007). *The graphic syllabus and the outcomes map: Communicating your course.* San Francisco: Jossey-Bass.

Nyquist, J., & Wulff, D. (2001). Consultation using a research perspective. In K. Lewis & J. Lunde (Eds.), *Face to face: A sourcebook of individual consultation techniques for faculty/instructional developers* (2nd ed., pp. 45–62). Stillwater, OK: New Forums Press.

O'Banion, T. (1997). *A learning college for the 21st century.* Phoenix, AZ: Oryx Press.

Olsen, D., & Crawford, L. (1998). A five-year study of junior faculty expectations about their work. *Review of Higher Education, 22*(1), 39–54.

Olsen, D., & Sorcinelli, M. D. (1992). The pretenure years: A longitudinal perspective. In M. D. Sorcinelli & A. E. Austin (Eds.), *New directions for teaching and learning: No. 50. Developing new and junior faculty* (pp. 15–25). San Francisco: Jossey-Bass.

O'Meara, K., & Rice, R. E. (2005). *Faculty priorities reconsidered.* San Francisco: Jossey-Bass.

Ory, J. C., & Ryan, K. E. (1993). *Tips for improving testing and grading.* Newbury Park, CA: Sage.

Ouellett, M. L., & Sorcinelli, M. D. (1995). Teaching and learning in the diverse classroom: A faculty and TA partnership program. In E. Neal & L. Richlin (Eds.), *To improve the academy: Vol. 14. Resources for faculty, instructional, and organizational development* (pp. 205–217). Stillwater, OK: New Forums Press.

Ouellett, M. L., & Stanley, C. A. (2004). Fostering diversity in a faculty development organization. In C. M. Wehlburg & S. Chadwick-Blossey (Eds.), *To improve the academy: Vol. 22. Resources for faculty, instructional, and organizational development* (pp. 206–225). Bolton, MA: Anker.

Palmer, J. C. (1991). Nurturing scholarship at community colleges. In G. B. Vaughan & J. C. Palmer (Eds.), *New directions for community colleges: No. 76. Enhancing teaching and administration through scholarship* (pp. 69–77). San Francisco: Jossey-Bass.

Palmer, P. (1998). *The courage to teach: Exploring the inner landscape of a teacher's life.* San Francisco: Jossey-Bass.

Parks, S. D. (2000). *Big questions, worthy dreams: Mentoring young adults in their search for meaning, purpose, and faith.* San Francisco: Jossey-Bass.

Pascale, R., Milleman, M., & Gioja, L. (1997, November/December). Changing the way we change. *Harvard Business Review, 75*(6), 127–138.

Pathways to the profession of educational development. (n.d.). *About the project.* Retrieved November 28, 2007, from www.iathe.org/pathways/eng/about.asp

Patrick, S. K., & Fletcher, J. J. (1998). Faculty developers as change agents: Transforming colleges and universities into learning organizations. In M. Kaplan & D. Lieberman (Eds.), *To improve the academy: Vol. 17. Resources for faculty, instructional, and organizational development* (pp. 155–169). Stillwater, OK: New Forums Press.

Paulsen, M. B. (2002). Evaluating teaching performance. In C. L. Colbeck (Ed.), *New directions for institutional research: No. 114. Evaluating faculty performance* (pp. 5–18). San Francisco: Jossey-Bass.

Pearlman, M., & Tannenbaum, R. (2003). Teacher evaluation practices in the accountability era. In T. Kellaghan & D. L. Stufflebeam (Eds.), *International handbook of educational evaluation* (pp. 609–642). Norwell, MA: Kluwer.

Pellegrino, J. W., Chudowsky, N., & Glaser, R. (2001). *Knowing what students know: The science and design of educational assessments.* Washington, DC: National Academy Press.

Peters, D., Schodt, D., & Walczak, M. (2008). Supporting the scholarship of teaching and learning at liberal arts colleges. In D. R. Robertson & L. B. Nilson (Eds.), *To improve the academy: Vol. 26. Resources for faculty, instructional, and organizational development* (pp. 68–84). San Francisco: Jossey-Bass.

Peterson, M. F., & Smith, P. B. (2000). Sources of meaning, organizations, and cultures. In N. M. Ashkanasy, C. P. M. Wilderon, & M. F. Peterson (Eds.), *Handbook of organizational culture and climate* (pp. 101–115). Thousand Oaks, CA: Sage.

Peterson, M. F., & Spencer, M. G. (1990). Understanding academic culture and climate. In W. G. Tierney (Ed.), *New directions for institutional research: No. 68. Assessing academic climates and cultures* (pp. 3–18). San Francisco: Jossey-Bass.

Phung, B. (2007). *A contrastive rhetorical study of Chinese and Mexican perspectives of their native writing instruction and its implications for ESL teaching and learning.* Paper presented at the first annual Mesa Community College Conference on Teaching and Learning, Mesa, AZ.

Piaget, J. (1963). *Origins of intelligence in children.* New York: Norton.

Plank, K., Kalish, A., Rohdieck, S., & Harper, K. (2005). A vision beyond measurement: Creating an integrated data system for teaching centers. In S. Chadwick-Blossey & D. R. Robertson (Eds.), *To improve the academy: Vol. 23. Resources for faculty, instructional, and organizational development* (pp. 173–190). Bolton, MA: Anker.

Polanyi, M. (1966). *The tacit dimension.* New York: Doubleday.

Polya, G. (1957). *How to solve it* (2nd ed.). Princeton, NJ: Princeton University Press.

Pondy, L. (1983). The role of metaphors and myths in organizations and in the facilitation of change. In L. Pondy, P. Frost, G. Morgan, & T. Dandridge (Eds.), *Organizational symbolism* (pp. 157–166). Greenwich, London: JAI Press.

Porter, E., Lewis, K., Kristensen, E. W., Stanley, C. A., & Weiss, C. A. (1993). Applying for a faculty development position: What can our colleagues tell us? In D. L. Wright & J. P. Lunde (Eds.), *To improve the academy: Vol. 12. Resources for faculty, instructional, and organizational development* (pp. 261–272). Stillwater, OK: New Forums Press.

Potter, B. A. (1998). *Job burnout: What it is and what you can do about it? Summary.* From *Overcoming job burnout: How to renew enthusiasm for work* (pp. 1–2). Ronin Publishing. Retrieved August 28, 2007, from www.docpotter.com/art_bo-summary.html

President's Commission on Higher Education. (1947). *Higher education for American democracy.* New York: Harper Brothers.

Prochaska, J. O., DiClemente, C. C., & Norcross, J. C. (1992). In search of how people change: Applications to addictive behavior. *American Psychologist, 47,* 1102–1114.

Quinlan, K. M. (2002). Inside the peer review process: How academics review a colleague's teaching portfolio. *Teaching and Teacher Education, 18*(8), 1035–1049.

Reder, M., & Gallagher, E. V. (2007). Transforming a teaching culture through peer mentoring: Connecticut College's Johnson Teaching Seminar for Incoming Faculty. In D. R. Robertson & L. B. Nilson (Eds.), *To improve the academy: Vol. 25. Resources for faculty, instructional, and organizational development* (pp. 327–344). Bolton, MA: Anker.

Reder, M., & Mooney, K. (2004, November). *Getting started in small college faculty development.* Roundtable at the 29th annual meeting of the Professional and Organizational Development Network, Montreal, Quebec, Canada.

Reindl, T. (2007). *Hitting home: Quality, cost, and access challenges confronting higher education today.* Washington, DC: Jobs for the Future, Knowledge Center/Publications.

Reynolds, A. (1992). Charting the changes in junior faculty: Relationships among socialization, acculturation, and gender. *Journal of Higher Education, 63,* 637–652.

Rhem, J. (2006). The high risks of improving teaching. *National Teaching and Learning Forum, 15*(6), 1–4.

Rhoads, R. A., & Tierney, W. G. (1990). Exploring organizational climates and cultures. In W. G. Tierney (Ed.), *New directions for institutional research: No. 68. Assessing academic climates and cultures* (pp. 87–95). San Francisco: Jossey-Bass.

Rhodes, F. H. T. (2001). *The creation of the future: The role of the American university.* Ithaca, NY: Cornell University Press.

Rice, R. E. (1996). *Making a place for the new American scholar: Inquiry #1.* Washington, DC: American Association for Higher Education.

Rice, R. E. (2005a). It all started in the sixties: Movements for change across the decade—A personal journey. In D. R. Robertson & L. B. Nilson (Eds.), *To improve the academy: Vol. 25. Resources for faculty, instructional, and organizational development* (pp. 3–17). Bolton, MA: Anker.

Rice, R. E. (2005b). The future of the scholarly work of faculty. In K. O'Meara & R. E. Rice, *Faculty priorities reconsidered* (pp. 303–312). San Francisco: Jossey-Bass.

Rice, R. E., Sorcinelli, M. D., & Austin, A. E. (2000). *Heeding new voices: Academic careers for a new generation.* Washington, DC: American Association for Higher Education.

Richlin, L. (2001). Scholarly teaching and the scholarship of teaching. In C. Kreber (Ed.), *New directions for teaching and learning: No. 86. Scholarship revisited: Perspectives on the scholarship of teaching* (pp. 57–68). San Francisco: Jossey-Bass.

Richlin, L., & Essington, A. (2004). Faculty learning communities to prepare future faculty. In M. Cox & L. Richlin (Eds.), *New directions for teaching and learning: No. 97. Building faculty learning communities* (pp. 149–157). San Francisco: Jossey-Bass.

Roberts, P. (1999). Scholarly publishing, peer review and the Internet. *First Monday, 4*(4–5). Retrieved December 10, 2007, from www.uic.edu/htbin/cgiwrap/bin/ojs/index.php/fm/issue/view/104

Rogers, E. (1995). *Diffusions of innovations* (4th ed.). New York: Free Press.

Rothwell, W. J. (1996). *Beyond training and development: State-of-the-art strategies for enhancing human performance.* New York: American Management Association.

Rothwell, W. J., Sullivan, R., & McLean, G. N. (1995). *Practicing organizational development: A guide for consultants.* San Francisco: Pfeiffer.

Rousseau, D. M. (1990). Assessing organizational culture: The case for multiple methods. In B. Schneider (Ed.), *Organizational climate and culture* (pp. 153–192). San Francisco: Jossey-Bass.

Ruben, B. D. (2004). *Pursuing excellence in higher education.* San Francisco: Jossey-Bass.

Ruben, B. D. (2005). The Center for Organizational Development and Leadership at Rutgers University: A case study. *Advances in Developing Human Resources, 7*(3), 368–395.

Sackmann, S. A. (1991). *Cultural knowledge in organizations: Exploring the collective mind.* Newbury Park, CA: Sage.

Sackmann, S. A. (Ed.). (1997). *Cultural complexity: Inherent contrasts and contradictions.* Thousand Oaks, CA: Sage.

Scheibe, M., Skutsch, M., & Schofer, J. (1975). Experiments in Delphi methodology. In H. A. Linstone & M. Turoff (Eds.), *The Delphi method: Techniques and applications* (pp. 262–287). Reading, MA: Addison-Wesley.

Schein, E. H. (1991). What is culture? In P. J. Frost, L. F. Moore, M. R. Louis, C. C. Lundberg, & J. Martin (Eds.), *Reframing organizational culture* (pp. 243–253). Newbury Park, CA: Sage.

Schein, E. H. (1995). *Kurt Lewin's change theory in the field and in the classroom: Notes toward a model of managed learning.* Retrieved August 10, 2007, from www.solonline.org/res/wp/10006.html

Schein, E. H. (1996). Culture: The missing concept in organizational studies. *Administrative Science Quarterly, 41,* 229–240.

Schein, E. H. (1999). *The corporate culture survival guide.* San Francisco: Jossey-Bass.

Schein, E. H. (2004). *Organizational culture and leadership* (3rd ed.). San Francisco: Jossey-Bass.

Schlossberg, N., Lynch, A., & Chickering, A. (1989). *Improving higher education environments for adults: Responsive programs and services from entry to departure.* San Francisco: Jossey-Bass.

Schoenfeld, A. H. (1985). *Mathematical problem solving.* New York: Academic Press.

Schulz, M. (1995). *On studying organizational cultures: Diagnosis and understanding.* New York: Walter de Gruyter.

Schuster, J. H. (1989). The personal dimension: Faculty development. *Thought and Action, 5*(1), 61–62.

Schuster, J. H., & Wheeler, D. W. (1990). *Enhancing faculty careers: Strategies for development and renewal.* San Francisco: Jossey-Bass.

Seidman, E. (1985). *In the words of the faculty: Perspectives on improving teaching and educational quality in community colleges.* San Francisco: Jossey-Bass.

Seldin, P. (1990). Academic environments and teaching effectiveness. In P. Seldin (Ed.), *How administrators can improve teaching: Moving from talk to action in higher education* (pp. 3–22). San Francisco: Jossey-Bass.

Sell, G. R., & Chism, N. V. N. (1991). Finding the right match: Staffing faculty development centers. In K. J. Zahorski (Ed.), *To improve the academy: Vol. 10. Resources for faculty, instructional, and organizational development* (pp. 19–32). Stillwater, OK: New Forums Press.

Senge, P. (1990). *The fifth discipline.* New York: Doubleday.

Shapiro, E. D., & Coleman, D. L. (2000). The scholarship of application. *Faculty Medicine, 75,* 895–898.

Shih, M., & Sorcinelli, M. D. (2007). Technology as a catalyst for senior faculty development. *Journal of Faculty Development, 21*(1), 23–31.

Shulman, L. S. (1993, November/December). Teaching as community property: Putting an end to pedagogical solitude. *Change, 25*(6), 6–7.

Shulman, L. S. (1999). Professing educational scholarship. In E. Lagemann & L. S. Shulman (Eds.), *Issues in education research: Problems and possibilities* (pp. 159–165). San Francisco: Jossey-Bass.

Shulman, L. S. (2000, October). *Fostering a scholarship of teaching and learning.* Paper presented at the 12th annual Louise McBee Lecture, Athens, GA.

Shulman, L. S. (2000a). From Minsk to Pinsk: Why a scholarship of teaching and learning? *Journal of the Scholarship of Teaching and Learning, 1*(1), 48–52. Retrieved December 3, 2007, from www .iupui.edu/~josotl/VOL_1/NO_1/SHULMAN.PDF

Shulman, L. S. (2000b). Inventing the future. In P. Hutchings (Ed.), *Opening lines: Approaches to the scholarship of teaching and learning* (pp. 95–105). Menlo Park, CA: Carnegie Foundation for the Advancement of Teaching.

Shulman, L. S. (2004). *Teaching as community property: Essays on higher education.* San Francisco: Jossey-Bass.

Shults, C. (2006, October). *Towards organizational culture change in higher education: Introduction of a model.* Paper presented at the meeting of the Association for the Study of Higher Education, Anaheim, CA.

Simon, D. P., & Simon, H. A. (1978). Individual differences in solving physics problems. In R. S. Siegler (Ed.), *Children's thinking: What develops?* (pp. 325–348). Hillsdale, NJ: Erlbaum.

Singer, S. R. (2002, Fall). Learning and teaching centers: Hubs of educational reform. In J. L. Narum & K. Conover (Eds.), *New directions for higher education: No. 119. Building robust learning environments in undergraduate science, technology, engineering, and mathematics* (pp. 59–64). San Francisco: Jossey-Bass.

Slavin, R. E. (1990). *Cooperative learning theory, research and practice.* Needham Heights, MA: Allyn & Bacon.

Smart, J. C., & St. John, E. P. (1996). Organizational culture and effectiveness in higher education: A test of the "culture type" and "strong culture" hypothesis. *Educational Evaluation and Policy Analysis, 18*(3), 219–241.

Smith, B. L. (1993). Creating learning communities. *Liberal Education, 79*(4), 32–39.

Smith, B. L. (1998). Adopting a strategic approach to managing change in learning and teaching. In M. Kaplan & D. Lieberman (Eds.), *To improve the academy: Vol. 18. Resources for faculty, instructional, and organizational development* (pp. 225–242). Bolton, MA: Anker.

Smith, W. F., & Fenstermacher, G. D. (Eds.). (1999). *Leadership for educational renewal: Developing a cadre of leaders.* San Francisco: Jossey-Bass.

Solem, M. N., & Foote, K. E. (2004). Concerns, attitudes, and abilities of early career geography faculty. *Annals of the Association of American Geographers, 1*(4), 889–912.

Sorcinelli, M. D. (1988). Satisfactions and concerns of new university teachers. In J. G. Kurfiss (Ed.), *To improve the academy: Vol. 7. Resources for student, faculty, and institutional development* (pp. 121–133). Stillwater, OK: New Forums Press.

Sorcinelli, M. D. (1994). Effective approaches to new faculty development. *Journal of Counseling and Development, 72,* 474–479.

Sorcinelli, M. D. (2002). New conceptions of scholarship for a new generation of faculty members. In K. J. Zahorski (Ed.), *New directions for teaching and learning: No. 90. Scholarship in the postmodern era: New venues, new values, new visions* (pp. 41–48). San Francisco: Jossey-Bass.

Sorcinelli, M. D. (2002). Ten principles of good practice in creating and sustaining teaching and learning centers. In K. H. Gillespie (Ed.), *A guide to faculty development: Practical advice, examples, and resources* (pp. 9–23). Bolton, MA: Anker.

Sorcinelli, M. D. (2004). The top ten things new faculty would like to hear from their colleagues. *National Teaching and Learning Forum, 13*(3), 1–5.

Sorcinelli, M. D., & Austin, A. E. (Eds.). (1992). *New directions for teaching and learning: No. 50. Developing new and junior faculty.* San Francisco: Jossey-Bass.

Sorcinelli, M. D., & Austin, A. E. (2006, November). Developing faculty for new roles and changing expectations. *Effective Practices for Academic Leaders, 1*(11), 1–6.

Sorcinelli, M. D., & Yun, J. H. (2007). From mentors to mentoring networks: Mentoring in the new academy. *Change, 39*(6), 58–61.

Sorcinelli, M. D., Austin, A. E., Eddy, P. L., & Beach, A. L. (2006). *Creating the future of faculty development: Learning from the past, understanding the present.* Bolton, MA: Anker.

Sorenson, D. L. (2000). Student collaboration in faculty development: Connecting directly to the learning revolution. In E. C. Wadsworth (Ed.), *To improve the academy: Vol. 8. Resources for student, faculty, and institutional development* (pp. 97–121). Stillwater, OK: New Forums Press.

Springer, L., Stanne, M., & Donovan, S. (1999). Effects of small-group learning on undergraduates in science, mathematics, engineering, and technology (health sciences): A meta-analysis. *Review of Educational Research, 69*(1), 21–51.

Stafford, G. (2001). The college campus as a web of sociality. In V. Miller & M. Ryan (Eds.), *Studies in education and spirituality* (pp. 173–181). New York: Peter Lang.

Sternberg, R. J., & Grigorenko, E. L. (2002). The theory of successful intelligence as a basis for instruction and assessment in higher education. In D. F. Halpern & M. D. Hakel (Eds.), *Applying the science of learning to university teaching and beyond* (pp. 45–54). San Francisco: Jossey-Bass.

Stevens, C. A. (2007, January). *Do more with less: The well-rounded faculty's guide to integration of teaching, service and scholarship.* Paper presented at the Society of Park and Recreation Educators Teaching Institute, Clemson, SC.

Stevens, C. A., & Wellman, J. D. (2007). Establishing a national board for the peer review of scholarly teaching: A proposal for the Society of Park and Recreation Educators. *Schole: A Journal of Leisure Studies and Recreation Education, 22,* 1–16.

Stevens, C. A., Wellman, J. D., DeGraaf, D., Dustin, D., Paisley, K., & Ross, C. (2007). Proposal to establish blind peer review of scholarly teaching for park and recreation educators. *SPRE Teaching Professor: Issues and Innovations,* 7–9.

Stone, M. E., Jacobs, G., & Hayes, H. (2006). Supplemental instruction: Student perspectives in the 21st century. *Student standpoints about access programs in higher education. Center for Research in Developmental Education and Urban Literacy Monographs, 6,* 129–141.

Stone Fish, L. S., & Busby, D. M. (1996). The Delphi method. In D. H. Sprenkle & S. M. Moon (Eds.), *Research methods in family therapy* (pp. 469–482). New York: Guilford Press.

Super, D. E. (1990). A life-span, life-space approach to career development. In D. Brown, L. Brooks, & Associates, *Career choice and development: Applying contemporary theories to practice* (2nd ed., pp. 197–261). San Francisco: Jossey-Bass.

Swanson, R. A., & Holton, E. F., III. (2001). *Foundations of human resource development.* San Francisco: Barrett-Koehler.

Tagg, J. (2003). *The learning paradigm college.* Bolton, MA: Anker.

Theall, M., & Centra, J. A. (2001). Assessing the scholarship of teaching: Valid decisions from valid evidence. In C. Kreber (Ed.), *New directions for teaching and learning: No. 86. Scholarship revisited: Perspectives on the scholarship of teaching* (pp. 31–43). San Francisco: Jossey-Bass.

Thorn, P. M. (2003). *Bridging the gap between what is praised and what is practiced: Supporting the work of change as anatomy and physiology instructors introduce active learning into their undergraduate classroom.* Unpublished doctoral dissertation, University of Texas, Austin.

Tice, S. L. (2005). Preface. In S. L. Tice, N. Jackson, L. M. Lambert, & P. Englot (Eds.), *University teaching: A reference guide for graduate students and faculty* (pp. xi–xii). Syracuse, NY: Syracuse University Press.

Tichy, N. M. (1983). *Managing strategic change: Technical, political and cultural dynamics.* New York: Wiley.

Tierney, W. G. (1988). *Organizational culture in higher education: Defining the essentials.* Journal of Higher Education, *59*(1), 2–21.

Tierney, W. G. (Ed.). (1990). *New directions for institutional research: No. 68. Assessing academic climates and cultures.* San Francisco: Jossey-Bass.

Tierney, W. G. (1999). *Building the responsive campus: Creating high performance colleges and universities.* Thousand Oaks, CA: Sage.

Tierney, W. G. (2006). *Trust and the public good: Examining the cultural conditions of academic work.* New York: Peter Lang.

Tierney, W. G., & Bensimon, E. M. (1996). *Promotion and tenure: Community and socialization in academe.* Albany, NY: State University of New York Press.

TLC Web site. (2007). *Teaching and Learning Center, North Seattle Community College: NSCC scholarship of teaching and learning initiative.* Retrieved August 22, 2007, from http://webshare.northseattle .edu/tlc/forfaculty_sotl.shtm

Toma, J. D., Dubrow, G., & Hartley, M. (2005). *The uses of institutional culture.* San Francisco: Jossey-Bass.

Torraco, R. J., & Hoover, R. E. (2005). Organizational development and change in universities: Implications for research and practice. *Advances in Developing Human Resources, 7*(3), 422–437.

Trice, H. M., & Beyer, J. M. (1991). Cultural leadership in organizations. *Organization Science, 2*(2), 149–169.

Trice, H. M., & Beyer, J. M. (1993). *The cultures of work organizations.* Upper Saddle River, NJ: Prentice Hall.

Trigwell, K., Martin, E., Benjamin, J., & Prosser, M. (2000). Scholarship of teaching: A model. *Higher Education Research and Development, 19,* 155–168.

Trower, C. (2005). How do junior faculty feel about your campus as a work place? *Harvard Institutes for Higher Education: Alumni Bulletin.* Cambridge, MA: Harvard Institutes for Higher Education.

Turnbull, S., & Edwards, G. (2005). Leadership development for organizational change in a new U.K. university. *Advances in Developing Human Resources, 7*(3), 396–413.

University of California. (1991). *The university-wide task force on faculty awards.* Retrieved January 26, 2008, from www.universityofcalifornia.edu/senate/reports/pisterreport1991.pdf

University of Oklahoma. (n.d.) *Campus profile 2007–2008.* Retrieved March 11, 2008, from http://go2.ou.edu/documents/07CampusProfile.pdf

U.S. Department of Education. (2006). *A test of leadership: Charting the future of U.S. higher education.* Washington, DC: Author.

van Emmerik, I. J. H. (2004). The more you can get the better: Mentoring constellations and intrinsic career success. *Career Development International, 9*(6/7), 578.

Vaughan, G. B. (1989). *Scholarship: The community college's Achilles' heel.* Virginia Community College's Association Occasional Paper Series, No. 1. (ERIC Document Reproduction Service No. ED 313 081)

Vaughan, G. B. (1991). Scholarship and the community college professional: Focusing the debate. In G. B. Vaughan & J. C. Palmer (Eds.), *New directions for community colleges: No. 76. Enhancing teaching and administration through scholarship* (pp. 3–15). San Francisco: Jossey-Bass.

Vygotsky, L. S. (1978). *Mind in society: The development of higher psychological processes.* Cambridge, MA: Harvard University Press.

Warzynski, C. C. (2005). The evolution of organizational development at Cornell University: Strategies for improving performance and building capacity. *Advances in Developing Human Resources, 7*(3), 338–350.

Watson, G., & Grossman, L. H. (1994). Pursuing a comprehensive faculty development program: Making fragmentation work. *Journal of Counseling and Development, 72,* 465–473.

Weick, K. E. (1969). *The social psychology of organizing.* Reading, MA: Addison-Wesley.

Weimer, M. (1990). *Improving college teaching: Strategies for developing instructional effectiveness.* San Francisco: Jossey-Bass.

Weimer, M. (2002). *Learner-centered teaching.* San Francisco: Jossey-Bass.

Weimer, M. (2006). *Enhancing scholarly work on teaching and learning: Professional literature that makes a difference.* San Francisco: Jossey-Bass.

Weimer, M. (2008). Positioning scholarly work on teaching and learning. *International Journal for the Scholarship of Teaching and Learning, 2*(1), 1–6. Retrieved January 15, 2008, from www.georgiasouthern .edu/ijsotl/v2n1/invited_essays/Weimer/index.htm

Wenger, E. (1998). *Communities of practice: Learning, meaning, and identity.* Cambridge, England: Cambridge University Press.

Wergin, J. F. (2003). *Departments that work: Building and sustaining cultures of excellence in academic programs.* Bolton, MA: Anker.

Wheeler, P., Haertel, G. D., & Scriven, M. (1993). *Teacher evaluation glossary.* Kalamazoo, MI: Center for Research in Educational Accountability and Teacher Evaluation.

Whitt, E. (1991). Hit the ground running: Experiences of new faculty in a school of education. *Review of Higher Education, 14*(2), 177–197.

Wiggins, G. (1998). *Educative assessment: Designing assessments to inform and improve student performance.* San Francisco: Jossey-Bass.

Wilhelm, W. J. (2001). Alchemy of the oracle: The Delphi technique. *Delta Pi Epsilon Journal, 43*(1), 6–26.

Wilkins, A. L., & Dyer, W. G., Jr. (1988). Toward culturally sensitive theories of culture change. *Academy of Management Review, 13*(4), 522–533.

Wilson, R. C. (1986). Improving faculty teaching: Effective use of student evaluations and consultants. *Journal of Higher Education, 57*(2), 196–211.

Wilson, R. C. (2007, September 12). AAUP goes to bat for "freedom in the classroom." *Chronicle of Higher Education.* Retrieved November 12, 2007, from http://chronicle.com/daily/2007/09/ 2007091202n.htm

Witman, P. D., & Richlin, L. (2007). The status of the scholarship of teaching and learning in the disciplines. *International Journal for the Scholarship of Teaching and Learning, 1*(1), 1–17. Retrieved January 14, 2008, from www.georgiasouthern.edu/ijsotl/v1n1/essays/witman/ IJ_witman.pdf

Wolcott, H. F. (1994). *Transforming qualitative data: Description, analysis, and interpretation.* Thousand Oaks, CA: Sage.

Wolcott, H. F. (1999). *Ethnography: A way of seeing.* Walnut Creek, CA: Alta Mira.

Worthen, B. R., Sanders, J. R., & Fitzpatrick, J. L. (1997). *Program evaluation: Alternative approaches and practical guidelines.* New York: Longman.

Wright, D. L. (2000). Faculty development centers in research universities: A study of resources and programs. In M. Kaplan & D. Lieberman (Eds.), *To improve the academy: Vol. 18. Resources for faculty, instructional, and organizational development* (pp. 291–301). Bolton, MA: Anker.

Wright, D. L. (2002). Program types and prototypes. In K. H. Gillespie (Ed.), *A guide to faculty development: Practical advice, examples, and resources* (pp. 24–34). Bolton, MA: Anker.

Wright, M. C. (2005). Always at odds? Congruence in faculty beliefs about teaching at a research university. *Journal of Higher Education, 76*(3), 331–353.

Wright, R. (2006). Walking the walk: Review of learner-centered teaching, by Maryellen Weimer. *Life Sciences Education, 5*(311), 312.

Wulff, D. H., & Austin, A. E. (Eds.). (2004). *Paths to the professoriate: Strategies for enriching the preparation of future faculty.* San Francisco: Jossey-Bass.

Yen, J. W., Lang, S. E., Denton, D. D., & Riskin, A. (2004, June). *Leadership development workshops for department chairs.* Paper presented at the meeting of Women in Engineering Programs and Advocates Network Conference, Albuquerque, NM.

Yun, J. H., & Sorcinelli, M. D. (2007). *Mellon Mutual Mentoring program guide.* Retrieved November 24, 2007, from www.umass.edu/ofd/guide

Zahorski, K. J. (2002). Nurturing scholarship through holistic faculty development: A synergistic approach. In K. J. Zahorski (Ed.), *New directions for teaching and learning: No. 90. Scholarship in the postmodern era* (pp. 29–37). San Francisco: Jossey-Bass.

Ziglio, E. (1996). The Delphi method and its contribution to decision-making. In M. Adler & E. Ziglio (Eds.), *Gazing into the oracle: The Delphi method and its application to social policy and public health* (pp. 3–33). London: Jessica Kingsley Publishers.